Character: Writing and Reputation in
Victorian Law and Literature

EDINBURGH CRITICAL STUDIES IN LAW, LITERATURE AND THE HUMANITIES
Series Editor: William MacNeil, Southern Cross University
Senior Deputy Editor: Shaun McVeigh, University of Melbourne
Deputy Editor: Daniel Hourigan, University of Southern Queensland

Editorial Board
Dr Maria Aristodemou (Birkbeck, University of London)
Associate Professor Fatou Kine Camara (Université Cheikh Anka Diop de Dakar)
Professor Daniela Carpi (University of Verona)
Dr Susan Chaplin (Leeds Beckett University)
Professor Andrew Clarke (Victoria University)
Dr Stella Clarke (University of Melbourne)
Professor Penny Fielding (University of Edinburgh)
Mme Justice Hon Jeanne Gaakeer (Erasmus University Rotterdam)
Professor Peter Goodrich (Yeshiva University)
Professor Elizabeth Hanson (Queen's University at Kingston)
Associate Professor Susan Sage Heinzelman (University of Texas at Austin)
Professor Bonnie Honig (Brown University)
Professor Rebecca Johnson (University of Victoria)
Dr Orit Kamir (Hebrew Union College)
Associate Professor Lissa Lincoln (American University Paris)
Professor Desmond Manderson (Australian National University)
Professor Panu Minkkinen (University of Helsinki)
Dr Anat Rosenberg (IDC Herzliya)
Professor Renata Salecl (Ljubljana/Birkbeck London)
Professor Austin Sarat (Amherst College)
Dr Jan Melissa Schram (University of Cambridge)
Professor Karin Van Marle (University of Pretoria)
Dr Marco Wan (University of Hong Kong)
Professor Ian Ward (University of Newcastle)
Professor Alison Young (University of Melbourne)

Titles available in the series:
Judging from Experience: Law, Praxis, Humanities
Jeanne Gaakeer

Schreber's Law: Jurisprudence and Judgment in Transition
Peter Goodrich

Living in Technical Legality: Science Fiction and Law as Technology
Kieran Tranter

Imagined States: Law and Literature in Nigeria 1900–1966
Katherine Isobel Baxter

Outlaws and Spies: Legal Exclusion in Law and Literature
Conor McCarthy

Criminality and the Common Law Imagination in the Eighteenth and Nineteenth Centuries
Erin L. Sheley

Sensing Justice through Contemporary Spanish Cinema: Aesthetics, Politics, Law
Mónica López Lerma

The Play of Law in Modern British Theatre
Ian Ward

Earthbound: The Aesthetics of Sovereignty in the Anthropocene
Daniel Matthews

A Theological Jurisprudence of Speculative Cinema: Superheroes, Science Fictions and Fantasies of Modern Law
Timothy D. Peters

Character: Writing and Reputation in Victorian Law and Literature
Cathrine O. Frank

edinburghuniversitypress.com/series/ecsllh

Character: Writing and Reputation in Victorian Law and Literature

Cathrine O. Frank

EDINBURGH
University Press

For my son, Oliver

Edinburgh University Press is one of the leading university presses in the UK. We publish academic books and journals in our selected subject areas across the humanities and social sciences, combining cutting-edge scholarship with high editorial and production values to produce academic works of lasting importance. For more information visit our website: edinburghuniversitypress.com

© Cathrine O. Frank, 2022

Edinburgh University Press Ltd
The Tun – Holyrood Road
12(2f) Jackson's Entry
Edinburgh EH8 8PJ

Typeset in 11/13pt Adobe Garamond Pro
by Manila Typesetting Company, and
printed and bound by CPI Group (UK) Ltd,
Croydon, CR0 4YY

A CIP record for this book is available from the British Library

ISBN 978 1 4744 8570 8 (hardback)
ISBN 978 1 4744 8572 2 (webready PDF)
ISBN 978 1 4744 8573 9 (epub)

The right of Cathrine O. Frank to be identified as the author of this work has been asserted in accordance with the Copyright, Designs and Patents Act 1988, and the Copyright and Related Rights Regulations 2003 (SI No. 2498).

Contents

Acknowledgments   vi

Introduction: Character-Building: Narrative Theory, Narrative Jurisprudence, and the Idea of Character   1

1 Incriminating Character: Revisiting the Right to Silence in *Adam Bede* and *The Scarlet Letter*   31
2 Gossip, Hearsay, and the Character Exception: Reputation on Trial in *The Tenant of Wildfell Hall* and *R v Rowton*   83
3 Defamation of Character: Anthony Trollope and the Law of Libel   116
4 Dignity, Disclosure, and the Right to Privacy: The Strange Characters of Dr. Jekyll and Dorian Gray   165
5 The English Dreyfus Case: Status as Character in an Illiberal Age   207

Works Cited   225

Index   238

Acknowledgments

Research for this book was aided early on by a Minigrant from the University of New England and by two sabbaticals. I'm grateful for the focused time for scholarship and hope the next book won't take as long. Thanks to Nan Goodman, Gary Watt, and Kieran Dolin whose invitations and editorial oversight gave me the opportunity to work up initial thoughts about portions of this book, and to Caroline Shaw who looked over proposals and fomented conference panels. Likewise, I thank Anat Rosenberg and Gordon Bigelow for a memorable ASLCH dinner conversation about Trollope, Stevenson, and Wilde, which sent me home with new things to read. Warmest appreciation goes to Nora Frank whose visits made it possible for me to attend conferences at all.

Bill MacNeil's enthusiasm for the project has been a real boon. An email from Bill, from whatever part of the world he happens to be in, brims with cheerfulness or wry observation, and I read it, encouraged. Thanks also to the anonymous readers who pushed me to answer questions I suspected I ought to say more about, pointed me towards new reading, and let me know I was on a right road. And of course thanks to Laura Williamson and Sarah Foyle at Edinburgh University Press for shepherding the project along.

An earlier version of Chapter 2 appeared as "Gossip, Hearsay, and the Character Exception in Victorian Law and Literature" in *Law and Humanities*, vol. 9, no. 2 (2015), pp. 172–202 and is reprinted by permission of the publisher (Taylor & Francis, Ltd, http://tandfonline.com). A portion of Chapter 4 originally appeared as "Privacy, Character, and the Jurisdiction of the Self: A 'Story of the Door' in *The Strange Case of Dr. Jekyll and Mr. Hyde*" in *English Language Notes*, vol. 49, no. 2, pp. 215–24. Copyright 2010, Duke University Press. All rights reserved. Republished by permission of the publisher. www.dukeupress.edu. Likewise, my discussion of George Edalji's case appeared first in the chapter "Narrative and Law" in *Law and Literature*, edited by Kieran Dolin, Cambridge University Press, 2018, pp. 42–57. Reproduced with permission of the Licensor through PLSclear.

Finally, I thank Oliver. This book has grown along with him—often right next to him, in fact, during this last, strange year—and while I didn't always appreciate his input, including the insertion of a friendly cat, I suspect he was more patient than it seemed. I know he already understands the satisfaction of completing a book.

Introduction: Character-Building: Narrative Theory, Narrative Jurisprudence, and the Idea of Character

> The real effective education of a people is given them by the circumstances by which they are surrounded. The laws are the great schoolmaster, as the ancient statesmen and philosophers well knew, and it is time we should again learn the lesson. What shapes the character is not what is purposely taught, so much as the unintentional teaching of institutions and social relations.
>
> J. S. Mill (1846)[1]

> That we shall know with whom we have to do, is the first precondition of having anything to do with another.
> Georg Simmel, "The Sociology of Secrecy and of Secret Societies" (1906)

Character-Building in the Nineteenth Century

When John Stuart Mill declaimed that "The laws are the great schoolmaster," he yoked law to education in a way that emphasized its formative and normative functions for "a people," but he needn't have looked to the ancients for the view, also expressed by the eighteenth-century magistrate Patrick Quolquhon, that "What education is to an individual, the laws are to society" (qtd. in Wiener 47). These links between education and law, individual and society not only frame out the first half of the nineteenth century, they also reveal a shared foundation in what historian Martin J. Wiener describes as "the character-building task of law" and law's often tacit moral agenda (53).[2] Indeed, Mill's comment that law's lessons were best experienced as an

---

[1] Qtd. in Carlisle, *John Stuart Mill* 147. The passage comes from one of Mill's leading articles on Ireland in the *Morning Chronicle*.

[2] Mill's belief that structural reforms could change social relations, and hence the kind of character "a people" could develop, places him in an interesting relationship with other

"unintentional" form of instruction informs the nineteenth-century shift from public spectacles of punishment and their explicitly deterrent objective towards this subtler moral management. Yet Mill's use of the passive voice and his focus on "a people" render the collective body a passive object of political philosophies and policy reforms that, as he well knew, relied on the *individual's* cognizance of the socio-legal landscape, his *active* effort to contain or direct his impulses in appropriate ways, and his *responsibility* for the harms that resulted from a failure to do so. Secular utilitarianism and Christian evangelicalism thus shared an ethic of self-denial which also informs law's moral agenda *and* identifies character-building as an ongoing practice. From James Mill to James Fitzjames Stephen, the dominant if sometimes implicit view was that "consequentialism would build character" (55).[3]

To the extent that character-building implies a movement away from an underdeveloped or misaligned moral state towards a valued ideal (a Charles Kingsley school of Muscular Christianity), drawing attention to it inevitably invites the term's conservative associations.[4] I am less interested in the evaluative dimensions of character, however, than I am in the narrative processes through which character is built or, to follow the many compound forms listed in the *OED*, the way character is "drawn," "formed," "made," "moulded," "read," and "trained"—all of which usages (with the exception of "character-drawing" and "character-making") are illustrated by citations dating initially from the nineteenth century.

But what precisely was the thing thus acted on? Certainly, to speak of character itself can carry moralistic connotations, but the character concept has been known by a variety of terms whose conflation risks underappreciating their historical usage and connotative variety.[5] In writing about character,

---

social reformers who downplayed determinism in order to highlight individual capacity (Wiener 48).

[3] See Wiener on law's relation to what he refers to as *the* broader discourse of character (38–45) and internal reforms that supported the character-building function (52–83).

[4] See Hall. See also Blinka on character as "social, cultural, and ideological battleground" (90).

[5] See Amelie Oksenberg Rorty on the wide range of terms for character and the danger of trying to make one historically specific variant serve as the single best name for the "class" to which it belongs (537–53). For example, "Person" comes from drama and law and theology, "the unified center of choice and action, the unit of legal and theological responsibility" (542), but "character" lacks this unified core and consists instead in a set of "traits," "dispositions," and "habits" that determine how one responds to environmental circumstances and experiences and therefore the roles for which one is best suited, that is, those which are best calculated "to bring out his potentialities and functions" (539–40). This latter understanding seems to suit a status-bound social model in which the external observation of how a person fulfils his role is the way "to know what sort of character a person is," whereas

I will also use the more neutral terms individual, reputation, disposition, personhood, and personality because these are reflected in Victorian discussion of that thing which is at once a graphic sign, an ethical category, a professional reputation, a dramatic role, a moral quality, a fictional entity, and a mode of taking cognizance of oneself and other social beings. Still, in spite of this variety, the Google N-gram Viewer (the Google Books tool that can search its digital library for specific terms and phrases) provides tantalizing justification for "character" as the preferred moniker. The viewer shows that between 1779 and 1899 reference to "character" remained above .0250%. It peaked at .037% in 1834 and did not begin a steady descent until 1848 (at a rate of about .010% per fifty-year period). Thus, the graph suggests that writing about character reached its height in the middle of the nineteenth century and, although usage fell off, remained consistently higher than terms like "person" (which only intersected with and surpassed "character" in 1938).[6] To investigate the meaning of "character," one will be quite at home amid what political historian Stefan Collini calls the nineteenth century's "popular character-talk" (103).[7]

The fact that character-talk *was* popular and that so many disciplines had something to say about it demonstrates character's magnetism. As Janice Carlisle notes in her exhaustive study of Mill's writing on the subject, "character"—what he took to be "the central fact of human experience" (*John Stuart Mill* ix)—drew in science, philosophy, religion, politics, and literature where its "public dimensions" consistently took center stage (3). In this sense, character signifies both individual interiority and social "realtionality," but as Jonathan Farina observes, the Victorians' rhetorical repertoire even extended character-talk beyond a humanist emphasis into the world of things as well

---

"person" fits a more liberal, contract-oriented conception of society and of the distinct individuals who live in it.

[6] This contrast between character and person brings to mind John Frow's recent book of that name, *Character and Person*. I choose "character" not to argue with Frow or even to dispute the growing importance of "personhood" in the nineteenth century, but to illustrate the mobility and malleability of "character" by contrast to many of the other terms for referring to people. Frow's own definitions of fictional character include "quasi-persons" (vii) or "a person-shaped figure made salient by a narrative ground" (25). More substantially, he disputes ideas of character as a "substance," preferring an "instance of an operation within a social assemblage . . . a moment of an apparatus for the mobilization of subjectivity within the terms of an ethical or legal or religious or civic mode of action and understanding" (ix).

[7] A still more tantalizing finding, however, is that the downtrend reverses itself in about the year 2003 (going from .010% in 2000 to .012% in 2007). This resurgence in writing about character recalls Nicola Lacey's analysis of the trend in criminal jurisprudence and invites comparison of the Victorian and contemporary conditions that have renewed interest in this particular formulation. See discussion of Lacey in Chapter 5.

("Character" 609). Across discourses, character functioned as both "a distinct form of knowledge and [a] style of representation" (609).

How do knowledge and representation intersect in the term? The *OED*'s first definition of character is the literal one: "a distinctive mark impressed, engraved, or otherwise made on a surface" (I.1) which is typically understood in connection with "a set of symbols used in writing or printing to represent linguistic elements" (I.3a). In a literal sense, writing is always concerned with and depends on character.[8] This basic unit of representation and communication has many more figurative meanings, however, the first of which ("a distinctive indication, a visible token, evidence"), although now obsolete, was ready to hand for Robert Louis Stevenson whose depiction of Edward Hyde provides one of the dictionary's two Victorian citations. Character also figures forth a set of "moral and mental qualities strongly developed or strikingly displayed" (9b) on the basis of which an individual acquires a reputation (II.9b) so that to speak of someone's character "without further context" by default implies "good reputation or estimation" (II.13) and assumes an evaluative usage. Thus, character becomes an outward, portable, and descriptive sign of inner potential (as in the idiomatic *having* or *giving* of a character [12a]) put to evaluative effect.[9] More strikingly, character is defined as "the sum of the moral and mental qualities which distinguish an individual or a people, viewed as a homogeneous whole; a person's or group's individuality deriving from environment, culture, experience, etc.; mental or moral constitution, personality" (9a) as when Cardinal Manning writes in 1875, "The character is that intellectual and moral texture into which all our life long we have been weaving up the inward life that is in us" (52). Here character, as applied to individuals, races, or nations, becomes unitary and distinct, each defining feature an exponent of the next. In the *OED*'s second edition, this sense of character was defined, not merely as "deriving from," but as being "*impressed by nature and habit* on man or nation" in the same way character's first meaning denotes marks "impressed on . . . a surface." Whether human text, personified surface, or ideological structure, in Manning's conception this character develops through an active "weaving up" (52) that makes dispositional qualities cohere.

In *Character: Writing and Reputation in Victorian Law and Literature*, I explore how the writing up of characters in novels encouraged

---

[8] See also Farina's study of Victorian prose style and characterization as a mode of knowledge production in *Everyday Words and the Character of Prose in Nineteenth-Century Britain*.

[9] See Collini's discussion of the "descriptive" and "evaluative" meanings of character used in the *OED* 95–7. See also Carlisle's analysis of the *OED*'s citation of Mill on "individuality" as a synonym for character (*John Stuart Mill* 2).

nineteenth-century readers to recognize their own distinctive traits and capacities and bring them together in a way that could grow and preserve individual personality without unduly or dangerously exceeding a shared, communal identity. This lifetime work of "weaving up" one's inner life has its corollary in an equally crafted outward life of reputation. Because Victorians so often wrote of character in this "irreducibly public" sense (Carlisle, *John Stuart Mill* 2), this emphasis on *making oneself known in the world* raises questions about what parts of one's inner life it would be advantageous or appropriate to publicize or to keep private, as well as how to do it. If the novel fostered an impulse in both characters and readers to make these decisions for themselves, moral philosophy, political and evolutionary theory, socio-economic conditions, and law established the possibilities and monitored the parameters within which to do so. From the privilege not to incriminate oneself to legal protections of privacy (both of which recognize and limit external pressure to disclose personal information), from rules regarding character evidence in criminal law to libel laws that shielded one's reputation (both of which concern permissible kinds of speech or evidence about public character), nineteenth-century legislation and legal practice formed a second, material system, alongside literature, for organizing the telling of people's stories.

Although my particular focus in this book will be on the interrelation of literary and legal forms of "character-talk," it is worth pausing at the year 1859 to note the publication of *The Origin of Species*, *On Liberty*, *Self-Help*, *A Tale of Two Cities*, and *Adam Bede*.[10] All concerned with questions of individual disposition, with the capacity to adapt to or resist social demands or natural environments, and with the consequences of individual actions for the group, these diverse works offer a snapshot of both a multidisciplinary investment in questions of character as well as key tensions within the discourse. In his study of changing conceptions of criminality, historian Martin J. Wiener observes that as relationships between people became dominated by relationships between institutions, moral agency—the idea that individuals had the capacity to formulate, consider, act on, or resist their desires—began

---

[10] Some years ago, the Victoria ListServ, the discussion board on Victorian culture hosted by Indiana University in the United States, posted a question about where scholars might divide the era. Robert Lapides pointed to the publication in 1859 of *The Origin of Species*, *On Liberty*, *Self-Help*, and *Adam Bede* (Tennyson and Dickens make the cut as well) as works that "fostered a new perspective or addressed a cultural turning point." Figuring this shift symbolically, Lapides contrasted the death of the great historian Macaulay with the creation of Big Ben, a monument to time's passage that would need a new chronicler. Rather than emphasizing a chronological turning point in the era, however, I take these works as a synchronic snapshot of perspectives on and contributions to the Victorian discourse of character.

to resonate less strongly. Scientific studies of criminal behavior, for example, contributed to a reconstruction of "character" as "identity" and necessitated a shift in the legal sphere towards more lenient models of punishment for crimes whose origins might lie outside the individual (Wiener). This deterministic stance towards identity is perhaps best captured by that strand of Darwin's evolutionary thinking which replaced the theological idea of design with a natural selection whose effects were always in the making but which could not be predicted and would not be visible within an individual lifetime (Beer 42). Against the backdrop of a biological theory which "deliberately excluded" the human—and certainly the human will to control the future (Beer 44)—Samuel Smiles's *Self-Help* starts to look delusional. Even as Smiles's biographies of famous men (or the men made famous by his biographies) shared the retrospective, cause-and-effect structure of evolutionary narrative on a micro-scale, his model of volitional progress countered the exigencies of working- and middle-class life with an appreciation for those who showed themselves able to surpass them.[11] It was precisely the power of circumstance to influence or form character that prompted J. S. Mill's development of the new science of ethology, however, and informed his belief in the efficacy of social reform: change the circumstances in which people (especially marginal groups) live, and one changes their character.[12] By contrast to this social program (recognizable in twentieth-century strands of Legal Realism and Critical Legal Studies), Mill's best-known work of political theory *On Liberty* called individual readers to resist the tyrannies of "prevailing opinion" and "custom" (8) and to embrace "eccentricity" in the interests of diversification of thought and action (67).[13] And in literature, Dickens placed a wedge between moral character and external identity in *A Tale of Two Cities* through the repetition of the code-name "Jacques" (shared among Monsieur Defarge and his fellows in the Jacquerie) at the beginning of the novel and again at the end through Sidney Carton's far, far better substitution of himself for Charles Darnay (itself an alias for Evrémonde) on the scaffold. By contrast, in *Adam Bede* Eliot develops an argument about the attribution of criminal responsibility that hinges on ideas of intrinsic character, "nature," and consequentialist

---

[11] Smiles's work tracks with Darwin's: the sequels to each, *The Descent of Man* and *Character*, both appeared in 1871.

[12] Carlisle, "Ethology as Politics," *John Stuart Mill* 127–67. Mill conceded to convention by abandoning the term "ethology" in favor of "education" (125).

[13] In the field of psychology, Mill's colleague Alexander Bain would re-evaluate the then dominant mode of scientific character study, phrenology, in *On the Study of Character* (1861), while James Sully would publish "The Aesthetics of Human Character" in 1871, his idea that there could be an "aesthetics" of character reminding us of its place in that other great nineteenth-century enterprise, the novel.

theories of human action. One path this book will trace is through the novel's relationship with various social, cultural, and political understandings of character in order to follow their impact on developments within the genre, but also to trace how the novel's understanding of character—the people it depicted as much as those who read it—contributed to the notion of human complexity that new political and scientific theories were trying to understand and that law sought to regulate.

To begin with the idea of development, especially its meaning for the relationship between the novel as a genre, narrative as a mode, and character as an idea that I've been showing had such wide currency across dimensions of nineteenth-century culture: As Clifford Siskin has pointed out, the very idea of development was an "intergeneric" Romantic strategy for "mak[ing] change appear to make sense" (126). Found in Wordsworth's poetry and Austen's novels, development as "formal strategy" used a notion of "probable behavior" to reform, by naturalizing, "forms of social and literary experience" (140). Supported by demographic changes that yielded a more youthful population, development seemed especially relevant both for childhood as a distinct stage of human growth and for groups who were beginning to experience their inherited, status-bound social placement as being too limiting. For Siskin, "Development's function is not necessarily to undermine hierarchy, but ... to naturalize its instability as a sign of maturation" (142): classes, as with kids, will want to grow up. In this context, it is not surprising to find historian Dror Wahrman and literary critic Nancy Armstrong bracketing their respective studies of "modern identity" and "individualism" with analyses of Sir Joshua Reynolds's portraits of children, or locating the sources of social and political change in cultural forms like the visual arts and the novel with their changing depictions and narratives of character.[14]

Armstrong's argument that in order to "produce an individual" the novel had to eliminate or marginalize other forms of subjectivity (and the genres that made them) parallels Andrea K. Henderson's argument that other forms of Romantic identity were occluded by the emphasis on psychological depth (which also reinforces Siskin's earlier point that development is a historical and political, rather than natural, construct). Yet Armstrong's analysis of the misfit cum hero fits within Siskin's developmental model of change that makes sense. "Anything dealing with improvement," she writes, relied on the new idea of the individual, not the social position, as being the well-spring of desires and abilities, including the ability to craft a life in which the two might

---

[14] Wahrman 282–90 includes analysis of "Master Hare" and "Penelope Boothby" (1788). Armstrong reproduces as cover art for and opens *How Novels Think* with "Master Bunbury" (1780–1).

better align (28). What Siskin calls the "lyricization" of Romantic genres and a new definition of the self as "a mind that grows" (11, 3)—often past the bounds of traditional hierarchies—becomes, via Armstrong, a novelization of character or narrativization of individuals who in the nineteenth century confronted political structures that could not dismiss them but might not be able (or want) to accommodate them, either.

Dror Wahrman's distinction between the *ancien régime* and modern meanings of identity as "selfhood" (nodding towards difference and uniqueness but also towards "identicality," or the sense of inclusion in a group) (xii) is instructive here. Under the *ancien régime* of identity (prior to the age of revolutions), identity was outward facing and focused on social relationships held together through the workings of sympathy (187). Focused on "generic categorization" or groups, identity was fluid; persons assumed the characteristics of whatever group they joined, and a single person's nonconformity was relatively easy to miss or dismiss (278). However, in the modern regime, categories such as race, class, and gender "contributed to the generation of unique identity *before* they generated the identicality of a collective group" (278, emphasis mine). As with development, so now difference was naturalized. Within this understanding of identity, such markers could not be ignored because they were believed to be the very differences that made a person unique or individual and justified their subsequent assemblage into a collective and stable group identity.

Two points bear making: one concerns narrative and development (that is, development as something *to* narrate) and what Armstrong and Alex Woloch especially demonstrate to be the ways these new conceptions of character are deployed in the narrative form of the novel. Wahrman's observation that what made individuals unique could also make them part of a group sits a bit uneasily alongside Armstrong's observation that in the nineteenth century, deference to the social body, as something larger than and superior to specific forms of affiliation, required individual conformity. That this larger social group lived by "bourgeois morality" in service to the nation (27, 54) specified the limits on individualism, or just how far the surplus energy of eighteenth-century individuals had to be put to the work of self-discipline for the sake of the greater good. This version of maturation, to recall Siskin's observations about development and my own emphasis on character-building, makes social coherence the surrogate for personal fulfillment. That is, an emphasis on self-realization or self-fulfillment starts to seem selfish (or sectarian or factional) in the degree to which it risks social welfare. (By contrast to both notions of the "group," i.e. as a coherent whole or definable category, mobs or masses presented the prospect of an indiscriminate group made frightening by virtue of its resistance to or defiance of categorization as much as by its volume.) The trick to managing these interests, as Wahrman suggests, lay again in the developmental model of human growth best represented by the child whose individuality would be shaped by education—including reading habits, which Siskin contends made *what* one read an index to *how* one developed (147)—and would result in an adult with a "personal history" that begged for "retrospective recounting . . . in the form of a connected narrative" (Wahrman 289). Autobiography, yes, but also the novel.

The second point concerns the political implications and new social arrangements affected by this modern conception of difference and identicality; specifically, the idea of a coherent social body concerns the ways in which identicality was deployed by *non*-members of that group in service to the idea of a coherent social body. At the same time that identicality encouraged a new awareness of one's horizontal relationship with others, it was also used ideologically by elites to define out of personhood those very racial, ethnic, and gendered traits that constituted membership in that group. As Wahrman says of the age of revolution, rights talk makes sense only when a person capable of possessing rights exists. I take up this question explicitly in my discussion of personality and the right to privacy (Chapter 4) and implicitly in my discussion of responsibility attribution as legalistic modes of character-making (Chapters 1 and 5). My more immediate point is that formal strategies of characterization in the novel contributed to the novelization of character outside of strictly literary domains. The realist novel in particular took the Romantic idea of the development of character as a mode and a subject of narration, but the questions of which persons had characters worth narrating, how that value was determined by naturalized difference, and how such narration might proceed remained.

Character, Narrative Theory, and Narrative Jurisprudence

In *Aspects of the Novel* (1927) E. M. Forster reversed the Aristotelian priority of plot in the order of narrative importance and devoted two chapters to "people." This rhetorical change, by which characters cease merely to *refer to* but become *identified as* everyday people, suggests familiarity not only between novelists and their creations, but also between readers and the other people they encounter in the pages of fiction. If we play along with Forster and approach *homo fictus* as a regular person, we might expect him to demonstrate what J. Paul Hunter describes as "an intensified consciousness, individual by individual, of what selfhood means" (24), but this heightened reality-effect is produced only by "round," not "flat" characters, whose dimensions depend entirely on what Alex Woloch refers to as the author's "distribution of attention" within the narrative field (15).[15]

In *The One vs. the Many: Minor Characters and the Space of the Protagonist in the Novel*, Woloch develops two narratological categories to redress the under-theorization of character in narrative studies, more specifically, to synthesize structuralist views of character (as an effect of language and form) with a humanist approach to mimesis (character as referring to human personality) (17). Thus, "character-space" refers to "that particular and charged encounter between an individual human personality and a determined space and position within the narrative as a whole" (14), while "character-system" describes "the combination of different character-spaces or of various modes *through which* specific human figures are inflected into the narrative" (32). As his subtitle indicates, some characters' development is curtailed so as to create more space for a central one or few, not because some characters are intrinsically more interesting than others, but because they are allowed to become so under the realist novel's "labor theory of character" (26). "Minor characters are the proletariat of the novel" (27), he argues, because their work goes to the realization of major characters; their "specialized roles" are mobilized to serve the system at the cost of their personal development. Only through such a division of labor, he argues, can the realist novel achieve its unique combination of depth and breadth, psychological specificity and social panorama (33).

Woloch's focus on "modes through which" character is distributed in the novel provides a springboard for this study's approach to reputation as being sometimes synonymous with character and as *a mode for distributing* character that takes both written and oral forms. In the context of nineteenth-century character-talk, with its topical or thematic focus *on* character, the narrative control *of* talk offers a structural complement to allocating attention and forming character. For example, Hester Prynne and Hetty Sorrel are exhorted to confess or answer charges before a legal tribunal. Helen Huntingdon (arguably guilty of kidnap) counters oral gossip about her marital status and suspect identity by giving Gilbert Markham her redacted diary. Phineas Finn

---

[15] Hunter dismisses "character" along with "realism" and "individualism" as the distinguishing marks of the novel (22–3), but his emphasis is a bit misleading. "Individualism, Subjectivity" comes in at number six in a ten-point list of "agreed-upon" features of the genre:

> The crucial difference between individuals in romances and novels involves the degree and quality of self-consciousness in novels, a strikingly different awareness of the processes of thought and feeling that affect individuals in relation to their world and their experiences in it. The subjectivity of the novel involves not just a raised status for the individual self but an intensified consciousness, individual by individual, of what selfhood means. (24)

obtains an injunction to prevent a libelous publication, while Cousin Henry reluctantly sues a paper whose libels are meant to draw out his secrets. Jekyll's lawyer hides a "mad will" (Stevenson 30), and Dorian hides his criminality in the portrait. To varying degrees and in different combinations, all of the novels I discuss, from *The Scarlet Letter* to *The Picture of Dorian Gray*, provide access to character through dynamics of secrecy and disclosure or through the allocation of responsibility or liability for wrongdoing, both of which hinge on this control of talk as a narrative mode (including but not limited to dialogue) and the circulation of reputation—for example, when a criminal defendant or a stranger in town is called on to explain herself to the assembled community; when someone speaks for or about her if she refuses; in the response to gossip or to printed libels that damage reputation, and through the arrangement of conditions under which an individual may determine for him- or herself what facts, information, feelings, or ideas to disclose. To claim that these dynamics are primarily legalistic is not to deny how other discourses such as theology or psychology would explain them, but to declare my focus. For example, if having access to an inner life signaled that one was in the presence of or experiencing fictionality—where both the access and the inner life suggested by it were the product of literary fiction making—we should ask how law participated in the creation of that inner life, how it protected it, and under what conditions it could assume the power to access it or compel disclosure.

Literary works that explicitly focus on legal actors, themes, or contexts obviously invite the thematic consideration of law in literature, and when they (implicitly) underscore the different rules by which law regulates character-talk, they invite analysis of law as literature. Both views of the interrelation of law and literature highlight the socio-historical plane in which their forms operate, but they also suggest the value of what Peter Brooks has imagined as a "narratology of law" ("Narrative Transactions"). This narratology is not quite the same as the storytelling turn pursued by scholars of narrative jurisprudence, but of course it overlaps with and has implications for it. What I propose is to bring together recent trends in narrative theory that combine structural, representational, and ideological analysis of character, with calls such as Christine L. Krueger's for a historicized narrative jurisprudence, in order to think of law itself as a character-system through which individual persons are made round or flat and to focus on the particular ways this system worked in Victorian England.[16]

---

[16] No two histories of the law and literature movement are precisely the same, but "narrative" looms large in all, traceable throughout as a general attention to stories about law (law in literature), linked with rhetoric as a mode of argument and persuasion in law (law as

The way material persons are mobilized in legal narrative depends on formal manipulations and ideological foundations, including legal ideas about character, as much as the characters in a novel do. My discussion of self-representation and the right to silence, character evidence and reputation, and privacy shows these to be among the legal ways of rounding or flattening out character that occupied Victorian writers and thinkers when the idea of character was in the ascendant. To take the issue of the right to silence, for example, one of the most often cited arguments in the 1850s against allowing the accused to give sworn evidence was that even if they did not succumb to the temptation to lie, they would tell their story badly. Unpacking this objection through the tools of narrative theory raises questions about the ways in which narrative attention is apportioned and directed under a jurisprudential theory of character. For example, what does it mean for a party to a case to tell his or her *own story* badly? Would the facts in issue or the events themselves be different so as to change the elements of story? How would the telling itself change when narrated in the first-person by a third-party witness (say, the minor character with his or her own sub-plot) or in the third-person by counsel (Welsh, *Strong Representations*; Schramm; Grossman; Rodensky)? What should we make of counsel's address to the jury? Is counsel a character in the trial, functioning as the intradiegetic narrator of his client's story for an equally framed set of jury-characters, or is he outside that story, commenting on opposing counsel's representations and rearranging elements to persuade jury-"readers"? How does legal discourse itself narrativize the events of the story (Fludernik)? What are the master plots informing auditors' reception of the story (Scheppele)? What evidence must be excluded?

These questions are taken up piece-meal in the chapters that follow and more centrally in Chapter 5. In what follows, however, I want to start to develop a conversation between literary and legal character-systems that each use multiple modes and sometimes overlapping conventions for drawing attention to character. These modes include theoretical questions or

---

literature), taken as the linguistic object of interpretation (hermeneutic), but also identifiable as a discrete strand of jurisprudence that calls attention to "'outsider' narratives." The term "outsider jurisprudence" is Mari Matsuda's in "Public Response to Racist Speech: Considering the Victim's Story," *Michigan Law Review*, vol. 87, 1989, p. 2320, qtd. in Scheppele 2084. Robin West includes law and literature, critical legal studies, feminist legal theory, and critical race theory as examples in *Narrative, Authority, and Law* 424. See also Robin Wharton and Derek Miller's "New Directions in Law and Narrative" that identifies a third strand of scholarship, in addition to acts of storytelling and rewriting, that focuses on stories that "constrain and define the possibilities of legal practice" (4). I discuss Krueger's work in *Reading for the Law* in Chapter 1.

meta-analyses at the discursive level about what character is and how best to access and represent it. When narrators interrupt their narratives to talk about character, or when judicial opinions and parliamentary debates parse its meanings, we see character discourse in the making. Character modes also include thematic explorations within the story, for example gossip, hearsay, libel, secrecy, privacy, and disclosure, where characters wrestle with the differences among and implications of these kinds of character-talk. In many cases, these themes become a third mode and work as structuring devices or founding premises as when a novel's major conflict centers on an imbalance in the narrative control of character-talk that the story attempts to recalibrate.

At the macro-level all chapters begin from these observations or premises: first, in the nineteenth century, and again today, character signifies an essential quality of personhood, as external sign and as interior disposition, even though the nineteenth-century idea of consistency or core character seems anachronistic now and may be applied more frequently to the character of groups.

Second, character also carries rhetorical value that makes it a springboard for shaping and sustaining communal boundaries in the sense that, when mobilized, "character" opens up discussion of the kinds of knowledge people do or don't need, especially outside of personal relationships or the context of local reputation, in order to live among one another. Twenty-first-century readers of social media will be familiar with the contrary pull of character-talk, or the ways in which an empathic vision of character solicits stories of individual experience in order to celebrate diversity, commiserate suffering, or correct representational imbalances by distinction to an agoraphobic vision of character as the constellation of negative traits separating "us" from groups of "them."

Third, the Victorian novel promulgated new concepts of character and dramatized this discussion through a heightened attention to fictionality that made the experience of novel-reading different to the made-upness of other, non-literary fictions. In the chapters that follow, the novel draws attention to its fictionality through historical displacement, gothic fantasy, and topical treatments of reputation that enact discursive comparisons between the way literature and law do their character-work. Conflicting attitudes towards the sociological value of hearsay, for example, suggest literature's confrontation with law, but the representation of legal remedies for libel positions law as a mediator between literature and other discourses such as journalism. These different discursive alignments suggest that while the realist novel and specific areas of legal practice share some conventions, their use-value differs across systems, sometimes contradicting, complementing, or even reinforcing one another.

Fourth, Victorian legal discourse constituted law as another character-system wherein specific examples of character-talk, for example the character rule or the character exception, joined what I am considering as other character-oriented areas of law such as libel. In this system, rules or procedures about character apply to multiple branches of law (the character rule applies primarily to criminal trials without specifying the nature of the crime), and even areas of law obviously oriented towards character could touch on others less immediately or apparently so (in a way that points towards the wide-ranging effects of law on conceptions of personhood that circulate outside the professional legal community). Thus, privacy attaches to a privilege against self-incrimination, but it can also attach to libel. In this respect, it can be helpful to think less about strict definitions of criminal versus tortious acts in favor of positioning libel, privacy, evidence, and testimony as demarcating character-spaces within the legal character-system that are mobilized to draw attention to specific issues, or to specific aspects of legal actors, or indeed that are put to different work in the interests of supporting the overarching system.

This idea of mobilizing character is an important reminder that character does not develop solely out of description or analysis. When investigation of the constitutive relationship between person and event occupied so many thinkers, as my brief look at the year 1859 suggested, it's easy to move, as Forster does, from character to plot and back again. As I've suggested, many of the novels I discuss build a thematic interest in character on a structure that allocates narrative attention according to the same idea, in other words, the dynamic and the topic overlap within the narrative field. Where Woloch sees a labor theory of character behind this allocation of narrative attention, I see a jurisprudential theory of character informing, and sometimes in tension with, an author's literary distribution of attention. What are the structures that support or narrativize character? What does this jurisprudential theory look like in practice?

Woloch is among a cadre of literary critics whose work over the last twenty years has revived an explicit interest in character by reconciling formal analyses which treat character as an aspect of narrative structure with "humanist," mimetic, or ethical theories that treat character as the representation of a particular type of individuality. Instead of asking only who characters *are*, these critics ask how they are made, how they work in relation to other formal properties of genre, how readers consume or interact with them and, importantly, how specific cultural, historic conditions determine these answers.[17]

---

[17] For an overview of the changing status of character in narrative theory, see James Phelan's chapter in the 40th anniversary edition of *The Nature of Narrative* (283–336). See also Rita Felski's introduction to the special issue of *New Literary History* focused on character (v–ix);

One view which scholars working in areas as diverse as early modern literature and the realist novel share, however, is that even at its most individuated, character always emerges out of relation with other persons or entities in a shared system.[18] (This is the formal dimension of their work. Their particular insights come through the ways that the narrative system itself is shown to be part of a broader ideological or cultural framework.) Elizabeth Fowler's reading of Chaucer's *General Prologue*, for example, demonstrates how the characters of the knight and the prioress emerge through the arrangement of familiar "social persons" within "maps of social meaning" (11). Functioning like genre in human dress or a "collective imaginative technology" (17), the social person creates complexity on a one-dimensional plane. Absent the psychological depth of their nineteenth-century counterparts, early modern characters become "coordinates" on a map, which makes reading character into a kind of literary orienteering akin to the formal distribution of character-space and narrative attention that involves nineteenth-century readers in the creation of character depth.[19]

As noted, one character's roundedness depends on controlling the potential for roundedness in minor characters. In her work on fictionality and nonreferentiality, Catherine Gallagher observes one way this distinction is achieved in the paradox through which proper names—one of the earliest signs of a novel's realism—claimed the reader's attention. "Novelistic names not only help us to sort characters into major and minor, round and flat, serious and comic but also prompt us to begin—or not to begin—the intense imaginative activity of reading character," she writes; the more specific, indeed

---

Jonathan Farina "Character" (609–12) and Jill Galvan, "Character" (612–16), both in the recent Keywords issue of *Victorian Literature and Culture*, vol. 46, no. 3/4 (Fall/Winter, 2018); and Frow v–xi.

[18] Jill Galvan describes recent emphasis on character as "a dynamically relational form: a mobile entity shaped by interaction—whether with the reader, other characters in the storyworld, or both" (612).

[19] Fowler's insight about *character as being always relational* works against the idea of character as core or continuity, yet it is in keeping with the novel's complex and populous social world in which attention has to be differently distributed. The premise of *The Canterbury Tales* pulls in two directions: towards the inequality assumed by competition and towards an equal distribution of attention (each pilgrim gets a portrait, tells a tale, and in theory has a chance to win). That some tellers are more frequently interrupted and some tales better received than others is a reminder of the former, and an early sign, perhaps, of the kind of distribution to come with the novel. See also Dror Wahrman's remarkably similar discussion of the masquerade as the epitome of eighteenth-century expressions of identity before the modern idea of selfhood took hold: this "pre-self" is "a set of positions within which one identified oneself—a set of coordinates, or a matrix" (168). See also John Frow's formulation, "Fictional character is a person-shaped figure made salient by a narrative ground" (25).

banal, a name is, the greater its "promise of subjectivity" (353). Gallagher's observation that reading character involves a process of "sorting" connects to Elizabeth Judge's argument that the early novel instructed readers in a "praxis of credibility" by teaching them both to attend to the internal probability of a given narrative and to test the credibility of its teller, or the character of those who bear witness (33). In essence the novel helped readers learn how to sort out whom they could trust and therefore what they could believe (2). Judge's focus on the uses of character in the novel and the courtroom likewise calls to mind Deidre Shauna Lynch's emphasis on the "pragmatics of character" in a market-based economy where practices of character reading, whether in the context of pre-Romantic social semiotics or in Romantic-era formulations of reading as personal development, joined with commodity culture and market forces to reconfigure social relationships and divisions (4–5). This sorting depended on the ability to recognize increasingly subtle outward markers. Judge's "credibility indicia" (25)—from demonstrations of rhetorical skill to involuntary physical expressions (42)—become, for example, matters of discrete dress in the early nineteenth century (Lynch 163). Lynch's emphasis on the class basis of these distinctions points towards the capital behind ideas of cultural capital and, with it, the idea of access. The canny reader gains access to cultural capital when he or she learns what to look for.

These studies of the eighteenth-century novel focus on the instrumentality of the genre in developing new ideas about fiction, as Gallagher explains, and negotiating ideas about character that, in Judge's and Lynch's analyses, emphasize the reader's experience of novel-reading as a new way to navigate non-fictional discourses of character where ideas about roundness and flatness also obtain. I want to shift perspective from the reader back onto the orchestrator of this narrative attention, however, in order to reconnect these outward (physical or performative) displays of character to the idea of reputation and to the crafting of reputation as a deliberate form of access. Reputation offers a window onto specific aspects of interiority and makes them do public work, and in this sense reputation always results from manipulation (certainly by screening out or making private other aspects of one's inner life). However, the novelist who depicts this dynamic at work, or subjects characters to public scrutiny and comment, or employs omniscient narrative modes manipulates character in another sense. However subtle any single outward mark of inner character is made to appear, the novel paradoxically flaunts its ability to grant readers this kind of access *to* character and indeed to mediate the kind *of* character that has this inner, complex, rounded life.

That readers are able to access something that looks like an inner life is itself a sign of a Romantic strand of novel theory and the growth of fictionality. It is not my purpose to rehearse the so-called rise of the novel; Siskin's "generic history" reminds us that the rise of any genre has more to do with its prominence among the different kinds with which it is associated at a given time than with a singular, developmental history (11). However, I do want to linger over Gallagher's observation that "accessibility means fictionality" (356) because of its implications for the novel's relationship to other discourses, especially legal discourse about both public reputation and private character. Gallagher observes that the novel helped school eighteenth-century readers in "cognitive provisionality" or a way of temporarily accepting non-facts for a practical purpose (e.g. as with legal fictions). This "expedient fictionality" (347), although it sounds at first like Lynch's "pragmatics of character" (4) or Judge's claim for the novel's pedagogical value as a primer in credibility testing, is not immediately concerned with character, however. Rather, it shifts the novel's usefulness from the practical to the pleasurable in the sense that the novel allowed readers to relax their vigilance against deception, to indulge belief without negative repercussions, and, importantly, to *choose* to engage with the novel's fictions and set them aside when finished (Gallagher 347).[20] Coleridge's willing suspension of disbelief thus entailed suspension of the skeptical side of disbelief and encouraged enjoyment of the playful side of make-believe.

At the same time, the Romantics also taught readers to think of characters as individual persons with psychological depth and agentic power (Lynch 8–9), and to think of reading not only as escapism from their own "social context" (6)—including the skepticism Gallagher describes—but also as a deep-dive through which they "found themselves and plumbed their own interior resources of sensibility" by exploring that of fictional characters (10).[21]

[20] See David A. Brewer, *The Afterlife of Character, 1726–1825*, on the many ways eighteenth-century characters proved irresistible to readers who, far from relinquishing the fiction, crafted new storylines to keep the character alive.

[21] Lynch thus reminds us that, starting with the Romantics, professional, literary critics developed and countenanced the rise of the novel *theory* which has yoked the genre to the rise of individualism since the early nineteenth century, made "verisimilitude of character" the apotheosis of both, and granted "literariness" and canonical status to works in that tradition (4). At the risk of a tautology: Forster can make character the most important aspect of the novel *because the novel had already made character that way, that is, because previous critics had already decided a referential, realistic, psychologically oriented model of fictional character defined the novel.* In this sense, the lectures rehearse a tradition. It is also important to note that Lynch's reminder does not undermine connections between liberal individualism, realism, interiority, and the novel. Rather, it historicizes and de-naturalizes them by showing them to be the "by-products" of social processes that included the reasons for and the ways in which readers approached reading (6). Thus, although she wants these meanings "to take a back seat" (4), they're still along for the ride. Ideas about character as personal, deep, coherent, agentic do belong to the nineteenth-century novel; Lynch argues that we should

This combination of risk-free speculation and hypothetical thinking with vicarious experience and self-examination raises questions not only about the experience of novel-reading, but also about the ease with which readers switched off habits or attitudes gleaned in the pleasurable encounter with literary fiction.[22] How might the novel's fantasy of getting behind a character's reputation to explore its private character and interior resources activate a sense of one's *personal* depths and influence one's thinking about the very relationship *between* inner and outer character? If reading novels encouraged in readers a habit of imagining themselves this way, how did this habit interact with ideas about public and private character in legal discourse, especially Victorian ideas about distinguishing the two but protecting both?

Thinking about accessibility as a sign of fictionality highlights the irony that while in law a lack of privacy inhibits the development of character, the novel's character development depends on that lack, making it a defining feature of the genre. The notion of an omniscient narrator, or the use of indirect discourse to focus a character's thoughts and convey them in his or her idiom are among the surest signs that readers are moving in a fictional world. The deeper readers get into characters' mental states, the more they are reminded that these characters are being created through the text (Gallagher 356). Gallagher's point that these narrative modes of access create an "unreal knowability" should underscore why it is that such access to a real person is never so easily gained. After all, people can be spoken about, and in no way more convincingly than by intimates best acquainted with their turns of phrase or trains of thought, but some do not have, because others do not grant, this kind of access. In the real world of knowability, law sets limits on access and disclosure by allowing individuals to restrict what can be known about them. On this thinking, if accessibility is a hallmark of fictionality, and excess access is a violation, then the novel, with its third-person narrators

---

pay attention to how they got that way. What stands out in these readings of the novel is the way eighteenth-century readers were called to involve themselves self-consciously in acts of reading, to use the novels, whereas the nineteenth-century novel presented itself to readers already habituated to these ways of reading. See Armstrong's discussion of "early nineteenth-century canonizers" (21).

[22] Lisa Rodensky's study of criminal intention and narrative omniscience is grounded in a similar question about the effects of such close, imaginative contact with the interior life of fictional characters: "What might the consequences of such representations be for social and cultural attitudes towards the basic elements of crime and toward criminal responsibility more generally?" (7). I discuss Rodensky's work in *The Crime in Mind* in Chapter 1. See also Blinka on the futility of instructing twenty-first-century juries to turn off their culturally influenced ways of thinking about character, for example (148).

flaunting their omniscience, by definition must be an invasion of privacy. It cannot operate in a world where privacy actually, or at least always, works.[23]

One formulation of this foundational irony is that the absence of privacy becomes a condition of the novel because the novel cannot otherwise create characters with psychological depth. And characters of undifferentiated depth start to look more like the Chaucerian "social persons" Fowler describes, each with their own turn to take, than like the properly named character about whose plausible experiences readers could speculate in a risk-free environment of make-believe. (And if this is true of all flat characters, a cast of all round characters would leave no room for plot.)[24] A slightly different formulation is that, instead of privacy's absence, it is the prospect of privacy's loss, or the threat of exposure, or the voluntary relaxation of its boundaries (e.g. through the extension of intimacy) that is a fundamental condition of the novel. That sense of having something to conceal, whether dangerously criminal or merely embarrassing, becomes a source of psychological depth that has the secret as its signpost. Secrets (whether their content is revealed to the reader or not) act as mystification or suggestion of immanence. They may function as a kind of possession, or take the form of greater knowledge (both of which are useful for blackmail plots), but in each case, having a secret—like having excess energy—becomes a supplement that draws attention to one character or set of characters more than to another; it rounds them.[25]

---

[23] Gallagher 357 observes that narratives told in the first-person make sure to limit their knowledge of other characters in a way that prevents readers from reaching certainty about other characters or identifying with them. I might put this as protecting the privacy of "the character who is the object of desire" (e.g. Kurtz as Marlow's desired object) by placing him or her outside the narrator's grasp while also showing how susceptible he or she is to just this kind of intense speculation; just because others can't really get at you doesn't mean they aren't trying. The modernist example is especially pertinent since by the time these narrative modes come to dominate fiction, we've also reached greater legal protection for privacy, perhaps as a function of the very habits of reading created by the realist novel.

[24] To imagine a world of round characters is to create a world of importunity, and the problem of accommodating or discriminating among (ideally equal) rights at the individual and group levels. See Woloch 31–3 on democracy; and Armstrong 20 on the idea of crowds and masses.

[25] See Alexander Welsh, *George Eliot and Blackmail*, especially "Part II: The Pathology of Information" in which he links the nineteenth century's booming "knowledge industry" and mass communication with new forms of crime prevention and circumstantial evidence. The former contributed to a climate of "threatening publicity" that enhanced the value of privacy and made private communications, like the secret, a "deliberate means to intimacy" (73). But secrets could be used for profit, too, and the nature of circumstantial evidence meant that not all secrets had to be deliberately shared.

The dynamic of secrecy and disclosure, the right to set limits on what to disclose and how much access to oneself to grant, is at the heart of privacy. By denying fictional characters the capacity to make this decision, novels imaginatively violate privacy. We can thus add a further paradox to Gallagher's analysis of fictionality: as long as the discourse of privacy made it essential to developing one's inner life or keeping one's personality inviolate, then the novel ought not to be able to create plausible characters by violating it. Yet that is what novels do. We take pleasure in having this kind of access and speculate with this increased knowledge. Our "ironic credulity" is heightened because we, as readers, have situational knowledge not shared by other characters (qtd. in Gallagher 346). We might borrow the language of finance (another discourse in which character meets credit) and say that our insider's knowledge reduces the risks of our particular speculations.[26] Furthermore, our attachment to these characters increases because they give us this experience and, in Gallagher's analysis, produce a sense of relief (like the feeling of waking from a bad dream and realizing that it wasn't real) that our own lives are not so alarmingly permeable (357). In other words, what we *don't* risk is our *own* privacy.

However, while fictional violations of privacy reassert privacy's importance for us as readers, it does not necessarily follow that we're right to be reassured. If anything, leaving the novel should mean returning to the world of skepticism and vigilance (where fictionality does not make itself so easily known) so that the experience of surveilling characters *in* the novel would heighten our desire for privacy *outside* the novel. In short, the privacy axis of access/disclosure can be a theme, a tool of characterization that helps to distribute attention, *and* a condition of the novel's character-system. It's another formal mechanism for creating character space within a character-system based on the legal protection of privacy.[27]

---

[26] Mary Poovey likens realism's "control of narrative attention" to the dynamics of secrecy and disclosure which animated nineteenth-century financial journalism, both of which cause readers "to focus on some details and ignore others" ("Writing about Finance" 52). Gallagher pursues a similar metaphor for novel-reading when she describes the novel as "a protected affective enclosure that encouraged risk-free emotional investment" (351). See also Finn. I discuss Georg Simmel's characterization of urban life as a credit-economy in Chapter 4.

[27] Critics who rely on a relational, distributional schema of character formation point out that the asymmetry or disequilibrium in these relationships is symptomatic of capitalist models of social organization. My turn towards law is consonant with those readings especially as regards property's foundational role vis-à-vis the legal superstructure. (Blackstone named property as one of the three basic rights, alongside life and liberty, neither of which meant much without it.) What do Warren and Brandeis do but postulate an inner life that must

References to privacy or private character may seem out of place in a book that is not primarily about privacy. After all, the title refers to writing and *reputation*. Privacy enters its pages repeatedly because of the close associations between character and an individual's decision-making power about how to distinguish between an inner life, a private life, and a public reputation. Privacy is not the same as secrecy, yet like keeping secrets, making something private lends an aura of immanence or depth to personal character and relationships, and the idea of "inviolate personality," made famous by Samuel D. Warren and Louis D. Brandeis, explicitly contends that privacy is a necessary condition of self-realization.[28] The self-determinism behind all of these privacy traits carries with it both the moral agency implied in early conceptions of character as well as the active synthesis of one's experiences that Cardinal Manning drew on in his metaphor of weaving. So while I do not begin with an interest in privacy per se, my interest in character and reputation and the way novels work paradoxically demands it. In order to develop these connections, I turn first to an overview of the different ways the Victorian novelists I study made character a thematic priority before looking at the way these themes become structures that may make the novel's development of character and its manipulation of reputation itself a violation of privacy. What I offer is not quite two versions of a chapter synopsis as much as an illustration that starts with the most obvious example of literary character-talk.

Woloch pointed to Elizabeth Gaskell's elevation of working-class characters into prominent positions as an example of the topical mode through which the character-system emphasizes some characters more than others. Extending this approach, I argue that a thematic interest in character as such is a sign of the novelist working out topically what he is doing formally in apportioning "attention" to his characters. Anthony Trollope's preoccupation with libel law best exemplifies this approach. A character's reputation assumes greater significance in Trollope's oeuvre because the characters themselves keep coming back, sometimes moving from central roles to become minor reference points (Lizzie Eustace comes to mind), sometimes having a second go at major-ness as with *Phineas Redux*, or sometimes stretching the

---

be protected by law so as to permit personal self-fashioning and flourishing, the further *development* of one's inner life? So long as this presumption of legal personality grows out of propertied notions of personhood (one has to *have* property to *be* inviolate and enjoy a right *to* privacy) and then remains associated with physical barriers between self and others (the right to set limits on access being reified into separate, private spaces), then the right to privacy remains unevenly distributed with the result that some will be allowed to develop that inner life, to become round, while others remain flat, a jurisprudential version of alienated labor.

[28] See Vincent; Lepore; and Pionke and Millstein.

bounds of their character-space through repeated use and heightened impact so as to become less minor as in the case of Quintus Slide. Fired by his newspaper at the end of *Phineas Redux* because he had become "too energetic for their purposes" (*PR* II.359), Slide re-emerges in *The Prime Minister* to plague Plantagenet Palliser's conscience, demonstrating that his energy was also too great for Trollope to set him aside. "Gossip" figures similarly as a tool that enables groups as different as the Wildfell gossips in Anne Brontë's novel and the narrator of Gaskell's *Cranford* to function as intradiegetic guides to the way communities control their membership, in a sense reflecting back to the author the way her narrative control of character-talk performs precisely this function for the novel. Likewise, a topical focus on defendants' speech, the right to silence, and the apportioning of criminal responsibility at the level of story in *Adam Bede* and *The Scarlet Letter* reproduces the formal apportioning of attention among character-spaces at the level of discourse. As criminal(ized) characters, Hetty and Hester are already eccentrics who by resisting their prescribed social function within the fictional community—what they're supposed to do *in* the story—help to emphasize what they do *for or to* the telling of the story. When their transgressions threaten the social order within the novel, these women surpass not only the "limits of individualism" ascribed to them, as Nancy Armstrong might put it; they may also threaten to exceed their narrative function. (Hester is recuperated, but Hetty is expelled and allowed to die, a doubling-down on the disciplinary power of law and the novel.)

The work of narrativizing transgressive characters offers an especially interesting mode of exploring the disciplinary potential of the novel and, more importantly, its capacity to *create* the excess energy that informs nineteenth-century conceptions of character as individualism.[29] This sense of individualism's having limits takes an ironic turn at the end of the century—exemplifying what Woloch refers to in fact as the "ironization of centrality" (33)—in *The Strange Case of Dr. Jekyll and Mr. Hyde* and *The Picture of Dorian Gray*. In these urban gothics the social expansiveness of the realist novel is thrust to the background, much as Hyde pushes out Jekyll or Dorian casts off Sybil Vane (who, interestingly, ceases to act her part(s) at precisely the moment her inner life, her love for Dorian, acquires complexity and

---

[29] Armstrong argues that unlike the eighteenth-century subject who confronted an arguably more malleable social order (one it could "ask" to accommodate eccentricities), the nineteenth-century subject, now one of a mass of individuals, must adapt "to a position more limited than its subjectivity, which constitutes an inner world apart and only partially expressed in social terms" (55–6).

claims attention). This is not to say that psychological depth, if attempted, is thereby *achieved*, however. Rather, both novels' exploration of the relationship between personality and privacy suggests that without the latter there can be no foundation for character. Instead of depth, there is parallel alterity. In the character-systems of these gothic novels, violate personalities are shown to force the expansion of their allotted character-spaces.[30]

How do Stevenson and Wilde respectively manage, contain, or distribute attention to these unconventional protagonists? Partly through surveillance and the negotiation of private spaces but also through contests over intellectual and artistic property, the material expressions of one's inner life, which pushed the concept of ownership onto more abstract ground and offered a legal argument for privacy. Closing a bracket opened by the right not to incriminate oneself, the right to keep one's inner life to oneself through the operation of privacy is a mode of self-authorship. In their efforts to determine for themselves whom to let into and what to let out about their inner lives, they can be read as characters who want to shape the boundaries of their character space themselves and whose struggle in particular exemplifies the way that theme becomes dynamic and structures the novel's development, or disintegration, of character.[31]

By extending Woloch's formal and ideological analysis of the way narrative works in the realist novel—as an aesthetic example of a labor theory of character—to legal narrative, it becomes possible to examine the workings of a jurisprudential theory of character within law's character-system, but this book also traces the permeability of that system, or the way legal ideas of personhood circulate within a broader cultural discourse of character, meet up with novel persons in literary fiction, and re-enter their respective domains newly informed by that contact. It would take a sociology of reading to

---

[30] See also Armstrong's chapter on *Dracula* and the romance as alternative "modes of subject formation" (11) against which the novel had to contend in order to maintain its conception of individuality and its generic status. Armstrong's point that anything which didn't look like liberal individualism had to be depicted "in phobic terms" describes Stevenson's and Wilde's gothic tales that explore the limits of inviolate personality, including the expanded conceptions of property on which it was based, and the foundation it provided for a new conception of privacy.

[31] When this self-authorizing impulse is explored through a fictional character, it shows the other side of what Woloch sees in Henry James's rueful acknowledgment of his own authorial obligation to curtail the "carrying power" many of his characters possess (22–3); that is, it depicts a kind of contest over authorial control. But if Mr. Croy settles for his fate, Jekyll/Hyde and Dorian do not.

understand how readers themselves manipulated these interactions.[32] What I offer here is an account of the way legal and literary ideas about character take practical shape in legal rules and procedures and in literary productions, or the way narrative theories of character become applied in particular ways at particular historical moments. Considered from the vantage point of narrative jurisprudence, the ethical ramifications of narrative choices—from the structure of the narrative to the mode of its telling and perspective of the teller—become clearer and more meaningful when the range of choices and conditions of selection are specified. In this respect, the chapters that follow are attempts to understand how changes within Victorian literary and legal practice contributed to the kinds of characters that could be formed and which even now frame our conception of what it means to be an individual and to live among others.

A secondary and more implicit aim of this study is to reinterpret the relationship between Victorian law and literature. The narrative, rhetorical, and interpretive foundations of law and literature make fellows of these two areas of writing and thought. The gentlemanly class to which Blackstone addressed his *Commentaries* and the man of letters Robert A. Ferguson found in the early years of America's Republic moved easily between them, and if a career in the law proved out of reach, many picked up a pen to write novels instead.[33] The felt similarities owe something to the ideas about character outlined above, namely, the early nineteenth-century assumption that individuals possessed moral agency, that character followed a developmental trajectory, that law and literature contributed to that development, and that the representation of these individuals was something lawyers and novelists especially did. If law and literature traveled together for as long as this conception of character obtained, the shift towards management of identities, bureaucratization, and the consolidation of a legal profession with its own separate rules and language, distinguished the goals and hence lessened the basis of comparison, sometimes putting law into competition with, if not in opposition to, literature.[34] However, to postulate that the relationship between the two is consistent is to ignore asymmetries in their relationship. As I explain further

---

[32] Richard Altick's *The English Common Reader* and John Sutherland's *Victorian Fiction: Writers, Publishers, Readers* come to mind. More recent cognitive theories of the way readers interact with character are germane as well.

[33] See R. A. Ferguson, *Law and Letters*. John Sutherland in *Victorian Fiction* counts 411 male novelists in the Victorian period with one out of five of them turning to literature after attempting a career at law (162).

[34] See Dolin for recent accounts of different configurations of the law and literature relationship.

in Chapter 1, to imagine literature as being always liberatory is to miss its disciplinary function or its overreach into areas of personhood that it helped to create but which also need protection; conversely, to imagine law as being primarily punitive or regulatory is to miss its world-creating function. As Woloch observes, literature's theory of labor depends on readers' acceptance of social inequality, but this inequality is the root of criticism in "outsider jurisprudence."[35] At the same time, legal rules to protect private character are formative, not just punitive. If contrarian theories of narrative can be synthesized as aspects of a single narrative field, then one can look at different ideological and formal positions of character within law and literature separately *and* within the combined discursive field of law and literature. In this sense I share Christine L. Krueger's view that abstract theories of how law and literature relate risk obscuring the historical realities of the way parts of law relate to parts of literature. The reinterpretation I offer is less grand narrative than specifically contextualized explorations across cognate areas of law in their relation to forms of the realist novel.

Chapter 1, "Incriminating Character: Revisiting the Right to Silence in *Adam Bede* and *The Scarlet Letter*," begins by revisiting F. R. Leavis's comparison of George Eliot to Nathaniel Hawthorne. Looked at from a literary-aesthetic and socio-legal perspective, *The Scarlet Letter* (1850) and *Adam Bede* (1859) offer a window into a mid-century discourse of character that coincides with contemporary legal discussion of witness competency and the broader effort to define and allocate responsibility for wrongful actions. Both Hawthorne and Eliot return to an earlier period to explore the effects of remaining silent in the face of pressure to speak, a pressure which the silencing of the accused had relieved by the time both novels were being written, but which was also being dismantled in the interests of gathering the best evidence. Accused of crime and compelled to speak, both Hester Prynne and Hetty Sorrel appear to exercise a right to silence that did not exist in the historical settings of either novel and that makes them the fulcrum for weighing the dangers of disclosure against those of silence. For readers in the 1850s, however, the right to silence offered a different way to interpret an absence of women's speech that would have resonated not only in the legal debate over

---

[35] Woloch comments that Forster's notion of character "registers the competing pull of inequality and democracy within the nineteenth-century bourgeois imagination" (31). At the same time that the formal focus on a protagonist or set of major characters is made familiar by the realities of social inequality—and therefore tacitly accepted by readers—a more democratic impulse acknowledges the (just) demands of minor characters and maintains readers' interest in them (31–3). The term "outsider jurisprudence" is Matsuda's in "Public Response to Racist Speech," qtd. in Scheppele 2084.

competency generally, but in the context of women's political speech, professional writing, and other forms of transgression.

When the defendant cannot or will not speak, as Hester Prynne and Hetty Sorrel do not, others must be relied on to provide the necessary character evidence. But what are the conditions and limits on the kinds of testimony a witness might give? Chapter 2, "Gossip, Hearsay, and the Character Exception: Reputation on Trial in *The Tenant of Wildfell Hall* and *R v Rowton*," examines legal objections to hearsay as compared with the novel's more liberal treatment of gossip. One of the most routine exceptions to the rule against hearsay is the character exception, or the idea that testimony as to general reputation can be admitted as evidence. However, even legal commentators of the day, responding to a controversial decision in *R v Rowton* (1865), lamented that the court's rejection of a witness's individual experience of the defendant—in favor of general reputation—reduced that testimony to little more than hearsay, or gossip. A reading of the legal decision is situated within discussion of Anne Brontë's *The Tenant of Wildfell Hall* and Elizabeth Gaskell's *Cranford* as novels which not only admit gossip but repurpose it for narratological and sociological goals of community building.

Where Chapter 2 discusses the way defense attorneys used objections to hearsay to protect their clients' characters, Chapter 3 changes orientation and considers how libel laws enabled character to go on the offensive. The forty years between Lord Campbell's Libel Act (1843) and the Newspaper Libel and Registration Act (1881) saw increased protections for that most public dissemination of character in the press, and many of the century's most publicized libel trials occurred after passage of the 1881 Act. While novelists certainly capitalized on the public taste for scandal and its interest in famous trials when devising plots, and while gossip is a mainstay of the novel's characters' communal knowledge, surprisingly few novelists seem to have taken up the issues of libel and slander explicitly. Anthony Trollope's ongoing engagement with the press (in *The Warden*, *Orley Farm*, and *Phineas Finn*, for example) makes him a notable exception. Chapter 3, "Defamation of Character: Anthony Trollope and the Law of Libel," situates Trollope's novels of the 1860s and 1870s within significant developments in libel law. Beginning with the period of Trollope's editorship of *Saint Pauls Magazine* and publication of *Phineas Finn* (1869) and *Phineas Redux* (1873), I argue that these years mark a historical junction of legal, literary, and journalistic concern with libel to which Trollope was particularly attentive because so many of his characters brought reputations with them from one novel to the next. Ending with *The Prime Minister* (1876), *Cousin Henry* (1879), and new legislation for enlarging freedom of the press, I argue that Trollope's method of literary characterization, namely the impact of the media on characters' self-concept, anticipated the limits of libel law and opened the way for what might be a more effective means of protecting character through privacy.

Chapter 4, "Dignity, Disclosure, and the Right to Privacy: The Strange Characters of Dr. Jekyll and Dorian Gray," reads Stevenson's and Wilde's novels through the lens of Samuel D. Warren and Louis D. Brandeis's 1890 *Harvard Law Review* article "The Right to Privacy" and examines the ways in which each novel explores the idea of controlling one's image by controlling the disclosure of or access to forms of intellectual and artistic property (the formula, the confession, the portrait) and with them the "personality" grounding privacy. Because ownership, no matter how broadly defined, continues as the foundation of inviolability, these novels raise questions about the integrity of the personality that could have such rights and under what conditions those rights become forfeit. Subjects of gossip on the one hand, on the other hand, both Dr. Jekyll and Dorian engage in acts of disclosure where the act emphasizes self-possession but the nature of the disclosure (or the failure to read it correctly) emphasizes an alienated self. Depicted through scenes of disarticulation and growing incoherence, Henry Jekyll and Dorian Gray thus provide a limit test of the premise of "inviolability" on which Warren and Brandeis build their privacy protection.

I conclude with Chapter 5, "The English Dreyfus Case: Status as Character in an Illiberal Age," which considers Arthur Conan Doyle's true crime writing in "The Strange Case of George Edalji" (1907) alongside Julian Barnes's novel *Arthur & George* (2005). Conan Doyle reclaimed Edalji's character by reconstructing the case and highlighting the impact of presumptions about race, ethnicity, and national identity, or group-based character, on determinations of an individual's capacity for criminal behavior. Pitting cosmopolitan coverage against local report and the Home Secretary against regional authorities, Conan Doyle's newspaper account also drew attention to the impact of the venues where it was tried. Julian Barnes's recreation of the relationship between Conan Doyle and Edalji enables a comparison of legal, journalistic, and fictional narratives of character. Further, the novel's timing coincides with what Nicola Lacey refers to as the "resurgence of character" or the return of "status" and "character determinism" to processes of assigning responsibility for crimes in ways that threaten all "who form easily identifiable objects of anger, fear, or resentment" ("Resurgence of Character" 173).

As this synopsis shows, I have tried to highlight chronology without ignoring analogy and to map a development of ideas without espousing a progressive (as in ever improving) history. Indeed, each chapter is comparative in nature. Conversations are played out between pairs or series of novels as well as between novels and legal concepts, essays, opinions, and statutes, and each isolates and recounts a specific legal history. However, while some issues come into focus, others only temporarily recede into a background in which the history of cognate areas is also being made. This dual awareness is reflected in my organization and in the selection of novels.

In terms of organization, each chapter engages a specific legal issue that leads logically or dialogically to a related question; if the distinction can be allowed, their relationship is causal without being determinative or allowing for only one effect. For example, the right to silence canvassed in Chapter 1 necessitates Chapter 2's attention to character evidence; attention to defendants invites a lateral focus on the prosecution. Similarly, oral gossip calls for consideration of libelous print, which in turn opens onto privacy issues. As broad constructs, character and character-talk inevitably lead into distinct areas of law, and my purpose has been to follow where it leads instead of concentrating on an extended history of one. To highlight a range of literary engagement with these issues, I have chosen novels that are thematically aligned and contemporaneous with the moment the legal issue becomes acute in an approach that takes for granted the value of historical specificity as a basis for comparison. That being said, a novel like *The Tenant of Wildfell Hall*, for example, draws together multiple issues, but these issues capture attention differently in different decades, and each chapter gestures towards those horizons.

Readers can reasonably ask why, given its comparative approach and the prioritization of legal matters, this book bothers with chronology or with the appearance of a traditional literary history. For indeed a rough literary chronology can be traced from the 1850s through the 1890s in chapters whose temporal edges, like their thematic focus, also overlap. I freely acknowledge that there are other ways to organize this study and rather than ignore them, I invite readers to pursue a syncretic or looped approach to reading in which each legal issue can be refracted through a different literary lens, and each novel can be understood in its relation to different permutations of the legal question of character. Reading the pre-history of the right to silence in Hawthorne's and Eliot's novels of the 1850s, for example, raises the logical question of how the court adapted to its own rules regarding the exclusion of the accused's testimony (who could provide the necessary character evidence?), but to begin answering this question, Chapter 2 moves both backwards to Anne Brontë's *The Tenant of Wildfell Hall* (1848) and forwards to the 1865 case of *R v Rowton*. Helen Graham's transgressions and selective silences could have earned her a place in Chapter 1, but one effect of the current organization is to see her simultaneously within the protective framework of non-incrimination and within a new framework focused on character as reputation, including the transactional relationship between one's own disclosures and communal speculations. Likewise, laments that the

Rowton decision effectively turned reputation into hearsay or gossip colors an ongoing discussion of libel, public benefit, and the press that, for Anthony Trollope, became acute in 1867 but which I don't take up until Chapter 3.

My point is that the thematic focus on legal questions means that while some issues were more critical at specific moments, it is often the case that they surface in novels from different decades or, if starting from the literary point of view, that Hetty Sorrel might have as much to say to Dr. Jekyll about crime and confession as Helen Graham has to say to Phineas Finn about how it feels to be an outsider or to be maligned by one's community.

I should also emphasize that leading with a legal question is not an attempt to disguise that this book remains grounded in literary criticism, a study of the way novels interact with law to do the work of character-building. In this respect, stopping off decade by decade to look at the ways novels changed their approach to character—from styles of narration, to modes of conflict, to reversals of the developmental integrity of character introduced earlier in the century—reminds us that literary history is embedded in and responsive to cultural history even as it recirculates a rhetorical history, as the late Susan Manning observed, that might free literary analysis from a compulsive linearity, especially one linked to national bias (xii).

Indeed, the particular comparisons I make are not meant to instantiate a hierarchy, either between law and literature as fields or between individual authors, novels, or national traditions (Manning and Taylor 75). Several of these concerns animate the field of transatlantic literary studies. As Meredith McGill has pointed out, where American Studies has felt the necessity of transatlantic approaches, scholars of British literary history have tended to view the study of transatlantic connections as an "optional extra" (164), and Joseph Rezek, implicitly addressing this sensibility, challenges scholars of British literature to explain why they *aren't* reading transatlantically (5).[36] The work that follows does not fully take up Rezek's challenge. Readers *will* see a mix of British and American, legal and literary, texts, but that mix is not uniform across chapters, either in terms of proportion, emphasis, or type and is guided instead by the correspondence of ideas, a surprising similarity, a shared reference point, or a pointed contrast. I cross the boundaries of literary fields when empirical evidence (e.g. contemporaneous book reviews, a comment in a letter) makes the comparison for me, but I also resist some leads precisely because they lead away from my focus. Character is an enormous concept, and I've leaned towards greater historical specificity to ground it.

---

[36] "[T]he burden of proof now lies with those scholars who still wish to treat literary history in strictly national terms" (Rezek 5).

More important than the specific novels, or even the other common law jurisdictions, I leave out, then, are the pitfalls I hope I've avoided: an exclusively westward movement of British influence on American writers (with the implication that British literature was always in the vanguard of aesthetic development), and an uncritical assumption that national character automatically inheres in the British (or English, Scottish, or Irish) novels I read. At best, they may help us see those associations in the making.

A methodological tension between a comparative analysis that emphasizes aesthetic forms and a historical study of those forms is not dissimilar to the tension Woloch observes between structural and mimetic analyses of character, and it's certainly recognizable in the history of the field of law and literature, and perhaps all interdisciplinary fields, that negotiate theories and methodologies that constitute the separate disciplines. If it seems that I'm trying to have my methodology both ways, it's because each has its virtues: a comparative study where the bases of comparison are historically grounded.

The works I bring together thus form the temporary edges of a field of inquiry that can reveal the ways ideas change, and new questions emerge, as they move through different discourses, across oceans, and over time. So, while I remain focused on Victorian England in the second half of the nineteenth century, readers should not be surprised to find *The Scarlet Letter*, or Nathaniel Hawthorne himself, there in the 1850s, too. Likewise, when Parliamentarians debated libel legislation in the 1860s, their own comparative politics included reference to U.S. approaches to free speech. No wonder Trollope considered America a fitter venue for Quintus Slide's tactics. And no wonder that American jurists Warren and Brandeis pieced through English precedents on libel and intellectual property in their search for a common law legal basis for privacy or, further, that their Continental sensibility might complement Oscar Wilde's Dorian Gray better than American conceptions of liberty.

One final reminder: a jurisprudential theory of character is not limited to a specific set of laws. It encompasses those that impinge on character, but it develops out of the textual interaction between legal thought and legal rules when they are represented, challenged, allegorized, or adapted in literary techniques for creating character. This study explores how a particular set of interactions around the idea of character produced a legal theory of character at work in the novel and a narrativized treatment of character at law.

1

Incriminating Character: Revisiting the Right to Silence in *Adam Bede* and *The Scarlet Letter*

> "Either I must have surrendered my secret,—or have returned an equivocating answer,—or finally, must have stoutly and boldly denied the fact . . . I therefore considered myself entitled, like an accused person put on trial, to refuse giving my own evidence to my own conviction, and flatly to deny all that could not be proved against me."
>
> Walter Scott (1829), quoted by George Eliot (1858)

Comparisons of Nathaniel Hawthorne and George Eliot began almost as soon as Eliot started writing fiction. In a July 1859 article in the *Edinburgh Review*, published just a few months after the appearance of *Adam Bede*, Caroline Norton noted that "Mr. Eliot resembles Hawthorne, the American author, more than any other writer with whom we are acquainted" (240) and gestured towards examples, particularly in *Scenes of Clerical Life*, that "[have] all the scent of the Hawthorne bough" (240). A year later, the *North British Review* elaborated on the comparison in "Imaginative Literature: The Author of *Adam Bede* and Nathaniel Hawthorne." Signaling Eliot's continued alias alongside the success of her first novel, the title draws readers into what is primarily a review of the two authors' most recent works (*The Mill on the Floss* and *Transformation*, as *The Marble Faun* was known in England) focused on "the relative power of these writers to delineate character" (180). Eliot herself had declared Hawthorne "a grand favorite of mine" and re-read *The Scarlet Letter* not long before commencing *Adam Bede*.[1]

---

[1] At least two letters mention Hawthorne. Most frequently cited is one from August 1852 as she waits for a copy of *The Blithedale Romance* (Haight II.52), followed by one from 1857 when she mentions reading *The Scarlet Letter* (Haight II.311n5). See Haight; Quick 287–8; and Casson 19. Hawthorne served as consulate to Liverpool from 1853 to 1857 and made his first trip to London in 1855 where he attended a "literary breakfast" hosted by poet and MP Richard Monkton Milnes (Milder 65). Eliot and George Henry Lewes returned from

Drawn by Eliot's own admiration for Hawthorne, literary scholars have continued to link them. In his 1961 Foreword to *Adam Bede*, F. R. Leavis commented on "that profound kind of influence" that works below the level of consciousness (x) and yet which produced, for Leavis, a striking set of similarities between Eliot's first novel and *The Scarlet Letter*. While I share Alexander Welsh's view that the question of authorial influences on Eliot, and Hawthorne's in particular, is secondary to the cultural and personal factors influencing her interest in secrecy (*Blackmail* 27), I revisit these comparisons to think about the two works as contemporaries, novels that bracket the 1850s and which in their representation of transgressive women not only worked to delineate fictional personae, as the *North British Review* emphasized, but also participated in the broader contemporary discourse of "character."[2]

Because this chapter depends on a transatlantic comparison, it's important to acknowledge the particular caution with which scholars in transatlantic studies approach the idea of influence because of the old tendency, particularly within linear literary histories, to position American literature, like the nation, as being derivative of English literature and, indeed, of England (the "lateness" of American Romanticism is a case in point).[3] On the face of it, pairing Hawthorne and Eliot reverses the customary direction of cultural influence in favor of the elder writer's influence on the new novelist, but if both authors were influenced by Scott and Wordsworth before him, a more circular relationship becomes visible, one that acknowledges, as Clifford Siskin observed, that every genre is connected to past iterations of that genre

---

an eight-month journey through Germany in 1855 (Henry 88–92) and took up residence in Richmond, but the two writers did not meet. Commentary on this missed opportunity is scarce. Raymona Hull describes a conversation between Hawthorne and Caroline Bray at a gathering in February 1860 (183). Hawthorne was eager to meet the Brays, who had hosted Emerson in 1848 and were close friends of Eliot (Henry 54). According to Hull, Hawthorne admired *Adam Bede* and regretted that he hadn't met the author, contrary to reports that he'd refused on moral grounds to meet the younger author. Commenting on similar reports, Hawthorne contemporary and biographer Moncure D. Conway describes a meeting in 1860 at James T. Field's house when Hawthorne expressed this disappointment and remarked: "'I mentioned my wish to meet her to several ladies in London in whose house I was a guest, but none were on visiting terms with her.'" Conway says, "he ascribed this to her irregular marriage to—or relation with—G.H. Lewes" (qtd. in Kalinevitch 6–7).

[2] For the most sustained comparison, see Stokes, especially 105–14, 122–46. See also Quick; Casson; and Gollin.

[3] See Robert Weisbruch on correspondences between the consolidation of the nation state as a geopolitical entity, stadial models of cultural development, and literature as a developmental index. For discussion of authors as national "property," see Straub 10. For more general introductions to the field of transatlantic studies, see Bannet and Manning; and Hughes and Robbins.

and that each exists in "a synchronically distinct set of relationships among different kinds" (10). Played out over both vertical and horizontal axes, this more fluid relationship between genres, or between Hawthorne's romance and Eliot's realism, is one example of the "matrix of influence and response" within which transatlantic scholars situate the literary text and which, they argue, requires a complementary, comparative methodology (Manning and Taylor 75). Of particular importance for my comparison is the way that a jurisprudential theory of character necessarily supplements literary history by bringing legal history within the matrix of influence and response as well. I bring Hawthorne and Eliot together, not to extol British over American literature (or law, for that matter), but because of their corresponding interests in the female offender's historical silence before the law, the stylistic and formal range of their treatment of it, and the implications of their conclusions for the relationship between public speech and character. By positioning these authors and their works as brackets around a legal question, I hope to avoid the evaluative tendency to which comparisons generally are prone.

The question then is what the comparison can reveal about a mid-century discourse of character. Character is a multivalent term, at once a graphic sign, an ethical category, a professional reputation, and a literary construct. Hester Prynne's embellished "A" graphically signifies her criminal deed and her internal, errant state, just as the accusation of infanticide and subsequent verdict against Hetty Sorrel radically change her status in the Hayslope community. Looked at from a literary-aesthetic and socio-legal perspective, *The Scarlet Letter* and *Adam Bede* offer a window into a mid-century discourse of character and practices of character formation that highlights their different literary modes and coincides with contemporary legal efforts to delimit the kinds of evidence that could be put before a jury, especially as regards witness testimony, and, more broadly, the larger effort to define and allocate responsibility for wrongful actions. The "character" of these women—how they are known, valued, and treated in their communities as well as how they respond to these characterizations—is made and remade through the legal processes of adjudicating their crimes and through the literary narratives that depict them.

In spite of shared moral culpability and equal violation of social codes, the two Hesters, rather than the two Arthurs, are brought before the law, however. Although various forms of transgression propel both novels (and play an essential role in the development of the novel as a narrative form), it is because the women are subjected to legal scrutiny, undergo legal process, and suffer legal punishment—and because their responses are markedly silent— that they concretize the problem of character as a narratological and evidential construct. There is certainly good reason to ask why criminals, and more particularly criminal women, should make the best objects for developing a theory of literary and legal character. As suggested in the Introduction, legal discussions of criminality and the administration of criminal justice became sites specifically for character-building in the nineteenth century at the same time that imaginative literature adopted a developmental model of personhood and embraced the idea of personal reform: to start with the criminal gives both law and literature somewhere hopeful to go.

The interest in criminal women is less straightforward though, not least because, as Nicola Lacey observes, nineteenth-century criminology typically associated criminal behavior (and consequently the capacities needed to reform it) with traits that were coded masculine (*Women* 2). By contrast, the "criminological image of the female offender" would seem to disqualify her from a central role in either law or literature: "passive rather than active; driven by emotion rather than reason; moved by impulses located in the body rather than the mind" (*Women* 3).[4] Yet Lacey observes a transformation in attitude towards women's criminality from the eighteenth to nineteenth centuries that is instructive for my own interest in Hester and Hetty because it hinges on the "social consequences of women's exercise of their agency and self-expression" (*Women* 6). Thus, it is not the historical, legal approach to the crimes of adultery or even infanticide, as gendered crimes per se, that interests me. Rather, I am drawn to the examples of Hester and Hetty because of the legal and characterological implications of their respective silence and how the knowledge gaps produced by it were, or might be, filled.

One of the more persistent problems to occupy legal scholars in the 1850s concerned rules of evidence and the prospect of allowing "interested parties," including defendants, to testify in criminal trials. American jurist John Appleton successfully advocated throughout the 1850s and 1860s for the removal of restrictions, making the U.S. state of Maine the first common law jurisdiction in the world to do so in 1864 (Gold 59), whereas specifically criminal defendants in England remained unable to give evidence under oath until 1898. In the absence of opportunities for the accused to be questioned at trial or to speak on her own behalf, other means of obtaining and weighing important evidence were necessary. The novel labored under no such restrictions, of course, and yet in these novels, which not only could admit the central characters' testimony and, indeed, exhort them to explain themselves,

---

[4] This is not to say that Hester and Hetty make equal claims to centrality. Hester might be "bad" and Hetty "mad," in accordance with tropes identified by feminist criminologists (Lacey, *Women* 3), but both women are set aside as the novels delve further into the hearts and minds of the two Arthurs.

the accused *will not* speak. Why not name Arthur Dimmesdale? Why not call Arthur Donnithorne to help or to explain?[5]

Brook Thomas provides a sensible reminder that literary scholars need "to repose the questions to which [a novel's] narrative is an imaginary solution" (7). Dramatic irony, omniscient narration, and the uses of conventional plotting create knowledgeable readers whose questions will differ from those of the novel's internal audience.[6] For the knowledgeable reader, the question Hester's and Hetty's silence raises is not so much one about facts—the birth of one child, the death of another, the paternity of either—as about the value of subjective knowledge and what its retention means, on the one hand, for the private individual's sense of interiority, including one's conscience. On the other hand, and against the demands of individuality and the privacy and self-determinism that were coming to define it, these novels also speak to the kinds of knowledge that are necessary to create and maintain communities, especially the most ethical and reliable modes of acquiring and sharing that knowledge.[7] In this respect, the biggest contemporary problem the novel dramatizes may be the tension between a right to silence and what happens or must result when that right is exercised, and this seems very like the quandary Appleton and other legal thinkers confronted. Following Thomas, I look to the way these novels undertake questions playing out in the legal discussions around them to better understand their literary solutions, as well as those problematic aspects of character that remain(ed) insoluble in literature as well as law.

What then distinguishes the literary-aesthetic from the socio-legal approach and in what ways is that difference significant? In *The Crime in Mind*, Lisa Rodensky starts with the Victorian novel's most pertinent feature: the ability of a third-person narrator to "go inside" the mind and, as she writes of Eliot's novels, to represent crime "from the inside out" (7). With no need to rely, as legal actors often did, on inferences from circumstances or on direct testimony, the realist narrator could produce evidence of mental states and

---

[5] Elizabeth Alsop asks a similar question: "Why should women be required to talk comparatively more often than men; why do men enjoy a greater freedom to remain silent?" (102). Although her short answer is the women's guilt (i.e. that the women have done something they *should* have to explain), it seems more descriptive than explanatory insofar as their guilty male partners aren't put to a similar task. For a comparative study of masculinity in Hawthorne and Gaskell, another contemporary, see Healy.

[6] See Stephen Railton on the distinction between reader, audience, and Hawthorne's "addressee" (481).

[7] See Korobkin's treatment of outward submission as an opportunity for private intellectual freedom, but also Sennett's and Lacey's arguments about urban life and the way semiotics replaces reputation (Lacey, "The Resurgence of Character" 159–60).

link it to acts in the world. Determining criminal responsibility in particular depended on a finding of criminal intention and its connection to a specific act, and while this focus on criminality is germane to Hester's and Hetty's cases, Rodensky points out that discussions of criminal responsibility were one vector of larger conversations about the "workings of the interior self" (8) and changing, increasingly psychologized conceptions of character during the nineteenth century. More than that, the fact that novels *could* access a character's mind and *could* hold up this departure from legal convention as a defining feature of the genre raised questions about whether it was ethical to go so far, or about what this knowledge might make actionable, or how it might change readers' thinking about crime even outside the novel (11).

Tellingly, Rodensky describes the narrator's access as a form that "transgress[es]" legal barriers to knowledge (11). As subsequent chapters on hearsay and privacy will show, these barriers may be self-imposed restrictions rather than epistemological problems, but when rules are self-imposed, the fact that a novel's narrator may by-pass them raises questions about narrative overreach, even if the superior access can provide richer, multidimensional pictures of character. And certainly when a novel chooses *not* to enter a character's mind and/or to preserve their silence, the seeming withdrawal of narrative attention pushes in the opposite direction and raises questions about character development. I share Rodensky's sense that insisting on one kind of function for the novel ("as a liberalizing force or as a disciplinary technology" [11]) or one kind of relationship between it and (in her case) the criminal law is to downplay the complexities of both. As a case in point, I want to consider what the novel's access means for contemporary arguments that tout the value of the novel's ability to give voice or to render the inside out.

A familiar if contested assumption among scholars of law and literature, and of narrative jurisprudence specifically, is that the opportunity to tell one's story is a good thing; to have a voice is desirable, and to be denied one, or to have it contorted into legal argument, is a demerit. Where this argument has been contested is in the claim for the salutary effects of literature's tendency to provide this opportunity to socially marginalized groups and points of view.[8] In light of renewed legal consideration of witness competency that was

---

[8] Kristin Kalsem characterizes Hetty Sorrel's trial as just this sort of missed, or ignored, opportunity for demonstrating feminist narrative jurisprudence (35). Christine L. Krueger goes further and complicates claims for the universal superiority either of direct representation at law or of the recuperative function of literature. As she asks of one woman's excruciatingly forthright suicide note, "Should those stories have been voiced instead? Could they have been comprehended even if they had been spoken?" (*Reading for the Law* 235). I am indebted to Krueger's approach to literary and legal history, and my analysis of

underway in the same decade that Hawthorne and Eliot were writing, their creation of an occasion for speech paired with a refusal to take advantage of it is perplexing: it doesn't fit a significant contemporary account of how the novel's narratives relate to (and, indeed, are to be preferred to) the trial's stock of stories. Instead, these novels complicate the assumption that telling one's story is a universal good and in the process tell a more varied story about the novel's relation to legal practice. As much as the courts were weighing the value of allowing the accused to testify or of continuing the prohibition, the novels I look at in this chapter also are weighing the costs of her disclosure against those of silence. Silence can offer a form of protection: for others, as with Hester's refusal to name Dimmesdale, and for oneself, as with Hetty's repression of her crime. For Hester, silence may be a form of protest or, for Hetty, a sign of incapacity. And silence certainly has narrative value proportional to the novelist's need for the conflict it perpetuates and the character study it therefore enables. On this view, Hawthorne and Eliot seem on the side of the legal status quo even if for different reasons. However, these novels also play out the negative consequences of the accused's silence in settings when the expectation to speak had existed, and which, at the time of composition, might again. Brook Thomas reminds us that novels are the "stories a culture tells about itself" (5), and while this conception holds true for fiction set in the readers' present day, it is nowhere more clearly to be seen than when the story is about a culture's past. What did the historical displacements of both novels—the opportunity to reflect on Puritan New England and provincial Old England—imply about legal and literary understandings of character in the 1850s when both novels were published?

The first section of this chapter takes up the legal status of character and witness competency. Legal debate in the 1850s about who could give evidence—either as parties to a case or nonparty witnesses, or on their own behalf or for the opposing side—revolved around a nascent right to silence that did not exist during the period of either novel's setting. Both Hawthorne and Eliot return to an earlier period to explore the effects of remaining silent in the face of pressure to speak, a pressure which had largely been removed before either novel was written, but which was re-emerging in discussions of witness competence on both sides of the Atlantic. The evidentiary gap produced by continued silence could be filled by other means, and this section explores the legal terrain of character evidence as one such possibility. By providing important context, character evidence could prevent a trial from

Hetty Sorrel's silence will skirt similar terrain. However, I take a broader approach to competency generally and to Eliot's literary contemporaries.

ever convening or could mitigate sentences, but the understanding of what precisely this evidence represented and how it could enter the court were equally subject to debate.

The second section of the chapter takes up Hester's Prynne's selective silences and reads them as acts of narrative control. Her refusal to name Arthur Dimmesdale contrasts other scenes in which she speaks forcefully, as well as her non-verbal work to change interpretations of the scarlet letter's meaning. Hester's silences require other voices to bear witness to her experience both in the seventeenth century of the plot and in its later historicizations. Less a sign of the novel's failed feminism or Hawthorne's reactionary response to nineteenth-century women's activism, however, the juridical need for other voices also emphasizes the need for community.

By contrast to Hester Prynne's self-sufficiency and strategic reticence, Hetty Sorrel's muteness works in tandem with a "willful blindness" to the realities of her situation. Demonstrating what Nicola Lacey identifies as "culpable ignorance," Hetty can be held responsible because she was unreasonable, her "fault . . . grounded in unreasonable character manifested in lack of self-knowledge, poor judgment or self-deception" (*Women* 122).

In the chapter's third section, I focus on both explicit and implicit uses of character in *Adam Bede*, particularly as they weigh in discussions of the relative influence of internal moral agency and external circumstance on individual behavior. Character is an essential concept in the novel's development of a theory of guilt and responsibility, especially when evidence of good character afforded defendants their best chance of receiving a less severe penalty. However, as a historical term meant to provide local color, "character" also conflicted with (or at least highlighted tensions within) mid-century discussions of the credibility of witness testimony: the closer to the crime or the greater the interest in the trial's outcome, the less reliable the evidence and, consequently, the greater the need for character witnesses.

Just as legal scholars debated the most reliable means of gathering relevant evidence, literary critics were discussing the relative merits of romance and realism as modes of developing character. The fourth section of the chapter looks to Eliot's and Hawthorne's respective theories of fiction, as given in chapter 17 of *Adam Bede* and in Hawthorne's "The Custom House," to better appreciate how their conception of character and its personal and communal value aligned with or departed from legal uses for it.

I conclude with more focused attention to Eliot and the professional and personal attractions of character as a subject for her work in *Adam Bede*. Legal discussion of the relationship between conduct and character, and its narratological corollary in plot and character, suggest that both law and literature need us to be bad; they need the conflict our transgressions generate for their narrative momentum. In Eliot's case the relationship between authorship, adultery, and transgression wrapped up in both novels raises the question about the cost of withholding explanations but equally of speaking out.

Competence versus Credibility: Witness Testimony in the 1850s

As suggested in the Introduction, both Hester Prynne's and Hetty Sorrel's silence makes reputation all the more important as a context for their actions and makes the testimony of respected others the only possible mitigation of their guilt. But the damaging inferences that could be drawn from the accused's refusal to defend herself in both the Puritan and Napoleonic settings of the two novels had been removed by the time Hawthorne and Eliot wrote them. Several histories of the criminal trial point to the Prisoner's Counsel Act of 1836, when defense counsel assumed full responsibility for presenting and interpreting the facts of the prisoner's case, as the mechanism which finally removed an accused person's responsibility for representing him- or herself or for cross-examining prosecution witnesses.[9] However, this legislation alone, while an important dimension of the growth of a right to silence, would not explain how a defendant who once had to speak and was then made unable to speak would by the end of the nineteenth century have a choice whether to speak or not. Rather, as Henry E. Smith explains, defense counsel can be situated within a number of "rules and maxims related to the subject of silence" (146), including the privilege against self-incrimination—what in the nineteenth century would become the right to silence.[10]

As a protective cover for defendants and nonparty witnesses alike, the privilege figured in broader discussions of witness competency and compellability—who may give evidence in their own defense or be called to testify by the opposing side—and still broader rules regarding the admissibility of evidence. Although defendants like Hester and Hetty might have welcomed the privilege (seeing that they assume it, anyway), the evidentiary

---

[9] See Schramm on changes to rules of evidence (62–6) and on central questions in the debate over defense counsel (102–3) and passage of the act (105–9); Langbein, *Origins* 277–84; Farmer on the "reconstructive trial" ("Trials" 459, 457–66); and H. Smith 162–9. See also H. Smith 170 on Jervis's Act of 1848, which required Justices of the Peace to caution witnesses during pre-trial questioning.

[10] Smith frames the right as an extension of a privilege that protected "third-party witnesses" or nonparties from incriminating themselves and concurs with Langbein's observation that a defendant who could no longer speak had little use for a privilege against self-incrimination (*Origins* 278). Smith points instead to *R v Garbett* (1847) and its merger of this witness privilege with the greater protections of the confession rule as the first articulation of a modern right to silence (174). For discussion of the confession rule, see Langbein, *Origins* 179.

gap thus created raises several questions: What opportunities were lost by the prohibition against giving evidence? What was the reasoning that disqualified potential witnesses, or made them incompetent to give evidence on their behalf? What inferences could judge, jury, and the public draw from a witness, still more the party to a case, who could choose to give information but chose not to? Were there particular calls to speak—a cultural or lay version of legal compellability—which *might* have engaged Hawthorne's or Eliot's sympathy for a privilege against self-incrimination?

To start with what was lost: The provision of defense counsel was an act of substitution, which meant that the opportunity to "test" the prosecution's case or to "reconstruct" its narrative of events was not lost precisely but shifted from the accused to her counsel (Langbein, "Historical Origins" 1048; Farmer, "Trials" 459). However, from 1827 at the latest, when Jeremy Bentham's *Rationale of Judicial Evidence* was published, Bentham had complained of the common law's exclusionary rules of evidence that made anyone unwilling to undertake an oath or affirmation, anyone convicted of crime or undergoing punishment for crime, anyone with a financial interest in the outcome of a case, and foremost the parties to a case incompetent to testify (Allen). Alert to, if not downright suspicious of, the additional work (understood as profit) these rules brought to the legal profession, Bentham's main objection was that withholding evidence increased the chances of "misdecision" (Allen 9, 99–100). A liar could be found out, but testimony withheld could not be judged. Christopher J. W. Allen explains that Bentham was especially strong on the incompetency of the accused—"'the one person in the world, who, if the fact be in existence cannot fail to know of it'" (128)—whom he thought not only could, but should be made to, give sworn evidence (127), for without this testimony, verdicts would be reached on lesser kinds of evidence.

Bentham's influence, if not exclusive, was nevertheless far-reaching, and efforts to extend witness competency in civil trials progressed through the 1820s and 1840s with the Evidence Act of 1843 (Lord Denman's Act), Lord Brougham's Evidence Amendment Act of 1851, and with reform of the rules regarding the competency of the accused in criminal trials beginning in earnest in 1858 (Allen 132). Where Bentham's influence was most clearly at work, however, was in the United States, according to Allen. John Appleton, who graduated from Bowdoin College in 1822 (one year after Hawthorne had matriculated) and joined the State of Maine's Supreme Court in 1852, had been advocating for the extension of competency since 1835 in a series of articles which were finally compiled as *The Rules of Evidence: Stated and Discussed* (1860). In its first chapter, meant to review the "arguments in favor of excluding witnesses for any cause" (9), Appleton holds forth on the evils of exclusion instead. Responding in particular to another Maine lawyer and Harvard Law Professor Simon Greenleaf's discussion of the "character of witnesses," Appleton disputes the implication that any judge or jury member ever did or could investigate the character of individual witnesses, including those whose testimony is *admitted*, in order to determine their credibility.[11] He therefore concludes that whole "classes" of witnesses should no more be excluded than an individual who was not "tested" in this way (16): "Of individuals or classes there is none of which falsehood can certainly be predicated in any particular instance. Exclusion because of anticipated falsehood, is decision without and before hearing,—adverse to the integrity of the witness" (11). Here, Appleton is speaking of witnesses generally and of the universal fear of perjury thought to follow from infamy or interest, but to pre-judge the value of testimony because of prejudices about a witness's character status is premature, the more so, as he will point out, because no one comes to court without an interest in the outcome of the case.

Like Bentham, Appleton was critical of the rationale for excluding parties to civil and more especially criminal cases. Advocates of the right to silence maintained that it relieved the accused either from telling the truth badly or having to concoct a lie, both of which could serve to incriminate. Once given the choice, however, the decision to speak or keep silent entailed challenges to the presumption of innocence: a silent defendant, it could be inferred, must have something to hide.[12] But Appleton argued that if an accused defendant was to be presumed innocent, then logically the prosecution must be suspected of falsehood, and yet the testimony of the ostensibly injured party, who could expect to benefit from a conviction, was allowed because the jury could gauge his credibility (123–4). As with Appleton's earlier objections, here he argues for equal treatment based on his own reliance, first, on the jury members' ability to read character at least as well as they do in their daily interactions outside the court and, second, on the judge's ability to guide them when in court (14–15). Appleton was nonplussed by the opposition's suggestion that by removing the restriction "silence [would be] tantamount

---

[11] See Blinka 129–31 on Greenleaf's revision of Thomas Starkie's treatise and his own treatment of witness impeachment.

[12] The defendant's silence was a tool for effecting the presumption of innocence. When the accused was legally prohibited from speaking, the question of his voluntariness or resistance was removed and could not lead to inferences of guilt. In addition to these "practical" objections to competency, see Gold on the "conservative" and "constitutional" objections in Maine to Appleton's proposed reform of evidence law (63–6).

to a confession" (129) because in his view only a guilty defendant wanted to be spared the exposure.[13]

These arguments are outlined in chapter 7, "Admission of Parties in Criminal Procedure," which Appleton first published in 1835 in the *American Jurist and Law Magazine* (Gold 61) and in which he showed himself alert not only to Bentham's influence but to Lord Brougham's proposed reforms as well.[14] In the revised collection of articles, Appleton cites Lord Brougham's introduction in 1859 of a bill to extend competency to the accused in criminal trials and open them to cross-examination, but this was one of a series of bills Brougham presented in 1858–60 and of his decades-long campaign to enable parties to give sworn evidence.[15] In what was mooted as a report on the returns from the county courts (a system whose development Brougham had spearheaded in 1845–6), for example, Brougham insinuates an argument for removing the disqualification of parties at criminal trials that built on the success, first, of Lord Denman's Act (which removed the disqualification for infamy and interest in 1843); second, on positive reports from county court judges about the efficacy of examining parties to civil cases; and, finally, on the results of his own efforts in 1851 to bring this practice to the superior courts ("Papers Moved for," cc. 313–17). Amidst these growing opportunities to receive testimony, Brougham railed against two rules that moved in the opposite direction, namely the witness privilege against self-incrimination (embodied in the Witnesses Act of 1806) and what he called the "pernicious practice" of magistrates who reminded the accused not only that their pre-trial testimony would be recorded and used at trial, but also that they could refuse to answer (c. 317).

---

[13] Gold notes that Appleton had no sympathy for the guilty and was happy to have juries act on this inference. The bigger problem lay with prosecutors and judges who drew attention to the defendant's silence in their closing arguments or in instructions to the jury. Maine adopted a statute in 1879, after parties gained competency, prohibiting such addresses, which were seen to compel the defendant and thus to work against the privilege (65–7). Allen refers to a speech before Parliament in 1876 in which this "American practice" is already referenced (160).

[14] In the original article, Appleton refers to the costs of prosecution and Brougham's example of one case in which they amounted to more than 10,000l. ("Rules of Evidence-No.6." 49).

[15] Appleton's note refers to Brougham's comments on cross-examination of the accused in the present tense, as being "now" advocated (*Rules of Evidence* 126). It's clear from Appleton's comments in the Preface to *Rules* that although the collection may suffer from the redundancy of hearing his basic argument repeated in each chapter, he did update the notes in accordance with changes in the law, including the implementation of some of the reforms first advocated in *Rules* (iv). See also Allen 133.

Brougham's excursion into witness competency met with surprise. Lord Cranworth commented on it explicitly and reminded him that magistrates were required by statute to caution witnesses (implicitly referring to Jarvis's Act of 1848). However, it's unlikely that Brougham had forgotten either that statute or Lord Cranworth's earlier offer to support any inquiry into whether the right not to incriminate oneself was sound legal principle (c. 319).[16] As promised, Brougham introduced a bill to extend competency to parties in criminal proceedings later in the same session, which included a clause to undo or limit the witnesses' privilege against self-incrimination. It was followed by another in 1859, and yet another in 1860, but each time the bill was delayed, either for further discussion or for lack of time (Allen 133). Meanwhile, Appleton was having better success, first in 1859 when the Maine State legislature permitted defendants for lesser crimes to testify and, most significantly, in 1864 with the passage of a "general competency statute" (Gold 61).[17] Lord Brougham's Evidence Act, otherwise known as the Criminal Evidence Act, would not become law in England until 1898, thirty years after Brougham's death.[18]

Looking at the 1850s, then, one notices not only Brougham's and Appleton's persistence—Brougham gave his famous speech calling for a Commission of Inquiry into law reform and civil procedure in 1828 (Eardley-Wilmot xxviii), and Appleton wrote his first piece on atheists' competency in 1829—but also the countervailing trends respecting speech and silence. On the one hand, the removal of disqualifications for infamy and interest of nonparties in 1843 (Denman's Act) and the extension of competency to parties in civil actions in 1846 (with Brougham's work on the county courts) represented what Henry E. Smith refers to as "silence threatening" measures (179–80). To these can be added the 1851 Evidence Amendment Act, which although it made parties to civil suits in the superior courts competent, also included express prohibitions against their extension to criminal cases.[19] By contrast, the decision in *R v Garbett* (1847) and passage of Jarvis's Act in

---

[16] Lord Cranworth had commented at the second reading of Brougham's Law of Evidence and Procedure Bill (1853) that while he himself would welcome an inquiry into "whether the rule of law, *Nemo tenetur seipsum inculpare*, was or was not a correct principle," the clause respecting the witness privilege should be struck from the present bill (Law of Evidence and Procedure Bill, c. 1379). On Jarvis's Act, see H. Smith 147; and Allen 124.

[17] In the 1860 Preface to *The Rules of Evidence*, Appleton lists "libel, nuisance, simple assault, simple assault and battery, or for the violation of any municipal or police ordinance" (iv).

[18] Great Britain, Criminal Evidence Act (1898).

[19] "Nothing in the act should make competent or compellable any person charged with a criminal offence, or render any person compellable to answer any question tending to criminate himself . . ." (Allen 103). Note Smith's clarification that "compellable" means able to

1848 added legal and statutory "silence promoting" measures to the ongoing disqualification of criminal defendants who remained unable to testify on oath at trial. The collision of these measures would only become problematic if the accused was made competent; as Smith puts it, "something was needed to ensure that the accused, once he was no longer required to keep silent, did not become required to speak" (180). That something would become a modern right to silence.

Both Allen (173–4) and Gold (69–70) suggest that mid-century emphases on "responsible individualism" influenced the extension of competency, but this worldview vied against a more paternalistic, protectionist stance towards witnesses and the accused, which in the eighteenth century sought to spare witnesses from "reputational harms" that might arise out of testimony but which by the early nineteenth century had boiled down to protection from subsequent criminal prosecution (H. E. Smith 158).[20] As advocates of the former, neither Brougham nor Appleton sympathized with the plight of those who had something to conceal—be it criminal or something "to disgrace and degrade" him—the revelation of which was essential to doing justice.[21] In their view, credibility and cross-examination would be the safeguard of competency.

As this brief history shows, the central problem in the competency debates was the need to gather the most relevant and reliable evidence and the fear that those who possessed it would surely lie to protect themselves, or so muddle their replies as to nullify their value as evidence or, worse, damage their cases. These are problems of proof, truth, and knowledge that are intimately linked to assumptions about character: if fiction appeared to have little to do with the former, it had everything to do with the latter. *The Scarlet Letter* and *Adam Bede* dramatize these and other possibilities as they engage in their own "silence threatening" and "silence promoting" strategies (J. Smith 78–9). Hetty's story as revealed to Dinah is incoherent because she cannot understand what happened and would only have hastened her conviction, while Hester's silence in the face of exhortations to speak—whether to protect or punish her partner—requires she bear the magistrates' punishment alone.

---

be called by the opposing party. Compellability understood as evidence given involuntarily only applies to confessions.

[20] See H. E. Smith 263n63. To the extent witness privilege remained concerned with reputational harms, its influence would have been felt in libel law.

[21] See Brougham, Law of Evidence and Procedure Bill, c. 1368, especially comments on the wide application of the privilege and on indemnification.

"Madame Hester refuseth absolutely to speak": Verbal Resistance in *The Scarlet Letter*

Readers cross two thresholds on entering *The Scarlet Letter*: one of the prison and another of the narrative. In the first, brief chapter called "The Prison Door," Hawthorne aligns the "threshold of our narrative" with a description of "that inauspicious portal" and prepares readers for the appearance of two prisoners: the story proper and Hester Prynne (37). Joining the site of crime to the site of commerce in chapter 2, "The Market-Place," readers cross a third, temporal threshold into seventeenth-century New England history when "religion and law were almost identical" (37), when punishment was a spectacle to be consumed in the marketplace, and when adultery betokened an immoral and illegal form of commerce. (The novel's immediate success in the literary marketplace is a separate point.)

To signal the prisoner's offense, the narrator comments on the particular interest taken by the "goodwives," "gossips," and other "matrons" in the crowd before the scaffold. Although the reader is forestalled from knowing whom they've assembled to see, these women are preparing to witness the "hussy" Hester emerge from the prison and commenting on what justice would have looked like had they had the authority to judge her. Laura Hanft Korobkin discusses the comic treatment of this female jury in the context of Hawthorne's modification of Puritan criminal procedure, but the narrator's comment on the "boldness and rotundity of speech among these matrons . . . that would startle us at the present day, whether in respect to its purport or its volume of tone" (38), sets up a strong contrast to Hester Prynne, whose appearance and whose reticence especially might make her seem more like a woman of 1850 than 1642.[22] Hester does not keep silent throughout the novel, however. Her impassioned defense of maternal rights before Governor Bellingham (chapter 8) and still more persuasive call for Arthur Dimmesdale (her minister, lover, and father to her child) to flee the settlement and "begin all anew," to say nothing of her eventual confession to the minister of her role in her husband Chillingsworth's campaign against him (chapter 17), all demonstrate Hester's powers of speech and restore some of that Puritan woman's verbosity and candor. However, these various verbal acts underscore the three-fold form of verbal resistance her initial silence represents—to

[22] Korobkin invites readers to see Hester as a white Northerner upholding the rule of law, not as a "surrogate slave" nor yet an abolitionist. But Hester's resistance and verbal skill recall other feminist figures, especially Transcendentalist author Margaret Fuller, and other activists involved in the Seneca Falls Convention (1848) about whose politics Hawthorne was ambivalent. See, for example, Hawthorne's attitude towards revolution and especially comments on Fuller in Reynolds 62.

Roger Chillingworth, the magistrates, and to Dimmesdale—in chapter 3, "The Recognition."

When, after long absence, Hester's husband Roger Chillingworth returns to the settlement to find Hester on the scaffold, they exchange glances of recognition. Placing a finger on his lips in a gesture of silence to her, he asks the townsman next to him to explain the circumstances of her public shaming. Asked specifically who is the father of Hester's child, the townsman responds, "Madame Hester refuseth absolutely to speak" (46). This early scene establishes a central tension in the novel between the demands to speak and the right to remain silent, or between the necessity of confession as a sign of penitence and silence, either as solidarity with her fellow sinner or as its own form of punishment. The only moral the narrator will eventually "put into a sentence" is "Be true! Be true! Be true! Show freely to the world, if not your worst, yet some trait whereby the worst may be inferred" (163). In this he appears to concur with the Reverend Wilson's assessment in this early scene that the shame is in the sinning, not the showing of it (48), hence the showing, through the scarlet letter, that removes all need for inference. However, it is not shame alone, nor yet her own shame, that Hester evinces as she stands on the scaffold.[23]

In the face of what Rev. Wilson characterizes as Hester's "hardness and obstinacy" (an assessment to be made of Hetty Sorrel, too), Rev. Wilson urges Dimmesdale to persuade her to confess her seducer's name (48). Dimmesdale has already suggested, off-stage, that they should respect what would be a woman's special shame in being compelled "to lay open her heart's secrets in such broad daylight, and in presence of so great a multitude" (48). Unlike the minister or the narrator in this putative respect for women's modesty (a modesty not evident among the assembled goodwives), Dimmesdale's arguments both deter and invite Hester's confession. On the one hand, he frames the argument in the conditional. Hester should name her partner *only if* she thinks it will increase the likelihood of her spiritual salvation. On the other hand, he reasons that unless she gives up her seducer's name, all "her silence [can] do for him" is to make the sinner into a hypocrite as well, since he evidently lacks the courage to speak out himself. Her non-verbal reply, a shake of the head, brings down the Rev. Wilson's warning that this resistance might be a new transgression to cost her "Heaven's mercy," whereas telling would relieve her of wearing the scarlet mark. However, and contrary to Dimmesdale's suggestion that she might want her partner's help to work

---

[23] See Welsh on the roles of guilt, shame, and secrecy in Chillingworth's and Dimmesdale's relationship in *Blackmail* 360.

towards salvation, Hester claims the letter as a part of herself, her own brand, through which to "endure his agony, as well as mine" (49). Hester thus refuses to answer the Puritan authorities, just as she declines to answer the mysterious stranger, her husband's, new charge to "Speak; and give your child a father!" (50). Having accepted his first admonition not to reveal *his* identity, she extends it into her own edict not to reveal her lover's identity, either.

Critics have commented extensively on Hester's silence, some reading it as a sign of Hawthorne's misogyny or his ambivalence about women's activism, and others seeing in it feminist agency. Among the latter, Leland Person interprets Hester's conspiracy with Chillingworth as an act of revenge suggested, ironically, by Dimmesdale himself (472). By contrast, Elizabeth Alsop characterizes the community's demands as an "expositional mandate" (101), a gendered form of "compulsory talking" that infuses Hester's silence with a "politics of non-explanation" (101–2). More specific than the civil disobedience Matthew Pringle finds in Hester (41), Hester's is a narratological resistance to being cast in a reductive story mold. But if Hester will not tell her story, who will?

Before answering this question, I want to point to those scenes in which Hester herself compels speech: first in the meeting with Gov. Bellingham and again in the forest with Dimmesdale. In this first scene, Hester makes a strong claim to her "indefeasible rights against the world"—as mother and as outcast for whom the child is God's "requital" of everything her earthly judges have deprived her—but confronted by the throng of men, Hester's impassioned language requires another voice, and so she commands Dimmesdale, "Speak thou for me"; "Look thou to it"; "Look to it" (76). Likewise during their meeting in the forest, she exhorts the ailing minister "Preach, Write, Act. Do anything, save to lie down and die" (127). These scenes confirm the selective nature of Hester's silences, but they also suggest the limits of her speech, or the need for another voice to supplement or corroborate her own—or just to be on her side. Simply put, if even her speech acts require supplementation, then her silences surely do, and it is this character evidence which Dimmesdale and, later, the townspeople supply and which to some extent even the magistrates consider when they determine her punishment.

As I've already suggested, both Hawthorne's and Eliot's novels explore theories of guilt, transgression, responsibility attribution, and retribution that take practical shape in the trial and punishment of guilty women, a version of what Alsop refers to as the "plot of female culpability" (86).[24] I want to build

---

[24] Alsop's work on female culpability in U.S. literature complements Lacey's in *Women, Crime, and Character* on the female offender in British novels. This chapter's transatlantic approach extends both, while subsequent chapters go beyond criminal offenses.

on Alsop's argument that a general "presumption of guilt" informs novels like *The Scarlet Letter* to argue that the specific legal contours of the narration, if not the plot (the rules and procedures more than the content of the offense), are important, for example the rights Hester would have had.

According to Edwin Powers's study of *The Body of Liberties* (1641), the governing legal code of the Massachusetts Bay Colony, defendants could choose a bench trial or to have their case heard before a jury whose selection they would be able to contest. Defendants could also invite witnesses to testify on their behalf, could supply documentary evidence that would hasten the trial process, and appeal verdicts (qtd. in Korobkin 430). Even in the absence of specific information about Hester's trial, the townspeople's reactions tell readers what they think about the magistrates' decision, seeing in it a "great mercy and tenderness of heart" (46) that some applaud but which others, as noted, find inadequate. Readers also hear snatches in Rev. Wilson's address of what has passed before Hester appears, which suggests that Hawthorne allowed Hester at least one of the rights outlined in *The Body of Liberties*, namely the right to counsel.

Two witnesses (or their equivalent) were needed in order to reach a conviction in capital cases such as adultery, the implication being that these were witnesses who brought or corroborated facts that told *against* the accused (Powers 93). Powers notes that in both civil and criminal cases, the defendant usually answered these charges on her own, but counsel was available in cases in which the defendant "findeth himselfe unfit to plead his own cause" (94). The counsellor had to be approved by the magistrates and could not be compensated for his advice, either by "fee or reward," but, most importantly, the provision of counsel did not obviate the need for the defendant's own testimony: "this shall not exempt the partie him selfe from Answering Questions in person as the Court shall thinke meete to demand of him" (94). Indeed, as Thomas Letchford commented, "'The parties in all causes, speake themselves for the most part'" (qtd. in Powers 433).[25]

Both the Rev. Wilson and Gov. Bellingham want Dimmesdale to address Hester because she is a member of his parish, which makes him responsible for her soul and gives him greater insight into her "natural temper" and therefore into the tactics most likely to work on her. Passing over the many ironies of this scene, I want to emphasize the important detail of proximity and personal knowledge the Rev. Wilson cites in what we learn *has been* a debate between himself and Dimmesdale: "I have sought, I say, to persuade

---

[25] This much comports with Eben Moglen's assessment that colonial courts followed English criminal procedure to the best of their ability, but see also his reading of the *Body of Liberties* and the "deprivation of defense counsel" (112).

this godly youth that he should deal with you," Wilson says; "But he opposes to me . . ." (48). Although addressing Hester, Wilson tells the entire crowd, including readers, that he and Dimmesdale have differed over who should examine Hester. I've already mentioned Wilson's reprisal of Dimmesdale's response, and it's worth pointing out that the latter's counterargument concerns the general character of women, not Hester specifically (and of course his interest in sticking to generalities is personally, as well as philosophically, motivated). Nevertheless, their argument shows that Dimmesdale has spoken on Hester's behalf—either as character witness or advocate—and defended what by itself seems an anachronistic right to keep back her "secret" on the basis of her character as a woman and women's special relationship to publicity (the implication being that in a less public setting Hester—and Dimmesdale—might be more willing to talk).[26] Whether her silence should be considered his "reward" is debatable.

At the end of the novel, as Hester listens to the sound of Dimmesdale's voice delivering the Election Sermon (prelude to his own confession), the entire scene is marked by music, sounds and voices: "The street and the market-place absolutely babbled" (157), and, inspired by Dimmesdale's "eloquence," the crowd gave a "shout" with enough "force and volume"

> to produce that more impressive sound than the organ tones of the blast, or the thunder, or the roar of the sea; even that mighty swell of many voices, blended into one great voice by the universal impulse which makes likewise one great heart out of many. Never, from the soil of New England, had gone up such a shout! (158)

A paean to Dimmesdale's unifying powers, the narrator's observation also marks the historical significance of the crowd's reaction just one chapter shy of the novel's conclusion in which Hester's own legacy will be described. These voices survive.

At the beginning of Hester's punishment, she feared being reduced to parable because it would limit her self-authorizing tendencies (Alsop 87). In one important respect, these early fears are realized in Surveyor Pue's archive (recovered from the Salem Custom House) which included statements, "drawn up from the verbal testimony of individuals, some of whom had known Hester Prynne, while others had heard the tale from contemporary

---

[26] What's surprising is that, according to one townsperson, the magistrates paid even more attention to her specific circumstances when deciding her punishment: "this woman is youthful and fair, and doubtless was strongly tempted to her fall:—and that, moreover, her husband may be at the bottom of the sea" (46). See Korobkin 433–4 on Hawthorne's defense of the magistrate's discretionary power.

witnesses" (163). Although this collection of first-person testimony about Hester includes hearsay evidence as well, the narrator takes it as his main "authority," claims that it "fully confirms" the preceding tale, and draws from it the one moral he will articulate as such: truth to self through truth to others. Although one can dispute the conclusion that Dimmesdale, the immediate object of this moral, offered no "trait whereby the truth may be inferred" (characters often remark on the hand perpetually over his heart), the minister's experience has so far differed from Hester's because her worst—her crime and her child—have been on display all along.[27] By the end of the novel, however, Hester has altered the substance of the lesson to be drawn from her life. As she had embellished the material A, that same letter "ceased to be a stigma . . . and became a type of something to be sorrowed over, and looked upon with awe, yet with reverence too" (165). My point is two-fold: One is that her refusal to speak is limited only to the authoritarian demand to give her lover's name. When the compulsion comes from within herself, she either demonstrates her own eloquence or commands Dimmesdale to speak for her, and she converses freely with the women who *ask* for her guidance. Second, when she is no longer able to speak for herself, character witnesses supply the facts that will allow her story to survive her. That she was able to change that narrative during her life, to see its success in the people "who refused to interpret the scarlet A by its original signification . . . [and] said that it meant Able" (106), restores enough of that self-authorizing ability to make this legend one she could endorse.[28]

"Hard immovability and obstinate silence": Hetty Sorrel's Missing Testimony and the Failure of Character in *Adam Bede*

F. R. Leavis's comparison of Hawthorne and Eliot seems something of an afterthought, a note left out of the "Great Tradition," while the point for later critics has been to establish a discursive history that in the case of *Adam Bede* has frequently been concerned with the meaning and significance of infanticide and the influence, not just of Hawthorne on Eliot, but of Wordsworth

---

[27] See Korobkin and Reynolds for divergent views on whether Hester's freedom of thought, instead of action, keeps the community together or whether the existence of these dissident ideas means that there is something worse than adultery and illegitimacy which Hester does keep hidden.

[28] See Nina Baym's review of feminist readings of Hawthorne, in particular her own insistence that "Had Hester never returned, she would have been forgotten. Had she returned and not worn the letter, she would have escaped the letter's meaning without changing it. Returning and wearing the letter . . . alters the way the letter is perceived, changes its definition" (550).

on them both.[29] The history of infanticide, more so even than that of adultery, is undoubtedly important, especially in terms of the way cultural narratives about motherhood and childhood condition readers' reception of Hetty and of the novel, just as they would have influenced judge or jurors listening to the case against an accused defendant. I want to acknowledge these crimes while setting aside their content to focus more specifically on the different discursive history of character that the process of allocating fault or attributing responsibility for crime enables.[30] How then does *Adam Bede* think about character, and what are its signs?

Even for a historical novel, *Adam Bede*'s first chapter startles by its specificity. No dashes disguise the time or place of this story, which readers join on June 18, 1799. Other references to British victories over the French and Napoleon's return from Egypt place the action in 1799, but the narrator alerts readers to a historical trial that foreshadows the trial at the novel's center. Following Mrs. Poyser's altercation with the old Squire Donnithorne over the lease of Hall Farm, the narrator comments that

> It is really too hard upon human nature not to imagine the death even of the king when he is turned eighty-three. It is not to be believed that any but the dullest Britons can be good subjects under that hard condition. (404)

This pointed reference to the treason trials of 1794—when "imagining the death of the king" was an indictable offense—is the first of several examples in which Eliot uses legal history to demarcate England's provincial past. The narrator's critical observation of the harsh legal construction that squashes imagination (and not a very active one, at that) in the name of fidelity to the Crown complements later remarks on the limitations of defense counsel in the "stern times" of Hetty Sorrel's trial.

---

[29] See especially Krueger, "Literary Defenses"; Berry; McDonagh; and Jones. Laura C. Berry and Christine L. Krueger both argue, with differing emphases, that *Adam Bede* removes the crime from a Darwinian to Wordsworthian context, which distances it from the bureaucratic responses to the crime that had developed in the sixty-year interval between its setting and completion. Josephine McDonagh compiles a long list of specifically literary antecedents for Eliot's treatment of the "child-murder theme" (229), including Scott's *The Heart of Midlothian* (1818), but she also takes a more oblique approach to child-murder as a historical "archive" (237) or "motif" (239) for encoding history. Miriam Jones discusses the novel's reproduction of middle-class professional discourse centered on the working-class woman, especially the narrator's prosecutorial handling of Hetty's case. For Wordsworth's impact on Hawthorne, see Pace.

[30] See Lacey on the distinction between the "conduct element" and "fault element" of criminal law ("Responsible Subject" 350).

This historical signposting does more than place the narrative voice in a later, ostensibly more lenient time, however; it also subtly introduces a definition of character that would have been operative during both Hetty Sorrel's and her real-life model Mary Voce's trials. It was Erskine's defense of Hardy that drew the attention of Mr. Sleigh, barrister for the defense, in the 1865 case *R v Rowton*, which revolved around the admissibility of certain kinds of character evidence. I discuss this case at length in Chapter 2. What's important to note here is that Mr. Sleigh cited Erskine's speech not only to explain why character evidence had been introduced but also because it offered "the best definition of character" (*Regina v Rowton* 1500):

> "You cannot," he [Erskine] says, "when asking to character, ask what has A.B.C. told you about this man's character. No; but what is the general opinion concerning him. Character is the slow-spreading influence of opinion, arising from the deportment of a man in society. As a man's deportment, good or bad, necessarily produces one circle without another, and so extends itself till it unites in one general opinion; that general opinion is allowed to be given in evidence." (1500)

Erskine's emphasis on character as "one general opinion" or reputation is one of several connected ways that character enters *Adam Bede*. For example, when castigating the Squire's heir Arthur Donnithorne and again when delivering his letter of farewell to Hetty, Adam reminds them both that if their relationship were made known, Hetty alone would "lose her character" (356, 375), understood here as her good reputation. In this sense, character circulates informally throughout the community (although Mrs. Poyser's reminder to the maid Molly to be grateful for having been hired "without a bit o' character" reminds readers of its more business-like uses, too) (137).

When reputation enters the courtroom, however, it assumes legal significance. Following John Olding's damning testimony at Hetty's trial for infanticide (an account that finally convinces Adam of her guilt) and the close of the prosecution's case, the Rev. Mr. Irwine gives evidence of Hetty's "unblemished character in his own parish, and of the virtuous habits in which she had been brought up" (479). As the narrator notes,

> this testimony could have no influence on the verdict, but it was given as part of that plea for mercy which her own counsel would have made if he had been allowed to speak for her—a favour not granted to criminals in those stern times. (479–80)

There is more to be said about the function of counsel, expectations regarding Hetty's ability to speak for herself, and even the desirability of her doing so. What is important to note first about these two uses of character, however, is that they are straightforward. They work to convey a familiar, common-sense understanding of the concept that is all the more unquestioned in these examples because, as the narrator's retrospective comment suggests, that usage is itself part of the historicization of the novel's subject; that is, used in this un-self-conscious way, "character" denotes the story's provincial, rural, and legal histories.

In itself, that historical usage raises questions about the status of character in the 1850s, but *Adam Bede* further complicates such common-sense usage through the openly interrogatory discussions between Mr. Irwine and Arthur, and again between Mr. Irwine and Adam, that delve into the interior qualities behind the outward designation of character. More specifically, their discussions of the relationship between nature and action and the correlative issues of guilt and responsibility all deal with wrongful actions and an individual's impact on a community. Not only does this tenor increase the sense that modern personhood presumes transgression, but a comparison of their conversations reveals both abstract and applied theories of responsibility attribution that get worked out through Hetty's trial.

Discussing the men's conversations about guilt may seem an unlikely way of understanding Hetty's character, but to the extent that they develop a theory of responsibility early on in the novel—when it is largely abstract—and return to it as it reaches its legal climax in Hetty's trial, they help raise a question as to *how* that theory applies to Hetty, the only character brought before a formal legal body and accused of crime. Indeed, Lisa Rodensky notes that Hetty's death sentence intensifies questions about *Arthur's* responsibility (103). No doubt, Arthur is compelled to acknowledge and share the guilt, but this emphasis also shifts narrative attention back to him, away from considering the effect of Hetty's sentence *on Hetty* herself, thereby further marginalizing her. In this section, I read Eliot's positioning of Hetty as an object lesson or legal test case of what Rodensky frames as the utilitarian theory of "consequentialism" (108), made real through a gendered division of Arthur's mental state and Hetty's conduct, his ruminations and her physical travails and actions.[31] Unlike Hester Prynne, Hetty becomes what Nicola Lacey called "doubly deviant" (*Women* 3), both bad and mad, and plays up the paradox of a female offender who is at once the actor at the center of the legal process but also peripheral, a victim at once too passive or impulsive for her actions to be explicable in the masculinized terms of nineteenth-century criminal

---

[31] This is a gap Rodensky first flags in her discussion of *Oliver Twist* in which Fagin's "vividly represented criminal intents" become Sikes's acts (37). Where Fagin becomes in legal terms an "accessory before the fact," Rodensky asserts that "Arthur is no Fagin" (119), however much Adam thinks otherwise, because his intent was seduction, not murder.

responsibility, represented in *Adam Bede* by the men's philosophizing about guilt. Indeed, Rodensky suggests that Eliot may have been "more interested in thinking through the complexities of Arthur Donnithorne's moral and legal responsibilities than she is in Hetty's" because her particular crime, infanticide, "raised ... questions of responsibility that admitted ... inconsistent answers" (103). The suggestion here is that Arthur's case provided Eliot more consistent ones, and although Rodensky's own thorough analysis of Arthur's conversations with Mr. Irwine shows the limits of that hope, the narrative decision to avoid or defer entering Hetty's mind, or entering her own testimony into evidence, raises the stakes for character evidence even as it reveals its limits, too.[32]

To begin with Arthur: Shortly after beginning his flirtation with Hetty, Arthur recognizes its inherent liabilities for her, as well as for his own social position and self-esteem, and resolves to end it. However, his good intentions are undermined when he meets her alone for the first time "In the Wood." The Chase of *Adam Bede* is no less a "moral wilderness" than the forest outside Boston where Hester Prynne and Arthur Dimmesdale make their revolutionary plan to flee the settlement, assume new identities, and "begin all anew" (Hawthorne 127), and while at this point in their respective tales Arthur Donnithorne has less to incriminate himself with than Arthur Dimmesdale does, the former is already becoming sensible of his weakness and resolves to make a pre-emptive confession to Mr. Irwine because, he surmises, "the mere act of telling it would make it seem trivial" (Eliot, *Adam Bede* 201). But the prospect differs from its reality. Without relaying "those little scenes in the wood" (231), Arthur cannot explain his position and goes from wishing "to secure himself" by telling (201), to protecting his reputation by *not* telling. In the first passage, telling trivializes; in the second, "those little scenes" are already trivial, and confession would only exacerbate their importance and increase his embarrassment.

Earlier in the chapter, the narrator remarks that "we don't inquire too closely into character in the case of a handsome generous young fellow.... It would be ridiculous to be prying and analytic in such cases, as if one were inquiring into the character of a confidential clerk" (186–7). The conversation

---

[32] Rodensky's topical focus on criminal intention and criminal character is thus invaluable whenever crimes are at the center of the novel's plot and even as the *sine qua non* of a modern personhood. In this way, her analysis of narrative omniscience as the novel's particular mode for confirming and getting at the inner life extends beyond criminal character. However, her analysis puts more pressure on the question of why Eliot in writing *Adam Bede* did not use this mode to represent Hetty at crucial moments and why, further, she exacerbates her legal position by silencing her.

with Mr. Irwine abides by this status-bound cover and the presumption of innocence that goes with it, partly because Irwine's own delicacy prevents him from being prying and analytic by pressing Arthur to explain his "danger" (235), and partly because Irwine himself relies on the fixed notions of Arthur's "character," especially the value Arthur places on public opinion (237). This missed opportunity stands out more strongly, however, against Mr. Irwine's warnings about human "nature" and action, or the relationship between conduct and the interior qualities it was felt to manifest.

Irritated by his own failure, Arthur complains about the inadequacy of good intention as a bulwark against the vicissitudes of circumstance and "moods that one can't calculate on beforehand" (235). Forethought—one's proleptic "reflections" and "determinations"—should count for more under his theory of guilt so that unintentional wrongdoing should be less blameworthy. Mr. Irwine seizes on the idea of being "ruled by moods" to explain that these also "lie in his nature," however (235). "A man can never do anything at variance with his own nature," he argues, because he "carries within him the germ of his most exceptional action" (235). In these passages, Mr. Irwine does not so much argue for heightened self-awareness or scrutiny of one's motives, which comes piece-meal and mostly in retrospect, as he does for a vigilant, forward-looking attention to consequence.[33] In effect, Mr. Irwine works from the assumption that regardless of one's disposition, those tendencies can be curbed by attending to consequences. Where that foresight is underdeveloped, or where it fails against more immediate temptations, as Arthur suggests, Mr. Irwine sees an object of deepest pity, for not only does this failure lead to "inward suffering," but those consequences are "hardly ever confined to ourselves" (235). In this hypothetical case, Mr. Irwine the magistrate might also have seen the basis of criminal character, defined in the early nineteenth century as the failure to restrain oneself or effectively "work on" one's character (Lacey, "Responsible Subject" 364).

Several points are worth remarking here. When Mr. Irwine asserts that "consequences are unpitying" and that "deeds carry their terrible consequences quite apart from any fluctuation that went before" (235), he is speaking as much in his capacity as a magistrate as he is as the rector of Hayslope and Arthur's friend and teacher. Drawing on the reasonable man theory, Mr. Irwine posits a rational decision-maker with the ability to foresee the likely, logical consequence of any action, which should encourage good

---

[33] See Rodensky's discussion of the role of states of mind in Arthur's theory (102) versus Mr. Irwine's emphasis on deeds (103). These represent, respectively, a subjective theory of responsibility based on "actual knowledge and intents" as against an objective test "based on consequences from which intention and knowledge are presumed" (95).

decision-making in the present.[34] Rodensky registers this distinction further in the difference between a consequence "foreseen" and one "foreseeable," an impulse unnoticed or one "unnoticeable" (105, 115). Thus, where Arthur might reasonably foresee pregnancy as a consequence of his actions—and be held responsible for it—the novel does not suggest he should have known Hetty would kill the child, much less that he would have meant her to do it (119). To be sure, there are significant distinctions here between moral and legal responsibility and between civil liability and criminal guilt that their general discussion of human "nature" elides. As Rodensky explains regarding criminal guilt, for example, the varied emphasis on deeds and intentions places *Adam Bede* at the beginning of

> a shift from an objective test for criminal responsibility—what is foreseeable to a reasonable man—to a subjective test that looks to actual knowledge, a test that makes responsibility much harder to affix because it is difficult to judge what someone else knew and when he knew it. (119)

Although Rodensky sees this shift most clearly articulated in Mr. Irwine's later conversation with Adam, this question of "what someone else knew and when" allows for comparison of the different contexts and outcomes of Arthur's and Hetty's respective silence—what they knew and *didn't* make known, or what they *ought* to have known and ignored—that highlights the novel's dynamics of secrecy and disclosure and in turn the creation of its characters' inner lives.

And it is relevant at this point in the narrative, too, even when (or because) no criminal offense has been committed. A dairy maid seduced by the Squire's son? A knowledgeable reader, inside and outside the novel, could predict where that plot leads, and had Arthur made the facts of his liaison known to Mr. Irwine, their conversation would have assumed a practical bent, as it does when Adam confronts Arthur. An infanticide? Even Mr. Irwine's recognition of the broader social harms that may follow from Arthur's treatment specifically of Hetty does not cue the reader to the criminal act to come. So one set of effects of Arthur's silence is that it leaves the discussion of his own responsibility in the abstract, thereby reserving it for a moral rather than legal context.

The second feature of assigning responsibility—judging what someone knew and when—is one that a third-person narrator might reveal, and in this example, we do learn what transpires in Arthur's mind. However, that access

---

[34] For a close reading of the "doctrine of consequences" in both Hawthorne and Eliot, see Stokes 141.

at the level of narration makes his decision not to reveal it at the level of plot, through dialogue, more notable. A second set of effects of his silence, then, is to distinguish his privilege not to incriminate himself from the very different outcomes of Hetty's refusal to speak which, as will be seen, requires and yet undoes the character evidence offered in its place and allows consequences to play out on the bodies of Hetty and their child.

Interestingly, "character" is not the operative term in Mr. Irwine and Arthur's conversation although in drafts of the novel, it had been. That is, where Arthur and Mr. Irwine place the source of action in one's "nature," Mary Waldron explains that in the original manuscript, Eliot gave "character" as this source. The substitution of "nature" for "character" raises a question about the associations *character* would have carried that made it the less applicable concept and made *nature* the better one. Waldron glosses the difference as being between "learnt behavior" and "inherited traits" respectively and suggests that Eliot agreed to the change prior to publication with Blackwood because she wanted to emphasize both Mr. Irwine's "secular cast of mind" and Arthur's "inability to change" (Eliot, *Adam Bede* 235n1). "Character" might indeed have connoted learnt behavior insofar as it drew on the idea of a flawed self that could be improved, but the ethical ramifications of this capacity to "work on" oneself, although consonant with Christian teaching, were not limited to it. In fact, the notion of natural determinacy reflected in the term "nature" seems to undermine both the adaptability essential to Darwinian thinking, as well as the political efficacy of reform (a way of altering circumstances) reflected in John Stuart Mill's early writing. Mill himself had described nature as "'the ensemble or aggregate of [an object's] powers or propensities: the modes in which it acts on other things . . . and the modes in which others things act on it'" (Carlisle, *John Stuart Mill* 1), but Janice Carlisle points out that for him character *was* nature applied to humans. As she explains, character, for Mill,

> signifies a thoroughly conditioned phenomenon known by its "powers and propensities," not by an unchanging essence imperceptible to others. Character involves how one human being acts or is acted upon by other human beings and by their shared circumstances. Character inevitably comprises one's thoughts, desires, and impulses, but it is known most accurately through one's choices and actions. (1)

The scope for choice in this definition resonates, not surprisingly, in utilitarian as well as evangelical calls for the kind of forward-looking self-control Mr. Irwine advocates and in legal definitions of manifest criminality. Writing of the criminal character specifically, Martin J. Wiener explains that in this consequentialist context, early nineteenth-century criminal law became a "character-building" institution that served the interests of a modernizing state (48). More than the difference between secular and Christian approaches to the question of responsibility, then, "character" reveals the tension between impulse and resistance—whether that impulse was explained in biological, moral, or legal terms. Arthur cannot change in the sense that he cannot remove the impulse, and in this sense confirms eighteenth-century assumptions about transgressive individualism, but there is no fatality in it, hence Mr. Irwine's emphasis on keeping the consequences of one's conduct for oneself and others firmly in view. Adam makes this latter point explicitly when, in his shock at discovering Arthur's relationship with Hetty, he blames the future Squire for jeopardizing the tenants whose welfare he is supposed to protect.

Like Arthur's focus on the role of intentionality and the force of circumstance as causes of action, however, these assumptions belong more to the time of composition than the novel's setting. In the novel's late eighteenth-century setting, character was the stuff of reputation, and reputation meant a localized history of past actions that indicated whether the accused was a corrigible member of that community (Lacey "Responsibility and Modernity" 257).[35] As suggested above, Arthur's past conduct works against the likelihood of his being guilty in this case, insofar as his desire to be respected disposes him to avoid bad behavior (this, even though his status deflects close inspection and makes license a social perquisite of the elite; if only Hetty had read *Pamela* or *Tom Jones*). However, Hetty also fulfills his desire to be liked and admired.

The application of this meaning of "character" works both ways: to warrant but also to preclude further investigation. Eliot subjects Arthur's behavior to an eighteenth-century theory of guilt based on an eighteenth-century theory of the self in which action and disposition are unified; conduct is inseparable from who one is because it's held to be the manifestation of disposition. One purely speculative explanation for the change from character to nature is that Eliot in effect transliterated the meaning of character for her contemporary audience, one that would have been reading Charles Darwin and Samuel Smiles simultaneously with *Adam Bede*. Nevertheless, in a year in which conceptions of "nature" and "character," determinism and self-determinism, were clearly in front of the reading public, *Adam Bede* seems irresolute about which sense should prevail as a way of understanding Arthur's and Hetty's behavior.

This ambivalence comes through in the narrator's speculation about why Arthur abandons his plans to confess: "Was there a motive at work under

---

[35] The answer to this "key question" lay in "the character and disposition which the alleged offense, along with other pieces of local information and the testimonies of character witnesses, suggested" (Lacey, "Responsible Subject" 362).

this strange reluctance of Arthur's," she asks, "which had a sort of backstairs influence, not admitted to himself?" (236). The question alone places motive within the self, but by also making it unavailable to conscious reflection, the narrator's question presumes a divided self that belongs to the nineteenth rather than the eighteenth century. This difference is elaborated through a pair of analogies that mechanizes, dehumanizes, and otherwise appears to reduce responsibility by untethering action from the individual's conscious deliberation and control, thereby breaking, as Rodensky observes, the link between internal mental state and external act that could make Arthur's moral lapse into a legal crime:

> Our mental business is carried on in much the same way as the business of the State: a great deal of hard work is done by agents who are not acknowledged. In a piece of machinery, too, I believe there is often a small unnoticeable wheel which has a great deal to do with the motion of the large obvious ones. Possibly, there was some such unrecognized agent secretly busy in Arthur's mind at this moment—possibly it was the fear lest he might hereafter find the fact of having made a confession to the Rector a serious annoyance, in case he should *not* be able quite to carry out his good resolutions? I dare not assert that it was not so. The human soul is a very complex thing. (236)

References to the modern, industrial State accentuate the narrator's stance as a historian making sense of the past for contemporary readers. At the same time, the pose of uncertainty (conveyed in question marks and double negatives) and bland conclusion together undercut the seriousness of her analysis of Arthur's mind. The soul may indeed be complex, but the tone implies that Arthur's behavior is transparent.[36]

If there is any sympathy for Arthur, it comes in the recognition of his plight as being a common one. Shortly after the interview between Adam and Arthur, the narrator asks whether this guilty Arthur can be the same one who met with Mr. Irwine. Answering that he is, "only under different conditions" (369), the narrator expands:

> Our deeds determine us as much as we determine our deeds; and until we know what has been or will be the peculiar combination of outward with inward facts, which constitutes a man's critical actions, it will be better not

---

[36] Rodensky's analysis of this same passage points up the way that "negations do important work" (115), as does the narrator's movement in and out of Arthur's mind, which signals the limitations of omniscience but also, in the closing line, "the kind of ironic bite that comes only with a very special knowledge of the mind in question" (115).

to think ourselves wise about his character . . . Europe adjusts itself to a *fait accompli*, and so does an individual character,—until the placid adjustment is disturbed by a convulsive retribution. (369)

This passage raises several questions, including *how* those inward facts become knowable and by whom, but its theory of the relationship between motive, conduct ("actions"), and the growth of individual character is most immediately striking. Mr. Irwine argued that succumbing to our worst impulse, particularly in circumstances likely to excite it, cannot excuse bad conduct, and the narrator's condescending assessment of Arthur in those early pages seemed to support Irwine's view. In this passage, however, the narrator's attention to the "combination of outward and inward facts" seems to corroborate Arthur's idea that a "combination of circumstances" (235) should be considered when attributing guilt. Moreover, reference to outward and inward facts mirrors the opening assertion that the sources of action lie both within us, as individual agency, and outside us, in the way we respond to our past actions when confronted by their results. According to this logic, we are self-determining individuals, but our deeds are not independent of one another; they have a cumulative, evolutionary effect that can only be suspended by "a convulsive retribution," a catastrophic disruption of punishing effect.[37] If this passage rings with nineteenth-century historiography, the narrator's reference to European politics also recalls the comparison of Arthur's motives to the invisible agent of the State and draws attention to the tendency of nations and individuals alike to rationalize past behavior to suit present conditions. Still, if one's immediate context guides the way any individual interprets her own past deeds, it also factors into the way others interpret the individual, a point Mr. Irwine makes when he tells Adam (mistakenly, as it happens) that Hetty's "youth and other circumstances will be a plea for her" (459).

---

[37] See Rodensky's discussion of John Locke's "forensic person" (40–1) with its emphasis on a consciousness that extends "'beyond present existence to what is past'" and links it to the present in one continuous "same self." If selfhood depends on consciousness in this way, then the reasonable man, by looking *forward* to consequences, seeks to extend consciousness into the future, to imagine a future self that would be consistent with the present. The possibility of reform, however, requires imagining a future self that would be different than the one who performed criminal deeds in the past and thus is not the same forensic person. One hears the rationale for excluding evidence of past acts, other acts or similar fact evidence in contemporary criminal trials (in order to isolate and try the specific charge) at the same time that the maneuvering around those exclusionary rules points to the ongoing conceptual appeal of continuity of character, or thinking of character as continuous over time. See Chapter 5 for discussion of contemporary approaches to character in other common law jurisdictions.

Mr. Irwine's meetings with Adam, first when relaying the news of Hetty's arrest (chapter 39) and again on the night before the trial (chapter 41), balance his earlier meeting with Arthur when the theory of guilt was abstract. Here it becomes all too concrete as Mr. Irwine learns of Arthur's role and recognizes the sub-text of that philosophical discussion in Arthur's failed confession. When Mr. Irwine presents the news to Adam, there is no doubt that the crime has been committed and that Hetty is guilty of it. Only Adam refuses to believe because he cannot credit that a baby was born and died at all. Once convinced of those facts, however, and working from his own assumptions about Hetty's character, his effort turns to mitigating her fault by inculpating Arthur as the guiltier of the two. Recurring to the discussion about responsibility and the distinction between content and fault, a new layer is added that specifies the "manifest" or "subjective" nature of criminality and the attendant aim of trial proceedings.[38] Let the crime be what it is, where does responsibility for it lie? What assumptions about the defendant will or should the court make when *it* judges Hetty?

Faced also with "facts which left no hope in his mind" that Hetty is innocent (459), Mr. Irwine works to lead Adam away from passions that could lead to his own wrongdoing. His rationale is not merely pragmatic (i.e. aimed at preventing Adam from exacting vengeance in the guise of justice); it also makes ethical demands on Adam's sense of empathy and the wellbeing of the community. Putting aside Adam's own possessiveness and mistaken idealization of Hetty, his outrage at Arthur is three-fold and derives, first, from Arthur's disregard for the likely consequences to Hetty of their relationship, second, his duplicity about the extent of their intimacy, and third, his cowardice (like Arthur Dimmesdale's) in letting her face punishment alone. Adam's main objects, then, are to "expose" Arthur (459), to make him "feel what she feels" (467), and to assume responsibility for *her* crime. By contrast, Mr. Irwine urges a more fluid view of the way communities are formed and how individuals interact in them. Emphasizing that no one can "isolate" himself "and say that the evil which is in you shall not spread" (469), he essentially repeats the earlier lesson to Arthur that consequences are never confined to the perpetrator of a bad act. But if he is consistent in this respect, his theory

---

[38] Lacey, "Responsibility" 361. Theories of manifest criminality assume that the fact of being indicted confirms not only that the crime was committed but also that the defendant did it. The trial is less about proving fault than doing exactly what Adam attempts here: bringing forward evidence of good character that will lessen the degree of guilt and hence the severity of the penalty. Subjective criminality, by contrast, requires the forensic, inculpatory work of proving guilt by linking the crime to the defendant's state of mind, motive, or intent. See also Rodensky 95, 119.

of moral and legal guilt is murkier. Indeed, one of the most interesting aspects of this discussion with Adam is the way the explicitly legal context of this conversation calls out the rector's clerical role in an inversion of the magistratical overtones of his earlier, ostensibly "moral" discussion with Arthur.

On the night before Hetty's trial is to begin, Adam continues to struggle with the degree of her responsibility and asks Mr. Irwine whether he thinks she's "as guilty as" the indictment says. Mr. Irwine's answer is equivocal: Guilt may "never be known with certainty" because of interpretive fallibility on the one hand and the limitations of evidence (the "want of knowing some small fact") on the other (468). By contrast, he is dogmatic about moral judgment:

> It is not for us men to *apportion the shares* of moral guilt and retribution. We find it impossible to avoid mistakes even in determining who has committed a single criminal act, and the problem *how far a man is to be held responsible for the unforeseen consequences of his own deed*, is one that might well make us tremble to look into it. (468, emphasis mine)

As advice to Adam, the immediate point of this response is to persuade him to let the courts and God sit in judgment of Arthur. One hears the pity he predicted for the hypothetical man struggling against temptation, but one hears also some backtracking from his earlier firmness that an eye trained on consequences of deeds, rather than excuses for them, could avoid most problems. (Adam provides the rejoinder: "What if he didn't foresee what's happened? He foresaw enough" [469].) As a more complicated reflection on the way moral philosophy and legal theory are operationalized or put to work in the temporal world, however, Mr. Irwine's comments distinguish between the procedures of judging and rendering verdicts on criminal acts—as legal processes—and the broader social and religious judgment of morality.

Insofar as juries decide guilt and judges hand down sentences, they certainly do "apportion the shares of moral guilt and retribution," and Mr. Irwine splits hairs when he says that it is outside the purview of men to gauge degrees of moral culpability and distribute punishment. His statement makes more sense when one recalls that the novel's action predates the creation of graduated prison sentences to correspond with new offense categories, but the provision of partial verdicts shows that juries did look for proportional forms of punishment and that character evidence could influence them (Langbein, "Historical Origins" 1062–3). Nevertheless, even by specifying *moral* guilt, he devalues the character evidence he's prepared to give on Hetty's behalf as a plea precisely for legal mercy (i.e. if her virtues evoke mercy in response to a legal offense, then there must be a difference between legal guilt and moral guilt). Further, his insistence that crime affects entire communities makes criminality a social "evil" so that efforts to disentangle legal process from its social context are as rhetorical as law's separation from morality. Like the change from character to nature, the distinction between law and morality encodes a particular historical difference. The tension between Mr. Irwine's legal and clerical roles signifies the unity but also the split between law and morality that came in the nineteenth-century turn towards legal positivism, just as the professionalization of law would relocate legal power from lay to legal actors.[39] At the time of *Adam Bede*'s setting, however, the differences Mr. Irwine puts forward are vaguely anachronistic and downplay the importance of character—or nature as he called it earlier—in this apportioning of blame.

Thus far I've paid close attention to the novel's discussion of responsibility as a moral and ethical concept, one that is supposed to gain clarity as it is applied to particular cases. Arthur's prospective application of this theory to his own future behavior is countered by Adam's retrospective judgment on its concrete effects. Hetty's is the only criminal act—and hence hers the only explicitly legal occasion for testing these theories of guilt and measuring out blame—and yet as Eliot draws her, Hetty is the least likely to offer such a framework for understanding and judging her actions. To be sure, she has a rudimentary sense of consequence that causes her to leave Hayslope, to contemplate suicide, and finally to kill her baby. The narrator's decision to enter Hetty's mind at the moment she resolves *not* to confess, and to comment on what she finds there, revives questions of what Hetty knew and when (Rodensky) as well as what she ought to have known (Lacey, *Women*). It reanimates the question of narrative overreach, but it also provides some explanation for why Hetty remains silent as long as she does and why the narrator allows her to, leaving her to the mercy of the court and the character witnesses designed to procure it.

Resorting to interior monologue, the narrator relates Hetty's outlook in which silence will shield her from shame, and suicide, by destroying the evidence of her body, will somehow undo her sexual transgression:

> Hetty felt that no one could deliver her from the evils that would make life hateful to her; and no one, she said to herself, should ever know her misery and humiliation. No; *she would not confess even to Dinah*: she would wander out of sight, and drown herself where her body would never be found, and *no one should know* what had become of her. (432, emphasis mine)

---

[39] See West in *Narrative, Authority, and Law* on the positivists' efforts to separate morality out of natural law to enable moral judgment of law.

Hetty imagines replacing knowledge of her promiscuity with no knowledge, an epistemological undoing that begins with silence and ends with her erasure. When the intention to kill herself is interrupted by the birth, she falls back on silence as the one remaining option for concealing her "misery and humiliation." In an obvious interpretation of the meaning of pride (the one available to Hetty's consciousness), the narrator comments that the prospect of having her pregnancy exposed is akin to what "the sick and weary prisoner might think of the possible pillory. They would think her conduct shameful, and shame was torture. That was poor little Hetty's conscience" (390). "Intolerable shame," the "dread of shame" (428): Hetty's willful blindness to everything but the loss of reputation and status makes the idea of resorting to the parish "next to the prison in obloquy" (428).[40] This form of pride reads like an aggravated form of vanity, but the narrator goes further by contemplating pride's anti-social potential as well.

The narrator prefaces Hetty's thoughts with a separate reflection on the circumstances that sometimes call forth the "strength of self-possession" that Hetty is about to demonstrate (432). Specifically, Hetty's self-possession is a symptom of despair: "Despair no more leans on others than perfect contentment, and in despair pride ceases to be counteracted by the sense of dependence" (432). A sense of dependence, as with a sense of responsibility, links one to a community, but despair severs this link, leaving only pride. This self-possession is not to be confused with the kind that Hester Prynne exudes, for all that their sins and their silences coincide, however. Hetty's is a self-destructive counterpoint to Hester's, which avoids rather than claims responsibility, pushing agency off onto "the evils that would make life hateful to her" instead of accepting that the "evil" of her pregnancy follows from her actions: to be "deliver[ed]" from evil, as in the prayer, requires being delivered of the unwanted child and the public censure to follow. Hetty's changed circumstances lead the narrator to ask, just as she did of Arthur, whether *this* Hetty could be the same "that used to make up the butter" (428), so transformative has her conduct been.

Rodensky refers to Arthur's as the "hard case" for weighing the relationship between intention and responsibility for consequences, but Hetty's is hard in a different way. Her conscience trained entirely on punishment with no reflection on her own responsibility, the effect is to render her a

---

[40] One broadsheet describes Mary Voce's fear of "public spectacle" and shame as impediments to her confession. "An Account of the Experience and Happy Death of Mary Voce, Who was Executed on Nottingham Gallows, on Tuesday, March 16, 1802, for the Murder of her Own Child." Rpt. in Eliot, *Adam Bede* 600.

moral cipher.[41] E. S. Dallas in his review of *Adam Bede* took Hetty to be the proof of Pope's premise in the "Epistle to a Lady" that women are characterless:

> She is one of those who is so much less than they seem to be, whose most significant acts mean so little, that it is not easy to fix upon any central principle in their nature, any strong point of thought, or work or act which belongs to them. (Rpt. in Eliot, *Adam Bede* 612)

Presumably Dallas means that Hetty's best and worst acts are equally capricious, driven by circumstance rather than principle, since it's "not easy" to find anything personally substantive to explain them or distinguish her. But many will try: the narrator, Dinah, the witnesses at court, and Hayslope's community of informal character witnesses are called to interpret and explain this inscrutable person whose silence creates the epistemological anxiety that necessitates other people's narratives.

As already noted, many critics have pointed to the discourse surrounding infanticide as providing just that narrative. Christine L. Krueger describes a sympathetic literary treatment of infanticidal mothers, the rhetorical features of which helped defense counsel protect mothers against new forensic medical testimony regarding their infants' bodies ("Literary Defenses" 275). Also attentive to the apparent surge in infanticide cases in the 1860s, Aeron Hunt links Hetty's market-based morality to a mid-century emphasis on economic motives that undermine sympathetic representations (84–8). By contrast, Kristin Kalsem emphasizes the way that a woman's character, more than her circumstances, affects her reception at law (36). Connecting Hetty's character to the figure of the "lewd woman" (33), Kalsem points to the way Eliot's omniscient narrator effectively builds a case *against* Hetty by revealing her as a vain, seductive, and selfish young woman with a cavalier attitude towards children (37–8). Similarly, Miriam Jones describes a narrator positioned, if not as prosecutor, than as "punitive courtroom spectator" (312) whose distance from the working-class Hetty (unlike Hester Prynne's jury of peers) informs the novel's strategy of minimizing her character by making sure that "anything about her that needs to be conveyed must be interpreted by the narrator, or by one of the articulate characters" (321).[42] That Hetty is an

---

[41] For discussion of the importance of self-reflection, in particular its links to social responsibility and communal moral standards, see Berger 310–16.

[42] For Jones, the novel's critique of gender and sexuality is subsumed under Eliot's focus on class, which may explain why she ignored available medical interpretations such as puerperal insanity and other "tropes of feminine irresponsibility" (314). In the context of my earlier discussion of responsibility attribution, this is a tantalizing omission. It's not clear, however, that these tropes would have availed Hetty in 1799; Bartle Massey only mentions

inarticulate character when she encounters the law leaves all of these possibilities open: her motives are shielded or mystified; she is exposed to both hostile and sympathetic interpretation, and her silence is taken for contempt.

Much of Eliot's representation of the trial and the days leading up to it depicts characters in a state of anxiety about Hetty's silence. The facts of the case undermine not only Hetty's place in the communal order but the order itself. Here is that "convulsive retribution" that by unmaking requires a remaking which the trial, especially Hetty's explanation, might supply.[43] The problem is that these narratives, like charges put to the accused, must be answered *by Hetty*. However, Hetty is absented from her own trial: presented first as a "white image . . . seeming neither to hear nor see anything" (473); then, like Hester Prynne, as the figure of local legend ("the neighbors from Hayslope who were present, and who told Hetty Sorrel's story by their firesides in their old age, never forgot to say how it moved them when Adam Bede . . . took his place by their side" [475]), and finally as the subject of others' testimony. Indeed, as a pair, "The Morning of the Trial" and "The Verdict," although occasioned by Hetty's crime, are more about Adam's experience of her trial and about the legal process than they are about her.[44] Where she refuses to speak, others must.

Of the three chapters Eliot devotes to the trial (which is three more than Hawthorne gives to establish Hester's guilt), "The Verdict" is the only one to take readers directly into the courtroom. The "elaborately reported" details of this chapter have led some to comment on its heightened realism (Quick 291), but while description and narrative omniscience are certainly dimensions of realism, this realism goes no further than other chapters have into Hetty's account of events, nor are readers shown Mr. Irwine's testimony on

---

that the doctor gave evidence, not what he said (472). What is clear is that Hetty would have had to articulate the defense herself or narrate her journey, as she does in her confession to Dinah, and hope that the court would hear her indecision and the baby's haunting crying more than her strong resolve "to get rid of it, and go home again" (494).

[43] See also Alsop's point about Hester Prynne's adultery, for example, that in order for stock explanations to work her accomplice also needs to be named. By keeping her secret, Hester keeps the community in a state of unrest, similar to Hetty's effect on Hayslope. By contrast, see Korobkin's argument that Hester's silence and isolation allows her to maintain community because she doesn't express her rebellious thoughts.

[44] What might be called the legal matter of the novel extends into the next three chapters, "In the Prison," "The Hours of Suspense," and "The Last Moment." Krueger configures these as "extralegal" moments occurring in "literary spaces" because they follow on the verdict and sentencing, in other words, after Hetty's speech could have had legal effect (*Reading for the Law* 235, 225–6).

Hetty's behalf.[45] For example, because Adam cannot bring himself to attend the morning session, Bartle Massey brings an account to him. Readers learn along with Adam about defense counsel's cross-examination of witnesses, the doctor's medical evidence, Martin Poyser's affecting appearance in the dock, and the prospect of Mr. Irwine's being a witness "by-and-by" (473). Bartle Massey's misogyny, although tempered by sympathy for Adam, colors his commentary on these details, but there is altogether less commentary on the events of the verdict.

Although all eyes in the court are trained on Hetty, the reader's eyes are focused on Adam who is present for the end of the one-day trial. This report is focalized chiefly through the narrator's description of his reactions and mental state. The two longest speeches belong to witnesses Sarah Stone and John Olding, and here even the narrator stands aside. These apparently unmediated, staccato monologues resemble nothing so much as trial reports whose narrative coherence derives from the questions tacitly posed by the prosecution. What stand out here, again, are the damaging effects of Hetty's silence. Mr. Irwine had twice referred to her "obstinate silence" (459–60, 464), and Bartle Massey echoes him. Telling Adam she would not enter a plea when asked ("so they pled not guilty for her" [473]), he foretells that "It'll make against her with the jury, I doubt, her being so obstinate: they may be less for recommending her to mercy, if the verdict's against her" (474). As predicted, Mr. Irwine's plea for mercy is ineffectual. Although the audience is surprised by the sentence, the narrator explains that "The sympathy of the court was not with the prisoner: the unnaturalness of her crime stood out more harshly by the side of her hard immovability and obstinate silence" (480).

These chapters show a kind of scrupulousness on Eliot's part in the service of her realism to capture the contours of the eighteenth-century trial: its brevity (one day) and the even shorter span given to jury deliberation ("hardly more than a quarter of an hour" [480]); counsel's ability to cross-examine witnesses but not to make a closing argument or even to require defense witnesses to appear in court. They also demonstrate a canniness that Hetty's story, if told, would be unlikely to help her legal case—inviting the "pious perjur[ies]" (Langbein, "Historical Origins" 1063) and other "cover stories" that Krueger discusses (*Reading for the Law* 203). Moreover, they tacitly rely on an understanding of how character evidence functioned in pre- and post-trial processes.

---

[45] See Quick 291 on the more romantic treatment of Silas Marner's trial. Quick distinguishes *Silas Marner* from *Adam Bede* in order to show the influence of Hawthorne's *The House of the Seven Gables* on Eliot.

Hetty's trial takes place at a crucial point in the history of the adversarial system: before the expectation that the accused would respond to the charges against her had wholly given way to an expectation that defense counsel instead would probe the prosecution's case. Indeed, as legal historian John Langbein explains, several aspects of eighteenth-century criminal procedure essentially forced the accused to speak: the gradual introduction of defense counsel and limitation of his role (e.g. the inability to speak to matters of fact or to address the jury); the *unsworn* testimony of defense witnesses; a different standard of proof that allowed doubt to work *against* the accused, and various impediments to preparing a case (starting with not being told the charges she had to answer until appearing in court).[46]

This expectation was nowhere so strong, however, as during the gathering of evidence before the trial. Although Christopher J. W. Allen finds evidence to suggest that from at least the 1820s onwards defendants were increasingly advised to keep quiet during pre-trial interrogation by the magistrate (124), Langbein describes the magistrate's examination as a "systematic extraction of self-incriminatory pretrial statements" which the accused resisted or denied at her peril (1061). In either scenario, character evidence would have been important at this stage of proceedings. Since a good reputation in the local community might have inclined judges not to commit the accused, the fact of being brought to trial consequently entailed a presumption of guilt (Lacey, *Women* 16). Character evidence might still be effective as a means of inducing the jury to downgrade their verdict (thereby requiring a lesser sentence), or afterwards as an argument for mercy or pardon, but when the inducement to such leniency depended on the severity of the crime and the "conduct and character of the accused" (Langbein, "Historical Origins" 1064), to refuse to represent oneself was a dangerous gamble.[47] Even Mary Voce, the twenty-four-year-old mother whose conviction and execution for infanticide Eliot took for her story, provided evidence at her trial. One broadsheet (most likely the story as told to Eliot by her aunt) depicts a Mary "hardened and impenitent" but still "denying her guilt" (i.e. answering the charges) until the evening following her sentencing when she made a full confession (Eliot, *Adam Bede* 600), whereas another notes that in answer to the judge's question,

---

[46] Langbein, "Historical Origins" 1048–54.

[47] When the only two available punishments for serious crime were death or transportation, juries looked for reasons to limit guilty verdicts to lesser charges. See Langbein, "Historical Origins" 1063; and Lacey, *Women* 14–15. Mr. Irwine's claim that men don't apportion moral guilt begins to make more sense when one considers that the "grading" of sentences would only arrive with the move towards new offense categories and the possibility of long-term imprisonment as a viable alternative.

Voce supplied a written refutation of the murder charge which she then recanted in an oral confession made on her day of execution (604–5).

And Hetty? She is detained miles from Hayslope; she refuses to give the constable her name (455), and more than once she baffles Mr. Irwine with her "obstinate silence" (459–60, 464). It is this apparently stubborn refusal to give up information that compounds all the other evidence and prejudices legal and lay auditors alike. Whatever other character evidence might have helped prevent a trial, her silence is interpreted as—becomes evidence of—recalcitrance that even Mr. Irwine's post-trial character evidence cannot soften. The narrator refers to Mr. Irwine's character evidence as being part of "that plea for mercy" in "those stern times" (480) and uses the demonstrative pronouns to create a temporal distance that makes legal process itself a form of historical signposting. By specifying the plea for mercy but also singling out Hetty's silence, the narrator not only distinguishes the present from the stern times when the defendant's silence could be an argument against mercy, she also singles out her "immovability and silence" (481) as being stronger indicators of character than all the rector can say in her favor. Under these circumstances, the comments on Hetty's behavior before the magistrate and reactions to her refusal to speak in court start to look like Hetty's presumption (added to her others about Arthur) of a right that does not exist; Hetty seems *to them*, that is, to be acting as though she has a right to silence, when on the contrary she was expected to explain herself. Langbein makes the implications clear: at a time when defendants were expected to answer the charges against them, a defendant's refusal "would have been suicidal," "a forfeiture of all defense" and the putative right to silence nothing more than "the right to slit your throat" (1048, 1054).

As the history of witness competency revealed, the triangular relationship between the accused's speech, character evidence, and the perception or credibility of the accused continued to trouble the courts. It continued to trouble literature, too, not only in immediate terms of plot development but also in respect to the goals and challenges of fiction writing. That is, while both novels dramatize a problem of getting at facts through the medium of character, Hawthorne and Eliot undertook the problem of representation directly: Hawthorne in "The Custom House" and Eliot in her famous chapter 17. What can their theories of fiction tell us that might explain why, since legal rules of evidence prohibited the defendant from testifying, their novels both *compel* the accused and show their contempt—the characters' and the novels'—for legal demands of disclosure? What object lessons do these novels provide about the implications of once again making defendants competent, to say nothing of compellable and subject to (cross-)examination?

In the Witness Box: Moonlight, Mirrors, and other Reflections on Fiction

Literary answers to these questions depend partly on the mode in which the novel was written (romance or realism) and on the kind of light to be cast on its characters and events.[48] Following description of his colleagues at the Salem Custom House and his discovery of Surveyor Pue's forgotten archive, an unusually forthright Hawthorne describes a pernicious bout of writer's block. Having accepted the ghostly Pue's commission, testified to the authenticity of the historical outline, and claimed the authorial prerogative to "imagin[e] the motives and modes of passion that influenced the characters who figure in it" (27), Hawthorne gets stuck. "My imagination was a tarnished mirror," he writes; "it would not reflect . . . the figures with which I did my best to people it." The classic image of realist representation, the mirror, joins with various sources of illumination (not to say lamps) to describe the conditions and aims of Hawthorne's authorial vision through which material realities become spiritualized, intellectualized, and acquire "dignity" (29). These modes of representation come together most concisely in the hearthside image of the quondam writer of romance:

> This warmer light [of coal-fire] mingles itself with the cold spirituality of the moonbeams, and communicates, as it were, a heart and sensibilities of human tenderness to the forms which fancy summons up . . . Glancing at the looking-glass, we behold . . . the smouldering glow of the half-extinguished anthracite, the white moonbeams on the floor, and a repetition of all the gleam and shadow of the picture, with one remove further from the actual, and nearer to the imaginative. Then, at such an hour, and with this scene before him, if a man, sitting all alone, cannot dream strange things, and make them look like truth, he need never try to write romances. (29)

When the most quotidian objects can be defamiliarized under these conditions, how much easier ought it to be to bring forth the "strangeness and remoteness" of Hester Prynne's history, he implies. However, Hawthorne chides himself for the "attempt to fling myself back into another age" (30) when her story, as history, is at a double remove from the present. It is too difficult to resist the present and the practical, to move beyond what is visible to what is hidden, past, unimagined, or otherwise absent. By contrast,

---

[48] See Jonathan R. Quick on metaphors of illumination in Hawthorne's and Eliot's literary criticism, as well as Hawthorne's influence on Eliot's own romance *Silas Marner*. See also Stokes 105–14.

non-fiction, such as the veteran shipmaster's narratives, or realist depictions of the contemporary world would have been more productive, if prosaic, modes of writing than historical or gothic romances. Here, too, Hawthorne admits his fault in failing "to seek, resolutely, the true and indestructible value that lay hidden in the petty and wearisome incidents, and ordinary characters" then surrounding him (30).

This second failure of imagination is one which Eliot in her own meditations on the purpose and experience of authorship does not commit, however much she shares Hawthorne's sense of the discrepancy between her idea and its achievement in the novel. In the much cited statement of Eliot's realism that interrupts chapter 17, the narrator addresses readers:

> I aspire to give no more than a faithful account of men and things as they have mirrored themselves in my mind. The mirror is doubtless defective; the outlines will sometimes be disturbed; the reflection faint or confused; but I feel as much *bound to tell you*, as precisely as I can, what that reflection is, *as if I were in the witness-box narrating my experience on oath*. (238, emphasis mine)

This passage could be a classic illustration of those arguments that the realist novel hands over the power to speak to the narrator, making him into an advocate just as, in Ian Watt's analogy, the reader becomes a jury member.[49] Here is that body of evidence supplied by the detached, omniscient narrator which apprises readers of events, of characters' private thoughts, and encounters between characters, which would affirm the point—made by Justice Appleton in respect of the jury's ability to recognize truthful testimony and by literary critic Alexander Welsh in his characterization of "strong representations"—that internal consistency is the hallmark of truth: we can know the truth when we hear it, just as we can recognize a lie (Welsh, *Strong Representations*). Yet in this example the narrator is not at all detached but formally engaged. He has sworn himself to give a truthful rendition of what he knows or sees; there is the obligation ("bound to tell") to give as accurate an account as possible—presumably so the reader can better assess the story as well as the teller's credibility—that assumes a pact between narrator and reader. Yet there is also the disclaimer (the defectiveness of the percipient mind) that the content of this testimony, albeit truthfully told, may not *be* the truth, that the method is not equal to conveying the content (a contrast to

---

[49] See Lacey's discussion of Watt's "realism of assessment" (*Women* 31–4), which also runs through Welsh's "strong representations" and Rodensky's (22–3) and Schramm's (138–44) studies.

Hawthorne's preference for the half-light under which realist objects acquire psychological depth).

One doesn't want to quibble too much by pointing out that in *this* passage the engaged narrator—that is, the narrator who reveals himself—is another witness, not the equivalent of defense counsel, which is important in terms of the kinds of relationship it creates with the reader. This narrator takes a legal analogy, claiming a warrant for his fictional narrative in the language of law, which aligns the two discourses. But if Eliot follows closely on the law when her narrator speaks in this direct manner, with the detached one, she opens up other possibilities for getting at character or for failing to do so (e.g. in the novel's depiction of confession and silence). This doubled narrative voice may be a feint on Eliot's part (a way of explicitly signaling a correspondence with law while tacitly marking out a difference); an attempt to have it both ways of the sort we saw in the narrator's analysis of Arthur's mind, or, more simply, the kind of inconsistency one might expect at a time when law and literature were renegotiating their relationship.[50]

Compared with the Hawthorne of "The Custom House" who struggles to see beyond the material, Eliot's narrator regrets the distortions of a "doubtless defective" mind (238) and vows to be as truthful to the image (albeit "faint," "confused," or otherwise "disturbed") as a witness testifying on oath. Indeed, in response to a hypothetical reader's request that this real world be "touch[ed] up with a tasteful pencil" (238), Eliot's narrator replies,

> I would not, even if I had the choice, be the clever novelist who could create a world so much better than this, in which we get up in the morning to do our daily work, that you would be likely to turn a harder, colder eye . . . on the real breathing men and women, who can be chilled by your indifference or injured by your prejudice; who can be cheered and helped onward by your fellow-feeling, your forbearance, your outspoken, *brave justice*. (239, emphasis mine)

Rather, this narrator advances a theory of "Art" devoted to "the faithful representing of commonplace things" (241)—again echoing Wordsworth, here in the Preface to the *Lyrical Ballads* (1802), as well as her own argument in

---

[50] Robyn R. Warhol uses "distancing" and "engaging" to describe the effect produced on "narratees"—the "you" of a narrator's address—by nineteenth-century women writers' techniques, including their attitudes towards characters and towards the practice of narration itself. Of the narrator's extended intervention into the story of *Adam Bede*, she claims that Eliot's insistence on truthfully representing Hetty's plight was designed to engage readers, make them identify with the narratees, share their sympathy for the characters, and extend that feeling into the extradiegetic world (814–16).

"Silly Novels by Lady Novelists" (1856). Now, there is a social project in this goal for the novel (using fiction to represent things as they are to create an opportunity for readers to cultivate their sympathy, extend it to the real world of action, and promote "brave justice") which does not animate Hawthorne's narrator. At best, he suffers from a malaise akin to Eliot's hypothetical readers who disdain the people around them, but while the Hawthorne narrator at least believes the quotidian world has a "deeper import" to fathom (48), he can't muster the interest to explore it.

A second explanation lies, as I suggested at the beginning, in the narrative value of silence: confession hastens the end of conflict and suspense in these novels. In both Hawthorne's and Eliot's novels, the desire to hear an account of *how* the facts—the birth of a child, the birth and death of another—came to be makes silence a form of momentum. Both women's silence, that is, engenders curiosity of a sort that compels readers to continue reading. At the same time, their silence allows both authors to dramatize precisely what happens when one kind of story is withheld. In the absence of direct explanation from the accused, other, differently reliable, forms of evidence must fill the void, and different stories be told. And when confessions are made, these novels are unwilling or unable to continue much beyond them, which suggests that the novel may be *equally as* open as, or even *less* open than, the courts were to hearing some stories, particularly when *other* stories—for example, about maternal instinct or spiritual leadership—that the reader well knows are themselves flouted by the nature of the crimes. If the novel is less interested in this sense in the good or at least repentant character, does this mean the novel as a form needs us to be bad?

Conduct and Character: Why (Law and) Literature Need Us to be Bad

Since Ian Watt at least, the history of the novel has been told via a history of the law (or at least through legal analogies to it) and I, too, have called attention to the coincidence of legal efforts to define and allocate responsibility for wrongful actions and the explosion of narrative fiction, which, like legal narratives, structure expectations and the ways we organize and interpret ourselves and our societies.[51] In the novel, plot and the expectations created by conventional storylines provide this structure. Indeed, observing that Hetty

---

[51] See Susan Heinzelman's reading of the gendered implications of Watt's analogy as well as her account of the use of law in literary history. See also Lacey on responsibility's "normative and constructive" function, a function emphasized by the plural "practices" of responsibility instead of the singular, metaphysical being responsible ("Responsibility and Modernity" 253). I extend this normative and constructive function to novel-reading, more particularly, to the expectations created by conventions of narrative plotting.

"had never read a novel," the narrator asks pityingly, "how then could she find a shape for her expectations?" (196). (Had Hetty been a more experienced reader, she may not have been blind to the clichéd nature of her relationship with Arthur.)[52] I am not attempting to resolve questions about the relative importance of action or character in the novel, but I do want to reinvigorate discussion of their relationship by suggesting that it is the same that troubled legal analysts in the nineteenth century, thereby positioning narratological discussions of plot and character as a corollary of the legal problem of "character": each discourse considers the degree to which character is a measure of doing or being, acts or mental states, and how it can be accessed. The larger question of this study is how legal attitudes towards character evidence spread to and influenced the broader culture, and conversely how the novel's conception of character crossed over into law.

Behind this question is the assumption that there has been some sort of wrong or transgression to prompt the legal question and bring the individual into law's formal arena. Where possessive individualism links one's state of being to acquisitiveness, so that having becomes a measure of being, in this case, both law and literature require transgressive individualism and the conflict or breach that will activate the ritual performance of their ordering functions. Thus, if in one sense character is an extant identity or confirmed reputation to be ascertained whole, it is also a designation that is created, modified, and deployed through both discourses' reliance on forms of representation.

Long before the professionalization of legal practice, the criminal justice system was administered by middle-class lay people, from Justices of the Peace to witnesses, who were also the target audience for novels, so that, Nicola Lacey suggests, "social attitudes reflected in the realist novels" could exert real influence on the practice of criminal law (*Women* 43). Paired with Nancy Armstrong's provocative contention that it's the novel's way of "thinking" which produced the modern subject or "self-governing individual" (3–6), their observations lead to the following scenario: to think like a novel is to imagine a kind of individual who, charged with more energy than his social limits can brook, tries to exceed those limits and must in a sense always be in some degree of conflict with his social world. This supplemental energy and the ensuing conflict is something the novel helps to generate—is, indeed, a condition of traditional narrative action (Miller)—but in the nineteenth century, the novel will also work to "contain and redirect" this energy in socially

---

[52] See Rachel Bowlby's discussion of the kind of novel she might have read, *Adam Bede* itself or its eighteenth-century precursors, such as *Pamela* (19).

acceptable ways (Armstrong 81).[53] Nicola Lacey makes the same observation about affinities between the novel form, the role of criminal transgression, and the new model of personhood that put "older form[s] of expression of individuality . . . at risk" (*Women* 48). Thus, the novel plays a key role in the creation of liberal individualism: if Bentham thought judges made work for the legal profession, novelists made work for themselves by creating an inner life—and an audience—engaged in this conflict of self-assertion among individuals and between individuals and forms of (social, cultural, legal, political, moral) authority.

Nevertheless, if the novel makes a form of transgression the condition for individuality and creates the transgressive individual, and if this conception of the modern subject exerts real influence on the practice of criminal law, then the court would seem to be placed in the position of presuming guilt rather than innocence, or at least of emphasizing the capacity for guilt. Put differently, if to be an individual in the modern sense means having transgressed in the first place, then in this secular version of The Fall, the modern subject can never be fully innocent. And that's exactly what the legal history bears out: from the presumption of guilt built into early modern concepts of manifest criminality to the role of reputation or character in eighteenth-century evaluations of conduct, and on to nineteenth-century attention to criminal capacity, basically, we have a modern subject who is both prone to transgress and called upon to exercise self-control and a form of literature bent on creating and directing, if not also containing, this energy.[54] So the issue becomes not only how law and literature together imagine and create the self-disciplined subject, but also what it must do to those who lack, resist, or escape the forms of restraint. As long as criminal actions in the legal world or violations of prevailing social and moral codes in the novel drive those narratives' plots, these disruptions of the social worlds of life and fiction must be met by efforts at resolution, whether a return to some pre-existing order or its revision and remaking into a new one. Like the readers in, and the readers of, *Adam Bede* and *The Scarlet Letter*, the curiosity and perplexity these

---

[53] See D. A. Miller's premise that only certain kinds of conflict are "narratable" (ix).
[54] Nicola Lacey discusses this connection across multiple works. Most relevant here are "Responsible Subject" 361 and *Women* 12, 25. Jan-Melissa Schramm complicates the idea that literature contains this energy, at least in ethical ways, when she notes that the entire enterprise of fictional narration was open to charges of manipulating evidence and giving false testimony: "Eliot's alliance of the oath and the conventions of narrative realism is designed to generate assent in the reader, but at the same time it compromises fiction by reminding us of its potential association with perjury" (139–40).

transgressions generate keep the readers looking for explanations, as long as no one confesses.

My project in this chapter has been to explore the effects of women's silence at a time when, as criminal defendants, they were expected to answer the charges against them and to think of the novels, especially *Adam Bede*, as shutting down women's speech instead of being open to it in the way narrative jurisprudence, for example, suggests non-legal forms can more readily be. For readers in the 1850s, though, the right to silence offered a different way of interpreting the absence of the accused's speech. It is hard to imagine in Hetty's case that this silence was meant to be a gift, but it does offer a way of imagining how much better off she would have been if her silence could have been interpreted differently. Krueger's analysis of "cover stories" showed one way in which defense attorneys depended on the accused's silence in order to craft more sympathetic identities for defendants in infanticide cases (*Reading for the Law* 203).[55] This dependency opens onto a more basic observation. When silence is mandated and voluntariness removed, a failure to testify could only have been read as compliance instead of contempt.

Calls for the competency of the accused in the 1840s and 1850s, however, promised to introduce voluntariness—the key component that had been lacking in both the accused speaks model of Hetty's trial and the compulsory silence instituted with the Prisoner's Counsel Act—*and* its attendant interpretive liabilities. On the one hand, voluntariness would make it possible to read Hester—and perhaps Eliot herself—as being engaged in political, civil, social, or narrative resistance. Their silence becomes empowering. But Hetty Sorrel represents the other possibility that guilt can be inferred from voluntary silence, thereby tacitly creating compellability, no matter how poorly the resulting story might be told or how humiliating its details.[56] That is, in order to avoid the negative inference, Hetty would need to speak whether she wanted to or not. This merger of competency into compellability plays out precisely the untenable position Henry E. Smith described of an accused "no longer required to keep silent" when questioned yet unable to resist answering, effectively *required* to speak (180). On these terms, "compellability," or

[55] See also Krueger's earlier analysis of the relationship between women's speech, legislative reform, and legal narrative in "Witnessing Women" 338–9.
[56] This possibility was recognized in the state of Maine when prosecutors and judges were prevented by statute from encouraging this view in their address or instructions to the jury. If Miriam Jones is right that Eliot's narrator takes a prosecutorial stance towards Hetty, then all his comments on silence (Jones argues for a male narrative persona) are made to foster precisely this inference, and the sympathy suggested by "poor Hetty" becomes a rhetorical sham.

the general availability to being called to testify by the opposing party, takes on the meaning associated with forced confession, that is, of evidence given involuntarily.[57]

Moreover, this merger carries particular implications for women's speech during the time of composition. One need only think of women's activism—from Seneca Falls in the U.S. (1848) to the Matrimonial Causes Act in the U.K. (1857)—as occasioning a demand to speak out or requiring, as Hester does, the supplemental voices of male MPs, to see that the imposition of silence was viewed as the more serious problem and one that many women ignored. But this activism also raises a question about the extent to which other liberal-minded women felt compelled to participate and the inferences that might be drawn about those who refused or whose participation was more muted. To take a different example, the necessity of giving evidence at the new divorce proceedings—the availability of divorce being a desired reform—made suffering the likely humiliation of publicity the cost of separation, another Hobson's choice.

If Hawthorne and Eliot thought giving their heroines a right to silence would help their fictional cases, the plan backfired. When Hester and Hetty refuse to speak, they assume a voluntariness which at law they do not possess and whose exercise ironically heightens their responsibility, making them appear more culpable. However, when taken as comments on contemporary debates about the privilege against self-incrimination and the right to silence, Hawthorne's and Eliot's novels seem to mandate silence in order to circumvent the association between choice, responsibility, and guilt. Rather than view this maneuver as an attack on liberal individualism or on the capacities assumed by the attribution of criminal responsibility, however, these novels

---

[57] Peter Brooks's observations about the Fifth Amendment to the U.S. Constitution hold true for Hester and Hetty. The existence of a right not to incriminate oneself says something about "how society wants to conceive the criminal suspect" and about "human dignity" more broadly, especially the tensions between "reduc[ing] the accused to a state of abjection, all the while maintaining that they must be unfettered to exercise their free will in acts of rational choice" (*Troubling Confessions* 5). Langbein points to *R v Jane Warickshall* (1783) that excluded testimony "'forced from the mind by the flattery of hope, or by the torture of fear,'" finding in it the "mature" confession rule that excluded involuntary confession (qtd. in *Origins* 179). Only confessions made voluntarily and in an "out-of-court" context could be admitted in criminal cases. As a rule designed to prevent pre-trial coercion, it offers another contemporary explanation for Hetty's silence before the trial. However, as it stands in *Adam Bede*, Hetty's voluntary admission *following* her sentence would only corroborate the appropriateness of the court's finding. And the rule has nothing to say about Hetty's refusal to answer charges during the trial.

argue for a different kind of freedom that comes from not having to make the difficult choice.

In this final section I turn to another dimension of literary production—literature reviews and the literary professional—and the impact of this public life on definitions of character. In doing so, I turn my attention more fully on Eliot. Her theory of fiction spoke to the challenges of writing as well as to more philosophical questions of the percipient mind and the ability to represent things as they are. As both novels have shown, Hetty cannot represent herself and Hester will not, but neither does Marian Evans. Those same reviews that compared the author of *Adam Bede* to Hawthorne also addressed the demands and pitfalls of publicity. Although Hawthorne was also "disinclined to talk overmuch of myself and my affairs" and marvels that "an autobiographical impulse should twice in my life have taken possession of me, in addressing the public" (7), I want to suggest that Eliot's fascination with both women's refusals to speak, and with the "wrongful actions" their silences would not explain, is akin to her own concealed identity and the projection of an authorial character. As woman author and as partner to an illicit romance, Eliot transgressed in multiple ways as she negotiated both her public and private identities.[58]

Following publication of *Scenes of Clerical Life*, when Eliot was writing *Adam Bede* and negotiating for its publication, Eliot's correspondence with Blackwood and others frequently recurs to the subject of her "incognito" (Haight II.419, II.505). In December 1858, she tells Blackwood of a new rumor, possibly originating with her family, and her wish that *Adam Bede* be released quickly so it could be judged "quite apart from its authorship" (II.505). In a postscript, she asserts that any direct question about her identity "will be met with direct contradiction" and invokes "Scott's opinion" on the value of silence:

> Either I must have surrendered my secret,—or have returned an equivocating answer,—or finally, must have stoutly and boldly denied the fact ... I therefore considered myself entitled, like an accused person put on trial, to refuse giving my own evidence to my own conviction, and flatly to deny all that could not be proved against me. (II.505n10)[59]

---

[58] See Welsh, *Blackmail* 113–27 for discussion of Eliot's attitudes towards the impact of her private life on her public, professional life. For a reading of "The Minister's Black Veil" and *The Lifted Veil* which builds on the idea of covering and the hazards of exposure, see Sheasby.

[59] Gordon S. Haight notes that Eliot's journal of that month shows she and Lewes were reading Lockhart's *Life of Scott*. The passage he cites comes from the General Preface to the *Waverley* novels (1829).

Fully alive to what in 1858 England had become a right to silence, Eliot, channeling Scott in 1829 Scotland, invokes the privilege not to incriminate herself, but she also confirms jurists' suspicions that extending competency would lead witnesses, to say nothing of parties to the suit, either to muddle their stories or to lie. To "deny all that could not be proved" is to invite furthermore the more ambiguous Scottish verdict of "not proven" (as opposed to "not guilty") and to admit that something may be true without being probative at law. In claiming this right, Eliot sets herself up as a hostile witness.[60]

The publication of *Adam Bede* in February 1859 only intensified curiosity. The review published in the July number of the *Edinburgh Review*, attributed to Caroline Norton and discussed in the Introduction, concludes with an account of the "disputes as to its authorship" that had filled recent newspapers, including a letter from the Rector of Kirkby that gave the rights to Mr. Liggins of Nuneaton, Warwickshire (242), an identification that was apparently taken to be true. However, Norton reports that the paper received

> a wrathful letter from "George Eliot" . . . asking (not unreasonably) whether "the act of publishing a book deprives a man of all claim to the courtesies usual amongst gentleman?" And adding "If not, the attempt to pry into what is obviously meant to be withheld—my name—and to publish the rumours which such prying may give rise to, seems to me quite indefensible, still more so to state these rumours as ascertained truths."(243)

The exchange continues, with another cleric reporting that money was being sent to the supposed author and with Blackwood finally denying Liggins's authorship and denouncing anyone's having received "'charitable contributions.'"[61]

Norton herself does not resist referring to "internal evidence" in support of the "latest suggestion" that the author is a *woman* from Warwickshire, confirmation of which might come with her next publication, but this final speculation is prelude to a much longer comment on the phenomenon of pseudonymous publication, celebrity, and public reaction to it. In a series of rhetorical questions, Norton characterizes the price of successful authorship: curiosity about one's "birth, parentage, and education" and recrimination for withholding that information; loss of the right not to be addressed "without an introduction"; and the application of one's writing talent to autographs. Although she commiserates with authors and agrees that the public

---

[60] Welsh also quotes a letter to the Cross sisters in which Eliot claims outright, "I am the criminal usually known under the name George Eliot" (qtd. in Welsh, *Blackmail* 126). See Haight VII.298.
[61] See Welsh's account in *Blackmail* 129–31.

"monomania" is as senseless as it is irritating, she nevertheless asserts that "while an author has clearly the right to deny his authorship and conceal his name," one who does "must take the chance of intrusive conjecture and stolen laurels" (245). One question is particularly relevant in the context of this chapter, though, and that is why this public persona—one can say character—should dominate consideration of the private, or as Norton asks it, "why is the inner man to be so much less sacred than the outward man?" (243).

This modern conception of human subjectivity as having both inner and outer dimension recalls my opening question about the relationship between conduct and character, doing and being, but here that "being" is further distinguished as the conjoined public and private selves. In spite of the continued importance of public figures and public achievements as subjects of important nineteenth-century genres such as biography and history, the era witnessed the rise in prominence of the private man and of the novel as the genre that could best capture that interiority. One does want to be careful about drawing too great a distinction between these two dimensions of personhood. As Richard Sennett explains in *The Fall of Public Man*, the principle of "immanence," which associated authenticity and meaning with the inner self, required external guides (21, 151). And in the legal arena, jurists charged with allocating responsibility for and punishing criminal acts struggled precisely with this issue of how to understand the relationship between a defendant's behaviors or conduct and their inner capacities, either to commit crimes or to be law-abiding members of a community.

The decision in the 1865 case *R v Rowton* (discussed in the next chapter) defined character as "reputation" precisely because of the difficulty of getting at "disposition" directly. As an opinion that was more widely held and for a longer duration than the experience of a single witness could produce, general reputation was more likely to be the best evidence of disposition. But critics of the decision argued that ruling out the testimony of direct, personal experience meant replacing it with hearsay so that reputation became nothing more than rumor, and legal evidence no different than the modes of proof that circulated among the public. The sociological value of gossip and the legal history of hearsay is the subject of the next chapter, but I do want to comment on the coincidence of Justice Erle's assessment of the evidentiary value of rumor, Eliot's own distinction in her letter to the *Edinburgh Review* between it and "ascertained truth" (243), and Walter Scott's much earlier comment on the costs of direct disclosure.

It might appear that as with the "outward man" of literary celebrity, conduct or actions were more valued in law as indices of character than the inner man or disposition. That is, the wrangling over the meaning of "character"—as general reputation or as disposition—at first appears to be an argument over a substantive difference between them where the first derives from the second, or where the second speaks to an inner quality that becomes manifest in the actions that are the basis of reputation. But the struggle to find language to describe the same thing, character, really results from the more difficult task of accessing that inner quality and bringing it before the jury to weigh. Direct testimony of personal experience is more like other admissible forms of evidence, but the inefficiency and impracticality, to say nothing of the potential abuse, of these forms of "opinion" make them bad evidence, according to *Rowton*. It takes consistency of conduct, the repeatability of opinion among a group of people and over time, to add up to reliable character evidence. As Cockburn's summation made clear, "what you want to get at is . . . But there's no way of asking that directly" (*Regina v Rowton* 1502). The inner man of Norton's question is *not* less sacred than the outward man, just harder to reach—which for Eliot, and Scott, was as it should be.

Eliot's comment shares this sense of the location of truth in an inner or at least private space, as well as the unreliability of unsanctioned statements ("rumours") based on partial information got by illegitimate means ("prying"). The main difference between Eliot's comment and the immediate context of *Rowton* is that the legal case is about bringing evidence of character forward whereas Eliot's is about the right to withhold it. Character takes on new meaning, for not only is Eliot "a character artist" of the highest skill, as one approving reviewer notes, "George Eliot" is also a role that enables Marian Evans (or Lewes, as she then referred to herself) to preserve her privacy.[62]

As already suggested there are many reasons that character was such a problematic concept in the 1850s. I've focused on the idea of transgressive individualism as a key point of connection between legal and literary conceptions of character and of representing that character through narrative. There is a rich tradition of scholarship about women writers that describes their authorship as transgressing acceptable gender roles, and in Eliot's relationship with George Lewes there is further reason to think about the role that transgression would have played in her sense of her own position, in the paths she drew for her characters, and perhaps the attraction of Hawthorne.

Eliot's argument for privacy against the demands of her reading community expresses a value for personal autonomy and self-determinism, liberty even, consonant with some strands of liberal individualism and certainly with the idea of character as a set of capacities to be developed. But the State,

---

[62] See Haight II.398n10 where Haight refers to the journal entry for June 22, 1857 as marking the "change of name" and subsequent estrangement from her brother.

the community, the *socius* had its claims, too. Eliot's need or right not to tell, in other words, did not foreclose others' need to ask and, in the absence of explanation, to supply their own. The silences of the women discussed in this chapter removed their voices from conversations about them, but they didn't stop those conversations. Rather, they opened onto a much broader field of potential knowledge, if not evidence, that functioned differently in the legal arena than in the community at large. What Eliot disparages as rumor may be false, but it may also be truth in a latent state, a yet-to-be-corroborated fact that nevertheless exerts influence in the world and can be acted on by it. As Chapter 2 will explain, where the law sought to *exclude* rumor and its cousin gossip through application of a new set of rules designed to protect character, the novel saw them as a valuable form of character evidence essential for negotiating relationships and shaping social boundaries.

2

Gossip, Hearsay, and the Character Exception: Reputation on Trial in *The Tenant of Wildfell Hall* and *R v Rowton*

[W]e were disputing, as we came along, a question that you can readily decide for us, as it mainly regarded yourself—and, indeed, we often hold discussions about you; for some of us have nothing better to do than to talk about our neighbours' concerns, and we, the indigenous plants of the soil, have known each other so long, and talked each other over so often, that we are quite sick of that game; so that a stranger coming amongst us makes an invaluable addition to our exhausted sources of amusement.

Anne Brontë, *The Tenant of Wildfell Hall* (1848)

What you want to get at is the tendency and disposition of the man's mind towards committing or abstaining from committing the class of crime with which he stands charged, but no one has ever heard the question—what is the tendency and disposition of the prisoner's mind?—put directly. The only way of getting at it is by giving evidence of his general character founded on his general reputation in the neighborhood in which he lives.

R v Rowton (1865)

Police notices in *The Times* for September 10, 1864 document the arrest and indictment of James Rowton, a forty-five-year-old private tutor from Grove-house, South Hackney, who was charged with the "indecent assault" of George Low, a fourteen-year-old office boy at the London and Northwestern Railway's Camden-town station ("Police-Rowton, James for Indecent Assault"). Three days later *The Times* printed the following clarification:

> Referring to the case which came before Marylebone Police Court on Thursday, Mr. Samuel James Rowton, of Grove-house school, South Hackney, asks to have it stated that he is the only person of the name of Rowton resident or a tutor in that establishment, and that he is not the

person who was charged before the magistrate. ("Rowton (Samuel James) Not the Rowton in the Police Court")

The James Rowton whose trial would hinge on the admissibility of certain kinds of character evidence (and whose conviction ultimately would be overturned because of it) was really a forty-six-year-old clerk in holy orders with a "superior education" and a raft of vicars, curates, and rectors to back him ("Middlesex Sessions," Oct. 1, 11). This mix-up about the right Rowton marks an ironic beginning to a case that called on judges to parse the meaning of "character" and related concepts, such as reputation and disposition, but it must have been in all seriousness that *Samuel* James Rowton confronted the threat to his professional reputation and personal moral standing that the misattribution posed. More than a question of any one man's social status or connections, however, the initial confusion about James Rowton's identity epitomizes a broader, cultural preoccupation with defining, assigning, and circulating character.

Like newspaper columns, Victorian drawing rooms, courtrooms, and the novels that depicted them were full of reports and testimonials from one character about another. How to measure the value of these reports and define the uses to which such information could be put, however, varied with the venue. As the realist novel expanded its internal communities and its reading audience, it created more opportunities for learning about the central character. Deploying "character" as the single most significant measure of personal identity and social currency, the novel explored gossip's potential as a constructive form of relationship building and a viable means of information sharing.[1] So it was at law where, before the centralization of the courts, a man's reputation was his best defense or biggest liability as the local judge either knew him personally, or could rely on the testimony of others who did, when deciding whether to indict.

However, nineteenth-century reform of the rules of evidence, informed partly by urbanization and the loss of local knowledge, created more stringent boundaries for the kinds of evidence that could be brought to court and by whom. These boundaries were particularly hard to set in relation to character because the concept had become more complicated, denoting at once an interior disposition as well as an outward reputation. Samuel James Rowton's alarm at finding himself named in the police notice reflected the increased importance of character in a new, urban world where reputation always precedes personal experience. Thus, while the novel is replete with what political theorist Stefan Collini calls "character-talk" (103), and while

---

[1] See especially Deidre Shauna Lynch, on the "pragmatics of character" across discourses (4).

certain legal issues actually rely on character evidence, the law had become generally more wary of untested report.[2] What can be learned about modern conceptions of personhood when approached through the development of the novel and legal rules of evidence? More specifically, how do the uses of gossip in the novel and the problem of hearsay at law impact the nineteenth-century concept of character?

This chapter looks at Anne Brontë's *The Tenant of Wildfell Hall* (1848) and, briefly, Elizabeth Gaskell's *Cranford* (1853) as novels which depict especially cohesive—and extremely talkative—communities that, through the use of gossip and character-talk generally, alternately create and foreclose space for the would-be protagonist and her story. More specifically, I focus on the figure of the stranger who enters these communities and who, like the legal subject separated from his or her reputation, must rebuild a character. In drawing attention to the hazards of being separated from one's reputation, I assume not only that the character it describes is a good one—according to the *OED*, "character" always did mean good character and required negative adjectives to mean otherwise—but that the relationship between character and reputation was clearly understood. Yet the 1865 trial report of *R v Rowton* showed that the meanings of reputation and character and the larger problem of "how to get at" them, as Chief Justice Cockburn phrased it, are far from clear. If communal structures for getting at character such as those represented in the novel are inadequate to law's regulatory purpose, how do legal rules of evidence circumvent or replace them?

By raising these questions about character and forms of testimony—for this is what gossip and hearsay are—I enter the terrain of narrative jurisprudence. Scholars of narrative jurisprudence have typically preferred the novel's treatment of stories precisely because the legal management of evidence rules crucial experiences, affects, and information out of bounds. The hearsay rule forecloses on speech, just as the novel's provision of gossip opens it up, in ways that neatly fit characterizations of the relationship between law and literature (this in contrast to Chapter 1's focus on novels that withhold defendants' speech). Of particular interest are the problems that existing cultural narratives always influence the way we interpret new stories, that not all stories can or are allowed to be heard in the first place, or that even when they are told, they can fail to be understood.[3] These problems face the newcomer in the novels as well as their readers who, like members of a jury (to invoke

---

[2] On the importance of character in trials, like Rowton's, for "homosexual offenses," see H. G. Cocks. Based on criminal petitions filed between 1829 and 1877, Cocks finds that the character of defendants and their accusers was a "principal issue" (36–7).

[3] See Cover; Brooks and Gewirtz; West, *Caring for Justice*; and Krueger, *Reading for the Law*.

Ian Watt's classic analogy in *The Rise of the Novel*), must discriminate good evidence from bad and make judgments about its source and its subject, the central character. But, facing those problems, the novel itself must manage the evidence it allows to come forward, especially when the provision of more evidence can put the legal issue in question, or increase its complexity and the difficulty of deciding it. The question here is not whether literature is categorically better for allowing these stories but how it makes sense of this mass of information. Can the novel recognize the legal problem and still find ways to supplement or work around it?

The Tenant of Wildfell Hall and *Cranford* offer two versions of the uses of gossip or hearsay, where Brontë's dramatization of the negative effects of gossip confirms the very reasons untestable report was excluded at law. Showing the hazards of gossip, Brontë finds other ways of making character visible where Gaskell, by contrast, offers a model for understanding how readers might relate to a novel's content—here, to stories about their own cultural past—in ways that highlight the constructive potential of character-talk. The pairing makes visible a further, more valuable response the novel makes to legal restriction, namely, the way the novel repurposes hearsay and finds other uses for it: a sociological one of creating and maintaining communal boundaries; an epistemological one of confirming, uncovering, or otherwise creating knowledge, and a narratological one of generating plot, all of which impinge on character. Though I risk a circular argument, it is in the nature of character as a moral, philosophical, literary, professional, cultural, and legal concept that it cuts across and conjoins all three categories in a cyclical relationship: communities tell, and retell, stories which adapt and recirculate knowledge that was necessary to their foundation and remains so for their continuation. What we know about character and how we share it are crucial to creating relationships among individuals and, to adapt Alex Woloch's phrase, to *make* one *out of* many.

Gossip at Work: Forming Communities in and through the Novel

The Tenant of Wildfell Hall offers a lot to readers interested in the law. Published in 1848, it is poised precisely between the Custody of Infants Act (1839) and the Divorce and Matrimonial Causes Act (1857), which together removed the greatest legal impediments to marital separation. But set in the 1820s, its depiction of Helen Graham's ill-judged marriage to a charming but increasingly dissolute and manipulative husband dramatizes all the reasons a woman might want to divorce alongside the most compelling reasons not to, specifically the loss of her child. However, in this chapter I turn from the novel's context in specific legislative reform to a less strictly legal dimension of the novel: the way communities constitute, regulate, and maintain themselves through narrative and, more specifically, the *exchange* of stories. My interests are broadly sociological, yet focused on specific rules of evidence through which the Victorian legal system managed information about people and imagined the individual's relationship to a community. Brontë's novel speaks directly to these issues, first, through its framing device and, second, through a set of explicit comments about the nature and function of gossip.

Analysis of *Tenant* typically recognizes its interest in gossip as a mechanism for communal structuring but with very mixed response. As a speculative language of indeterminate origin, gossip does not so much report on the "object of discourse" as replace it in what Jan B. Gordon calls "a collective conspiracy to gain access to that which is spatially or socially hidden" (723). By contrast to studies focused on the detrimental effects of gossip, Patricia Meyer Spacks extends the social function of "serious gossip" to establish intimacy and sustain relationships to the realist novel in which gossip defines a character's status in or outside the social context (4, 8). And Priti Joshi examines Brontë's uses of gossip as a corrective to upper-class isolation and hyper-masculinity and, more generally, as a valuable source of life-changing, narrative-shifting information (918). This chapter approaches gossip as a form of character evidence that is allowed to circulate within the novel in ways prohibited in the venues of law. Within these terms, Brontë's open criticism of specific legal policy extends to legal procedure, albeit ambivalently. That is, her censure of divorce and custody law has a partial corollary in the critique of legal procedure implied by her openness to evidence that at law would be dismissed as hearsay, even while her characters retain a preference for written modes of proof shared by an empirically minded legal profession.

Brontë's novel opens with a letter from the narrator, Gilbert Markham, to a friend who, having given a "particular and interesting account" of his life before they became friends, is injured by Gilbert's failure to respond in kind. Explaining that he hadn't been "in a storytelling humour" then (9), Gilbert now embarks on "a tale of many chapters" (10) that will serve as "proof of friendly confidence," thereby making amends for the offense. This frame story serves two purposes by providing its internal audience with an occasion for writing and setting out the terms by which Brontë's external audience should approach the novel. Noting his reader's preference for "particularities and circumstantial details," for example, Gilbert promises not to rely on memory alone, and cites other letters, papers, and "an old journal" as evidence of his tale's truth (10). Although the literary antecedents of the frame tale itself are many, the epistolary form and references to written documentation alert readers to the genre's eighteenth-century roots and the importance of what Alexander Welsh and others have treated as the testimony of its first-person narration.[4] Thus recalling the inter-textual nature of the early novel, the growth of literary realism, and the era's empiricist bent, Gilbert's promise to his reader is Brontë's cue to her own that they should attend to the form of the stories that circulate, to the evidence that supports them, and, most intriguingly, to their function, here, the effect that the stories have on the shape of the communities in which they circulate. Christine Colón suggests that by embedding Helen's diary in Gilbert's letter, Brontë reinforces her purpose of building community through telling stories that "others may identify with and learn from" (28). However, this charge becomes all the more urgent because the frame's emphasis on the exchange of stories and on written proofs (written, durable, and extensible beyond the immediate community versus oral, malleable, and localized) sets up a potential conflict that the novel dramatizes: for the premise offered by the frame is that stories cement relationships, but the promise that they also be true highlights anxieties about how to tell a true tale from a false one and about the quality of relationships based on unsubstantiated stories.

The novel's title *The Tenant of Wildfell Hall* emphasizes the place more than the person: the place is given a proper name; the person is no more than a role. Indeed, Wildfell Hall, with the "fell's" connotations of exposure and barrenness, signifies the remoteness of the moorland setting (and consequently the insularity of the local community), as well as the attention that anyone situated there would draw on herself. Throughout its early chapters, Gilbert refers to the tenant as "the fair recluse," "the fair unknown," "the fair young hermit," the "mysterious occupant," and other epithets that highlight her outsider status and the curiosity it engenders (14, 15, 21, 28). Gordon suggests that "the most pointed signifier of [Helen's] role as a potentially disruptive outsider in the community" is the amount of talk she generates and describes these early chapters as being "really nothing more than the attempt of gossip to come to terms with meaning" (721–2).[5] Gilbert effectively documents the difficulty of this attempt in the locals' many efforts to learn about

---

[4] On the testimonial forms of the eighteenth century novel, see Welsh, *Strong Representations*. See also Terry Eagleton on the novel as an "anti-genre" that "cannibalizes other literary modes" (1).

[5] Gordon reads the news of Helen's arrival as an interruption of Brontë's depiction of "ritual images of Victorian order ... whose meanings are communally shared and hence capable of being transmitted, more or less intact, to others" (721). But in this reading gossip, however much the locals resort to it, is not treated as one of those ways of making "communally shared" meaning. As an "interruption," Helen injects conflict and desire—the stuff of narrative—that makes her arrival equally an invitation to shift to a new mode of establishing meaning and preserving communal boundaries. See D. A. Miller's argument that "only conflict is narratable" (ix).

Helen and the equally many ways the new resident rebuffs them so that her identity and history remain as inaccessible as the wild, isolated house she rents. Like Gilbert's failure to return Halford's confidence, her failures to return calls quickly enough raise the communal eyebrow.

Helen's aloofness and reticence about her background become the occasion for gossip and more malicious rumor and remind readers that the stories circulating within the novel are directed to different audiences, for different purposes. First, the gossip: As suggested, Helen's arrival makes her the subject of general, largely harmless speculation, which Fergus, Gilbert's irreverent younger brother, classes among the "refined sources of enjoyment" (51). He jokingly excludes Gilbert from the "ladies and gentleman, like us,"

> who have nothing better to do but to run snooking about to our neighbours' houses, peeping into their private corners; and scenting out their secrets, and picking holes in their pockets, when we don't find them ready made to our hands. (51)

As a form of entertainment for the idle, gossip bands locals together as spies, hounds, and thieves in a way that makes the discovery of Helen's actual identity counterproductive—to fun, certainly, but also to the work of social maintenance that speculating and talking about her performs.[6] Gossip thus solidifies prior local relationships, but Fergus's facetious description also points to its negative impact on the objectified person, the way it violate codes of privacy and property, as the cost of this local cohesion.[7] Moreover, Fergus violates the community's internal codes. As will be seen in *Cranford*, the rules that govern the locality are shared and silent; knowing them acts as a kind of shibboleth, but Fergus flouts the rule when he tells Helen outright that "a stranger coming amongst us makes an invaluable addition to our exhausted sources of amusement" (54). Although he maintains that gossip is no more than a pastime, and although Helen herself laughingly meets his frankness with her own, Fergus's disregard for this secret operation evokes "apprehension and wrath" from his sister who tells him, with no sense of irony, to "hold [his] tongue" (54). Helen could become integrated, which would involve learning and living by these rules, but to give her the key outright, before she has

---

[6] According to Spacks, "Like other forms of gossip, it ['idle talk'] can also solidify a group's sense of itself by heightening consciousness of 'outside' (inhabited by those talked about) and 'inside' (the temporarily secure territory of the talkers)" (5). See also Joshi on gossip's "vital function of creating fellowship" (908).

[7] Gordon notes that gossip "tends to be subversive precisely because it challenges our private spaces, because it treats history as a kind of property" (723).

returned their confidence—hearkening back to the exchange of stories—is prematurely inclusive.

Gossip's more invidious cousin, rumor, begins to circulate as a show of community resentment. It acts as a form of policing communal boundaries and censuring the stranger whose efforts to integrate are felt to be insufficient, or who poses a more direct threat. Romantic rivalry explains the origins of the "idle slander" and "ill-natured reports" (66, 69) about Helen that begin when the two most marriageable women perceive her attraction for the two most eligible men. Rumor supplies the "character" that Helen Graham's silence, and even her alias, do not. She is placed in a different narrative context, and those new stories are passed among the "usual company of friends and neighbours" (67) as rumor, as when Miss Wilson, who makes a show of not wanting to sit next to Helen at a party, wonders that her hostess invited her at all. "Perhaps she is not aware," she suggests, "that the lady's character is considered scarcely respectable" (69), thus circulating an evaluation of character that is based only on speculation about her apparently widowed status. ("Can you tell me . . . who was her husband; or if she ever had any?" asks the same Miss Wilson.) Gossip thus serves an instrumental function in Brontë's novel: it "creates plots where none exist" (Gordon 724) and "derives from and generates a need to know the facts of the case" (Spacks 7–8) which is equally as important for the Misses Millward and Wilson as it is for Brontë's readers.

Spacks suggests that the information gleaned through gossiping is of greater importance than the speech act because these rumors now need to be disproved and thus supply a further occasion for writing. Two subsequent volumes attest to the need for more pages, but the mode of Miss Wilson's evaluation warrants greater attention as well. Although Jane Wilson is the source, her delivery denies that origin, displacing it onto what Gordon refers to as a "democratic 'anyone'" who cannot be held accountable yet the power of whose utterance grows "in direct proportion to the dilution of its authoritative base" (722–3). Offered as already-received opinion, the act of saying functions as a performative assertion of veracity similar to the realist novel's own claim for representativeness, its self-contained yet unselfconscious reproduction of lived experience. Further, the content *is* remarkable for its combination of banality and suasion: that Helen is cast in this particular narrative is really only interesting because it is surely one of the most conventional. The very obviousness of its motive, its content, and its mode of delivery makes it the least believable and opens it to the most skepticism, yet its power remains intact as Gilbert's own susceptibility to his rival's role in it demonstrates. One would have to question the premise of Miss Wilson's rumor and the fiction that envelops it in order to change either the direction of her story or the function of the novel. *The Tenant of Wildfell Hall* shows both the difficulty of this task and a possible way around it.

To manage this evidence both internally and for the reader, Brontë turns to other, less immediately interested characters (an equivalent to nonparty witnesses) for their reaction to the rumors. Rose Markham compares them to her own observations, but is troubled by her inability to confront the principal "scandal mongers" (76) because "they don't speak openly to [her] about such things" (82). She explains to Gilbert, "It is only by hints and innuendos, and by what I hear others say"—in other words, by hearsay—"that I know what they think" (82). Rose can examine the claims, but etiquette, or a friendship cooled by her relation to Gilbert, prevents her from questioning the source to reach a reliable conclusion. Rose's social circle thus denies her the cross-examination, to say nothing of the oath, provided under legal rules of evidence, which at the very least illustrates why the legal rule exists. How can the novel maneuver around this apparent epistemological shortcoming? What other forms or sources of evidence are adequate to the task of accessing character?

Undertaking his own investigation, Gilbert confronts the accuser and goes to Helen so that she can answer the charge (a remnant of the "accused speaks" theory of the trial). This answer comes chiefly through her journal (the same Gilbert cites in his opening letter to Halford), and although Helen gives him an expurgated volume, this textual evidence replaces oral testimony. The exchange of documents versus oral stories—Gilbert's romantic strategy of plying her with books matched here by her gift of (spiritual) autobiography—points to the value of textual forms of proof first signaled in the novel's frame. More importantly, it makes that text *a principal source of information about character*, understood here as Helen's moral interior. The diary may be a suspect form of proof as to facts, since it comes from the most interested party of all, and perhaps even to the psychological motive or legal intent of the writer, but its function in this novel is to provide a kind of evidence and a kind of story that cannot be told at law or even in the local milieu since it would expose her abduction of young Arthur.

Of course, Helen insists that she does not want the story to *be* disseminated. In the operations of privacy and the sharing of secrets, the diary is Helen's way of building a relationship specifically with Gilbert. So, rather than swearing to the veracity of her own textual testimony, she reverses the oath-taking when she calls upon Gilbert's "honour" to keep its contents to himself (109). But she does not wait for his answer. It would be splitting hairs to think that because he does not affirm her conditions (or at least Brontë does not show readers that he does), he should not honor them, and Priti Joshi is right to point out the physical proximity, in the arrangement of chapters, of Helen's entreaty to the evidence that Gilbert ignores it (914). Still, there is a sense in which Gilbert does honor Helen's wishes. In a gentle form of coverture (he says her diary becomes an "old journal *of mine*" [Brontë 10]), he absorbs her story into his own so that, as Joshi argues, his internalization of her moral influence turns the diary into a tool for reform.[8] In this respect, Helen has done no more than every Victorian housewife was meant to do by acting as the moral lodestar of the domestic sphere. Nevertheless, the initial act of lending her story was meant not to improve Gilbert's character but to confirm the goodness of her own and to justify her retreat from the world. If we turn from the diary's later influence on Gilbert to its function for Helen herself, then, we see that at the level of content, it offers a model for developing and conveying knowledge of *its author's* character and, more particularly, of her capacity to regulate herself.[9]

As technique, Helen's original act of writing, recording, and ordering experience was the cornerstone of spiritual autobiography and, as Melody J. Kemp has shown, a staple method of character formation (195). By reproducing Helen's diary, Gilbert's letter not only approximates her character-forming activity; it also provides Halford and Brontë's audience a model text to read. At once privatizing yet also providing this "methodized" history of her moral state and consequent actions, Helen's journal speaks to shifts in the definition of character from eighteenth-century emphases on conduct to nineteenth-century capacities for self-restraint and judicious action. Even when character is understood as conduct or a set of behaviors, rather than this later capacity or disposition, in other words, Helen's personal diary documents the many acts of her crusade against Arthur Huntingdon's personally and socially degrading vices.

Unlike *The Tenant of Wildfell Hall*, *Cranford* makes a village full of people rather than an individual its focus, and it is hard to imagine two groups more different than Huntingdon's cronies and the ladies of *Cranford*. In Linden Car we have physical isolation, in Cranford historical separateness: only "20 miles from Drumble by train" (1), its imminent entrance into the modern, connected world is a source of consternation. And instead of a woman gone into hiding, we have Lady Glenmire and Captain Brown whose aristocratic

---

[8] Joshi notes the characters' need for textual evidence as well as the naivety of their reliance on it, since the document is twice used to expose Helen's history, but as Joshi argues there is a meaningful distinction between the uses to which Huntingdon and Markham put their knowledge.

[9] On the shift from conduct to "capacity" as the basis for assessing character, see Wiener; and Lacey, *Women*. See Gordon on the limitations of an exchange of books "to get behind the community's gossip" (726).

connections and plainspoken plebianism respectively, while earning them a share of speculation, can be accommodated by the openness that characterizes their interactions with the locals. In spite of these distinctions, I place Gaskell's novel alongside Brontë's because both of their communities rely on gossip as a means of accessing character. Together they dramatize a nineteenth-century transformation of character into personality and the concomitant processes Richard Sennett describes of reading external appearances, on the one hand, to arrive at this inner state and, on the other, of concealing it to avoid being read (167). They are especially relevant examples of these trends insofar as both novels are set in the recent past (more recent than in *The Scarlet Letter* or *Adam Bede*) and thus illustrate for their Victorian readers the social changes occurring in their own lifetimes.

The nearest equivalent to Helen Graham in *Cranford* is Capt. Brown, but if he and his daughters are talked about, so is everyone else in the network of tacit fictions through which the community operates.[10] Rather, it is the narrator's own insider-outsider status that is more interesting because of the kind of relationship it enables, or requires, her to create between herself, her subjects, and her readers. Her ethnographic position within the Cranford community and her account of its doings for the benefit of a more urbane audience—an adaptation of what Joseph Rezek calls an "aesthetics of provinciality" (2)—make Cranford as a body, not the stranger to it, the subject of gossip.[11] One can compare the tone of Fergus's comments to the Cranford narrator's. Both are clear-sighted about their communities; both function as social satirists,

---

[10] Here Spacks's characterization of "serious gossip" as an essentially private mode of sustaining communal relationships is relevant: "Its participants use talk about others to reflect about themselves, to express wonder and uncertainty and to locate certainties, to enlarge their knowledge of one another." Although the ladies of Cranford appear not to reflect on themselves, seeking to hide their knowledge of one another's circumstances rather than "enlarging" it, the stories they do exchange perform the same function. As Spacks suggests, "gossip" "provides a resource for the subordinated" in the sense that "the relationship such gossip expresses and sustains matters more than the information it promulgates" (5–6). The exchange matters most, which is especially important in *Cranford* since the information is a set of fictions maintained in the face of contrary evidence.

[11] Rezek's argument that provincial writers are best understood in terms of their collective relationship to a book trade dominated by London reinterprets histories that emphasize their proto-national affiliations. Focused on Scottish, Irish, and American authors, his point that the representational strategies developed to negotiate this market "derived from geographically inflected cultural subordination" (15) can also describe the "two nations" of England and the way works such as *Cranford* selectively recirculate gossip to navigate between communal and national identities. See also Borislav Knezevic's discussion of *Cranford*'s "ethnographic imagination" (406), particularly his connection of Mary Smith's narrative to amateur collecting.

and both even make their observations to strangers. But where Fergus's audience and subject are the same, the ladies of Cranford are not shown to be aware that their idiosyncrasies are being exposed, even affectionately, to a strange, metropolitan audience. Readers thus become the greater gossips in the sense that the narrator "talks about" this quaint group of "Amazonian" women on the verge of extinction. Cranford's ladies become provincial, old curiosities whose difference from the contemporary, urban life of their readers is the proper subject of the novel and a key to the readers' creation of their own communities.

Sennett's comments on the role of nostalgia in shaping individual personality can be extended here to communal and national identity and provide a clue to the cultural function of such tales from the provinces and the interest readers might take in them. Nineteenth-century personality is grounded in a self-conscious effort to "formulate what it is one feels" by examining one's past, especially "known and finished feelings," and taking them as the best indices of personal identity (152).[12] This largely Romantic sensibility (best articulated by Wordsworth in his Preface to the *Lyrical Ballads* and again in the *Intimations* Ode) carries through to the Victorian period. If this self-assessment is vital to the individual character (and we see this in the value of Helen's diary keeping), it is no less so to cultural identity. As was seen first in Chapter 1's discussion of Hawthorne's and Eliot's historical fiction, the selection and framing of stories about the past create opportunities for contemporary readers to figure out what they feel about it—whether nostalgia, condescension, or contempt—and consequently who they are.

This mode of creating, communicating, and consuming knowledge about individuals thus extends to cultural character and in this respect is not confined to the novel. As Deidre Shauna Lynch explains, it was during the Romantic period that the nineteenth-century novel became a favorite locus for the "individuation of the individual," but notwithstanding its popularity it was only one among many "technologies of the self" (126). As my reading of Brontë and Gaskell has shown, the novel's meta-fictional treatment of "character" and the selective exchange of stories about it make the novel a form through which readers developed their own characters, as well as the character of their communities.[13] In turning to the case of the Queen versus James Rowton, I suggest that the laws of evidence offered another such

---

[12] See also Lynch's observation that it was in the Romantic period that reading became "an occasion when readers got to know themselves and their feelings" (126).

[13] See discussion of the naturalization of development in a range of generic contexts in the Introduction.

technology for establishing character that was controversial within the legal community because it seemed novel-like.

From "Character" to "Case": Hearsay Evidence and the Character Exception[14]

Rose Markham's description of hearsay underscores a shared investment in character, in law and literature, as a constituent part of legal action and the node around which stories form and advance. Information about character can change the audience's response to stories of individual wrongdoing or personal injury, and they can influence the way communities negotiate their boundaries. Because the force of even the most familiar stories is so powerful, as Gilbert's own inability to discount the rumors about Helen showed, Victorian trial procedure set strict boundaries around the kinds of evidence that could be allowed to define its central characters. The legal quip "Hearsay is no evidence" reflects the importance of proofs—the oaths a trial witness would make and the cross-examination he would undergo—to ground what would otherwise be loose talk (Wills 5).[15] Brontë's novel represents this very problem and, as suggested by its framing device, relies especially on written proofs both to substantiate Gilbert's account and to justify Helen's alias. The novel's textual realism thus correlates with legal rules of evidence as frameworks through which stories of character are crafted, conveyed, and weighed although, it should be noted, criminal trials would be concerned even more with oral evidence.[16] In a similar comparison, Rex Ferguson argues that nineteenth-century legal rules and realist techniques worked expressly "to safeguard experience from its impersonators: hearsay, speculation, and irrelevance" (30). I share his interest in the quality of knowledge a witness could bring to court, especially as that knowledge pertains to character and especially with the understanding that legal rules themselves are not simply or uniformly applied. Looking at the way their terms are interpreted reveals

---

[14] On the maxim "we try cases, rather than persons," see Cicchini and White 347.
[15] Wills mentions the "familiar maxim" as best expressing the rule that witnesses must relay only their "direct personal knowledge" rather than repeat other people's statements (5). See also John H. Wigmore who calls the hearsay objection that "most characteristic rule of the Anglo-American law of evidence" and "next to jury-trial, the greatest contribution of that eminently practical legal system to the world's jurisprudence of procedure" (458). But see also John Langbein's correction of Wigmore's account in *Origins* 180. Langbein's access to the *Old Bailey Sessions Papers* shows that Wigmore dated the development of the character and hearsay rules too early, in the seventeenth century.
[16] On the importance of written evidence in eighteenth-century civil law, particularly in respect to Geoffrey Gilbert's *The Law of Evidence* (1754) and its treatment of the "best evidence rule," see Gallanis.

the changeable nature of the structures and hence of the characters they support. Before turning to *R v Rowton*, then, it will be useful to contextualize its discussion of character in the rules of criminal evidence. What gave rise to the practice of excluding relevant evidence? Just how had the rules against character and hearsay developed, what connects them, and how far had the nineteenth-century application of these rules departed from or refined their original purpose?

As part of the secularization and rationalization of legal practice, changes in eighteenth- and nineteenth-century legal attitudes towards evidence were part of a broader epistemological shift (Gallanis 505), one that influenced the growth of the novel and, as we saw, operates self-consciously in Brontë's and Gaskell's works. As Thomas P. Gallanis explains, in the mid-eighteenth century, documentary evidence took pride of place over oral proofs. When Geoffrey Gilbert described the "best evidence rule" ("that a man must have the utmost evidence, the nature of the fact is capable of"), he was thinking of written texts, the basis of proof in the civil court (506). Showing comparatively little concern for the oral testimony that occupied the criminal side, Gilbert nevertheless cautioned against hearsay (508). In spite of this warning, however, Gallanis remarks that in both civil and criminal venues in the eighteenth century hearsay was "accepted almost without comment," largely "unregulated," and in some instances even necessitated by restrictions on who was competent to give evidence (512–14). Nineteenth-century legal theory inverted this emphasis. Witness testimony grew in importance since, according to Thomas Starkie's *Practical Treatise of the Law of Evidence* (1824), even written evidence required proofs which were usually given in oral evidence (519). If oral proof was to be more reliable, then the rules of evidence for admitting—and excluding it—would have to become both more voluminous and more precise.

The rule against hearsay bars one person's report of another person's statement from being taken as proof of the facts at issue because on principle second-hand speech cannot be the best obtainable evidence (because the original speaker was not under oath and was unavailable for cross-examination).[17] In his study of treatises from 1754 to 1824 that discuss the hearsay rule, Gallanis finds that the most significant changes to its application had already occurred by the start of the nineteenth century, a picture case law confirmed

---

[17] Sometimes hearsay *is* the best evidence obtainable, however. Testimony to dying declarations or as a substitute for witness incompetency are two examples. See Langbein, *Origins* 179, 238; and Gallanis 534.

as trial reports *up to* 1780 rarely mention it (533).[18] By contrast, Gallanis's examination of the trial reports at Westminster shows an average of eight objections per case as testimony in the early years of the nineteenth century was subjected to a new battery of regulations, among them the rule against hearsay and restrictions on character evidence (539).

This increase in the number of objections to evidence towards the end of the eighteenth century correlates with specific lawyers who appeared in both the criminal and civil courts and whose doubled duties were themselves indicative of what John Langbein calls the general "lawyerization of the felony trial" (*Origins* 203).[19] In his authoritative account of the origin of adversary criminal trial, Langbein argues that the introduction of defense counsel in the seventeenth century made a "structural change" that transformed the "very theory" of the trial from a refereed confrontation between accuser and accused towards the presentation and testing of a "case" (1–9).[20] Defense counsel at the end of the eighteenth century, however, faced a quandary: the nature of the adversarial system made him responsible for "gathering, selecting, presenting and probing" evidence, yet he was not permitted to address the jury and hence was unable "to explain away unsafe testimony or to disparage its reliability" directly (1). Criminal lawyers in particular were thus under pressure to defend their clients by *blocking* what their opponents could produce in evidence. Beginning arguably as compensatory strategies, then,

---

[18] This absence could be a matter of nomenclature. Langbein draws a line from hearsay back to the phrase "no evidence" and observes a trend towards disapproving hearsay as early as the 1730s—right alongside numerous exceptions, for example because the most knowledgeable witnesses were also interested parties, hence not competent to testify, or because the hearsay was offered as secondary, corroborative evidence of other sworn testimony (*Origins* 237–9).

[19] See Gallanis for discussion of the specific lawyers, notably James Adair and William Garrow (546–50). Gallanis counters the received view that the practice of excluding evidence began in the civil courts *before* moving to criminal trials and attributes it to the status and influence of lawyers who brought strategies developed in criminal practice back to the civil side (551).

[20] Langbein argues that just as defense counsel was introduced to balance out prosecutorial advantage following the treason trials of the seventeenth century, its redistribution of power would be called for again throughout the eighteenth century to redress similarly unfair techniques of prosecution that increased the likelihood of perjured evidence being brought against the accused, for example the advent of "reward-seeking thieftakers, leniency towards crown witnesses who gave evidence against their accomplices, and the general uptick in professional management of prosecutions" (*Origins* 4). Since this evidence was gathered in the pre-trial investigation, Langbein explains that many of the trial judges' decisions (e.g. to allow defense counsel to cross-examine witnesses or to challenge kinds of testimony) were a corrective to pre-trial corruption, error, or the inefficiencies of a private system of prosecution.

cross-examination and the evidentiary objection—typically based on the rule against hearsay—very quickly became the terror of prosecution witnesses and "the centerpiece of modern evidence law" (Gallanis 546, 537).[21] Indeed, the prioritization of cross-examination was used as an argument for making even interested parties competent, since now skilled lawyers could test their accounts (Langbein, *Origins* 246). However, while cross-examination could cast doubt on testimony, it could not make a jury un-hear it, making the ability to block evidence in the first place by calling it hearsay potentially the more effective strategy.

That said, most of the exceptions to the rule, among them a certain kind of character evidence, were also established during this period. Character evidence can be defined in two related but distinct ways: as an established exception to the hearsay rule which, like that rule, applies to both civil and criminal cases and, in a second, more limited sense as one of three "core" rules of criminal evidence that developed during the eighteenth century (Gallanis 517; Langbein, *Origins* 179).[22] In the first sense, character evidence, understood as one's general reputation, is not considered to be unverifiable, second-hand information (gossip) and therefore can be allowed. In the second sense, the criminal rule bars the admission of evidence of *bad* character specifically and is not immediately connected to the hearsay rule.

Thomas Starkie outlined the acceptable uses of character in 1824. Among these, evidence of a *witness's* character could be used in all cases "to impeach or support" his testimony (Gallanis 523).[23] In civil cases such as libel and slander or criminal conversation, that were materially *about* character and whose outcomes confirmed the loser's moral standing, character evidence might influence the award of damages, while in criminal trials, it "allow[ed] the jury to form a presumption about the accused person's guilt or innocence" (523). Comparing trial reports from the 1750s to the 1820s, Gallanis observes few restrictions on the use of character evidence in the early period, but by the 1820s limits on acceptable references to character had become a "prominent

---

[21] Although both Langbein and Gallanis discuss points of difference and overlap between the civil and criminal courts, their focus ultimately is on the impact that criminal courts had on the development of a law of evidence. The rule against hearsay may be the "the central enterprise of the mature Anglo-American law of evidence" (Langbein, *Origins* 233) because it applies in *both* civil and criminal courts; however, Langbein points out that treatise writers included it in their discussion of criminal evidence mainly when it had been used in criminal cases.

[22] Others are the corroboration rule (designed to deal with an accomplice's possible perjury) and the confession rule (Langbein, *Origins* 179).

[23] See also Blinka, "Character, Liberalism, and the Protean Culture of Evidence Law," especially 116–23.

oral-evidence topi[c]" (528)—not necessarily because they were hearsay and not even because they were irrelevant, but because they referred to facts that were not at issue in the case at hand (528).[24]

Although the scope and application of both rules governing the admissibility of testimony about character were increasingly tested and refined in the early 1800s, they could not prevent them from becoming entangled. As Gallanis's study suggests and as my discussion of *Rowton* will elaborate, the use of character evidence depended on the way the term "character" was understood, especially when "general reputation" was the only exception to the rule.[25] In criminal trials of the period, for example, a testifying witness's attempt to offer hearsay, "unless it fell within a recognized exception" was "routinely the target of an objection from opposing counsel or an admonition from the judge" (Gallanis 529). Taking general reputation as such an exception, however, even in the 1820s, witnesses freely testified to "what they had 'heard'" about the defendant's reputation (529). And if that general reputation were a bad one? Here the rule against hearsay and the exceptional status of general reputation confront the rule against evidence of bad character in ways that foreshadow the judges' debate in *Rowton*: when the general reputation was a bad one, the character rule might not withstand it.

According to the criminal law's character rule, the prosecution could not introduce evidence of a defendant's bad character unless or until the accused introduced evidence of good character, and even then (and as early as the 1750s) it could not venture into evidence of particular past acts.[26] This "rebuttal exception" made the rule against character evidence "a defensive option, not a prohibition" that allowed the defense counsel to decide whether evidence to good character, if brought forward, would outweigh any bad

---

[24] See also Langbein, *Origins* 191–2 and 198–9 on the "sub-rule against particulars."

[25] There is some discrepancy between Gallanis's account and Langbein's discussion of the growth of the character rule, partly in terms of timing but also the nuances of its definition. In spite of Wigmore's assertion that a rule against evidence of bad character had been established in the seventeenth century, Langbein estimates that it only began to be regularly enforced around 1715 and was not "fail-safe" before mid-century, although it did reach "maturity" in the eighteenth century (*Origins* 179). He concludes that even though recourse to character evidence may have been deemed unwise, that persuasion did not amount to a rule. Once defense counsel was present and able to query departures from practice, however, Langbein speculates that they may have standardized practice to the point that it could be recognized as a rule. This trajectory comports with Gallanis's characterization of the period between 1780 and 1799 as the time when the hearsay rule *and its exceptions* generated the most litigation and acquired its modern form, so that the early nineteenth century was more properly a period of "consolidation" than one of "innovation" (534, 536).

[26] See Langbein, *Origins* 190–203 for further discussion of the character rule as practiced in the seventeenth to eighteenth centuries.

the prosecution might then introduce (Langbein, *Origins* 179, 197). As an option, it exemplifies one way that trial judges made up for shortcomings of pre-trial investigation. However, the rule fell short in two significant ways. A defendant's decision not to produce witnesses to good character (not unlike a decision to remain silent when offered a chance to speak) could lead to unfavorable inferences. Under pressure by judges to produce witnesses, defense counsel who entered into character forfeited their ability to prevent the prosecution from entering its own. Worse, Langbein observes that as late as 1770, the Old Bailey showed "a seemingly unrestrained tolerance for character evidence against the accused" if it was given by the magistrate who himself had conducted the pre-trial investigation or by a third party who could describe that investigation, even when the description amounted to "character hearsay" (*Origins* 199, 201). Langbein speculates that there may have been greater tolerance for character evidence if it came out of what he calls "pursuit hearsay," or third-party testimony that pertained to the way the accused was "detected or detained" and which the court allowed well after the establishment of the hearsay rule (202). This "pursuit character evidence" thus appears to trample *both* prohibitive rules and in the process shows how closely entwined gossip and hearsay, and reputation and (criminal) character, could become.

How does this history inform our understanding of the novel's attitude towards the nature of character evidence and the lawyer's job of "gathering, selecting, presenting, and probing" it at trial? The shifting value of documentary and testimonial evidence is also germane to Brontë's treatment of character evidence and narrative reliability, especially in terms of the distinction between the written forms her characters rely on to combat loose talk and Brontë's own, arguably more circumspect, attitude about the way texts manipulate raw experience (Joshi 914). It is surely serendipitous that *Tenant*'s setting in 1826–7 occurs just two years after Thomas Starkie's *Practical Treatise* confirmed the transformation of an eighteenth-century concern with documentary proofs to a modern attention to oral testimony, for Brontë's novel plays out the same tensions between forms of proof and how to regulate them that Gallanis shows occupied the treatise writers and the courts.[27] Indeed, the novel may be said to enact an eighteenth-/nineteenth-century

---

[27] Told from the vantage point of 1848, the novel's main action takes place twenty years earlier, well after the major legal developments in evidence law had occurred. So, whereas Gilbert's objection to hearsay is fully contemporaneous with Starkie's prioritization and, hence, greater scrutiny of oral testimony, Helen's production of written evidence resonates with eighteenth-century attitudes. Again, the value for modes of evidence differs across civil and criminal lines. As I've argued elsewhere, registers of character such as a *written* last will and testament first required documentary form in 1837.

split in the evidentiary value of texts and speech, chiefly in terms of its frame story (which allows readers to see the earlier zeitgeist against the backdrop of a mid-century sensibility), but also in terms of Helen's and Gilbert's different attitudes towards those forms.

Helen's production of the diary replaces orality with written evidence and seems a throwback to earlier times—making the lovers and their proofs out of sync with the changes in exclusionary evidence law, and potentially out of sync with each other. One might speculate that Helen's insistence on the written form functions as a form of pleading: by emphasizing the kinds of evidence that dominated the civil courts, she asks Gilbert not to try her as a criminal. Their subsequent marriage and Gilbert's adoption of the written form provide his verdict, because although her character evidence might be "no evidence" in a court of law, these documents are just what Gilbert needs to exonerate her. At the same time, the conversational tone of the frame paired with the flimsiness of incomplete, written evidence may heighten the importance of talk in a way that highlights Brontë's re-evaluation of hearsay evidence: relevant, potentially unreliable, but still useful.

To review: the foregoing has shown how hearsay is repurposed in the novel to serve a broader set of objectives which may nevertheless entail some of the very traits that at law make hearsay "no evidence," or an impediment to discovering truth. But what of the discovery of character? Much of the development of the character and hearsay rules canvassed here has less to do with philosophical or metaphysical discussions of moral agency (at the root of nineteenth-century conceptions of character) than it does with the nature of knowledge and proof. Langbein's argument that the introduction of defense counsel changed the theory of the criminal trial from an altercation between actors to the probing of a "case" highlights the impersonal, technical quality of an encounter that makes questions of character appear to be beside the point. On the one hand, character ceases to be a state of being, a moral quality, or an expression of personality so much as a rule, a type of evidence, a matter of knowledge or proof. On another, *R v Rowton* shows how resistant to proof character might be.[28]

Rowton and Reputation: Forming Character In and Through the Law

In what would become a leading case in the rules regarding character evidence, *R v Rowton* (1865) set out to answer both a procedural question (on

---

[28] Recent analysis criticizes character evidence because character itself resists definition. Gabrielle Wolf and Mirko Bagaric describe character variously as "an illusory and incoherent concept" (590), one that "lacks any settled definition or empirical foundation" (567) and which makes any judgment based on it "speculative, misguided and arbitrary" (568).

the admissibility of testimony about a defendant's bad character) and a substantive question about whether the judge should have allowed the jury to consider it (Cockle 72–9).[29] Although the second question is interesting for the way it defines the relative roles of judge and jury and highlights how far the Victorian jury was from its self-informing predecessor, my interest in this case follows more from the first: the discussion of the admissibility of evidence of bad character led judges to talk about why evidence of character was allowed at all, how it came to be so, and what, after all, "character" was in ways that cut across the distinction between the character exception and the character rule. In the debate that ensued, the judges worked to distinguish key concepts such as "reputation," "disposition," and "rumour." Their difficulty in naming just what character was and the best way of ascertaining it led to a controversial holding that garnered negative commentary in the legal periodicals of the day and showed how the case accentuated, rather than assuaged, anxiety around the uses of character evidence.

The case against James Rowton was first heard in September 1864 when he was brought to trial for purportedly having "committed an indecent assault" on fourteen-year-old George Low. *The Times*' reports on the Middlesex Sessions for September 30 were more frank about details. Low is presented as a "very intelligent lad" who was reading a book during a lull at the Chalk-farm station when James Rowton approached from behind, asked twice if he was "reading about the girls," and then committed the offense ("Middlesex Sessions," Oct. 1, 11).[30] On examination at the police station, Rowton is reported to have apologized and said, under caution, that he "had no intention of putting [his] hand inside his clothes . . . It was the temptation of the moment, which ought to have been resisted." During the trial, Rowton's counsel blamed the boy's imagination for misinterpreting his client's behavior and suggested that Low's subsequent suspension from work reflected badly on his own character.[31] By contrast, a host of reputable witnesses were called to attest to Rowton's "general reputation for purity of mind and morality of conduct." In response, the prosecution called for witnesses to

---

[29] *Regina v Rowton* (1865) 169 English Reports 1497, 1499, subsequently referred to as *Rowton*. Cockle includes it in his *Leading Cases on the Law of Evidence* (1907).

[30] The sessions were held on September 30, 1864 and reported in *The Times* on October 1. See "Middlesex Sessions," Oct. 1.

[31] See Wills 57–8. The only two exceptions he notes are (1) that defendants in prosecutions for rape may call for evidence of the victim's "general bad character in respect of chastity and morality" and (2) the decision in *Rowton* that the criminal defendant may bring evidence of good character, "in the sense of general reputation," which the prosecution may rebut.

rebut this evidence of good character, giving rise to the substantive issue that would occupy Rowton's appeal.

Contrary to defense counsel's objections, Rowland Bateman, one of Rowton's former students, was allowed to testify. Asked about "the defendant's general character for decency and morality of conduct," Bateman relayed his and his brothers' personal experience. "I know nothing of the neighbourhood's opinion, because I was only a boy at school when I knew him," he replied, "but my own opinion and the opinion of my brothers who were also pupils of his, is that his character is that of a man capable of the grossest indecency and the most flagrant immorality" (*Rowton* 1499). Against further objections that this was "no legal evidence at all" (invoking the maxim about hearsay), the presiding judge, Mr. Payne, left it to the jury to weigh, which resulted in Rowton's conviction. On October 4, a new article on "The Case of the Clergyman Convicted of an Indecent Assault" appeared in *The Times* and recorded not only Mr. Payne's rationale for allowing Bateman's testimony but also some bickering with Mr. Sleigh as to which questions would be reserved for the Court of Criminal Appeal to decide (9).[32] The new trial was heard in November 1864 ("Middlesex Sessions," Dec. 8, 11), but "difference of opinion" among the judges led to a further trial before the full court the following January, during which time Rowton was held without bail.

On January 28, Sleigh and Tayler appeared before the full court, which overturned Rowton's conviction. In the week following the decision, *The Examiner* called the ruling "repugnant to common sense" and a safeguard to hypocrites whose good character is "the tool to get into men's confidence for the purpose of robbing them ("Evidence as to Character" 67). *The Saturday Review* called on Parliament to intervene in a decision that would "render evidence to character useless and absurd" with the result that "law will positively prefer hearsay evidence to direct evidence on a very important matter" ("Witnesses to Character" 133). *The Central Law Journal* took up this note when it called the evidence of reputation ("which consists in a witness stating not what he himself knows of the prisoner's character, but what he has heard others say of it") no less than "an authorization . . . of that kind of testimony generally most abhorrent to our rules of evidence—namely, hearsay" ("Evidence as to Character" 415).[33] As immediate reaction shows, commentators were most troubled by the judges' conception of character as reputation or,

---

[32] A subsequent article gives the Court for the Consideration of Crown Cases Reserved as the higher court, not the Court of Criminal Appeals. See "Law," *The Times* [London].

[33] Rpt. from the *Law Times*. An article of the same name, "Evidence as to Character-I," was published in the Criminal Law and Procedure section of *The Law Times* on Nov. 27, 1880 (with an article on the recent death of the Lord Chief Justice Cockburn who presided over

more properly, their decision as to the most reliable, and hence only admissible, way of bringing character evidence before the jury.[34]

Mr. Sleigh, arguing for the defense, explained that evidence to character was originally admitted as a plea for mercy in criminal cases but that even then only evidence of general character, not a witness's individual opinion, could be admitted (*Rowton* 1500).[35] Going further, he offered a definition of character and reputation (using the two terms synonymously) as "credit derived from public opinion or esteem" (1500). Quoting Lord Erskine's defense of Thomas Hardy in the treason trials of the late eighteenth century, he elaborated:

> You cannot . . . when asking to character, ask what has A.B.C. told you about this man's character. No; but what is the general opinion concerning him. Character is the slow-spreading influence of opinion, arising from the deportment of a man in society. As a man's deportment, good or bad, necessarily produces one circle without another, and so extends itself till it unites in one general opinion, that general opinion is allowed to be given in evidence. (1500)

In other words, character is the ripple effect of conduct and carriage, but it is important to note the gradualism of this development. By emphasizing

---

Rowton), but it focuses on the questionable value of character evidence as a defense and as a means of mitigating punishment (59).

[34] See Rodensky 236n35 for James Fitzjames Stephen's reaction to the "absurdity" of the case and subsequent courts' avoidance of the rule in his *Digest of the Rules of Evidence* (1876). Rodensky briefly discusses *Rowton* and concludes that its emphasis on general reputation (as perceived by a group of people) in distinction to individual observation of disposition lessened the probative value of the evidence. Mason Ladd, writing in 1939, echoed the idea that "The personal judgment of a qualified and reliable witness ought to be better than reputation of character based upon hearsay interchange of gossip of scandal in the community" (qtd. in Blinka 134). However, while this concern about the evidentiary value of character evidence is certainly reflected in the immediate reaction to the case, it seems less to indicate, as Rodensky suggests, "a move away from the introduction of character evidence into the courtroom" (45) than character's move into *other* forms of evidence. More recently, for example, Justin Sevier has defended the use of character evidence by pointing to studies in social psychology which "support the view that—as with hearsay—jurors make defensible decisions regarding when to credit or discount propensity evidence, and the public finds tribunals that allow the jury to consider propensity evidence more legitimate" (507).

[35] Sleigh's allusion to the value of character evidence as a mitigating factor in capital offenses is a reminder of the way it had since slid into the defense and sentencing of other criminal offenses. Boston attorney Elisha Greenwood, while approving that early "indulgence," criticized in particular its tendencies to distract from "the main issue" and warned against its further extension to civil cases (206). It also reminds us of Eliot's characterization of counsel at the time of Hetty Sorrel's trial.

the "slow-spreading influence of opinion," Erskine injected duration into the definition of character. Citing Lord Ellenborough in another State Trial, Sleigh concludes with his observation that reputation is categorically different than opinion: personal knowledge is relevant solely because "a witness who has known the defendant longest will have the best chance of knowing what his general reputation is" (1500). Again, length of time is a key constituent of this understanding of character, but the apparent conflation of character and reputation as terms elides any difference between character as a state of being and character as the report of that state, or the version of character whose value for the bearer depends on both its duration and its portability.

This attention to character as reputation became the source of disagreement in the legal discussion. Must reputation be founded on a certain number of individual reports? Must those judgments or opinions be consistent over time, and for how long a time? Must they be limited to generalities of opinion, or can they address particular instances of behavior or facts? Changing the terms of the discussion, Tayler argued for the Crown that the only reason to talk about reputation at all was because it showed a propensity towards certain behaviors. The original witness had provided evidence of "disposition," he maintained, "for that, and not reputation, is the sense in which the word character is used in these cases" (1500).[36] "Character means the general, uniform tenor of a man's conduct got at by witnesses giving their own judgment," he argued; reputation, by contrast, is only "estimated character" (1501). Indeed, to the extent that the witness's evidence "was hearsay of the judgment of others mixed up with his own judgment founded on his own observation" (1501), Tayler sought to disentangle the two and argued that personal observation and experience should be the only admissible evidence. Without that *direct* knowledge, the report would be nothing more than hearsay.

In his summation, Chief Justice Cockburn freely admitted the justice of allowing evidence of bad character to rebut the defense's provision of testimony to good character, but the fact that it could be allowed only raised the further question of what "evidence of character" would be (1502). His own view was that it meant reputation, not disposition. He writes:

> What you want to get at is the tendency and disposition of the man's mind towards committing or abstaining from committing the class of crime with which he stands charged; but no one has ever heard the question—what is the tendency and disposition of the prisoner's mind?—put directly. The only

---

[36] See also Justice Willes's remarks on disposition as the object of character evidence (*Rowton* 1507).

> way of getting at it is by giving evidence of his general character founded on his general reputation in the neighbourhood in which he lives. (1502)

"[T]he only way of getting at it": it is the mode of discovery that dictates what character can mean. Cockburn concedes that the substance of character is really one's propensities or disposition but the inaccessibility of that internal, moral, and mental state—and in particular the impossibility of asking a witness to testify as to what was in the defendant's mind—shifts attention to the externalized evidence of its workings, or the empirical evidence of reputation for deeds. And for that evidence to be strong, it must be corroborated by multiple people (the generality) and consistent over time. This being so, he concludes that evidence of bad character be confined to the same limits and recommended that Rowton's conviction be overturned.[37]

Justice Erle (Chief Justice of Common Pleas) offered the main dissent and opened the field for both kinds of evidence, that of general reputation *and* personal experience, the latter of which in his view "gives cogency to the evidence" (1504). His dissent is most interesting because of the way reputation slides into a new term, "rumor":

> You may give in evidence the general rumour prevalent in the prisoner's neighbourhood, and, according to my experience, you may have also the personal judgment of those who are capable of forming a more real, substantial, guiding opinion than that which is to be gathered from general rumour. (1504)

In light of Justice Cockburn's concern about the mode of discovering character, this substitution of "reputation" with "rumor" makes personal experience the main corroboration. The only better evidence of character would be the absence of any talk at all about it, "the best character [being] that which is the least talked of" (1504). Erle subtly changes the register of the conversation by linking reputation with gossip via rumor, an equation Justice Willes builds upon in his own remarks when he refers to "what people generally think of the prisoner" as "mere rumour" (1507). Both judges thus effectively remind the court of earlier warnings about hearsay.

A final dimension of Willes's remarks that is important to note concerns the nature of the offense and the likelihood of its being the subject of general

---

[37] Cockburn's admission perfectly illustrates Rodensky's point that the novel does not have to ask; it just does. His observation that no witness would ever be asked to testify as to the defendant's state of mind seems quaint in light of the medical and psychological experts who would be called upon to do just that. See Rex Ferguson on the increasing reliance on expert witnesses and the corresponding decline in the lay witnesses' character evidence.

comment: "because the prisoner was charged with an offense which would not only be committed in secret, if it were committed at all, but would be likely to be kept secret by the persons who were subjected to it" (1507). The only "way of getting at" this kind of disposition, to borrow Cockburn's phrase, is to call on the people with direct experience of its action or effects. In a burst of semantic ingenuity similar to Erle's conflation of reputation with rumor, Willes shifts the application of the term "generally": instead of the views of "people generally" (which leads to "mere rumour"), Willes locates the best evidence in "what is known of him generally in the judgment of the particular witness" (1507), in other words, not what the witness might say about particular facts but what he could say about the totality of his—and others'—experience of the defendant. And Willes makes these remarks at all because he wants to clarify that while he concurs in the decision, he worries that reliance on general reputation to the exclusion of personal experience will impose "a great hardship on prisoners" (1506).[38] While Willes takes the provision of character evidence as a right, rather than an example of law's mercy, his point is more instructive about the connection between the kind of offense, the likelihood of gathering evidence as to the alleged perpetrator's disposition, and whether character is a material or "collateral" issue.

Having looked at the possible meanings of character, I want to return to the kinds of structure that these rules of evidence provide for forming it. Willes's remarks on the nature of the perceived offense and the report about it recall the rumors about Helen Graham's moral character. As the accused, Helen's existing character is as material to the believability of the rumor as the rumor is to the creation of a new character. The problem for her and for the Linden Car community is that she comes without a reputation. We have only what she *reputes* to be, but there is none of the duration, breadth, or consistency of opinion Sleigh found necessary to qualify as reputation. Yet Willes identifies a new and perhaps greater obstacle to overcome than the questions of how to define character and how it can come before the court's hearing—and that is whether the witness who could tell it, will tell it and whether, telling it, it could be heard and understood. This, too, describes Helen's situation as defendant but also as victim and returns us to the aims of narrative jurisprudence. These novels are about the forms those narratives can take. Helen Graham is coerced into telling her "true" story and that in itself is problematic, but oral explanations do not suffice. In Brontë, textual evidence is needed to disprove rumor, evidence that draws attention to itself as a more

---

[38] The prisoner "may be of a shy, retiring disposition, and known only to a few; or again, he may be a person of the vilest character and disposition, and yet only his intimates may be able to testify that is the case" (*Rowton* 1507).

durable, yet still mobile, form of evidence than the oral forms of gossip: text trumps talk. *Cranford*'s narrator offers a different assessment. Her questions and direct address to the audience give the novel a precisely conversational tone, which maintains a value for gossip even amidst references to the textual activity of letter-writing. Where Gilbert Markham's textual evidence was put to the task of documenting personal history and verifying a potentially incredible story, the letters from Cranford are elevated by their kinship with talk. *Cranford* becomes a species of national archive in which the tone of a community is preserved through its stories which are themselves transmitted to modern readers through the narrator's chatty reminiscences.

Gossip, Hearsay, and Personality in Victorian Law and Literature

In chapter 8 of *The Fall of Public Man*, Richard Sennett discusses the difference between "natural character" and "personality" as social categories alongside the kinds of relationship between people—strangers, really—that personality's presumption of immanence required (152). Secrecy, privacy, withdrawal from others—all practices Helen Graham employs but also practices that govern social codes of decorum—are responses to what Sennett describes as the nineteenth century's secular "faith in immediate appearances": "personality is immanent in appearances," he writes, so that one person's reticence "puts pressure on others" to overreach those barriers and force an intimacy where more revealing or authentic interaction could take place (153).[39] We saw this idea at work in Patricia Meyer Spacks's discussion of gossip, in Gilbert Markham's pursuit of Helen, and in *Cranford*'s obsessive regard for etiquette. Together with the need to disprove rumor, this "compulsive intimacy" (153) informs the popularity of the novel's representation of privacy and interiority and the trial's probing of evidence of facts that connect conduct (acts as appearances) to aspects of character (personality).[40]

---

[39] "Natural character" is the Enlightenment conception of a "common thread running through all mankind" (Sennett 152). Control of this natural character meant "moderation of desires" or behaving in such a way as to (re)align with a character that was more or less fixed within oneself (but also within all people). Natural character is thus comparable to the legal ideal of the reasonable man. For specific commentary on the spectrum between "character essentialism" and a later, psychologized understanding of character that allowed for the contingencies of circumstance and "engaged capacities," see Lacey, "Resurgence of Character" 156, 152. See also Rodensky's discussion of the complicated relationship between conduct and character, even as terms (20).

[40] With these literary movements into the private sphere and the conscious mind, we also begin to see the development of privacy as a legally protected concept, what Samuel Warren and Louis Brandeis called the "right to be let alone" and founded on a concept of "inviolate personality" (193, 205). Warren's own experience as the object of compulsive intimacy

Intimacy connotes deep connection; however, we might ask what the object of this connection with others could be, or relatedly what it means to have an authentic self, in the context of the devaluation of character. The move from natural character to personality (understood as individuality or, perhaps more tellingly, as originality) represents a two-fold turn away from notions of common humanity and from the inherent stability of the self. It is a well-established argument that the idea of character shifted from the morally autonomous, self-authorizing person of the early nineteenth century to one whose being in the world was managed and identified by authorities external to the self.[41] Compulsive intimacy thus describes a search for connection and community (intimacy) necessitated (compelled) by barriers that are socially determined, but which, as the shift towards identity suggests, may also imply ontological emptiness. (The *attempt* to connect, foreshadowing E. M. Forster's mantra, stands in for its own achievement.)[42]

However, the repetition implied by compulsion acquires a less neurotic connotation when viewed as the work communities do to maintain themselves. My point in this chapter has been to show how specific novels use gossip to express the tension between social efforts to maintain a communal identity and individual efforts to retain the autonomy to define themselves that bespeaks character. This has been the sociological project in which gossip, in spite of its equivocal relationship to truth, nevertheless generates meaning and feeds the compulsion to narrate (or, indeed, makes compulsive narration a sign of compulsive intimacy).[43] It is precisely this relationship to facts and their lack of verifiability that changes gossip to hearsay and excludes it from courts of law, but as the history of hearsay and my analysis of *Rowton* have

---

prompted his search after a legal basis for privacy. See discussion of "The Right to Privacy" (1890) in Chapter 4.

[41] In addition to Wiener and Lacey, see also R. Thomas, *Detective Fiction* 11, 31.

[42] Defined more specifically, the semiotic relationship between personality and appearances (Sennett) parallels the forensic idea that links identity to an assemblage of physical signs (R. Thomas, *Detective Fiction*, especially ch. 1). By this argument, conduct might reveal character, but the fragmenting of natural character encouraged a focus in law on specific acts and their probable connection to states of mind (Rodensky) or "engaged capacities" (Lacey, "Resurgence of Character" 156) and in literature to isolated stories of experience or sensation as its own objective (Welsh, *Strong Representations* ch. 5; R. Thomas, *Detective Fiction* 34). High realism was certainly concerned with the inner workings of a character's mind, but once the concept of character developed a psychological, rather than primarily moral basis, it also became less coherent, consistent, stable—more Virginia Woolf's "moments of being" than a being consistent over time. See Schulkind. "Only Connect" is Forster's epigraph to *Howards End* (1910).

[43] See discussion of Georg Simmel's sociological study of secrecy, especially his analysis of discretion, in Chapter 4.

shown, the exceptional status of reputation and the importance of character evidence in other aspects of criminal defense suggest that it was hard to avoid gossip when constructing character even at law.

In drawing to a close, I want to return to the epistemological and narratological aims of this chapter and outline what it is that *The Tenant of Wildfell Hall, Cranford,* and *R v Rowton* suggest about the way law and literature negotiated the changes in character that Sennett describes. The broad strokes: The diminished value of the self-authorizing character is signified in both the trial and the novel by the narrative control of talk. The story of a person or character is inflected by who tells it to whom. Once we link character to orality and narrative control, then acts of narration, such as scenes of storytelling or gossip or witness testimony and oral argument, assume a family resemblance and can become the focus of analysis. On the one hand, Helen's persistent silence in *Tenant* foreshadows the silence of other outcasts and exiles like Nathaniel Hawthorne's Hester Prynne and George Eliot's Hetty Sorrel whose refusal to speak, the subject of Chapter 1, highlights legal debate in the 1850s about the *right* to silence that had replaced the requirement to speak. On the other hand, the interest in orality masks other areas and other ways in which law and literature contributed to the discourse of character.

Studies of the relationship between nineteenth-century narrative fiction and the laws of evidence are numerous, particularly relating to the development of the legal and literary professions, and oftentimes to competition between them in the shared enterprise of representation—not only of "things as they are," as in Eliot's plea for the realist novel—but of *people* as they are ("Silly Novels by Lady Novelists" 442). In the novel, the self-conscious development of character as a narratological construct modeled for readers a way of understanding their own subjectivity. Absorbed by the exploration of real-seeming characters navigating recognizable problems, readers of novels perpetuated a demand that novelists generously supplied, adding in the process to the range of cultural meanings of "character."[44] That there was such a range is indisputable, and one need not scour either end of the century to describe it. The coincidence of Charles Darwin's *Origins of Species,* Samuel Smiles's *Self-Help,* and Eliot's *Adam Bede* makes 1859 an exemplary year. The contrast between Darwin's model of adaptation and hereditary influence and Smiles's upwardly mobile, self-actualizing project is clear enough, but Eliot's first novel also hinges, at the level of plot alone, on the twin failures of a prisoner to defend her case and of character evidence to compensate for its

---

[44] See Grossman 26–36 on the evolution of print forms and the reader as consumer which tracks how legal practice spread beyond its institutional confines.

absence. Indeed, as Alexander Welsh, Jonathan Grossman, Lisa Rodensky, and Jan-Melissa Schramm have shown, the novel's innovations began as borrowings from and/or modifications of legal structures that also relied on and influenced cultural ideas about character.

As my discussion of the hearsay and character rules showed, the eighteenth century was a modernizing period: when changes to the structure of the trial altered its very theory and when the novel became new. Tracing this history of influence and modification from the eighteenth to the nineteenth centuries, critics have been especially attentive to acts of narration as such—who speaks to whom—and their impact on conceptions of personhood. In his groundbreaking work *Strong Representations*, Alexander Welsh describes a shift from first-person, "direct" testimonial narrative in the eighteenth century to professionally managed narratives of circumstantial or indirect evidence in the nineteenth, and links these to an epistemological re-evaluation of the basis of fact. In accordance with Langbein's characterization of the "accused speaks" model of the criminal trial (*Origins* 2), the early novel vested authority in its protagonist's first-person narration, but this reliance on empirical experience made evidence of "things not seen" more elusive (Welsh, *Strong Representations* ch. 1). Circumstantial evidence might fill this gap, but to be probative, Welsh argues, its elements had to be narrativized—ordered and connected in a chain whose strength depended on the lawyer's representation of its internal logic and the apparent inevitability of its conclusion (42). In similar fashion, the detached narrator of the nineteenth-century novel arranged events in a manner that led convincingly to a single conclusion.

Commenting on this mistrust of first-person accounts, Jonathan Grossman observes that the barrister's more convincing reconstruction of a defendant's story created an imaginative framework through which even ordinary citizens could recast their personal narratives and present them for judgment (22). Part authoritative judge, part party to a case, the barrister participated in the "art of narrating other people's minds" and resembled nothing so much as the novel's third-person narrator speaking in the particular idioms of its characters (23). Notwithstanding Grossman's observation on the "'mim[ic]' qualities of the barrister-narrator" (23), however, the emphasis here on plot and structure suggests that, for the first half of the century at least, character *in the novel* held the same diminished position that the accused did at trial.

There is of course more than one way to represent character; a novel does not have to be *auto*biographical to tell the story of a life. Helen's own progress through various communities and her efforts to realize an authentic self are indeed told in her diary, but they are also retold in her husband's letter. Then again, an omniscient narrator has direct access to characters' minds and provides what, following Rodensky, might be called novel evidence: the special access that comes "precisely because we are reading a novel" (22) and which produces evidence that interacts with circumstantial as well as direct, testimonial evidence provided by characters themselves (about both themselves and other characters). However, for Welsh, even the re-emergence of "stories of experience" at mid-century that allowed "the probing of the states of mind of the actors themselves [to] present their own claims to truth" bore the traces of this devaluation since in the move towards modernism, characters were shown to interrogate their own "experience of knowing" in ways that made objectivity an obsolete episteme (*Strong Representations* 42, 201, 298).[45] And yet as Rodensky's analysis shows, a narrator's access to characters' minds reveals more than a character's "experience of knowing." On the contrary, that access just as easily reveals what a character *doesn't* know or, as was shown in the case of *Adam Bede*, how a character deludes him- or herself. Moreover, that access is separate from any judgment or evaluation of character the narrator might make on the basis of its findings.

By contrast to Welsh's argument for the dominance of professionally managed, third-person narratives, Jan-Melissa Schramm points to the value of first-person testimony that persisted in nineteenth-century fictional trials because access to it had been "closed-off" in the courtroom (120). The provision of full legal representation in 1836 silenced the accused and enabled the novel to amplify its ethical difference from the law. "[I]n acting as a forum for the construction of an accused's story in their 'own words,'" she argues, "fictional trials illuminate both the ethical claims of testimony and comment self-reflexively on the reliability of the act of fictional narration itself" (123). Schramm's description of the dual function of fictional trials warrants separate analysis. First, Schramm's reference to fiction's reliability recalls an earlier observation that all fictional representation, in essence an author's report of what a character says or thinks, is itself susceptible to the objection of hearsay (21). If the suspension of disbelief activates and implicates readers in the novel's processes of judgment in a way that salvages reliability as she suggests, however, the more pressing question her comment raises is how any "story of a thing not seen" could avoid a charge of hearsay. Although this question

---

[45] As a quasi-biographical form, the novel substituted the protagonist's personal authority for failing institutional authorities. Pursuing plots of self-actualization, the bourgeois subject depicted in the realist novel simultaneously became a rogue figure in the detective novel which, according to Ronald R. Thomas, contained "the autonomy of [his] individual voice" by criminalizing it (*Detective Fiction*, 9). This "anti-biographical" turn of the novel participates in the same shift away from natural character that Sennett observes towards the importance of appearances.

clearly animates Welsh's study, especially insofar as he sees it informing scientific studies of natural origins and theological propositions of faith, his response that narrative coherence itself becomes probative makes it not so much an antidote to hearsay as another rule of exception.

Second, Schramm's emphasis on witness testimony, like Welsh's and Grossman's on the barrister's rhetorical skill, shares a fundamental and unsurprising interest in what she refers to as the "essential orality of English courtroom procedure" (20), but it bears emphasizing that they refer specifically to criminal trials. As noted earlier, law's civil side favored documentary evidence and took a "trial avoiding" approach in contrast to its "trial-centered" criminal side (Langbein, *Origins* 7). Thus, and notwithstanding the glaring exception of *Bleak House*, one might expect the majority of fictional trials to be criminal trials and *as criminal trials* to require more testimony or oral evidence than any civil trial would, which had used the pleading process to reduce the number of facts a jury considered. Furthermore, the question of the competency of the parties to a case was being actively debated in both England and America in the 1850s, the decade that separates *Tenant* from *Rowton*, with parties to a civil case being made competent by the passage of Lord Brougham's Act in 1851, decades before the Criminal Law Amendment Act.[46] I remark on this distinction equally as excuse, caution, and provocation.

The excuse: to the extent that *Tenant* straddles civil and criminal law, it explains the novel's mixture and testing of written and oral evidence, and, as with *Cranford*, points away from law's punishment of criminals to its constitutive and regulatory processes in the areas of property or family law, to name but two. The caution: the emphasis on the criminal trial in these analyses of narrative modes means that the connection between other aspects of substantive law, elements of procedure, and the form of the novel has been comparatively neglected. My own choice of *Tenant* and *Cranford* shows this tension insofar as there is no formal trial in either, no legal transgression at all in Gaskell's novel, and a set of legal issues (marriage, divorce, custody) that are not themselves part of the criminal law until Helen's "crime" of kidnap emerges but about which no other characters actually seem to care. Pointing towards other branches of law thus reminds us, first, that law had other means outside the criminal trial, and certainly outside the criminal branch,

---

[46] See discussion of witness competency in Chapter 1; Allen 110–22; and Gold 59. The state of Maine was the first commonwealth jurisdiction in the world to pass a general competency statute in 1864, the *same* year as *R v Rowton*.

for formulating character and representing intention and, second, that these means entailed other forms of evidence.[47]

In this context, my choice of *Rowton*, a criminal trial, might raise questions about its relevance to a discussion of gossipy novels. It's tempting to take the congress between the civil and criminal courts that Thomas P. Gallanis observed in specific eighteenth-century lawyers as a metaphor for how character itself moved between different branches of law. (A jurisprudential theory of character that recognizes how it moves through cognate areas of law does essentially this.) Nevertheless, one can be more specific by recognizing that the rule against hearsay cuts across civil and criminal distinctions so that untestable evidence could be excluded on both sides. As a corollary to gossip, in other words, hearsay was suspect in both legal contexts, which makes the difference between civil and criminal less significant than the difference between law's circumspect attitude to hearsay and the novel's embrace of gossip. In short, the ideas about character *Rowton* engages cannot be confined to the criminal trial because they are made to be reducible to what can be "got at." As a consequence of making general reputation or hearsay the best means for getting at character, the criminal court seems poised to operate by evidentiary rules (and standards of proof) already in the novel. If this struck the legal community as an epistemological fall from grace, Rodensky's analysis showed the problem to be exacerbated by the novel's omniscient narrator who outstripped the lawyer's ability to get at the core of character, an ability which would take the growth of expert witnesses for law to approximate.

The provocation: rather than pitting text against talk as forms of evidence, the more typical reading has emphasized the way one narrative performance replaces or corrects another: the lawyers' replaces and improves the accused's; the novel's narrator does the same for the barrister at law; the detective genre corrects the biographical novel. Following on a chapter about the value of silence, this chapter's focus on the idea of talk may seem either provocatively contrarian—or the next logical step. As discussed in Chapter 1, the 1850s was an important decade for weighing the benefit and liability of allowing the accused to testify, but *The Scarlet Letter* (1850) and *Adam Bede* (1859) depicted women who resisted the call to speak in ways that challenged claims for the novel's more expansive attitude towards evidence of character. Looking backwards from Justice Willes's concern in *Rowton*, one can see how those novels anticipated the way the nature of an offense lessens the likelihood of gathering evidence as to the prisoner's disposition because victims,

---

[47] On the history of inheritance law, the notion of possessive individualism, and the rise (and fall) of the testamentary novel, for example, see Frank.

or in this case prisoners, will be reluctant to come forward. Keeping their stories secret, these women ironically amplify Helen Huntingdon's redaction of her diary and suggest that, like reading someone's diary, reading novels that require their characters to speak, or delve into their minds when they refuse, might just be an invasion of privacy.

And what of *Rowton*'s pursuit of character and disposition, its attitude towards proof, and its need to delve into the defendant's inner state? To emphasize the social valence of personality, Sennett titled chapter 8 "Personality in Public," and notwithstanding his distinction between personality and character, it is tempting to take that phrase as a synonym for reputation, to speak of it as character in public. After all, character remained an important, functional term in utilitarian and evangelical discourse of the early century, which influenced the legal understanding of criminality and criminal capacity towards its end, and which *Samuel* James Rowton well understood when he asked *The Times* to clear his name. In the next chapter, I build on the importance of reputation by turning from gossip, especially the damaging sort that could constitute slander, to written forms of defamation or libel, in particular as they circulate in the press. This focus on the different discursive functions of journalism and the novel placed reputation at the center of debates about personal and public interest and at the center of Anthony Trollope's ethics of representation.

3

Defamation of Character: Anthony Trollope and the Law of Libel

No man may disparage or destroy the reputation of another. Every man has a right to have his good name maintained unimpaired. This right is a *jus in rem*, a right absolute and good against all the world.

William Blake Odgers, *A Digest of the Law of Libel and Slander* (1881)

What are the sufferings of the few to the advantage of the many? If there be fault in high places, it is proper that it be exposed. If there be fraud, adulteries, gambling, and lasciviousness,—or even quarrels and indiscretions among those whose names are known,—let every detail be laid open to the light, so that the people may have a warning.

Anthony Trollope, *Phineas Redux* (1874)

Anthony Trollope enjoys a series of superlatives: Dallas Liddle has said his work offers "the most sustained thematic engagement of any British novelist . . . with the genres and functions of journalism" (75), while Stephen Wall observes that he is the first to trace a character's development over multiple, distinct works, making him the "founder of the sequence novel proper" (152). In this chapter I want to explore a third: Trollope's investment in the different discursive functions of journalism and the novel paired with an artistic theory trained on what he himself called "the state of progressive change" in his characters' lives (Trollope 202–3) explains why Trollope is the only novelist to have written extensively, throughout his oeuvre, about the perils and consequences of libelous publication, not exclusively but most especially, libelous publication in the press.

The previous chapter showed how specific novels use gossip to express the tension between social efforts to maintain a communal identity and individuals' efforts to retain the self-determinism that bespeaks character. In this respect, the novel participates in a sociological project in which gossip, in spite of its equivocal relationship to truth, nevertheless generates meaning and works to create and maintain communal boundaries. And although it might seem that the legal rule against hearsay evidence controlled what for the courts was the *problem* of ungrounded talk, the so-called "character exception" made testimony regarding a defendant's general reputation admissible, in effect reducing evidence to hearsay, undermining its difference from gossip and, with it, a distinction between the courtroom and the novel. The central issue for this chapter remains the narrative control of one's character, but where Chapter 2 focused on control of talk or what was *said* of one's character, this chapter focuses on how private persons could control what was printed, made permanent, and circulated about them. Lest this distinction seem too slight, this chapter's turn from the orality of gossip and the trial towards the legibility of the novel and the press entails a shift from rules of courtroom procedure towards other areas of substantive law that regulate character, specifically, that of libel.[1]

By recognizing the importance of both private character and public benefit, Victorian libel law is an especially interesting ground for studying the relationship between individuals and the community largely writ. Furthermore, because libel by definition is concerned with character, developments in libel law over the century offer one of the best ways of assessing the status of character and identifying the most important bases of its legal protection, as well as the occasions when the ethical and pecuniary value of one's reputation came second to public welfare.[2]

At the same time, as a law of character, libel could be expected to draw the attention of novelists whose art or trade was precisely the observation of characters negotiating the public of their imagined communities. In this respect, Anthony Trollope stands out. The prospect of legal action for libel and, to

---

[1] It's worth noting that the distinction between slander and libel, especially remedies for the former, was addressed as early as 1843 when any words "tending to injure the reputation of another" became actionable (*Report from the Select Committee of the House of Lords* vii).

[2] Behind these concerns about how "to get at" character is an understanding of the ethical and pecuniary value of one's reputation as the "property" (per Malins V.C.) that determines how private persons interact with others as they negotiate public spheres. As a "property," reputation, character, and good name of course tie into ideas of possessive individualism as well as notions that there is something "proper" to the self, something that individuates the individual. It's not surprising that everything would seem like property to a judge in Chancery, but it is this "narrow," and nonetheless foundational, view of property that Samuel D. Warren and Louis D. Brandeis sought to expand in their justification of the privacy right. The inner life of thoughts and feelings must be included in the definition of property (as they are with intellectual property), but for the American jurists these inner qualities belong to and define an "inviolate personality" that can only flourish when (allowed to be) left alone. See discussion of "The Right to Privacy" in Chapter 4.

a lesser extent, slander informs works as various as *Orley Farm* (1862) and *Dr. Wortle's School* (1881) where defamatory statements circulate in heated encounters among characters or in private letters. However, Trollope's preoccupation with journalistic libel was far more pronounced, a fact made less surprising perhaps by his own professional engagements with the press and his novels' depictions of newspapermen (Liddle 77).[3] That libel specifically looms so large makes even more sense, though, because Trollope's characters keep coming back, bringing with them reputations that have been shaped in part by their representation in the newspapers.

Mary Poovey observes that Trollope's "imported plots" and reallocation of narrative attention among characters allowed him "both to create the impression that the lives of these characters continued even when the narratives stopped and to capitalize on information that readers had already gained from other novels" ("Trollope's Barsetshire Series" 38, 39).[4] Thus, Trollope's method of character development, paired with his journalistic experience and sense of competition between the two discourses, makes his novels especially good explorations of the impact on character of its circulation in the periodical press. Furthermore, although the body of Victorian libel law cannot rightly be called a "law of the press" (Mitchell, "Nineteenth Century Defamation"), nevertheless, the statutory emphasis on freedom of the press as an engine of public good accentuates the conflict between the one and the many that Trollope's novels explore.

The first section of this chapter surveys significant developments in libel law, including legislative change, developing case law, and their coverage in the periodical press. The second section focuses on Trollope's novels of the 1860s and 1870s, specifically *Phineas Finn* (1869), *Phineas Redux* (1873), *The Prime Minister* (1876), and *Cousin Henry* (1879). All three were written, serialized, or published at moments when specific legislation was making its way through parliamentary committees or debates, during observable spikes in the incidence of at least criminal prosecutions for libel, and when key decisions were reached in civil actions for libel. In the case of the two Palliser novels, this was also the period when Trollope served as editor of *Saint Pauls*

---

[3] See also Lauren Goodlad's chapter on Trollope and the civil service in *Victorian Literature and the Victorian State*.

[4] Recurring characters is one in a set of Trollope's innovations that Mary Poovey argues not only enabled disparate novels to appear as series, but also reduced and shifted the labor of building and evaluating character away from an intrusive narrator onto the characters, and readers, themselves. An increased use of free indirect discourse, a dialogic use of repeated scenes, and depictions of characters judging other characters are particularly relevant to my reading of the Phineas novels ("Trollope's Barsetshire Series" 39–41).

Magazine (1867–70), making these years a historical junction of legal, literary, and journalistic concerns with character. The third section of the chapter discusses the implications of a growing freedom of the press (and, indeed, of a growing press) on the kinds of information about character which had become acceptable to print. Although some of the most famous libel trials were still to come (Cleveland Street in 1889–90, the Wilde Trials in 1895), the 1888 Libel Law Amendment Act—legislation instigated and essentially written by representatives of the press for the press—extended and clarified the press's privilege. These liberties of the press were felt to infringe the dignity, if not also the freedom, of the individual, however, and, as the next chapter will show, potentially to violate the personality on which a right to privacy would be founded. If libel law was in a sense becoming a less reliable bulwark for character, privacy protections might put the decision about what to disclose or publicize back in the hands of the individual.

"For the better protection of Private Character": Private Character, Public Interest, and the Law of Libel, 1843–1881

In answering the question as to whether nineteenth-century defamation law was a "law of the press," Paul Mitchell observes that many of the most important court rulings were reached in cases that had no immediate connection to it and, when the press was concerned, that judges and legislators took very different approaches to its regulation: judges applied legal principles to cases, while legislators pursued a more programmatic list of specific do's and don'ts ("Nineteenth Century Defamation" 27, 32). Their sense of the interests being served or protected by the law also varied ("Nineteenth Century Defamation" 30). Notwithstanding Martin Hewitt's observation that libel was a "legal minefield" because of "the sanctity Victorians accorded to personal reputations" (158), a cursory observation of the major legislation reveals how much more explicit the concern for private character was when Lord Campbell introduced his bill in 1843 than in the 1880s when newspaper societies and others connected with the press had a greater hand in drafting and promoting legislation.

As this section will show, many factors contributed to this shift, among them the greater imperative of public benefit and the press's role in promoting it, especially in the context of an ever-expanding "public" and amidst finer distinctions between public and private character. Even when character remained an implicit concern, it was for that reason less obvious than the explicit focus on the newspapers' financial liability, a liability made worse by legislation that, for many proprietors, failed to appreciate how newspapers had to be run. When the gradual intervention of a press lobby won ground with MPs whose private careers were associated with the newspapers, "character" lost ground.

In its report to the House of Lords in 1843, the Select Committee appointed to consider the law of defamation and libel prefaced its recommendations by laying out the two central interests libel law needed to mediate: "the safeguard of character" and "the protection from vexatious proceedings of those engaged in communicating useful information to the public" (*Report*, 1843 iii). The committee's goal was "to afford protection to fair fame, to guard honorable men from vexatious litigation, and effectually to put down traffic in calumny" conducted by "certain disreputable weekly newspapers" (vi). So, although several of its recommendations applied to defamatory (spoken) words or to publication in forms other than the press, the committee was especially attentive to the kinds of defenses available to newspapers in both civil actions and criminal proceedings.

Among the most notable provisions of the Libel Act (or Lord Campbell's Act, as it came to be known), defendants could plead that defamatory content had been printed "without malice and without gross negligence," that they had apologized at the earliest possible opportunity, and that they would pay money into court with a view towards mitigating damages or avoiding an action altogether.[5] On criminal indictments, the defendant could plead the truth of the libel as justification if he could also show that it was for the public benefit to make the specific imputations known (double pleas) (s. 6) or, when pleading "not guilty," that the publication was made without his "authority, consent or knowledge" (s. 7). The Act also distinguished for the first time between degrees of offense by creating three separate classes punishable by fines and/or imprisonment and by reducing what could have been a twenty-year sentence to a maximum of three years. Such measures lived up to the Act's aim of "more effectually securing the liberty of the press," but other committee recommendations that might have "prevent[ed] abuses in the exercise of said liberty" fell by the wayside (e.g. the payment of securities at the Stamp Office to cover damages, which the committee thought might put the "pests of society" [*Report*, 1843 vi] out of business).

And what of the Act's first stated object, "the better protection of private character"? The many legal experts, solicitors, barristers, booksellers, and representatives of the press who gave evidence included "most of the editors and conductors of the more respectable newspapers in London and in the provinces," who as a body agreed that it was important for the integrity of the press "to put an end to the practice of invading the sanctity of private life, and attacking private character" ("Law of Libel," *Law Times* 236). Samuel Blackburn, editor of *The Globe*, "[laid] it down as a rule"—thereby drawing

---

[5] Great Britain, "An Act to Amend the Law Respecting Defamatory Words and Libel," s. 2.

an ethical distinction between reputable papers and those that "exist by slander" (*Report*, 1843 vi)—that although public character was a proper subject of discussion, "we have no business with a man's ledger or with a man's shut door; we have nothing to do with his private habits, and what his circumstances are we care not" (*Report*, 1843 168).

Going beyond practice, however, Thomas Starkie, Q.C. and author of *Treatise on the Law of Libel and Slander, and Incidentally of Malicious Prosecutions* (1830) (the same who wrote *A Practical Treatise of the Law of Evidence* (1824) discussed in Chapter 2), insisted that the true foundation of libel law was the *principle* of reputation. Asked what he perceived to be the areas of the current law most in need of reform, Starkie focused on the basis of criminal liability and maintained that "breach of the peace" (which made libel a public offense) failed to account for the injury to individual reputation. Arguing that libel was analogous to battery, Starkie opined that an injured party should be able not only to recover financial damages in a civil case (a loss incurred *as a result of* the libel), but also to seek redress for the substantive "injury" or offense of the libel itself: "the law ought to be extended to the protection of the private reputation of individuals, *for reputation's sake*" (*Report*, 1843 35, emphasis mine). Lord Campbell himself, who chaired the committee, amplified these arguments in his own statement. Private defamation was criminal, he argued, not because it disturbed the peace, but because, like "theft or battery of the person," libel injures a person whom the law is bound to protect (177). Thus, libel is prosecuted "with a view of vindicating the character of the party injured" (177) and punishing the libeler.

Starkie and Campbell both draw on already received ideas about the nature of damage and the reason, which the report took issue with, that slanderous words were actionable only when they imputed indictable offenses or contagious diseases, or when they *harmed someone in their trade or profession specifically*, thus occasioning loss of professional reputation and money. So, although they both sought to elevate legal recognition of private character as a principle, their analogies remained grounded in property and ideas of possessive individualism; property *was* the principle. According to the highly empiricist foundation of early Victorian thinking, then, libel should have been a crime because it robbed individuals of their character, where character was a property, or because it attacked personal security, where character was co-extensive with the body.[6]

---

[6] On the one hand, this association strengthens over the century and anticipates arguments for reputation as property, as when Malins V.C. argues in *Dixon v Holden* (1869) that a man's "mercantile reputation" is "property of the most valuable description" (358), a case which brought the issue of libel within Chancery jurisdiction. On the other hand, the

Although the bill presented to the House of Lords did not fully resolve the question of how libel should be classified, according to a report in *The Law Times*, the changes it did propose were met with "unanimous applause" ("The Law of Libel," *Law Times* 265). Its benefits to the public included the new schedule of punishments and the requirement that judge and jury would have to determine whether the publication of even true libels benefited the public. At the same time, the press benefited from new methods of mitigating damages and reducing court costs. The bill received its first reading in July, was passed into law in August 1843, and although further reforms were attempted, it remained law for almost forty years before any significant amendment was made. For example, Lord Campbell put forward a second bill in 1858 to extend protection to accurate reports of public meetings, even if the reports contained libelous matter, but it failed, and even Sir Colman O'Loghlen's proposal, which in one form or another occupied the House between 1865 and 1869, came to nothing.[7]

In spite of the failure of O'Loghlen's bill to become law, the discussion surrounding his proposal is nevertheless important because it helps to show (1) how broad the potential for libel was, or was felt to be, by the press, and (2) how the interests of private character, public benefit, and the press were being framed at the time Trollope assumed his new role within the world of journalism. What, then, was the field O'Loghlen entered? General commentary on libel in the first half of the 1860s rehearsed the typical tensions between private interest and the press's function as an engine of public good, which many felt remained hampered in spite of Lord Campbell's Act by concerns for private character. Advocating freedom of the press as a national virtue, *The Times* complained that there was no "tenderness" in the law for newspaper proprietors, nor among jurors, who failed to consider "how much their own daily lives would be affected for the worse if the Press were thoroughly emasculated, and reduced to the proportion of a Court and commercial chronicle" ("State Prosecutions" 9). The *Leader and Saturday Analyst* seconded this view of the English paper in particular as being "the first of influences for good" chiefly because it respected privacy as far as public good allowed ("Alleged Libels" 589). Steering clear of "details of private life and personal scandal" by endeavoring to "pronounce on acts without deciding on character," the *Leader* nevertheless took note of the many actions brought

---

property analogy, even when extended to intellectual property, is precisely the one Warren and Brandeis found too limiting in their own search in the 1890 article for the basis of privacy.

[7] See O'Loghlen's speech in the Second Reading of his bill (Libel Bill, Bill 33, Second Reading).

against newspaper proprietors for personal libels. In some respects the *Leader* blames "ungentlemanly," or simply unskilled, journalists for failing to couch their observations in less risky language, but the more immediate difficulty lay in the latitude allowed for reporting on a magistrate's statements while an investigation was in progress (590). Anticipating the growth of expert testimony, the *Leader* advocated that papers needed specialist reporters versed, for example, in "medical jurisprudence, in international law, [and] in general and applied science" so as to prepare jurors for their work (590). "If a few dispassionate and judicious newspaper articles had a little ventilated the subject," newspapers would have been instrumental in forming a "special jury ad hoc" (590). According to these articles, newspapers might report, but "the Press" must also educate, even adjudicate, and in order to do that effectively, the law would have to further clarify the extent of privileged communications.[8]

If the *Leader* found the law respecting judicial proceedings obscure, *The Times* by contrast declared "Nothing Can be Simpler than the Law of Libel," yet its discussion of fair comment specifically raised questions about what the test of fairness might be (9). The immediate occasion for writing was the recent decision in *Campbell v Spottiswood* (1863), concerning two members of the press. Campbell was a dissenting minister and editor of *The British Ensign* in which he published both a series of letters promoting Christianity in China and a list of subscribers to the paper to distribute it, thus spreading news of the evangelical project. Spottiswood, himself printer for *The Saturday Review of Politics, Literature, Science and Art*, published a response titled "The Heathens' Best Friend" in which he accused Campbell of stuffing the list of subscribers in order to increase circulation of the periodical and with it his personal financial gain.[9] Although the jury found that Spottiswood believed

---

[8] *The Cornhill Magazine* was explicit when discussing the decision in *Hunter v Sharpe* (of the *Pall Mall Gazette*). The Lord Chief Justice's summing up in that case endorsed and paraphrased the defendant's argument which, by suggesting the judge had nothing further to add, substantiated James Fitzjames Stephen's observation in *The Cornhill* that "Of late the courts have been disposed to regard newspapers as being invested with a sort of quasi-judicial position, involving privileges not unlike those which are possessed by regular tribunals" ("The Law of Libel" 36).

[9] *Campbell v Spottiswood* (1863) 122 English Reports 289, subsequently referred to as *Campbell*. Chief Justice Cockburn held, "I think the fair position in which the law may be settled is this: that where the public conduct of a public man is open to animadversion, and the writer who is commenting upon it makes imputations on his motives which arise fairly and legitimately out of his conduct so that a jury shall say that the criticism was not only honest, but also well founded, an action is not maintainable. But it is not because a public writer fancies that the conduct of a public man is open to the suspicion of dishonesty, he is therefore justified in assailing his character as dishonest" (291).

his allegations to be true, it also found those statements to be a libel on Campbell. Lord Cockburn, in his decision, rehearsed what had become the common view (that a belief in the truth of a comment is all that's required to publish it), but found also that

> the public have an equal interest in the maintenance of the public character of public men; and public affairs could not be conducted by men of honour with a view to the welfare of the country, if we were to sanction attacks upon them, destructive of their honour and character, and made without any foundation. (*Campbell* 290)

Responding to the defense's argument that the *Saturday Review* article was privileged, Justice Blackburn also challenged popular perception when he defined privilege as an attribute of the speaker, not the meeting. "Privilege" means that "a person stands in such a relation to the facts of the case that he is justified in saying or writing what would be slanderous or libelous in any one else" (*Campbell* 292). *The Times* criticized this way of parsing "privilege" in particular and concluded that "it is not so easy to render the Press harmless to individuals, and yet leave it powerful for good" ("Nothing Can be Simpler" 9). More sanguine than *The Times*, *Fraser's Magazine* saw nothing in the decision to challenge the right of free discussion of public matters. If Spottiswood's criticism of Campbell's professional conduct was a Trojan horse for registering other personal complaints, then there could be no question that his attack was libelous; however, the real issue was how to regulate public discussion of the public conduct of public men ("Liberty of Criticism" 36).

Thus, when O'Loghlen (MP for Clare, Ireland) introduced his bill to amend the law "for more effectually securing the liberty of the press" in February 1865, he sought to redress a range of complaints, including not only the defensibility of a defendant's belief in the truth of the statements he reports (discussed in *Campbell*), but also the kinds of meetings the reports of which would carry a privilege (Libel Bill, Bill 33, First Reading, c. 561). More than this, O'Loghlen's bill sought both to distinguish the original issuer of libelous statements from the "after publisher," who was currently held responsible for reporting someone else's defamatory remarks, and to make plaintiffs who recovered small sums in damages carry the burden of the newspaper's court costs—all this to reduce the likelihood that a civil action could be undertaken and to lessen the financial cost to the papers if it was (c. 562).

In terms of criminal proceedings, O'Loghlen proposed raising the threshold for bringing a criminal indictment and making the defendant competent to testify—something he couldn't do in other criminal trials (as we saw in Chapter 1) and which, O'Loghlen suggested, actually motivated private plaintiffs to prosecute criminally "for the malicious purpose of closing the defendant's mouth," thereby preventing him from speaking to the truth or falsity of the charge (c. 787). As he explained in the bill's second reading in May 1865, many of its provisions were drawn from Lord Campbell's 1858 bill, which had itself been an effort to effect provisions left out of the original Act of 1843. Nevertheless, the bill was withdrawn and not reintroduced until March 1867, ahead of the much anticipated debates over the Reform Bill.

True to his word, O'Loghlen used the reintroduction of his bill as an occasion to repeat many of the recommendations made by the Lords Select Committee in support of Campbell's failed 1858 bill. However, his declaration that "the law as it stood was entirely opposed to the principles of a free press" (Libel Bill, Bill 11, Second Reading, c. 1717) negated the earlier, placatory language about the good effects of Lord Campbell's original Act. Twenty years on, the defense of character was still strong, but the question of whom to make responsible for libel had become even stronger, especially in the case of public meetings. Since public meetings were the most likely to warrant public interest (of the kind that justified reporting), the discussion of character emphasized the imperative of a free press in a way that downplayed the interests of private character that had been so prominent in the 1843 Act. For example, the aspect of the bill that drew most commentary from the press in its regular coverage of politics was its proposal to shift the liability for defamatory statements away from newspaper proprietors onto the original speaker whose words had been recorded and printed. O'Loghlen rejected the idea that the original speaker could not be made party to a libel action for having committed what was really the more ephemeral and localized wrong of oral slander. Instead, he echoed Lord Chief Justice Thesiger's oxymoronic comment, before the 1858 Select Committee, that "talking libels in public" was essentially the same as writing them out for publication and should open the speaker to the same responsibility (Libel Bill, Bill 11, Second Reading, c. 1720). If amidst the pell-mell management of reporters, messengers, printers, and editors, newspaper proprietors could not be relieved of a rigidly interpreted law of libel (which held any *written* statement tending to bring its subject into "hatred, ridicule, or contempt" to be libelous), then their only protection, O'Loghlen implied, would be self-censorship: quoting Edward Baines (MP for Leeds), "if perfect security is required against the publication of libels, the only effectual security is to be found in the censorship of the press" (cc. 1717, 1721).

To stand back for a moment: On the one hand, the question of where to place liability or whom to make responsible for libel follows naturally from the premise that private character/reputation should be protected and that there should be a remedy when it isn't. The emphasis on whether to blame the author of a slander or the newspaper proprietor (the person of record) might be just that, a shift in emphasis only. On the other hand, this shift in emphasis went hand-in-hand with a change in register (in the language of the legislature if not also in the courts) that elevated the institutional importance of the press and heightened the sense of wrongs done to it at the expense of the individual, whether that person be the injured party himself or the slanderer whose words *became* libel when printed.

Although no MP opposed a second reading of the bill, the two most circumspect responses to its proposed freeing of the press rested precisely on its effect on individuals. Charles Newdegate, Tory MP for North Warwickshire, situated the bill within recent legislative trends that he said "had enormously increased the liberty and power of associations, but . . . had done very little for individual freedom" (c. 1731). Faced with a bill that stood to "widen the freedom of the press," Newdegate had to ask, "but how would it affect the freedom of individuals?" (c. 1730). Thomas Chambers, Liberal member for Marylebone, amplified this concern. "There was no conceivable engine capable of being employed for the purpose of inflicting wrong on private character comparable in power to the press," he cautioned, "and its power had in many years been increasing in geometrical ratio by reason of the immense multiplication both of newspapers and of their readers" (c. 1733). John A. Roebuck (MP for Sheffield) ridiculed the "solemnity" of their concerns, but his own view tended rather to substantiate their sense of the danger to individual freedom posed by the shift in legislative sympathies towards associations or corporations. Somewhat ironically, given his own history with members of the press, Roebuck portrayed a "poor unfortunate newspaper proprietor" assailed by money-grubbing lawyers and their dishonest clients, since in his view an honest man would bypass the courts and simply seek redress from the paper directly (c. 1735).[10] More moderate voices spoke to the bill's particulars and recommended they be committed to a Select Committee (to which Roebuck and others more favorable to the bill were nominated).

Reaction to the debate was typically divided. *The London Review* deplored "observations injurious to character" but limply suggested that journalists should be protected when they've acted reasonably, should be liable when

---

[10] The *Dictionary of National Biography*'s entry on Roebuck characterizes him as being politically independent and generally opposed to whomever was in power, so it's worth taking his comments circumspectly. Nonetheless, it's ironic that "Tear 'Em" Roebuck would chastise Chambers's criticism of the press when in 1835 Roebuck himself had been challenged to a duel by the editor of the *Morning Chronicle* for having "denounced newspapers and everyone associated with them" (Rae 96) in one of his *Pamphlets for the People*, a collection Roebuck edited. See Rae. It's likely that the pamphlet referred to is Francis Place's "The Taxes on Knowledge."

they haven't, and that the difference should be decided on a case-by-case basis ("Newspaper Reporting" 351). *The Saturday Review* pointed out that public office holders already enjoyed fewer protections than private men (an effect of the tacit extension of privilege to parliamentary reports), but it maintained that because newspapers were held "as liable for the record as the original speaker was for the utterance of a libel," then newspapers at least took care to send reporters able to massage the content of those utterances so as to avoid repeating the slander ("The Law of Libel," *Saturday Review* 600).[11] The present bill, however, was "designed to make libeling an easy . . . proceeding" and offered "a glorious prospect to the profession of provincial slanderers." Reporting later that summer, after the bill had come out of committee and been presented to the House, *The Times*, by contrast, maintained that it really didn't offer much that was new or which would effect a reputable paper. Speaking in the characteristic first-person plural, the paper insisted that

> For ourselves we have nothing to demand . . . The meetings whose proceedings it is our duty to report are just those in which gross breaches of courtesy are very rare, and some of our provincial contemporaries have probably much greater reason to welcome the proposed limitation of their liability. ("The Libel Bill Which Passed" 8)[12]

In answer to Mr. Neate's concern that new freedom might lead to abuse, *The Times* quipped:

> it is public sentiment, far more than legislation, which determines the tone of journalism in all its forms. It was never more truculent than in the days when the Press was under stringent regulations, and the secret of its present moderation is to be sought in the improved temper and taste of society. (8)

If journalism was never more truculent, then this tone, according to the article, was not because of the regulations themselves but because of the mood of the public (which one can imagine was exacerbated if not caused by restrictive legislation). If journalism had now reached a state of "moderation," the passage suggests, this is because readers' temper and taste have improved. But what

---

[11] This argument is essentially what opponents of the bill meant when they said loosening restrictions would harm freedom of the press. The middle steps are that greater freedom could mean less responsibility. Less responsibility means shoddier production, which could lead to more public outcry followed either by stricter regulation or by changes in practice (specifically, the end of anonymity) that would inhibit free speech. See Ayrton's comments on the "demagogues, or those who considered themselves the leaders of the people [and] who most resented the attacks of the press" (Libel Bill, Bill 215, Third Reading, c. 1056).

[12] On the discursive features of the leading article, see Rubery; Willson; and Liddle.

has created this new taste? *The Times*, keen to demonstrate its superiority, has already pointed out that its "professional reporters," unlike "amateurs" and/or those employed by "provincial contemporaries," would not be called on "by the editor of any public journal to chronicle the scandalous conversation of Mrs. Gamp and her neighbours" (9). Repeated references to the status and designation of individual papers—here and in the debates—clearly show that not all periodicals or the social echelons they reach have improved. Rather, it is readers of *The Times* whose tempers have improved, and it is hard to ignore the coincidence of their improvement with the removal of the taxes on knowledge and on the increased protections offered by Lord Campbell's Libel Act. Put differently, the proof of social improvement lies in the freedom of the press, not (or not only) as a general principle, but as a specific function of papers like *The Times* to create and shape public taste—a power which Trollope, as will be seen, was especially anxious to moderate or contain and which legislators had long feared was spreading among less reputable papers as well.

O'Loghlen's bill passed its third reading in August 1867 (with a sixty-one-vote majority) but not before Acton Ayrton (Liberal MP for Tower Hamlets) spoke against the principle of the bill, which he felt would ultimately, if unintentionally, diminish freedom of the press. Two parts of his argument warrant special attention, including an extended discussion of the category difference between slander and libel and its effects on how words are received, and his more ethical objection about how to attribute responsibility for words spoken at a public meeting: whether to the paper or, as the bill proposed, to the original speaker. This latter concern centered on the idea that granting the press exceptional legal status would require other modes of assigning responsibility, for example by ending the practice of anonymous publication which otherwise helped to secure freedom of expression, in his view. Without some such mechanism of accountability, he argued, the bill risked eliminating the credibility and influence of even the best-run publications to the detriment of real liberty of the press. Of course, shifting the blame to the original speaker, what Charles Newdegate called "a vicious principle," was intended as just such an alternative (Libel Bill, Bill 215, Third Reading, c. 1060). Like him, however, Ayrton objected to making a *speaker* responsible for a *printed* report because it confused slander with the more serious offense of libel in order to free newspaper proprietors from the responsibility that attached to all others "who entered into commercial enterprises for their own profit and advantage" (Libel Bill, Bill 3, Second Reading, Apr. 1, 1868, c. 667).[13] Three issues

---

[13] See also Robert Collier's assessment that the bill was "an attempt to establish something intermediate between slander and libel; and it would make the character and liability of

intertwine in this complaint: in addition to the basis of the legal difference between spoken and written defamation and their remedies, Ayrton injects into the question of responsibility the multipurpose, multifaceted identity of the press as both public benefactor (or servant) and private, commercial enterprise.

Against accusations that Ayrton had deliberately stalled the bill's progress at the eleventh hour, Newdegate defended him by pointing out that in fact the bill had been rushed through without adequate discussion because the House had been so much occupied "by another and a great question" (Libel Bill, Bill 215, Third Reading, c. 1059).[14] Since that question was the further extension of the franchise (which received the royal assent just one week after the Libel Bill had its third reading), it is curious that so little direct comment was made about the links between the Reform Bill's democratizing aims and the libel bill's provisions to reduce the liability of the press, especially liability for costs brought on by that bugbear "vexatious proceedings." This lack of discussion might not be surprising as regards passage of the first, Great Reform Act when, as Ian Loveland explains, parliamentary privilege barred the press from any "legally guaranteed entitlement even to report, still less to comment upon or criticize, the beliefs or behaviours of MPs" (19). But following as it did on the decision in *Campbell*, which restricted the meaning of political libel by expanding the "public-interest" served by such information (24), one might have expected more substantial commentary than the discussion reflects on the press's role in informing this expanded public. Instead, O'Loghlen's reminder that only the first three clauses applied to the press, while it rightly points towards the many other forms libel could take and which the bill addressed, also wrongly implies that newspaper libel could have little to do with the franchise (Libel Bill, Bill 215, Third Reading, c. 1059). However, his immediate reference to the sanction given to the bill by the Provincial Newspaper Press Association that represented some 200 proprietors—sanctions he later reiterated in Committee to answer charges that the bill was introduced at the aegis of "ill-conducted journals"—highlights the significance of those first three clauses and undercuts his

---

spoken words depend on the mere accident of a reporter being present" (Libel Bill, Bill 3, Committee, c. 609).

[14] Newdegate kept up this focus on procedure throughout the Fall, however, when he moved that O'Loghlen should not have brought the amended libel bill for its second reading during the short session called in November, which had been called specifically to inquire into the government's handling of "the Abyssinian Expedition." See Libel Bill, Bill 3, Second Reading, Nov. 27, 1867, c. 310.

suggestion that the bill was *not* primarily concerned with the Press.[15] After all, it was to safeguard liberty of the press that O'Loghlen introduced the bill back in 1865; it was the newspaper clauses that attracted most, if not all, criticism throughout its years-long progress through the House, and it was the value for free discussion—in public meetings as well as in a free and responsible press—that motivated *opponents* of the bill. But this is not how the bill's proponents framed it.

Whatever rhetorical complacency *The Times* might exude in defense of its institutional importance and its relationship to the public, the bill's clemency towards "the poor unfortunate newspaper proprietor" tended to focus, in contrast, on the injustice of his financial vulnerability.[16] Ayrton said as much when he ventured that "it would almost appear that the Bill had been drawn up by newspaper proprietors for their own protection, utterly regardless of the interests of society" (Libel Bill, Bill 215, Third Reading, c. 1052). Personal interest, not public benefit, motivated the extension of privilege to which Ayrton especially objected on the grounds that "a person who published *for his own profit* what another said was not to be made liable for what he so published" (c. 1052, emphasis mine). He was not alone. Thomas Chambers argued before the House Committee that those in the journalism "trade" "ought to be as much responsible for what they did in the way of their calling as the chemist or the druggist for what he sold in the way of his business" (Libel Bill, Bill 3, Committee, cc. 595–6). In other words, a paper can be allowed to profit from healthy reportage, but if it dispenses bad medicine, it should also be made to account. The underlying assumption here is not that serving the public good and making a profit are necessarily at odds, but that in the interests of vigorous circulation, proprietors would either publish

---

[15] See Libel Bill, Bill 3, Committee, c. 604. In discussion of a committee of the house, Charles Neate (MP for Oxford) repeatedly referred to the bill's bad timing. Already opposed to relaxing the press's "legal responsibilities," he emphasized the danger of doing so "especially at the present time, when newspapers were read more and more by a lower and more ignorant population, who might easily be guided or misguided by what they read in those publications" and, he continued, when the scope of the bill would encourage the growth of "a press of a less high moral character" than existed under the present laws (Libel Bill (re-committed), Bill 112, c. 540).

[16] Francis Larkin Soames, solicitor to *The Times*, testified before the 1879 Select Committee of the House of Commons that between 1872 and 1879, twenty-one actions had been brought against the paper. Fourteen had been abandoned before the trial, and of the seven that went forward, damages were awarded to only three of the plaintiffs. Soames estimated that the total costs for eighteen "mostly vexatious and speculative" actions were between £3,100 and £3,500, and the *Times* had been able to recover no more than £130 in costs. See *Report*, 1879 107.

libels to increase sales (the "traffic in calumny" Campbell had hoped to block in '43) or would simply rush to get out the news.

In any case, the tension between these ethical and financial arguments continued for the next two years as others blamed the newspaper "combination" (Neate) or "the importunity of the press" (Whalley) for the bill's ostensible leniency (Libel Bill, Bill 3, Committee, cc. 597, 605).[17] Chambers put the point most neatly when in March 1869 he contrasted the preamble to Lord Campbell's Act—"An Act for the better protection of Private Character, and for more effectually securing the liberty of the Press, and for better preventing abuse in said liberty"—with O'Loghlen's: "Whereas it is expedient to amend the law of Libel" and denied that the press had any grievance substantial enough to warrant altering constitutional principles affecting "the liberty of the subject" (Libel Bill, Bill 17, Second Reading, c. 1610).

What was that liberty of the subject? What could it mean to represent, if not the "people," then individual persons? In the midst of discussions about cost, the question of private character and the effect of damaging words was very often left implicit, yet, to return to the first of Ayrton's concerns, Ayrton had wondered about the repercussions for the individuals whose words were reported and those whose character they harmed when he challenged the bill's recategorization of slander as libel. He and others expanded on the problems entailed by this confusion: speakers would be made responsible for having said something which may have been taken out of context (Ayrton), or misattributed, or not attributed at all, or otherwise inaccurately reported (Newdegate, Libel Bill, Bill 215, Third Reading, c. 1060). Nevertheless, such reports would be spread over town and country by a reporter, opponents feared, whom the speaker may or may not have known was present and who certainly was not acting as an agent of the speaker.[18] In fact, Ayrton cautioned speakers in both Houses to consider whether their own pronouncements might not open them to an action if they were printed, since "half the

---

[17] See speeches by Charles Neate (MP for Oxford) and George Whalley (MP for Peterborough) at Libel Bill, Bill 3, Committee, cc. 597, 605. Stephen Gaselee "hoped [the bill] would go back to Ireland and never show its face in that House again" (c. 613). Whalley had suggested during the bill's second reading in April '68 that because O'Loghlen, who represented Clare, had prepared the bill in Ireland it necessarily favored "another system of laws" than those in England (c. 664). Since Whalley also persisted in the idea that the Jesuits were "at the bottom of the matter" and intended to "fetter the newspapers which went against Jesuitism, by converting slander into libel" (Libel Bill, Bill 3, Committee, c. 600), one has to assume that this is the source of his sense that because the bill was an Irish law it "struck at the root of freedom of speech" (Libel Bill, Bill 3, Second Reading, Apr. 1, 1868, c. 664).

[18] Newdegate stated that "this was in fact making a man responsible for the acts of another, and that other not his agent" (Libel Bill, Bill 3, Committee, c. 593).

speakers held up those who did not take their view of a subject to ridicule and contempt" (Libel Bill, Bill 215, Third Reading, c. 1053).

And what of the person slandered or libeled, as the case might be? Opponents to the third clause specifically argued that while a speaker would find such reports hard to dispute, the person defamed would find, even worse, "there was more difficulty in proving spoken than in proving written words" if the slander had not been attributed at all. Prefacing these remarks, Sir John Duke, 1st Baron Coleridge and soon to become Solicitor-General, observed in Committee in May 1868 that the law already privileged "public comments upon public acts of public men . . . It was only when private character was attacked that the law was stringent" (Libel Bill, Bill 3, Committee, c. 600):

> Why should a private, harmless man be dragged out of his privacy by the publication of a slander in a newspaper? Why should he be put to the annoyance and expense of defending his character? Why should he be put to the trouble of writing a long letter to a paper to refute that which would not be worth the trouble of a refutation *but for the importance given to it by its appearance in print*? (c. 600, emphasis mine)

Coleridge's remarks return private character to the forefront of debate and, tetchiness notwithstanding, typify the reasoning that made libel a more serious offense than slander. Spoken words might be hastily uttered, but in a localized context they could be condemned and retracted just as quickly, went the argument. The object of the comments might not even experience an injury, either because he was absent and didn't hear what was said, or because he was present and had the benefit of context—the "character, conduct, and tone of the speaker"—to aid interpretation (Ayrton, Libel Bill, Bill 215, Third Reading, c. 1054). Not so with a printed report. "Where was the protection in the report that that impression should be conveyed to those who read it in a newspaper," asked Ayrton in debate on the third reading, "because the reporter would not be called upon to give a dramatic account of the wild mode of delivering the speech or of the violent conduct of the speaker?" (c. 1054). The reporter, we might say, was no novelist. Taken together, the discourse of journalism, the deliberation implied by the preparation of a written report, and its widespread dissemination changed a speech "that might not have compromised the character of the accused in the slightest degree in the minds of those who were present" into an apparently "wise, well-considered, and effective one, of the most damaging description to the person attacked" (c. 1054), which placed the onus of correction, as Coleridge lamented, on the "private, harmless man."

This question of how an aggrieved person might get his remedy had been further complicated in June 1867 when, before the House Committee,

O'Loghlen proposed to add a new clause that would give to a range of parliamentary proceedings—specifically reports published in *Hansard's Debates*—the same qualified privilege already enjoyed by reports on judicial proceedings and which the House had just agreed to grant to public meetings. To illustrate, he referred to Rigby Wason, former MP for Ipswich, who had brought fourteen civil actions against *The Times* for having reported reaction to a petition, presented on Wason's behalf to the House of Lords in February that year, that Wason claimed maligned him (Libel Bill (re-committed), Bill 112, c. 544). Although O'Loghlen's clause was withdrawn (only to be reinserted in November and withdrawn again), Wason was to become an important object lesson in the law of libel and came to figure not only in the remaining discussion of the libel bill, but also in the decisive case of *Wason v Walter* (1868) of *The Times*.[19] Indeed, *The Times*, commenting in November 1867 on the bill's postponed reading, repeated its assertion that "we have no special indulgence to ask ... Libellous speeches are seldom made at such meetings as we report," but in a veiled jab, it continued, "litigious persons, moreover, think more than once before they proceed to extremities against those who are not to be intimidated into submission by the fear of costs ("The Libel Bill, of Which the Second Reading" 8). Although Wason had failed to win a summons against the publisher of *The Times* when O'Loghlen cited him in June, his criminal case was set to be heard before the Court of Queen's Bench at the end of December, less than four weeks after *The Times* puffed its feathers.

What followed was a brief but fascinating interplay of the press, the legislature, and the bench on the question of libel, fair comment, and parliamentary privilege. While Wason sued for libels against himself, *The Law Times Reports*' publication of the report, and two leading articles about it, revealed what the Lords considered Wason's own attack on the character of Sir Fitzroy Kelly, the newly appointed Lord Chief Baron of the Exchequer. Wason accused Kelly of having lied to an election committee in 1835 and

---

[19] *Wason v Walter* (1868) Law Times Reports 17 N.S., subsequently referred to as *Wason*. After an unsuccessful attempt at a second reading in November 1867, O'Loghlen moved to postpone to the next session in February 1868. The bill received its second reading in April 1868 and was discussed at length in a committee of the House in May, which was to resume the same week. However, in February 1869 Sir Edward Baines (Leeds) presented the bill for its first reading in the new session, the earlier bill having been withdrawn and O'Loghlen in the interval having become Judge Advocate and thus no longer able to shepherd it. The second reading was held on March 17, and included discussion of the impact of the *Wason* decision. That debate was adjourned and resumed the following month, but no further records point to its result. As had happened in 1865 and again in '68, the pressure of other business appears to have been stronger, and libel would not become a significant legislative discussion again until the end of the next decade.

to have obtained his former position as Solicitor-General through fraud, but the Lord Chancellor, Lord Chelmsford rejected Wason's petition for Kelly's investigation and ouster. Instead, *The Law Times* reported, Lord Chelmsford deemed Wason's petition itself a belated attempt at revenge, which in fact had "vindicated the character of the right honorable gentleman which he had branded in 1837" but which now constituted "a perpetual record of his [Wason's] falsehood and malignity" (*Wason* 386).[20] This "perpetual record" is not to be found in Hansard's, however, where a headnote to Wason's petition explains that between the current state of libel law and Parliament's express rejection of the extension of privilege, "Mr. Hansard holds it within his discretion to restrict his report" to the "essential part of the discussion": "the vindication of the Lord Chief Baron's character" (Petition of Rigby Wason, Esquire, c. 260).

As noted, O'Loghlen pointed to Wason's case as evidence of the need to protect the press when it circulated fair and accurate reports of parliamentary proceedings, whatever their content. Wason, presenting his grievance to the court, referred to "the inquiry on the libel law" that had been before both Houses in 1857–8 and the recommendation of Lords Chelmsford, Lyndhurst, and Wensleydale that when defamatory statements were made in parliamentary proceedings, the press should be liable for reporting them.[21] Noting that "the bill to relieve them [the press] from that liability was thrown out by a large majority," he pointed to more recent debates in the Commons and Joseph Henley's view, expressed in Committee in June 1867, that the new clause respecting privilege would leave aggrieved persons with no remedy, since any member could issue "'a great stroke in slander of absent persons'" which the press could report with impunity (*Wason* 387).[22]

---

[20] Wason first made the charges in 1837 and refused to respond to Kelly's "challenge." As a result, Wason was "posted as a slanderer and a coward," which Chelmsford concluded was "the source of all this rancorous malice which the petitioner has nourished up for a period of four and thirty years" (*Wason* 386).

[21] Wason was most likely referring to evidence given before the Select Committee on the "Privilege of Reports," set to meet in May 1857, and which Lord Campbell refers to in February 1858 on presenting the libel bill to the Lords. See Libel Bill, c. 686. See also the motion for a second reading and discussion (Libel Bill, Second Reading), when the second reading was postponed a further six months.

[22] Wason's (or the reporter's) quotation differs from Henley's speech as reported in Hansard's: "So long as the matter stated was confined within the walls of the House the party was not injured, unless he was present to hear what was said; but if it got into the papers, and was thus disseminated over all the world, the person aggrieved would have no remedy. It would be almost tempting people to do a good stroke of abuse, and give it a wide circulation" (Libel Bill (re-committed), Bill 112, c. 545).

The case did not go Wason's way. In his decision, Lord Cockburn took note of the practice of both Houses not to assert their privilege but rather to allow reports on their proceedings. "It is of such vital and essential importance to the public that these proceedings should be fully reported," he argued,

> that though it may occasionally happen that when the conduct of an individual is impugned before either House of Parliament and though it may be painful and injurious to him that what has been said to his detriment should be disseminated over the length and breadth of the land, yet the interest of the public must be preferred to that of the individual, and not that of the individual to that of the public. (*Wason* 389)[23]

Cockburn's respect for public interest demonstrates a resurgence of utilitarianism that Paul Mitchell speculates was connected to the newly expanded franchise ("Nineteenth Century Defamation" 31) and which Ian Loveland undoubtedly links to Cockburn's "moral topography" wherein "the massed rank of voters to whom the information is directed" overshadow libeler and victim alike (30). Certainly, the decision tips the balance between "protection of private character" and liberty of the press in the latter's favor on the grounds that the public should be "instructed and enlightened," but Cockburn's decision went further by extending the privilege to *comments* on the reports. Fair comment on parliamentary as well as judicial proceedings would sustain "the power of public opinion," which Cockburn found "so valuable in inspiring the sense of duty in public men, and keeping alive in them in the discharge of their public functions that sense of duty" (*Wason* 389). In short, the press could keep public men honest by keeping the public apprised of their character and conduct.

When Edward Baines brought the libel bill back in March 1869, he cited Cockburn's decision in *Wason* as having settled the matter of privilege, and although Thomas Chambers agreed with the court's decision (because "character formed the whole subject of the debate"), he disputed that it authorized "'sifting'" a man's character to sell copies, or excused editors from due diligence in the interests of timely production (Libel Bill, Bill 17, Second Reading, cc. 1599–1617). Reviving discussion of newspaper publication as a business enterprise, he further argued that "it could not be put as if it were the function of the Government or the action of a court of justice, or a debate in the Houses of Parliament" (c. 1613). In Chambers's increasingly

---

[23] Paul Mitchell, commenting on Cockburn's utilitarian preference for the general good, links the decision to the recently passed Reform Bill ("Nineteenth Century Defamation" 31). For discussion of the Reform Bill's various aims, see Carlisle, "On the Second Reform Act, 1867."

retrograde view, businesses should not govern, adjudicate, or legislate, yet this trend is precisely what James Fitzjames Stephen observed in *The Cornhill Magazine* when he noted that "of late the courts have been disposed to regard newspapers as being invested with a sort of quasi-judicial position, involving privileges not unlike those which are possessed by regular tribunals" ("The Law of Libel" 36). These were questions about the value of personal reputation, about what was truly in the public interest to know, as well as about the function and status of the so-called fourth estate.

Thus far, this chapter has been concerned with the implications of legislative debates for ideas about character. Why the 1860s in particular should have witnessed such a spate of legislation is rather beyond its scope, but the parliamentary record leaves several hints which it is worth pausing to consolidate before moving to the next section. Thomas Chambers's comments in 1869 recall those he made in 1867 that pointed out the dual, potentially dichotomous, identities of the press as an engine of information sharing and as a money-making venture, which mirrored the dual roles of several MPs whose public roles as representatives of the people coincided with private roles as owners of newspapers. Reducing liability for libel would increase what could safely be printed, in service to the first objective. So could eliminating the extra expense of litigation, but it's hard not to imagine that the money thus saved served the second objective by increasing the value of a proprietor's investment as well (or even by prefiguring a redefinition of private individual as corporate concern, that is, of imagining a corporation as an individual).

Beyond jockeying for circulation numbers, a second consideration is the status among newspapers that hinged on their audience and market: metropolitan versus provincial, upper-crust or low-brow. Thomas Chambers had commented in March 1867 on the "immense multiplication of newspapers and of their readers" (Libel Bill, Bill 11, Second Reading, c. 1733). Coming just months and even weeks before the vote on the Second Reform Bill, we have to add expansion of the franchise to the context of the libel bills. The voting "public" was growing, and the same class-inflected criticism which held that less affluent, less educated, less well-informed men should not have the responsibility or the privilege of voting was mooted in discussion of the press, as with Charles Neate's anxiety that "a lower and more ignorant population" could easily be preyed upon by "a press of a less high moral character" which would follow if the industry's legal responsibilities were diminished (Libel Bill (re-committed), Bill 112, c. 539).

Less obviously but perhaps more intriguingly (especially in light of Trollope's Irish hero, Phineas Finn) is the way Irish politics of the 1860s, specifically Colman O'Loghlen's and hence the bill's Irish origins, may also have played a role. As noted above (n17), at least two MPs registered their objections to the bill's content by reference to its Irish antecedents. Casting the bill as an effort to prevent newspaper criticism of "Jesuitism," George Whalley (MP for Peterborough), for example, linked the bill to what he saw as Irish, Catholic resistance to the political influence of "Protestant associations" in England which could be silenced if proprietors of "newspapers that went against Jesuitism" were held liable for printing slander (Libel Bill, Bill 3, Committee, c. 600). This debate occurred in the May session of 1868 when, Whalley notes, he had made the same argument "session after session, for five years" because O'Loghlen, "who was undoubtedly inspired by the Jesuits" had been so dogged (c. 600).

When religion and politics were so deeply entangled, however, "Jesuit" might just as easily have meant "Fenian." Robert Warren, Attorney General for Ireland, agreed with the objection that proprietors ought not to have the additional protection mooted by the bill and cited the possibility that papers would be enabled to print "second-hand libels," including "slander or treason spoken at a legally convened meeting in New York and reported in the American papers" (c. 602). Former Attorney-General for Ireland James Lawson's more pointed reference to a "Fenian meeting in New York" (c. 603) recalls American support for the Irish Republican Brotherhood (IRB) and the failure of just such an uprising as had occurred outside Dublin in March 1867, the same month that O'Loghlen reintroduced the bill (Rafferty 258). The timing of the bill's second reading, in the run-up to discussion of the Reform Act in England, thus highlights the comparative inattention to calls for expanded suffrage such as those made by the IRB in their Proclamation of an Irish Republic.

Setting aside Whalley's characterization of O'Loghlen's motives, the excursion into Irish politics reveals an even stronger, not to say stranger, link to the issue of libel, insofar as it was Lawson himself who, during his own tenure as AG, had shut down the Fenian newspaper *The Irish People*. Established in 1863, the paper was suppressed in 1865, and its organizers charged with treason-felony (Campbell 10). The trials that followed, which "made deadly use" of evidence gathered from the paper's offices and the evidence of the paper itself (Campbell 11–12), lasted until 1867 and would have been fresh in the minds of MPs—including Lawson, who had been elected Member for Potarlington and served on the Select Committee that studied the libel bill—thinking about how newspapers served the people, and which people.[24]

---

[24] See Sarah Campbell on coverage of the trials in the British press and parliamentary debate (13–14 and 20–1 respectively). Campbell refers to James Lawton [sic] as the Solicitor General for Ireland, but both Hansards and the *DNB* confirm James Lawson was MP for Potarlington with the *DNB* adding that he was Attorney General and responsible for closure

I will not attempt to calculate to what degree these varied interests combined to inspire the legislation, but Wason's case (to return) marked an interesting termination to the bill that Colman O'Loghlen first brought forward four years earlier. The case established a qualified privilege for reports of parliamentary proceedings, but there would be no statutory reform of the libel law for another decade.[25] (When debate on the second reading was resumed in April 1869, it was committed for discussion the next day but falls out of the record.) To the extent that it involved Fitzroy Kelly's public character, as the holder of high public office, it shifted the discussion of reputation away from private character (protected under Lord Campbell's Act). However, *The Times*' report, which included commentary about *Wason* that Hansard thought too risky to print, gave life to the category difference between words spoken at a public meeting and the written, potentially libelous report of them that had so much occupied debate over the questions of slander and libel and of responsibility. Furthermore, Cockburn's preference for the general good, when viewed in the context of the Second Reform Act, entailed an expanded sense of the "public" whose interests were being thus served. However, Cockburn's faith that the public could make up its own mind was not universally shared, especially as regards *The Times*, which Anthony Trollope claimed had become "The Press" in England ("The Press" 35). As Trollope warned, it was hard to reconcile the press's ideal function of informing the public, and thereby enabling liberty of thought, with the public's tendency to be led by *The Times*' leading articles.

Trollope on the Liberties of the Press

From his earliest ideas about the public function of journalism in "The Press" (1855–6), to his editorship of *Saint Pauls Magazine* (1867–70), and of course the serialization of his own fiction, Anthony Trollope relied on, participated in, criticized, and consumed the periodical press. Although the same can be said of many Victorian novelists, Trollope's fascination found its way into what Dallas Liddle estimates to be some fifty "formal representations and analyses of journalists" in the novels, making them just as important as the MPs, clergymen, courting couples, and lawyers for which his fiction is known (76). A survey of just some of his novels, for example, reveals an explicit concern with editorial prerogative, with acts of reading the paper, with the

---

of *The Irish People*. See Boase. As AG, Lawson also spoke on the treatment of Fenian prisoners held in Waterford. See "Ireland—Fenian Prisoners at Waterford—Observations" c. 444.

[25] Henry Raikes introduced an ill-fated bill to add hard labor and flogging to the list of punishments in 1872. See "Defamation of Private Character Bill," *Law Times* 95, 106; and Defamation of Private Character Bill, Bill 99.

power of the press generally—and *The Times* specifically—to influence policy as well as public opinion, and especially with its powers to infiltrate readers' minds and become the "whispering conscience" of characters who found themselves represented in its columns.[26] This, notwithstanding that in the last decade of Trollope's career he became what Graham Law refers to as a "newspaper novelist" with novels serialized and syndicated in weekly papers such as *The Graphic* in which *Phineas Redux* had its run (47, 49).[27] More even than this general interest in things connected to the press, the period of Trollope's editorship of *Saint Pauls Magazine* (1867–70) is especially interesting, not only because Trollope's many roles overlapped, but also because they did so when Colman O'Loghlen's bill was before the House, when *Wason v Walter* was decided, and when criminal cases at the Old Bailey experienced a surge— all factors to suggest, in short, that libel acquired more than its usual topicality at the moment Trollope became an editor and introduced his Irish MP to the editor of a penny paper (*PF* 1.241).[28]

---

[26] Matthew Rubery takes this passage from *The Eustace Diamonds* for the title of his chapter "The Leading Article: The Whispering Conscience in Trollope's Palliser novels" (94).

[27] See Goodlad's reading of *The New Zealander* (143); and Rubery. See also Andrew Willson on Trollope's critique of newspaper discourse, especially the uncritical reader's response to its authoritative tone, in *The Warden*. Willson focuses on the anonymity of writers of "leaders": "overstatement of authority" and "overinvestment of credibility" (172) are connected to the convention of anonymity, which by contributing a transcendence to the views expressed, discourages readers from imagining the writer as a material person whose views could be challenged—or, going further, who might even be made to account for them in an action for libel.

[28] Between 1860 and 1880, 19,226 cases were heard at London's Central Criminal court, and of those 1,682, or just under 9%, fell within the offense category "breaking the peace." More than 1,200 of these (75%) were cases of wounding, while libel, together with assault, riots, and threatening behavior, comprised the remaining 25%. All told there were 154 prosecutions for libel in the twenty-year period. However, if the number of libel trials is comparatively insignificant, the number of guilty verdicts is not: 152 verdicts were rendered, and the defendant was found guilty in over 100 cases. Generally speaking, punishment took the form of fines or payment of sureties more often than imprisonment (57% compared with 39%). The more important outcome, however, was the restoration of the victim's good name. With more than two-thirds of cases decided in the victim's favor, the odds of winning redress through the legal system must have seemed good. Still, in most years, fewer than ten libel cases were tried. The biggest bumps occurred in the years 1869, 1873, and 1874, when Trollope's novels *Phineas Finn* and *Phineas Redux* were in serialization, which saw ten or more cases each, totaling over 22% of all cases heard in the twenty-year period. A keyword search of the Sessions Papers revealed only seventeen cases between 1860 and 1880 that involved newspapers or editors, but thirteen of these defendants were found guilty, thus conforming to the trend.

When *Phineas Finn* began its run in October 1867, Trollope the editor also outlined his vision of what the magazine genre could do (namely, to mix the useful with the sweet by offering an eclectic blend of politics as well as lighter literature) (Trollope, "Introduction" 1). Using the magazine as a testing ground for new ideas about "editorial discourse" (Liddle), Trollope penned a series of short stories called "Editors' Tales," serialized *Phineas Finn*, and began work on *Phineas Redux* whose staff-writer-turned-editor Quintus Slide is among the most recognizable of his fictional newspapermen. And what came of these experiments? Dallas Liddle suggests that these fictional explorations of the professional role Trollope also occupied brought home the different priorities of those who edit a periodical and those who own it, "one understanding the periodical as an entity of discourse, the other as an entity of economic and legal interests" (89). Although it is hard to say what Trollope's precise knowledge of the (libel) law was, any proprietor would have relied on his editor's ability to manage content so as to increase circulation and reduce the publication's liability. (That James Virtue closed the magazine because it wasn't making money suggests Trollope was better at the latter.[29]) Indeed, the Palliser novels reflect at the very least a working knowledge of the risks a paper might take, as well as the prerogatives it enjoyed. For example, the second installment of *Phineas Finn*, in which Slide is introduced, immediately follows Leslie Stephen's assessment in "Anonymous Journalism" of the advantages papers enjoy in any "quarrel with individuals" (219), and in *Phineas Redux*, Slide exercises the privilege to report on parliamentary proceedings and on the progress of Phineas's trial in *The People's Banner*, even as he treads the more slippery ground of extortion.

More dismayed by *liberties of* the press than worried about restrictions on its freedom per se, Trollope's libel novels explore how the conventions of the paper's various genres (e.g. leading article) work on readers, thus linking public, discursive forms—especially those whose content is also about character—to the development of private character. Moreover, these novels explore the ways in which editors shape the ethos of the publications they manage, thereby humanizing, individuating, and potentially deflating what critics have identified as the depersonalized, transcendent voice of authority that conferred extra credibility on the views expressed (Rubery; Willson; Liddle). In this context "freedom of the press" actually means freedom *from*

---

[29] Before taking the position, Trollope warned Virtue that if he were to run the magazine as he saw fit, it was likely to cost a great deal without yielding a significant return on investment. Of its failure, Trollope wrote, "I do not think that the failure . . . arose from bad editing. Perhaps too much editing might have been the fault. I was too anxious to be good, and did not think enough of what might be lucrative" (*An Autobiography* 184).

critical reading practices, which the paper's ostensibly "unmediated" reportage (per Willson) exacerbates. For example, although Trollope himself may have been more interested in "good" than "lucrative" copy, his portrait of Quintus Slide shows a different sensibility at work, especially regarding his treatment of Phineas Finn, where the paper exerts its presumed authority in personally damaging, if not also legally libelous, ways when it concerns individual character.

Nevertheless, Trollope's editors are not all the same. If Trollope worried about how readers consumed papers and how editors promulgated a worldview that was more responsive to circulation numbers than to principles (Slide's notorious flip-flop of the political bent of *The People's Banner* is a case in point), his exploration of different types of editors tempers what might otherwise seem like wholesale disapproval of the profession. Indeed, *Cousin Henry* provides an exact counterpoint to the Phineas novels because the editor of the *Carmarthen Herald* risks charges precisely to draw the bad actor Henry out of hiding. Rather than offering a reductive view of the profession and its discourse, Trollope works on a case-by-case basis that judges particulars rather than types.

Furthermore, representing these editors offered Trollope an occasion for scrutinizing his own practice as a writer of fiction. Andrew Willson has argued convincingly of *The Warden* that Trollope's narrator, by demonstrating gaps in knowledge and confessing to the stresses of composition or editorial pressure, educates readers in the mediated nature of the reality his novels represent. By importing samples of journalism, Trollope also shows readers that these too are mediated, not only by his novel but by their own journalistic conventions as well. One striking lesson to draw from the comparison, for Willson, is how much more space, and hence more nuance, the novel can give to its character-portraits of men like Septimus Harding than is possible in the truncated forms of the "paragraph" or even the "leading article" (notwithstanding their outsized "impact") (177). As compelling as this observation is, however, a larger set of questions is whether, or how, this strategy of conscious "mediation" continues into later novels and whether it consistently works in the novel's favor, or even in one direction. What, if anything, does the narrator learn from the editor, for example? Might the act of mediation—for Willson of presenting and commenting on Tom Towers's article, but in the Phineas novels of developing Quintus Slide—exert its own pressure on the narrator, reversing the effect of criticism or undermining critical reading by drawing the narrator into the logic he represents?

Considering the way that Trollope complicates his narrator's posture of omniscience, it's necessary to pay attention to the way he maintains critical distance, for himself and for readers, from the characters Trollope the author lived with "in the full reality of established intimacy" and of whom he must know "whether [they be] true or false, and how far true and how far false" (*An Autobiography* 150). His admiration for but lack of sentimentality about Mrs. Proudie is a suggestive analogy. Cognizant of her flaws yet appreciating her complexity, he did not hesitate to kill her off to satisfy his readers' taste, as he explains in the autobiography (177). Quintus Slide is less complex than the Bishop's wife, but as he does with her, Trollope allows Slide to return over multiple novels and takes pains to articulate his motives, however delusional, as well as his reactions to events that don't transpire in the ways he used the paper to effect. Yet as with Mrs. Proudie, the narrator's unsentimental view works to disentangle the author's attachment to his characters from his practical sense of the exigencies of plot, audience, and editorial demand.

Not one to condone the press's methods or its rhetorical stance, even when the substance of a report might be true, Trollope's narrator voices the effects of negative publicity on characters as they internalize, reject, or reshape their self-concept—their characters—in response to images circulated in the papers. In *The Warden* (1855), Septimus Harding resigns his post as the warden of Hiram's Hospital because of "thunderbolts" launched by *The Jupiter*, that "all powerful organ of the press" (chapter 7) whose charges are impossible to answer because "What the Czar is in Russia, or the mob in America, that the *Jupiter* is in England" (60). In *The Prime Minister* (1876), Plantagenet Palliser agonizes over whether to notice repeated charges of corruption made against him in *The People's Banner*, which the Duchess numbers among "these dregs of the newspapers, these gutter-slanderers" (III.483). Dr. Wortle contemplates bringing an action against *The Broughton Gazette* for its implied aspersions on his conduct of the school in *Dr. Wortle's School* (1881), but is still more incensed by his Bishop's warning when he discovers its basis to lie not in reports in "the metropolitan press" (149) but in *Everybody's Business*, a provincial rag of the sort criticized in parliamentary debate on every libel bill (the point being that the Bishop could credit the report of such a publication in spite of his personal knowledge of Dr. Wortle's character).[30] And Henry Jones is cajoled into bringing an action against Gregory Evans, editor of the

---

[30] In *George Eliot and Blackmail*, Alexander Welsh mentions *Dr. Wortle's School*, specifically the use of letters to blackmail the Peacockes, as an indication of Trollope's interest in "the management and exploitation of secrets" in the later novels (4). Welsh focuses on the letters, with their obvious links to Trollope's work in the postal service, but alongside this blackmail plot is Dr. Wortle's libel plot and Trollope's other occupation with the periodical press. Welsh explains his focus on blackmail as distinct from libel and slander because libel and slander deal in untruths. However, Lord Mansfield's proposition that the worst libels *were* the true ones undercuts this distinction, as does the use of truth as justification.

Carmarthen Herald, "for the publication of various wicked and malicious libels against himself," which Henry knows actually to be true and which sicken him to have to challenge (*Cousin Henry* 189).

There is more to say of *Cousin Henry*, particularly in relation to debate leading to the 1881 Libel and Newspaper Registration Act, but Trollope's most individuated treatment of an editor is also the most sustained, occurring over multiple novels. In *Phineas Finn* (serialized 1866–7; 1869), editor Quintus Slide uses *The People's Banner* to make his first attack on the title character in the form of a critique of rotten boroughs. Phineas wins election to the borough for which Slide intended to stand and Slide, who views Finn's election and more especially his refusal to give Slide a turn in the next session as a betrayal, makes Finn the exemplar of political corruption. Perhaps a true libel of the sort contemplated by Campbell's Libel Act, this publication marks the beginning of Slide's malicious use of the paper to harm Finn. In the novel's penultimate chapter, abbreviated to "P.P.C." (for *pour prendre congé*), Slide and Phineas take their leave of one another but not before Slide apologizes for the paper's "little severities" (338) and offers to pay Phineas to write leaders for the *Banner of the People* (as it was then called and of which Slide has just become editor). Phineas instead accuses him of printing lies and, in response to threats, instructs Slide "to do [his] punishment at the office of the Banner" (339), since he will "prefer to do it print" than with physical blows, a preference Slide confirms as he leaves, "concocting his article as he went" (339).

Five years later in *Phineas Redux* (serialized 1873–4; 1874), Quintus Slide returns and intervenes in the disintegrating marriage of Lady Laura Kennedy and former MP Robert Kennedy. Trollope had already completed the novel in March 1871 and was negotiating a contract with the *Graphic* when *The Saturday Review* raised the alarm that "it might almost be supposed from the reports of the law courts that everybody had been seized with an uncontrollable passion for libeling everybody else" ("Legal Epidemics" 213). Although the article blames excessive litigiousness more than the actual growth of damaging articles, Trollope's portrait of the vindictive editor shows where such an "epidemic" could have had a start.

Slide receives a letter from the deranged Kennedy (a statement of perceived wrongs inflicted by Lady Laura and her father but which also implicates Phineas) who asks him to print the "public appeal" in the hope that outside pressure would secure his wife's return when his personal appeals had not. Slide threatens Finn with publication in *The People's Banner* if he cannot induce Lady Laura to return to her husband. Three times in this interview, Phineas calls the letter a libel and assures Slide "of course there would be a prosecution. Both Lord Brentford [Laura's father] and I would be driven to that" (*PR* I.201), but Slide remains assured that "Mr. Kennedy would hold us harmless." Slide's comment suggests that he has thought through the legal implications of printing the letter: Kennedy would not prosecute for a libel against his wife and she of course could not sue him.[31] Yet his condition is designed to fail so that whether Finn attempts to reconcile the couple or not, the piece will be printed. What's to be gained by provoking Finn? Personal revenge, certainly, but also increased circulation for *The People's Banner*. Asked the very question, Slide claims moral rectitude:

> We shall be able to say that we've done our best to promote domestic virtue and secure forgiveness for an erring wife. You've no notion, Finn, in your mind of what will soon be the hextent of the duties, privileges, and hinfluences of the daily press. (I.202)[32]

Plus, "I needn't tell you that such a letter as that would sell a great many copies, Finn" (I.203).

The narrator describes Slide's fantasy of syndication—the letter "would no doubt be copied into every London paper, and into hundreds of provincial papers"—every one of which would have to credit *The People's Banner* (I.235) because Slide, editor and typesetter in one, has addressed it to himself. Looking forward to "some half-dozen leading articles" that could follow, Slide refrains from publishing it the next morning, as threatened, because of what the narrator describes as "some inadequately defined idea that he could do better with the property in his hands by putting himself into personal communication with the persons concerned" (I.235–6). But Slide gets it wrong.

Phineas's efforts to persuade Kennedy end in a shooting, and Phineas, without calling in the police, secures an injunction against the paper that "was of such potency that should any editor dare to publish any paper therein prohibited, that editor and that editor's newspaper would assuredly be crumpled up in a manner very disagreeable, if not altogether destructive" (I.234). Characterizing "the whole transaction" of Kennedy's letter as "the very goods and chattels of the *People's Banner*," Slide considers that "the paper had been shamefully robbed of its property" (I.237).[33] Describing the affront first

---

[31] See S. M. Waddams, who notes that the typical plaintiff was a married woman. However, the common law doctrine of coverture removed the right to sue from married women: the Old Bailey cases discussed above show this principle at work and Lady Laura's return to England is predicated on advice from friends and lawyers alike that her return, coupled with her own action for separation, or her father's action against *The People's Banner*, are needed to answer the accusations (*PR* I.252, I.282).

[32] He specifies: "the morning daily press, that is; for I look on those little evening scraps as just so much paper and ink wasted" (I.202).

[33] Slide's thinking implicitly depends on anticipation of copyright and the money to be gained through publication, but at this point the more relevant category is intellectual property.

in Slide's own idiom—"He had been 'done'—'sold'—absolutely robbed" (I.236)—the narrator then changes tack to observe that

> Newspaper editors sport daily with the names of men of whom they do not hesitate to publish almost the severest words that can be uttered;—but let an editor be himself attacked, even without his name, and he thinks that the thunderbolts of heaven should fall upon his offender. (I.236)

The remark is at once a comment on professional hypocrisy and on the power of the press to inflict harm. More importantly, it creates an opportunity for Trollope to demonstrate the novel's difference from journalism by complicating what might otherwise be a caricature of Slide and an implicit claim of the novel's superiority. We should ask, following Liddle, where Slide sits in relation to the newspaper as a form of discourse or as an economic and legal entity, and further, following Willson, how Trollope's narrator makes his own discursive choices and limitations visible to readers in pursuit of what might be called an ethics of representation.

The chapter in which Slide discovers his betrayal is called "An Editor's Wrath." His prospects frustrated by Finn and "the meshes of the law, which are always infinitely more costly to companies, or things, or institutions, than they are to individuals" (I.237)—the opposite of Leslie Stephen's view of the balance of power—Slide's wrath grows when he is scooped by another paper's coverage of the shooting. The incident of the shooting of course plays a critical role in Phineas's trial for murder, but so does Slide's disappointment and his ensuing search for a legal way to use the paper as a "thunderbolt" against Finn. (In fact, Slide's effort to "gain preferment" by withholding the letter already puts him on the wrong side of the statute [ss. 4–5].) As noted, Slide thinks of the letter as a property, hence one he can manipulate and one which stands to promote *his* profits and professional status, but he also views it as an occasion for promoting "the interest of the People"; "he and his newspaper formed together a simply beneficent institution, any interference with which must of necessity be an injury to the public" (I.238). Here, the narrator interrupts the narrative proper to call attention, first, to Slide's conception of the press's role in securing the public good, thereby implicitly invoking a key

---

See Warren and Brandeis on "ownership" of personal letters in "The Right to Privacy." Kennedy has warrantied Slide's publication, in this sense apparently ceding ownership, but what neither has a property in is Lady Laura's, or certainly Phineas Finn's, private character. By itself the exchange of the letter between third parties is a libel; broadcast in the national press, the "public" becomes the third party and the question is whether Slide's publication is motivated by that public's interest or by his own malice. Trollope's narrator shows that Slide doesn't see or ignores the difference.

justification or defense in the law of libel, and, second, to Slide's conception of what it means to be an editor. "It must be acknowledged on behalf of this editor," the narrator notes, that Slide genuinely believes his construction of events:

> The whole practice of his life had taught him to be confident that the editor of a newspaper must be the best possible judge—indeed the only possible good judge—whether any statement or story should or should not be published. Not altogether without a conscience, and intensely conscious of such conscience as did constrain him, Mr. Quintus Slide imagined that no law of libel, no injunction from any Vice-Chancellor, no outward power or pressure whatever was needed to keep his energies within their proper limit (I. 238)

These comments reveal facets of Slide's character, for example the exaggerated sense of conscientiousness that causes him to "imagine" that editors in general, and himself in particular, can and ought to be self-regulating, that they know best what a "proper limit" is and can abide within it. They also reveal the narrator's sense of obligation to be fair or at least comprehensive in his depiction and thereby to uphold an ethics of representation that implicitly asks readers to compare the newspaper editor with the narrator/author of the novel they're reading.[34] Opening with a maxim, "it must be acknowledged," the narrator refers to an authority, whether belonging to the genre or to his own conscience, which requires that he speak "on behalf of this editor" the description of whose actions up to this point have spoken against him. However, the ambivalence of the passage amounts to a weak defense. In one sense, the narrator speaks in depersonalized terms that emphasize Slide's professional role and membership in the class "editors," but the emphasis on "this" editor clarifies that Slide's example does not necessarily represent the profession. It is not the practice of editors generally, that is, but "the whole practice of his [Slide's] life" that leads him to pit his judgment against that of the Vice-Chancellor. By acknowledging that Slide possesses a conscience, the narrator personalizes the figure of the editor and gestures towards the decision-making and judgment entailed by the job. However, the dubious reference to "such conscience as did constrain him" contrasts with Slide's own outsized notion of rectitude. The vagary of this reference may illustrate the narrator's limited knowledge and suggest that his reading of Slide is more intuitive than empirical until one recalls that we have met Slide before.

---

[34] Andrew Willson describes the comparative move Trollope makes in *The Warden* as an effort to expose the mediated nature of both fiction and journalistic writing with a view towards cultivating more critical reading practices.

Not only has he tried blackmail, he also left the earlier novel vowing to punish in print. Rather, whether the narrator knows the actual scope of the constraint is less important than his conviction that it is smaller than Slide himself "imagines."

Mindful of the obligation to speak on Slide's behalf, however, the narrator retreats from more explicit criticism. If Slide suffers from a degree of false consciousness, the narrator rationalizes, "it is not only in Mr. Slide's path of life that the bias of a man's mind may lead him to find that virtue and profit are compatible" (I.238). The passage is notable on two counts. First, this extenuation doesn't so much relieve Slide of the narrator's disappointed cynicism as cause others to share in it, and not just others who find ways to justify their profits, but also that public whom, as Andrew Willson observed, Trollope sought to make more critical readers through the fiction. Second, direct, third-person narratorial statements such as this one merge into almost parodic extensions of the line of thought they introduce, a merger that complicates the narrative tone and consequently the ethics of representation. Can the Trollope narrator speak convincingly on Slide's behalf, or is this obligation only grudgingly fulfilled? Can he represent a line of thinking without turning it into a joke or, more insidious, without succumbing to its logic?

As a case in point, the narrator begins by commenting on what "Mr. Slide" and others like him think through the form of a declarative statement and the formal *politesse* of a title, both of which distance himself from that line of thought. As a further mode of distancing, the representation of this logic is punctuated by rhetorical questions: "What are the sufferings of the few to the advantage of the many?"; "And how can such circulation be effected unless the taste of the public be consulted?" (I.238). Although they appear to characterize Slide's way of thinking, these questions can also create doubt, however, about who has convinced whom, about whether the Trollope narrator has been caught up in the argument he set out merely to describe. Put differently, the slippery rhetoric of the open question and the circular argument represents the kind of double thinking or false consciousness that otherwise characterizes Slide and offers a grammatical way of distinguishing these ideas from the narrator's declarative statement. Yet it can be hard to discern the point at which the narrator shifts from ventriloquizing to commenting on Slide's views or, as Matthew Rubery puts it, how Trollope "translates" [a character's] sentiments into authorial discourse by way of the narrator's voice" (95). This shading of one view into another is more especially tricky to demarcate when the concluding sentiment is a view the narrator is more likely to hold insofar as it aligns, here, with the perfunctory tone of his opening defense, "it must be acknowledged." For example, according to Slide's logic, "profitable circulation" allows the press to benefit the public, but to secure that circulation it must also measure public "taste." Following arguments made in "The Press," as well as Slide's proprietary attitude, Trollope recalibrates the editor's meaning of public interest, defining it as appetite instead of the "benefit" named in the statute.[35] Since this viewpoint is supported by other critical, apparently more spontaneous comments about Slide—ones not prefaced by the maxim "it must be acknowledged,"—we can take the critical comments to belong to the narrator, and the open-ended questions to be further evidence of Slide's thought processes.

When Phineas fails to gain office in the new government, he blames the professional setback as much on bad press as the rancor of a rival MP:

> Mr. Quintus Slide, with his *People's Banner*, and the story of that wretched affair in Judd Street, had been as strong against him probably as Mr. Bonteen's word . . . A wretched charge had been made against him which, though wholly untrue, was as it were so strangely connected with the truth, that slanderers might not improbably be able almost to substantiate their calumnies. (I.329)

Loaded with equivocal language and double negatives ("probably," "as it were," "might not improbably," "almost"), the passage voices Phineas's (and the narrator's) intuitive understanding of the slippery interaction between Slide's printed innuendo, Westminster gossip, Phineas's general reputation, and "the truth," such that the article might become evidence of the prior existence of facts which *The People's Banner* was actually instrumental in producing *as* fact in the first place. In this model of circulation, print generates talk, but talk also catches the ears of reporters and editors (II.100), as it does to striking effect after Phineas is arrested on suspicion of murdering Bonteen. The story of the shooting

> had been talked about, and had come to the knowledge of reporters and editors. Most of the newspapers had contained paragraphs giving various accounts of the matter [the shooting]; and one or two had followed the example of *The People's Banner* in demanding that the police should investigate the matter. (II.106)

Although no investigation follows, mention of this earlier report appears in the same chapter in which characters form camps regarding Phineas's innocence and in which Phineas is held over for trial. Here, reports on Phineas's

---

[35] See Trollope's acknowledgment of the circular relationship between press and public [opinion] in his chapter "The Press" in *The New Zealander*.

plight recall the earlier incident thus highlighting, as above, Slide's skillful use of his paper to indict Finn without opening himself to libel charges:

> The *People's Banner*, though it prefaced each one of its daily paragraphs on the subject with a statement as to the manifest duty of an influential newspaper to abstain from the expression of any opinion on such a subject till the question had been decided by a jury, nevertheless from day to day recapitulated the evidence against the Member for Tankerville, and showed how strong were the motives which had existed for such a deed. (II.107)

Trollope takes every opportunity to showcase how the newspaper might exercise its privilege, here to report on judicial proceedings as it had done on parliamentary affairs, ostensibly in the public interest but to show also how Slide uses public interest as a ploy for persecuting Finn.

When the trial comes on, the narrator addresses readers directly about the tedium of attending a trial in person, especially in no greater figure than "one of the British public," and concludes that "it may be better for you, perhaps, to stay at home and read the record of the affair as given in the next day's *Times*" where "impartial reporters" and "able editors" will have "preserve[d] for you all the kernel" of the proceeding (II.186–7). Among these reporter-editors is Slide, whom the narrator notes has himself been a court reporter and who, more ominously, comes to court in the full conviction of Phineas's guilt. Not only does Slide find it natural that "a man who had openly quarreled with the Editor of *The People's Banner* should come to the gallows" (II.187), he also "gave himself considerable credit for having assisted in running down the criminal." The equivocal "may" and "perhaps" of the narrator's initial suggestion that readers might be better served by reading reports in *The Times* is unequivocally negated by this image of Slide. Here, Phineas's crime is not the murder but his quarrel with an editor who uses the paper as an engine of revenge, topping the "quasi-judicial" function James Fitzjames Stephen saw being accorded to the press with an outright punitive capacity to try and condemn ("The Law of Libel" 36).

Having adopted such a stance, Slide's reaction to the turn events actually take, in spite of his best efforts, requires another flip-flop. Although the editor's second maneuver is less agile than his first (II.284–6), it does provide a more clear-cut comparison of the editor–narrator functions. Unlike the narrator's grudging defense of Slide in the novel's first volume, here in the second, the narrator remains in the declarative mode: no rhetorical questions and no subjunctives disarm the reader or prevent her from seeing the distinction between him and Slide. Rather, the narrator reminds readers of the editor's habitual animus towards Phineas and names the specific, indeed, generic conventions of a Slide diatribe. In "various short articles," Slide has first announced a journalistic principle, pointed at unscrupulous competitors who fail to abide by it, and then had himself "contrived to insinuate" or "been very careful to recapitulate" details tending towards Phineas's conviction (II.285), in short, sailing very close to the wind of libel. The narrative pattern of these articles is disrupted, however, by the three-fold successes of Slide's "enemy of enemies" (II.284): the telegram, the acquittal, and the re-election. Stunned into silence by the first, by the end Slide abandons, or loses, the acumen that characterized his reporting on the trial. As the most obvious mode of distancing himself from the editor, the narrator imports one section from "among a few other remarks which Mr. Slide *threw together*" (II.285, emphasis mine), their implied disunity and hasty construction a sign of Slide's inner strife.

The chapter concludes with three paragraphs' worth of these remarks in which Slide is left to defend himself and justify his past reportage, typically by recapitulating arguments made against Phineas, reasserting his own past motives (or revising them without any apparent sense of contradiction), and redeploying old arguments to suit the new circumstance. More significantly, the paragraphs also betray the degree to which Slide's guiding principles have been unsettled. The *indirect discourse* revealed Slide's sense of the effrontery of "crowning him [Phineas] with a political chaplet because he had not murdered Mr. Bonteen" (II.285). The *quoted paragraphs* shade into bafflement. "We cannot understand," he writes, "why the late member should be thought by the electors of Tankerville to be especially worthy of their confidence because he did not murder Mr. Bonteen" (II.285). What's noteworthy is that while the offset, quoted paragraphs physically distinguish Slide's remarks from the narrator's, their repetition of comments just offered by the narrator as characterizing his way of thinking confirm the difference between their points of view. The implication is that the narrator's statements are substantially grounded in what he has already observed. Put differently, views which at first are presented as being omniscient, or which the reader encounters as coming from an omniscient narrator, are made into interpretations once the empirical source—Slide's newspaper text—is appended and re-mediated in the novel's narrative.

What do these differences between the editor and the narrator have to do with libel? Part of what Trollope seems to be doing as he examines the different discursive functions of journalism and the novel is to explore the components of ethical representation, particularly representation of character, alongside the habits of mind that working in a given mode fosters. Slide is not likeable, and *The People's Banner* is not *The Times*, but the editor knows his trade. One needn't answer whether temperament and aptitude enable him to write stinging leaders, or whether writing in that mode develops such a temperament, so much as acknowledge their coincidence, as Trollope does in the essay "On Anonymous Literature" (1865) where his discussion of the difference between political journalism in newspapers and other kinds of periodical literature not only entails thinking about the effects that publishing conventions have on the writerly frame of mind, but also goes directly to the question of ethical representation.

In the (signed) essay, Trollope argued that anonymity was permissible, indeed necessary, to political journalism of the sort conducted in newspapers because the genre was meant to "instruct and inform" along ideological lines. Its views ought not to be reducible to individual perspectives, as they would be if signed by the author, he argued, but presented "as an expression of concrete wisdom from a condensed mass of political information and experience" (493). "Anyone can understand that a leading article in the *Times* must be written as part of a combined whole," he continued; "It must support certain views to which the *Times* is committed. It must be subject to, and compatible with, the prevailing spirit of the *Times*" (496). However, familiarity with the long-standing convention of one genre can make for lazy readers, not just because they resign their powers of critical thinking or fail to vary their reading (the argument of "The Press"), but because a kind of genre-confusion can lead to misplaced expectations, or even to editors who "break through their own rules" (494). In contrast to political journalism, he maintained that "stand alone" literature, especially criticism, ought to carry the author's name, "for the sake of the public," so that readers "may know how to hold a balance between the critic and the criticised" (497).

This last observation is especially important for understanding Trollope's depiction of Slide and more particularly its resonance with the libel debates. As discussed in the previous section, O'Loghlen's bill foundered on the question of whom to make responsible for libelous matter: the paper that reported it, or the speaker who first uttered it. Opponents to the bill feared that an aggrieved person would be unable to find a defendant if proprietors were relieved of responsibility or indeed, as Acton Ayrton suggested, that grievances might only arise *because* words had been taken out of context by reporters unexpected to give a "dramatic account" (Libel Bill, Bill 215, Third Reading, c. 1054). Trollope was equally concerned with public utility but argued that it was differently served by different genres or types of publications, the authority of which depended quite literally on whether their author was named or anonymous, an individual or an institution.

The part of his argument more salient for the libel discussion is the way anonymity mediates the relationship between authority and responsibility. Trollope's sense that public utility is best served when writers take responsibility for their *individual* views confers an exceptional status on political journalism. Of course, newspapers have names, as do proprietors, and I am not suggesting that Trollope freed political journalism from responsibility; he simply doesn't talk about libel per se in the essay. However, Slide's ethical shortcomings become more precise when viewed against Trollope's ideas about the authorial voice of persons versus publications. *The People's Banner* is essentially a one-man show masquerading as "the combined efforts of various minds" ("On Anonymous Literature" 491). With the exception of "old Rusty" whose departure allows Slide to become editor (*PF* 337), printers, typesetters, assistant editors, reporters, and staff writers all disappear behind Slide who could "edit *his* paper . . . and write telling leading articles himself" (*PR* I.195). What Trollope's portrait reveals is not the shared voice of a recognizable political point of view, in other words, but the personally motivated expression of individual malice.

In this sense, Slide as editor doesn't so much "break through" his own rules as traduce professional ethics altogether. In the novel's final chapter, the narrator describes Slide's persistent attacks on Phineas which, by dredging up Lady Laura's name, lead to her brother's libel action. "The paper had to pay damages and costs," and, the narrator adds in a rare reference to others concerned with *The People's Banner*, "the proprietors resolved that Mr. Quintus Slide was too energetic for their purposes" (II.359). Left to work as staff writer for another paper, he contemplates "seeking his fortune in New York" where, as had been noted disparagingly in the legislative debate, the laxity of libel law allowed the press to operate with far fewer restrictions and less responsibility.[36]

This "poetic justice" would seem to mark the end of Slide's career in London as well as the narrator's need for a foil to his own discursive methods. What then has the use of this foil achieved? Of course, Trollope's portrait of Slide has been fundamentally critical, sometimes satiric, but also not unrelenting. My point has not been that readers should think better of Slide, or that Trollope, in developing his character, has made him out to be worse than he is, or that there's any confusion about the quality of Slide's character. On the contrary, the narrator's expressed obligation to try what a more rounded version of Slide might look like demonstrates a sense of narrative ethics which, however grudgingly or tenuously applied, is still greater than Slide's own. Even allowing that Slide's narratives are limited by genre conventions or that the work of perfecting those forms has called out specific traits

---

[36] Ian Loveland notes that while Cockburn's focus on "public interest and political accountability," as evidenced in *Wason*, marked a high point from which English law declined over the course of the nineteenth century, U.S. jurisdictions embraced the ethos (36). The Palliser novels, as political novels, are most concerned with political journalism (the purview of the newspaper) and hence with political libel.

of their author (in effect training Slide to think like and believe his own narratives), Trollope's elevation of character development to the principal object of the novel points towards that genre's greater capacities as a forum where one character's self-concept can be illuminated alongside other characters' and the narrator's external views.[37]

The more complicated point has been to trace *how* (and how well) Trollope distinguishes the narrator's work from the editor's and/or what the novelist may learn from the editor he satirizes. Has he been less susceptible to the formal conventions of his genre than he's shown Slide to be to his? Trollope's chosen ending is neat to the point of being predictable, a retrenchment from the exploration of character pursued in the body of the narrative, but then this is what the novel's convention requires. Forced to conclude, the narrator retreats from the difficulty (the danger, even) of fully realizing a character's logic. Slide's comeuppance at the end of *Phineas Redux* also recalls the objectives of Lord Campbell's Libel Act to secure liberty of the press but also to prevent abuses in its exercise, especially regarding abuses of private character. That Slide meets with legal as well as poetic justice shows how the law and the novel can sometimes align, that in the shifting relationship of the press, the law, and the novel, Trollope uses the legal decision to ratify a character judgment his narrator has already reached.

The artificiality of this ending, and of endings generally, is made plainer two years later in *The Prime Minister* (1876) when Slide returns as editor of *The People's Banner* and continues to serve public interest by exposing corruption in Palliser's government and bringing down Phineas Finn and the Prime Minister together. "Phineas Has a Book to Read" depicts Slide's efforts, not merely to threaten Phineas with publication as in the earlier novel, but actually to publish an article that will goad him into bringing an action for libel. Indeed, throughout this chapter and elsewhere, allusions to events in the previous novels confirm that Slide is a known quantity, but Trollope ignores the tidy conclusion of *Phineas Redux*.[38] Not only is Slide once again editor of *The People's Banner*, but when Lord Chiltern urges Phineas to bring the action,

---

[37] See Rubery on Slide's, or journalism's, "suppression" of multiple points of view as compared with the novel's (106). This argument parallels those made about the (generally critical) difference between law and the novel, where "law" replaces "the press" as a discourse which, notwithstanding the adversarial system's necessarily conflicting views, reduces speech to law's language.

[38] Unembarrassed by inconsistencies in plot because of devotion to character (*An Autobiography* 150), Trollope's theory of characterization requires that characters develop over multiple novels, yet he doesn't expect readers to remember details from one novel to the next as well as he does. One novel "will be forgotten even by the most zealous reader almost as soon as read" (228) and in this sense, readers lose out on or can't enjoy the full complexity of

he is allowed to forget that he himself has already *won* an action against Slide specifically for libels against his sister. (At the same time, favorite metaphors carry over from one novel to the next as when Phineas warns Chiltern to "leave a chimney-sweep alone . . . Should he run against you, it is one of the necessary penalties of clean linen that it is apt to be soiled" [*PM* 535]. From the beginning, Slide the sweep has been "not remarkable for clean linen" [*PF* I.242].) As before, Slide's motive is to grow the paper's circulation. In a passage already replete with "ifs" and subjunctives, the narrator speculates that Slide "must have been very well aware" of the likelihood of legal action (533); he "no doubt calculated" that attacking men of high status would rally public support. Declaring "there is no better trade than that of martyrdom," the narrator concludes "All this Mr. Quintus Slide was supposed to have considered very well" (534). "Was supposed" by whom? Although the narrator resorts to the same speculative mood that characterized earlier presentations of Slide's thinking, he abandons any attempts at amelioration. Slide is a known opportunist who has been resurrected specifically to hound more morally complex characters who, as Rubery points out, can be distinguished from villains like Slide by their conscientious consideration of opposing points of view (95).

By contrast to the abruptness of *Phineas Redux*'s conclusion, Slide's departure from *The Prime Minister* is more gradual. His presence *in propria persona* dwindles to a few references to the title of the paper—*The People's Banner* claims the Duke's resignation would be his best service yet (612)—or to "the editor." The last mention of either comes in "The New Ministry" where

> The triumph of the *People's Banner*, as to the omission of the Duke, was of course complete. The editor had no hesitation in declaring that he, by his own sagacity and persistency, had made certain the exclusion of that very unfit and very pressing candidate for office. (671)

However, for a character whose predations have been integral to the personal and political life of the eponymous prime minister, this diminution of narrative attention amounts to a loss of circulation.[39] Slide will not be martyred, as he had hoped, and *The People's Banner* will gain no ads to boost its stature.

Palliser's changing character (229). Slide returns and grows worse so that Palliser can grow better; the fact that Slide had been fired is secondary to this need.

[39] See Mark Turner's chapter "The Editor as Predator in *Saint Pauls Magazine*" in *Trollope and the Magazines: Gendered Issues in Mid-Victorian Britain* (183–226). Turner's reading of "An Editor's Tales" as "eroticized stories about editors and contributors" (201) is also suggestive for Slide's resentful attitude towards Phineas. Phineas is an enemy because he rejects Slide's offer to "contribute."

Slide's political libels are pushed aside because of his mercenary and vengeful motives, but the idea that the press might provoke warranted *crises de conscience*, even where public interest is more narrowly defined, is a central feature of *Cousin Henry* (1879). Like Slide, Gregory Evans uses the *Carmarthen Herald* to precipitate a libel action, but gauging the narrator's criticism of the press depends on understanding his attitude to the characters who gain and lose by it, as well as the editor's motives. Considering that *Cousin Henry* was serialized in *The Manchester Weekly Times* and *The Glasgow Weekly* (Law 52), the publishing venue may also have influenced Trollope's more sympathetic portrayal of powerful provincial papers by contrast to Slide's metropolitan and less reputable title. In *Cousin Henry*, the last of the novels I discuss, the *Carmarthen Herald* publishes a series of "minute accounts" of wrongdoing concerning the will of Indefer Jones. The leader opines that "Circumstances will from time to time occur in which it becomes necessary on public grounds to inquire into the privacy of individuals" (143), and the disinheritance of a much loved local figure for a Londoner of suspect morality is offered as such a case. In this passage, public welfare is weighed against individual privacy, a notion of decorum that sounds very much like nascent privacy rights (discussed in the next chapter). However, this explicit justification for publishing is really calculated to draw Henry out of his silence about the last weeks of the old Squire's life. If Henry would seek "legal redress" from the paper, then he might be "made to confess" under skillful cross-examination (143); once in the court, the law might work *against* him.

The problem for Henry here, as it is for Mrs. Mason in the earlier *Orley Farm* (1862), is that he is guilty of at least some of what he's been accused of, and he *is* afraid to face the court. As Matthew Rubery explains, the leading article by definition was "a mode of discourse whose very purpose might be characterized as provocation . . . through defamatory insult" (106). Yet the family lawyer tells Henry that while he must bring an action for libel, it should not be "with the view of punishing the papers" (*CH* 156). Rather, he must accept the editor's "challenge," show himself willing to appear in court, and answer the public's questions (read: charges) (160). In the build-up to the coming assizes, when the *Herald*'s editor Gregory Evans will be indicted for defamation of character (219), Henry quails at the prospect of facing Mr. Cheeky and undergoing the notoriously intimidating tactics of an Old Bailey practitioner. The dramatic discovery of the hidden will and the avoidance of trial hardly improves his frame of mind, however. Although the lawyer is able to prevent the trial through Henry's acknowledgment that he is not the true heir, the costs of the trial remain as, indeed, does the question of libel. As the editor remarks, "the libel, if a libel, would be just as much a libel whether Mr. Henry Jones were or were not the owner of Llanfeare" (259). And, we might add, the paper's campaign has so effectively roused the public that they continue to believe not only in Henry's guilt, but also that "to kill him and to sell his carcase for what it might fetch towards lessening the expenses would not be too bad for him" (260).

It has been said that in a novel whose focus is so fully trained on the exploration of character, interest in the inheritance plot or its critique of lawyers and trial practice is warranted only by their capacity to heighten Henry's internal debates.[40] On this logic, one could argue that the libel plot is equally contrived to assist the novel's development of character, to which my answer is, yes, because libel law is a law *about* character. I have suggested that Trollope's treatment of Evans and the *Carmarthen Herald* offers a foil to the better known portrayal of the resentful Slide, and indeed just as the status of the *Carmarthen Herald*—that "bore a high character throughout South Wales" (142)—contrasts *The People's Banner*, Trollope reuses multiple motifs from *The Prime Minister* to create, in Henry Jones, Plantagenet Palliser's bathetic double. As with the political libels, newspaper libel functions as the *bête noire* Henry Jones cannot resist:

> It was said of him that the *Carmarthen Herald* was the only paper that he saw, and declared of him that he spent hour after hour in spelling the terrible accusations which, if not absolutely made against him, were insinuated. (144)

Lest readers doubt the gossip, Trollope leaves another clue when, on the night Henry resolves to burn the hidden will, he places his candle "on an outspread newspaper" to leave no trace of the ash (232). In their focus on these acts of reading, both *The Prime Minister* and *Cousin Henry* examine the destabilizing experience of encountering depictions of oneself in the press, whether the libels are true or not. Indeed the point of both novels is to bring characters to re-examine their actions, their consciences, and their own sense of self in the light thrown by these external views.

In spite of these and other important similarities, however, my point is not that we get another *Prime Minister*. In fact, Trollope's disappointment in that novel's reception, noted in an 1878 addendum to the *Autobiography* (228), suggests either that he might not want to try the experiment again or that he would need to alter the approach significantly. In *Cousin Henry* the entire world of the novel, from its setting to its timeframe, is condensed, and this constriction, marked most clearly by Henry's friendless seclusion in the book-room, intensifies the portrait's inward turn, while simultaneously

---

[40] See Julian Thompson's introduction to the Oxford World Classics edition (viii).

heightening the futility of Henry's attempt to separate his private moral cogitations and sense of self from an outside world mediated by the press and the lawyers.[41] (Phineas comes closer to Henry's experience during his imprisonment in *Phineas Redux*, but of course he does have friends working on his behalf, whereas Henry has none.) Perhaps in exchange for the wider world of politics and London life in which libel jostled with other plots, Trollope gives readers a more explicit, not to say thorough, description of how libel might work. In this sense newspaper libel is both a theme and a mode, a device for defending one's character but also, as the lawyer ApJohn knows, for achieving the ultimate object of showing that Henry cannot. Three examples of the novel's treatment of the press, the law, and their combined effect illustrate this dynamic.

In the chapter "An Action for Libel" (immediately following "The *Carmarthen Herald*"), the lawyer Mr. ApJohn tells Henry, "you must go and be a witness about yourself" in order to counter the paper's accusations (144). Not only does Trollope include the text of the paper, as he had done in earlier novels, but he also creates an auxiliary narrator in ApJohn who reads its list of questions aloud before Henry, "in a low, plain voice, slowly, but with clear accentuation, so that every point intended by the questioner might be understood" (158). This "questioner" is the lawyer himself, who by repeating the text of articles, which are themselves "only an echo of the public voice" (157), creates a buffer between those views and the novel's narrator that allows the latter to focus on Henry's reaction. Two of the eight questions, which "the editor was supposed to ask the public generally" (157), make their intent explicit: "Has Mr. Henry Jones any idea why we persecute him in every fresh issue of our newspaper?"; "Has Mr. Henry Jones any thought of prosecuting us for libel?" (158). Nevertheless, it takes the lawyer to move Henry from paralysis ("What am I to do?") to action or else risk a tacit admission of guilt and submit to public censure.

Although the chapter title refers to a civil action for libel, ApJohn has always wanted to pursue a criminal indictment, and Trollope devotes a lengthy paragraph to the relative merits of each proceeding (187–8). ApJohn's stated rationale is that because a criminal indictment carries no damages, it would signal that Henry "simply wished to vindicate his own character" (187). It's not clear why ApJohn tells Henry he would be unlikely to win damages in a civil case, but he uses the specter of then having to pay costs to dissuade him from that route. The ulterior motive Trollope outlines is that the criminal

---

[41] Robert Tracy groups *Cousin Henry* among what he calls Trollope's later "novels of obsession" whose focus on characters in isolation contrasts his "panoramic novels" (69–70).

prosecution would "bind" "the poor victim" (of the libel and of his lawyer) to appear in court, if necessary by police action (188). ApJohn's success earns him the community's approval, including the editor's, who has become "quite the leading man of the hour" (191) and "something of a hero" (195) and the sales of whose paper have skyrocketed. These two leading figures in the campaign against Henry meet in the chapter "Mr. Cheeky" in which they carry on an unorthodox conversation about the probability of Henry's guilt and the likelihood of the verdict. The narrator has already mentioned that the two, although on opposing sides of the legal argument, "were not hostile to each other in the matter" (189). Although ApJohn insists he will see Evans guilty of libel if Henry can show himself innocent of tampering with the will, they have both used the press to foment legal action in what amounts to their de facto collusion.

The final chapters of the novel have less to do with libel than with what might be called the cognate issue of privacy. Henry's awareness that all of Llanfeare believes him to be guilty—and his sense that he cannot adequately answer their charges—drives him into isolation. Secluded in his book-room where the will is concealed in a volume of sermons, he studies a tell-tale spot on the book's binding (107) and compulsively watches its "hiding place" (212). The book becomes the objective correlative of his own inner turmoil, and the book-room, not unlike Dr. Jekyll's cabinet or Dorian Gray's attic nursery, the space in which Henry studies his own transformation from an obscure London clerk to a hated usurper and would-be felon. More than the newspaper, however, it is the lawyer whose hounding finally precipitates Henry's collapse. In spite of his own procedural understanding that "a man's house is his castle, let the suspicion against him be what it may" and that it cannot be invaded without legal warrant (213), invade it—*and* find the will *and* physically assault Henry in order to secure it—is just what the lawyer does. As to the libel prosecution, the lawyer assures Henry it must go on unless he is prepared to admit the "libels" were true: a serious and costly admission, he says, "but perhaps that won't signify, seeing what your position as to character will be" (252). However, Henry cares little for his local reputation now:

> He was again a London clerk, with a small sum of money besides his clerkship and the security of lowliness into which to fall back! If only they would be silent;—if only it might be thought by his fellow-clerks in London that the will had been found by them without any knowledge on his part,—then he would be satisfied. (255)

"They" refers to the lawyers' silence, and it is hard to know whether the centripetal force of a provincial paper like the *Carmarthen Herald* would carry the news of Henry's fate to London. More striking, though, is the idea that Henry's private character may be better protected by the "security of lowliness" than by the limits of the press, in other words, that his social obscurity would preclude any interest readers, and hence newspapers, might take in violating his privacy.

From Libel to Privacy: Alternative Protections and the Libel Law Amendment Act (1888)

Why might Trollope take this turn, or make these kinds of changes to his earlier treatment of character and of libel? In Henry we have the private affairs of a private person whom Lord Campbell's Act dictated had to be protected. Even allowing that a country estate might be something more than one man's castle (given its role in the local economy), the private libels against him are just the sort that most newspapermen interviewed in the 1843 Select Committee said fell outside their ambit. Nevertheless, throughout Trollope's career, libel legislation and select legal judgments had been strengthening the press and complicating the distinction between public and private character. "Public" figure was coming to mean, not just the holder of public office whom Cockburn contemplated in his decision in *Wason*, but anyone who made a figure in public or in whom the public might take an interest, where "interest" was as likely to mean appetite or curiosity as benefit.

The case of the *Town Talk* libels illustrates this point and is especially noteworthy because it coincides with John Hutchinson's (MP for Halifax) formation of a new Select Committee on the Law of Libel, which published its report in August 1879.[42] The new committee was charged to inquire into the best way to prove the publication of libels as well as to the relative merits of civil and criminal proceedings as means of holding proprietors and publishers responsible. As before, representatives of metropolitan and provincial papers, solicitors, and other experts gave evidence. Asked whether he thought that holding a proprietor (as opposed to an editor or reporter) liable to criminal proceedings, Albert Kaye Rollit, speaking for the Provincial Newspaper Society, testified that it was a hardship. Even if the proprietor had himself authored the libel, Rollit thought that punishing the purse, not the person, would be more effective and speculated that if criminal prosecution for libel were abandoned in favor of civil actions, then juries might be more inclined

---

[42] "Report from the Select Committee on the Law of Libel: together with the proceedings of the committee, minutes of evidence and appendix." The committee submitted an extensive minutes of evidence taken but provided no report per se because it ran out of time. Instead, it recommended reconvening the committee in the next session. See Odgers on *Purcell v Sowler* (1877) which he argues gave rise to the Newspaper Libel Act of 1881 (722).

to award even heavier damages, thus making the protection "more complete" (*Report*, 1879 7).

This protection was nowhere more needful than from the so-called "society papers." Committee Chairman B. B. Hunter Rodwell himself raised the subject with reference to "the lowest of the low class of papers, viz. 'Town Talk'" (7).[43] Although Rollit suggested that reports in such papers were not likely to be credited, the best protection an individual could have would be the award of damages so heavy as to put it out of business. William Flux, solicitor and himself proprietor of a country weekly, feared that even categorizing *Town Talk* as a newspaper jeopardized the status of the English press. "Any foreigner coming to this country would receive the impression that 'Town Talk,' and some other things like it, were the prevailing literature of this country," he conjectured. "It is paraded everywhere, and it is simply disgusting" (61).

On October 20, 1879, Edward Langtry, husband of socialite-turned-actress Lily Langtry, appeared in London's Central Criminal Court to give evidence against Adolphus Rosenberg of *Town Talk* whose paper had circulated several reports about an imminent Langtry divorce (Trial of Adolphus Rosenberg). Langtry testified that he had neither petitioned for divorce from his wife, nor named the Prince of Wales as co-respondent, nor been offered a diplomatic posting. Rosenberg plead guilty to publishing the libels but not to knowing them to be false (i.e. not to having published them maliciously), but he was found guilty and sentenced to eighteen months' imprisonment.

He was also found guilty of publishing libels about another society beauty, Patsy Cornwallis-West, and both trials were covered by a world-wide press. In London, *The Saturday Review* condemned *Town Talk* for going further than any other society paper to satisfy the growing "appetite for personalities," what it called "the worst phase of modern journalism" and an "abuse of the privilege of the press" ("The Town Talk Libels" 527). Conceding that public demand was also to blame, the *Review* predicted that public taste thus piqued would not be satisfied with milder fare and that "the progress of the journal towards the freedom of libel becomes under these circumstances merely a question of time" (528). The *New York Times* picked up the story of both suits in "Libeling the Beauties" and smuggled in the offending article, which characterized Patsy Cornwallis-West as running a photographic cottage industry and, in a series of innuendo-laden metaphors, trading on her good looks. More serious than either article, however, *The Spectator* discussed

---

[43] Flux's observation that society papers "have advertisements and are put before the public as newspapers" seems to suggest that carrying ads is a defining feature of newspapers and not of other periodicals (*Report*, 1879 61).

the limitations of a libel law that could not protect one's "personal dignity" ("Libels on Personal Dignity"). Published two days before Langtry's case was heard, the article speculated that in the Cornwallis-West case in particular, what was harmed was not so much the lady's reputation as her self-respect and, going further, that while such an attack was "brutal," it might not be criminal under existing law.

Of course, *The Spectator* was not to know that Rosenberg would be found guilty of all charges and that the libel law as it stood would protect her private character in this instance. However, its observations that something more than libel law might be needed, or that something more than reputation might require legal recognition, is germane both to Trollope's observations of the destabilizing effects of the media and to the coming interest in privacy protections. Calling *Town Talk*'s treatment of Patsy Cornwallis-West an insult and a moral outrage, if not a crime, *The Spectator* wrote at length:

> It is a brutality perpetrated either to injure or for gain, and serving no public purpose whatever, and ought, therefore, to be suppressed. The law, however, usually fails to avenge insults. The law of libel was prepared in times when penny papers were not, when an over-numerous public had not been turned by rapid communication and a habit of gossip into a larger servants'-hall, and when, to tell the whole truth, more rapid and brutal methods of prevention had not become offensive to the community. It was intended for another condition of manners and another set of circumstances, and it may be questioned whether it does not now seriously fail in securing the privacy which ought to be a social right. (10)

Taxes on knowledge have been repealed. Dueling has been outlawed. A "public" made too big—through mass literacy, through extension of the vote, through the unifying effects of mass transit and mass communication—has reduced conversation to gossip and lowered the general moral tone. *The Spectator* does not conceal its status-inflected nostalgia for different standards of social decorum (or for narrower means of communication and rule by a literate elite, nor yet for severer penalties), but if the present law of libel was a holdover from the past, so too was the model of character it protected. In other words, this model of decorum depends on an understanding of character that itself had undergone cultural change and to which, I want to suggest, the tenor of debates over libel had contributed.

Everywhere in *The Spectator* piece, the failure of current libel law is linked to "dignity" and "privacy," not to character per se, but as stand-ins for the concept, privacy and dignity denote dimensions of character that had been forgotten or supplanted by more mercantile or professional variants that libel law *could* protect. One need only recall that "the better protection of private character" was the first object of Lord Campbell's Act to see how the weight had shifted rhetorically and practically towards protecting liberty of the press in subsequent legislation. I am not suggesting that these changes moved inexorably in one direction, that old libel law was uninterested in a person's trade (it was) or that current discussion ignored the difference between everyday people and those in public life (witnesses before Hutchinson's Select Committee did not). Clearly, old notions of character had not disappeared from public discourse, either. If anything, articles such as that in *The Spectator* stood to revive attention to the old measure of libel as any written statement bound to "expose" its subject to "hatred, ridicule, or contempt," the opposite of dignity.[44]

What I am suggesting is that to the extent that legislative and public discourse around libel focused on relieving the press, and less on other forms of and venues for libel or on the person harmed, it re-routed the discussion of character into other areas of law. As has been shown, English MPs resisted the example of French and American libel law when drafting legislation, but *The Spectator*'s references to Continental jurisprudence called for an even greater culture shift than the ones just described. The strong French attitude towards libel may have grown from French "forms of outrage" (11), but the growth of papers like *Town Talk* that "import" these forms renewed calls to look abroad for ways of combatting them, too, by restoring dignity to character, if not through libel laws, then through privacy.

Cousin Henry punctuates the intrusive potential of newspaper libel through a violation of physical space. In an author I've argued is concerned with the ethics of representation, this shift might be an evasive move that directs attention to the lawyer rather than the editor. But the psycho-social ramifications of Henry's encounter with the press (its ability to follow him into his retreat, into his mind, and perhaps back to his social circle in London) suggest that Trollope's investment in character and method of probing consciousness is more persistent, which raises questions about the coming literary aesthetic.[45] Matthew Rubery suggests that Trollope was ahead of his time because he demonstrated for readers the way their own character formation depended on a triangulated vision of their inner lives—a way of seeing their "reflections" or public selves as a third party might (104). Although his "scenes of newspaper readers" anticipated much of the coming anxiety over mass media (the same anxiety which prompted jurists Samuel Warren and Louis Brandeis to scour English precedent for a principle that would

---

[44] See Mitchell for this standard definition of libel (*Making* 15).
[45] See Sean Latham on twentieth-century libel cases involving the *roman à clef* and the impact on aesthetic standards of the court's effort to delimit fact from fiction.

warrant a right to privacy in their 1890 *Harvard Law Review* article of the same name), it is worth pointing out that this vision need not entail a negative consciousness. The press need not always inspire anxiety or manufacture guilt. Looking ahead to another smear campaign conducted in private letters and newspaper columns, we can recall the 1903 criminal case against the solicitor George Edalji and Arthur Conan Doyle's use of the *Daily Telegraph* to mount his own popular appeal to secure Edalji's pardon. Still, as Trollope observed in *The Way We Live Now* (1875),

> censure is infinitely more attractive than eulogy . . . No man was ever called upon for damages because he had attributed grand motives. It might be well for politics and literature and art—and for truth in general, if it was possible to do so. But a new law of libel must be enacted before such salutary proceedings can take place. (340)

Indeed, there would be two.

The Newspaper Libel and Registration Act (1881) offered what Baron Pollock called "a sort of settlement between the public on the one hand and newspaper proprietor on the other" (qtd. in Odgers 724). But William Blake Odgers, who quoted Pollock in his *Digest of the Law of Libel and Slander* (1881), maintained that although the act had been brought about by agitation in the newspaper world over the decision in *Purcell v Sowler* (1877), discussed by a Select Committee populated by associates of the press, and rushed through Parliament, "the public got the best of the bargain" (724). The act reinstated the rule (repealed in 1870) that the names of newspaper proprietors be registered so that complainants could identify someone to hold responsible for the libel. But this move towards allocating responsibility was offset by the statute's expanded list of privileged communications which papers could cover—including divorce proceedings and libel cases (Latham 81)—as well as its high bar for prosecution: only a Public Prosecutor could allow a criminal prosecution for libel against a newspaperman to begin.[46] Odgers argued that the privilege regarding public meetings remained largely theoretical because it was hemmed in by conditions that undermined the editor's ability to produce the paper at all, for example that he could not assume

---

[46] Great Britain, Newspaper Libel and Registration Act (1881); Great Britain, Law of Libel Amendment Act (1888). On the third reading of the 1881 libel bill [Bill 5], Sir Hardinge Gifford complained that "they were to have the Home Office, the Public Prosecutor, and the Attorney General to exercise a fiat in relation to these [criminal] indictments." In cases of a "semi-political character," he felt this provision would be especially harmful because it would "seriously curtail the liberty of the subject." See Newspapers (Law of Libel) Bill, Bill 5.

that because a meeting was public everything said in it was also in the public's interest to know (725). The decision of *Pankhurst v Sowler* (1886) (again focused on *The Manchester Courier*) denied the paper's privilege unless the jury found "that it was for the public benefit that the actual libel complained of should be published, broadcast and read at every Manchester breakfast table." As Odgers explains, Sowler and other friends in the press approached Sir Algernon Borthwick, Chairman of the Newspaper Press Fund, who introduced the bill that eventually became the 1888 Law of Libel Amendment Act (726, 732). And as Paul Mitchell observes, many of the bill's supporters in the House of Commons owned papers or were formally affiliated with press organizations; even the House of Lords followed recommendations made by the National Association of Journalists ("Nineteenth Century Defamation" 30). In the end, the press got its way.

What remained for the private person? Mitchell describes a judicial approach to abuses of the press that differed from legislative latitude. Development of the so-called "new journalism" of which *Town Talk* was an example, led to stricter rules for publishers and distributors alike ("Nineteenth Century Defamation" 31). In an important sense, the tenets of Lord Campbell's Act "for more effectually securing the liberty of the press" and for "better preventing abuses in exercising said liberty" were being split between two types of journalism, the gap between which was widening. Nevertheless, as *The Spectator* had suggested, the more libel law neglected personal dignity, the more urgent the need for a privacy protection became, hence Warren and Brandeis's emphasis specifically on intrusive society papers. As will be seen in the next chapter, their concept of "inviolate personality" raises interesting questions for the coming modernist aesthetic and its probing of consciousness: might the novel's exploration of character be an invasion of a newly defined right to privacy?

4

Dignity, Disclosure, and the Right to Privacy: The Strange Characters of Dr. Jekyll and Dorian Gray

> All the more intimate and delicate relations of life are of such a nature that to submit them to unsympathetic observation, or to observation which is sympathetic in the wrong way, inflicts great pain, and may inflict lasting moral injury. Privacy may be violated not only by the intrusion of a stranger, but by compelling or persuading a person to direct too much attention to his own feelings and to attach too much importance to their analysis. The common usage of language affords a practical test which is almost perfect upon this subject. Conduct which can be described as indecent is always in one way or another a violation of privacy.
> James Fitzjames Stephen, *Liberty, Equality, Fraternity* (1873)

> The common law has always recognized a man's house as his castle, impregnable, often, even to its own officers engaged in the execution of its commands. Shall the courts thus close the front entrance to constituted authority, and open wide the back door to idle or prurient curiosity?
> Samuel D. Warren and Louis D. Brandeis, "The Right to Privacy" (1890)

When eminent Boston lawyers Samuel D. Warren and Louis D. Brandeis penned their famous treatise "The Right to Privacy" (1890), they were responding, albeit some years later, to precisely the kinds of negative publicity endured by the Edward Langtrys and Cornwallis-Wests, which had prompted *The Spectator* to denounce the rise of "Libels on Personal Dignity." Unlike comments reputable papers might make on public figures for public benefit, the so-called *Town Talk* libels of 1879 (discussed in Chapter 3) concerned society beauties who, while certainly in the public eye, held no official, political, or professional position that might warrant examination of their public doings or, least of all, their personal habits.[1] *The Spectator*'s lament about the harms of printed defamation drew on libel as providing the nearest legal remedy for the excesses of the press. By linking libel to dignity, however, *The Spectator* highlighted a key term in Continental discussions of privacy that could extend the protection of character offered by libel to something more than one's reputation or good name, that is, to one's dignity or self-respect. The upper-crust Warren and Brandeis could commiserate with these social elites, more especially as increasingly sophisticated technologies like recording devices and flash photography had enhanced the press's methods of intrusion into the lives of the rich or famous. However, like *The Spectator* their sense of the injury inflicted by such publications entailed a wrong which was not strictly material and which encompassed all private citizens whose personal dignity was threatened by a style of journalism poised to lower the moral tone of a whole society.

Warren and Brandeis did not rest their right to privacy on the defense of honor alone, however; nor did they confine themselves to harms committed by the press. Although the press remains vital to Warren and Brandeis and others writing about intrusive publicity in the 1890s—when, as David J. Seipp notes, "restraint of the press was among the least developed areas of privacy protection" ("Right to Privacy" 1909)—their route towards a privacy protection depended upon treatments of intellectual and artistic property that established an individual's right to control publication, not merely in the interest of securing profit (as with statutory protections of copyright) but, as James Q. Whitman explains, in the ability "to control our public face" and to circulate "a public image of our own making" (1168). What distinguished these proprietary interests from other forms of property, or this public face from reputation, and thereby weakened the applicability of libel law? As Warren and Brandeis explain, and as will be discussed at greater length, what is really at stake in the protection of "thoughts, sentiments, and emotions expressed through the medium of writing or the arts" is not private property but "the right to one's personality" (205, 207). And unlike "reputation," which they argued concerned the opinions of others and one's relation with them, the protection of personality was tied more closely to a man's "estimate of himself" and his injured feelings (197). Thus, where libel suits were brought because material damage had already been done, privacy, as Warren and Brandeis imagined it, would either pre-empt these invasions or, if not, create a new cause for action (perhaps a new kind of "special damage")

---

[1] See Jessica Lake's discussion of Warren and Brandeis's article within the context of women's efforts to control their image.

in the harm to one's personality and the infringement of a broader right to be let alone.[2]

The plight of Oscar Wilde, perhaps more than any other figure of the 1890s, brings together the concerns of public image and reputation, libel, artistic property, personality, and privacy. From his flamboyant public image as a celebrated author and aesthete to the libel trials that exposed his private life, from his imprisonment for gross indecency to pamphlets advertising the auction of his Tite Street home, the story of Wilde's exposure and downfall is marked by what might be called a failed attempt to control his public face, or a failure of privacy.[3] My concern in this chapter is not with Wilde himself, however, but with two novels that explore the idea of controlling one's image by controlling the disclosure of and access to forms of intellectual and artistic property and, with them, the personality grounding the right to privacy. In *The Picture of Dorian Gray* (1890) and its precursor, Robert Louis Stevenson's *The Strange Case of Dr. Jekyll and Mr. Hyde* (1886), logs, letters, wills, narratives, diaries, portraits—all sorts of "personal writing" and "personal productions" according to Warren and Brandeis's categories—are composed, concealed, sought after, or shared with devastating effect by characters patrolling the limits of what they let out and who they let into their personal information circles.[4] Only through this control could one preserve the physical space and the mental repose Warren and Brandeis found necessary to human flourishing.

However, the nature of the secrets Dr. Jekyll and Dorian embed in these textual and aesthetic forms makes these novels a limit test of the premises on which the lawyers founded their privacy right. Through their depictions of

---

[2] "It is not for injury to the individual's character that redress or prevention is sought, but for injury to the right of privacy. For the former, the law of slander and libel provides perhaps a sufficient safeguard. The latter implies the right not merely to prevent inaccurate portrayal of private life, but to prevent its being depicted at all" (Warren and Brandeis 218). See also Whitman on the "Warren and Brandeis tort" 1208. On special damage, see Waddams 17.

[3] Certainly, Wilde's original libel suit against the Marquis of Queensberry proved to be a miscalculation and was abandoned when it became clear Wilde could not win. See Ellmann; Hyde; and an account of the first trial specifically by Wilde's grandson, Merlin Holland.

[4] See Whitman on the four forms of privacy tort: "intrusion upon seclusion" (space), "appropriation of name or likeness" (image), and "public disclosure of private facts" either without warrantable public benefit or "to portray victims 'in a false light'" (1202). Seipp observes that nineteenth-century English privacy law utilized a "convenient fiction" to extend the protection offered by physical boundaries to personal or confidential communications ("English Judicial Recognition" 337), but "intangible personal information" (341) presented the most challenge. See also Vincent, especially chapter 8 on "Virtual Privacy"; and Welsh, *Blackmail*, in which he notes that blackmail plots "register the translation of reputation into information" (82–3).

the dynamics of disclosure (what gets revealed, to whom, where, and under what circumstances), both novels raise questions about liberal individualism and the nature of nineteenth-century personhood, beginning with the idea of "inviolate personality." Warren and Brandeis define it as the "immunity of the person, the right to one's personality" (207), but as with other forms of immunity or negative right (e.g. "the right *not* to be assaulted or beaten, the right *not* to be imprisoned, the right *not* to be maliciously prosecuted, the right *not* to be defamed" [205]), the connection between the right "to be let alone" and the concept of ownership complicates whose personality may be deemed inviolate and who, therefore, is free to flourish.[5] When, for example, felons and women who married underwent a change in legal personality and simultaneously altered or forfeited their property rights, did they retain a right to privacy? Hard as Warren and Brandeis work to broaden the foundation of privacy by broadening the kind of property it protects, the right remains bound up with quite conventional associations between privacy and the control of real property, or personal and professional space.

Despite what might therefore be considered limitations, these spaces form the backdrop for broader applications of ideas about intellectual and artistic property which Warren and Brandeis maintained was the surer route towards the privacy protection. Behind the closed doors of the laboratory and the nursery, Jekyll concocts his secret compound, and Dorian hides the "diary of [his] life" as written on Basil's painting (Wilde 185). The important question is not does Jekyll have a right in his formula, or even whether a picture *of* Dorian makes it *his* picture or *Basil's* painting or both (although (mis)interpretation of what precisely is represented in the picture matters a great deal). Rather, the important question these novels enable us to ask regards the integrity of the personality that could have such rights, including the ability to set limits on disclosure and thereby to preserve one's dignity.

Depicting characters whose personalities are already violate, in other words, *The Strange Case* and *The Picture of Dorian Gray* invite questions about the immunity of the person, or the right to those particular personalities, without which they have no right to privacy. Like the lawyer ApJohn's search and seizure of the lost will in Trollope's *Cousin Henry*, Utterson's pursuit of Hyde and Basil Hallward's demands of Dorian—all actuated by claims of morality and justice—dramatize violations of physical space in pursuit of personal facts which under normal circumstances would constitute gross

---

[5] A similar question can be put about children, the intellectually or mentally disabled, and enslaved people who never had such immunity. A separate question is whether this immunity can be alienated. Warren and Brandeis have more to say about the commodification of privacy and the limits of copyright. See also Whitman 1176.

violations of personality as well. In one sense the novels justify these intrusions by criminalizing the pursued; for example, Utterson is on safe ground as long as he chases the murderer Hyde, just as Basil can point to Dorian's relationships with young men as grounds to confront him.

In another sense, however, these intrusions disrupt or sever connections within the "complex, multiform creature" Dorian takes for his model of man (Wilde 175) and precipitate both Jekyll's and Dorian's undignified deaths. Looked at as scenes of disarticulation, the separation of Hyde's body from Jekyll's and of Dorian from his picture are left to be interpreted either as murder or as suicide, the ultimate self-violation. These bodies thus become the last of a set of unintelligible texts that the narrative has produced. The fact that both novels end with acts of misreading or an inability to assimilate the revealed knowledge further blocks something that might be called an 'inviolate' ending to the narrative—closure—and that ambiguity at once signals modernist aesthetics and with them the perhaps equally dangerous attractions of prying too closely into other people's private selves but also of letting them alone.

The chapter is organized as follows. The first section discusses the paradoxical connection between reputation and privacy before turning to Warren and Brandeis's concept of "inviolate personality" as the foundation of forms of property and of privacy that together define nineteenth-century conceptions of personhood. Where the writing of Warren and Brandeis's legal text creates an inner life (its logical and rhetorical movement from control of property inwards towards a self-determining center), the second and third sections analyze how Stevenson's and Wilde's novels reverse this direction, assuming an inner life made untenable by violations of private space. The section on Stevenson discusses his novel's emphasis on physical spaces, especially as sites for containing the proliferation of documents, and the involuntary disclosures forced by violations of that space where even access to the facts will not solve the mystery. The section on Wilde picks up on the image of the secret text, but while its disclosure is voluntarily made, the failure to read it correctly—to understand whose it is and what it means—leads to a similar breakdown of personality.

As with Chapter 1's discussion of the right to silence in Nathaniel Hawthorne's and George Eliot's novels, this chapter also crosses the Atlantic (and the Channel, for that matter). However, the documented attention to authorial influence that united those authors in contemporary reviews does not connect Stevenson, Wilde, and Warren and Brandeis, who were near contemporaries but geographically distant. This can raise methodological questions about the basis of comparison on two counts: too temporally near to one another to exert influence but too culturally distant to share context.

David J. Seipp's analysis of the privacy right both in nineteenth-century America and in England up to the late twentieth century shows a long-standing value for privacy in England that nevertheless fell short of being recognized as a right or even a "unified" body of law ("English Judicial Recognition" 370). Hampered on the one hand by judicial reliance on other doctrines (such as those related to private property and defamation) and legislative reluctance to limit freedom of the press, this "interstitial and incomplete protection of acknowledged privacy interests" formed the context for Stevenson and Wilde (345).[6] By contrast, U.S. courts had already found for an individual's right to privacy, so named, in a host of contexts (including private property, confidential communications, and personal information) and yet, as in England, stopped short at curtailing the power of the press (333). However, Warren and Brandeis's article, Seipp argues, provided a necessary "catalyst" for extending existing protections to prevent "publication of truthful information of a personal nature" (326). I have said that our novelists offer a limit test of the premises of Warren and Brandeis's right. It can also be said that viewing these contemporary works side-by-side highlights how Stevenson and Wilde use the gap in English recognition of privacy that neither legislation would fill, nor judicial ruling had filled, to practice what Colm Tóibín refers to as the "art of being found out."[7] That is, they explore the separate privacy protections that Warren and Brandeis were trying to unite and to extend (yet which even they had to supplement with Continental theories) in a process fueled by what Tóibín describes as a "need to make duality seem unstrange."

Looked at this way, both the legal text and the two novels make legible the interiority that will constitute a right and produce a story. At the same time, the novel seems to transgress the very boundaries it sets up: first producing the interiority that needs legal protection by showing its violation (this within the world of the novel as well as in terms of the reader's access to the inner lives of characters), then judging when such incursions into another's private life may be justified, and in the process questioning the model of

---

[6] Indeed, Seipp speculates that one reason English lawyers as late as the 1980s resisted recognizing a privacy right lay in the "uneasy feeling that privacy law in the U.S. [had] run rampant and [had] intruded into older, settled categories of the law" (331). Legislative protection was no more viable because of the "organized power of the newspaper press" that blocked it (327).

[7] In the essay of the same name, Colm Tóibín characterizes the "art of being found out" as a theme not only in literature of the period but in an "English public life" defined by "doubleness, secret selves, and the possibility of discovery." Tóibín focuses on the outsider status of writers like Stevenson, Wilde, Conrad, Ford Maddox Ford, and Henry James and the necessary doubleness of forging successful literary careers in England. In Stevenson's and Wilde's "fantasies" in particular, Tóibín reads a "need to make duality seem unstrange."

inviolate personality. Is this relationship between the making of an inner life and its exposure a necessary paradox? How does this paradox compare with those others of ownership and the alienation of property (i.e. that ownership is most palpable at the moment of relinquishing it), or to the sharing of secrets that, by sharing, are no longer strictly secret? The bureaucratization of law, with its attendant gathering of personal information and recordkeeping, suggests an interest in the "identity" of legal subjects, which at first blush compares unfavorably with the novel's investment in developing and representing the fuller "character" of its characters.[8] The care taken by law to safeguard this information, however, might make us consider whether the novel, especially in the context of psychological realism and the emergence of modernist aesthetics, is not more invasive. In other words, is the legal construction of inviolate personality increasingly violated by the novel so that modernism itself is guilty of an invasion of privacy?[9]

Private Properties: Warren and Brandeis on Personality

The legal question Warren and Brandeis set themselves to answer was whether there were any foundation in existing law to support the protection of the "privacy of the individual" and, assuming such a principle could be found, what the "nature and extent" of that protection might be (197). The modern liberal subject being a propertied one, Warren and Brandeis find the right embedded, not surprisingly, within property rights, but they emphasize an evolution in the idea of property itself with law's "recognition of man's spiritual nature, his feelings and intellect," an acknowledgment of "the legal value of sensations" that allows the term "property" to compass "every form of possession—intangible, as well as tangible" (193).[10]

To find this foundation, Warren and Brandeis turn first to libel and slander because they are the closest kin to the kind of harm experienced by an invasion of privacy. David J. Seipp observes that an invasion of privacy could be challenged by bringing a libel suit, but not only could such a suit be counterproductive (precisely by drawing further attention to the "truth or falsity of a damaging disclosure"), libel doctrine itself had not caught up with the new forms of invasion that most concerned Warren and Brandeis (Seipp, "Right to Privacy" 1908). Even though the pair ultimately rejects defamation because of its strictly material emphasis (that is, on financial damage resulting

---

[8] See Seipp, "Right to Privacy" 1906–7.
[9] For discussion of the protection of personal information, including changes in American census questions, see Seipp, "Right to Privacy" 1904, 1906. For discussion of literary invasions of privacy, see R. Thomas, "Strange Voices" 80.
[10] See also Bezanson 1138, 1142; and Moddlemog 341.

from harm to professional reputation), it's important to note, first, that the development of a privacy tort was meant to extend those protections to other aspects of personhood.[11] Second, nearly all the limits on applying a right to privacy and all the remedies for its infraction remained connected to the law of libel. The upshot is to see privacy and libel as two sides of the protection of character, understood as public reputation and private personality, so that what libel can't protect, privacy might, and what doesn't concern privacy per se might be handled under libel. For example, reputation was outward looking, a form of being in public, a relation with others, and an acknowledged public opinion about oneself with financial and professional ramifications to be protected under the law of libel. By contrast, personality offered a way to think about the individual's contemplation of him- or herself as an inward-looking corollary of reputation that deserved its own form of protection.

Writing about the right to reputation just a few months before Warren and Brandeis, lawyer and founding editor of *The Nation* E. L. Godkin connected the modern invention of privacy with the multiplication of private spaces that conferred on propertied men "the power of drawing, each man for himself, the line between his life as an individual and his life as a citizen" ("Rights of the Citizen" 65).[12] This was no metaphoric line. By contrast to the Continental emphasis on "freedom from determinism," American ideas about liberty, or "freedom from tyranny," drew this line at the front door of the private house (Whitman 1181). Common law respect for the sovereignty of the private dwelling was not exclusively a concern for physical safety (thus bringing together the three tenets of liberty, security, and property) but also, Godkin continues, one of "respect for his personality as an individual, for

---

[11] "[O]ur law recognizes no principle upon which compensation can be granted for mere injury to the feelings. However painful the mental effects upon another of an act . . . yet if the act is otherwise lawful, the suffering inflicted is *damnum absque injuria*" (Warren and Brandeis 197). This view was likely true in theory, according to Seipp, but less so in application:

> In theory, invasion of privacy by the press could be distinguished from defamation; in a civil action for libel, the truth of the matter published was a complete defense, but the sting of an invasion of privacy was precisely that the personal information published was true. In practice, however, courts effectively extended the civil libel remedy to substantially true accounts . . . The damages a successful plaintiff recovered could include compensation for emotional distress as well as for loss of reputation. As long as a newspaper account contained some inaccuracies or omissions, both loss of privacy and loss of reputation could be remedied by a libel suit. ("Right to Privacy" 1907)

[12] For Godkin's subsequent review of Warren and Brandeis's article, see Godkin, "The Right to Privacy."

that kingdom of the mind, that inner world of personal thought and feeling in which every man passes some time"—and the most useful men more than that ("Rights of the Citizen" 65).[13]

Both changes—the broadening constitution of property and individuality alike—give new meaning to the idea of self-possession. Where the absolute possession of property assumed moral agency and afforded legal scope to do what one likes with it, self-possession signaled a similar ability to control oneself, to keep one's wits as well as one's secrets, or to control the flow of personal information that was central to Warren and Brandeis's conception of privacy. However, as William M. Moddlemog explains, while the discourse of privacy thus worked to "fortify the bounds of the self," it also had to check the potentially "radical subjectivism" that could threaten the authority of law by locating privacy in the home or, more specifically, using the home as a metaphor for the "ideal legal subject" (338–9).

This more expansive notion of property and respect for the individual's feelings, for all that it draws from the discourse of domesticity, thus entails a quite conventional reliance on real estate. The modern world too much with them, Warren and Brandeis claim "solitude and privacy" as conditions of wellbeing: "The intensity and complexity of life, attendant upon advancing civilization," they write, "have rendered necessary some retreat from the world, and man, under the refining influence of culture, has become more sensitive to publicity, so that solitude and privacy have become more essential to the individual" (196). The solitude they imagine here, as the epigraph to this chapter also indicates, requires a space, a home—and not just residence in a house, but the control that comes of ownership. But if the legal subject, being propertied, was therefore male, then, according to the logic of separate spheres, it was men of a certain class who most required "solitude and privacy." Godkin had said as much when he argued that the "kingdom of the mind" ("Rights of the Citizen" 65)—again, that notion of sovereignty—must be respected so that personal dignity could be maintained. Speaking of dignity in much the same way Warren and Brandeis would frame inviolate personality, he added that it was the outward sign of those individuals who were most likely to contribute to their societies' "moral and intellectual

---

[13] The second of Whitman's "two cultures of privacy," this understanding of privacy as liberty is an explicitly American one. As such, attempts to remedy invasions of privacy on the Continental grounds of insult or the rights to one's image run afoul of American protections of free speech and the free market (1208). The press cannot be censored, and an individual cannot be prevented from selling even embarrassing images when they are in demand. See also Whitman 1211–19 on the centrality of the home in the American tradition.

growth," hence the state's interest in protecting individuals whose refinement also made them more sensitive to intrusion.

This distinction between those who may or may not invoke a right to privacy will become more significant in my reading of the professional spaces in *Jekyll and Hyde*. To return to the legal value of sensations, however: It is because civilized man is more finely wrought—overwrought, perhaps—that he is more susceptible to "mental pain and distress," which Warren and Brandeis consider more grievous than "mere bodily injury" (196). Although they argue that in cases of defamation, for example, the impact of an injurious publication on one's feelings is irrelevant (the basis of legal action lying exclusively in the material damage to reputation), their concern clearly lies with finding a way to protect those feelings by allowing the disclosure of all sorts of communications ("thoughts, sentiments, and emotions") in all manner of modes ("whether it be by word, or by signs, in painting, sculpture, or in music") to be determined by the individual who originates them (197, 199).

Drawing on intellectual property for this principle, however, creates the conundrum of how to value private communications when "value" can't be determined except by circulation in a market that perforce undermines privacy.[14] The way out is to redefine "value" and "profit." Emphasizing both the distinction between statutory and common law protections of intellectual property, along with the difference between artistic and "domestic" publications (i.e. those whose context is strictly domestic), they argue that value consists of "the peace of mind or the relief afforded by the ability to prevent any publication at all" (200–1).[15] The new problem they perceive, however, is that the analogy must break down; the right which would create this peace of mind cannot be understood as a property right in the conventional sense (where "the quality of being owned or possessed" inheres); rather, it must be an example of the "more general right of the individual to be let alone," recast here as the principle of "inviolate personality" (205).

Brook Thomas traces the origin of this problem in the nineteenth-century shift from status to contract, the flowering of a market economy, and their consequences for the conception of both property and the individual that

---

[14] See B. Thomas 62 for discussion of the relative relationship of private and public, for example the private market as distinct from public government.

[15] "The aim of those statutes [copyright laws] is to secure to the author, composer, or artist the entire profits arising from publication; the common-law protection enables him to control absolutely the act of publication . . . The statutory right is of no value *unless* there is a publication; the common-law right is lost *as soon as* there is a publication" (Warren and Brandeis 200, 201).

made the relationship between property and individual privacy practically irresistible (59). If Warren and Brandeis's point of framing personality as inviolate, read in Lockean terms as "inalienable," was to keep aspects of oneself out of circulation, then, as Thomas surmises, "the inability to disassociate the right to privacy from property" in most discussions of it (e.g. from case law, to political theory, even to discussions of the earning power of reputation) offered a strong argument against their success.[16] However, the creation of the right is what gives substance to the individual, or creates the kind of personality that can be protected by law. Distinguishing between a "right to" and a "right of" privacy, Thomas explains:

> [A] right to privacy implies that unless people are guaranteed the right to be left alone they will not be able to maintain an inviolate personality, whereas a right of privacy . . . implies something that an inviolate personality has as an inalienable possession. A right to privacy is more a creation of the law, a right of privacy more an appeal to natural rights. (61)

Warren and Brandeis, who from the outset of their essay frame privacy as a necessity of complex, modern civilization, argued for a "right to."[17] But what exactly is this inviolable personality and how did other discourses alongside law conceptualize it?

In "The Sociology of Secrecy and of Secret Societies" (1906), German sociologist Georg Simmel analyzed the mechanics and the value of secrecy, which he dubbed "one of the greatest accomplishments of humanity" (464). The tension between a person's conscious decision to conceal information and the internal pressure to reveal it is especially relevant to my reading of *Dorian Gray*. Of more immediate interest, however, are Simmel's prefatory remarks on the structure of acquaintanceship because his reliance on the concepts of "discretion" and "honor" help to illuminate *The Spectator*'s discussion of dignity and explain the nature of the affront that prompted Warren and Brandeis. Like Godkin and Warren and Brandeis themselves, Simmel reflected on the complexities of modern, especially urban, living that he characterized as being "in much more than an economic sense, a credit-economy" (446). From intimate relationships to acquaintanceship to highly structured professional and scholarly endeavors, the communal need for mutual knowledge and trust

---

[16] James Q. Whitman describes "The Right to Privacy" as Warren and Brandeis's failed effort to imbue American privacy law with a Continental value for dignity and personality that foundered because there's no exporting one set of culturally dependent rights into a context where different values prevail (1204).

[17] Godkin saw personal dignity as a natural right but one which wasn't shared equally ("Rights of the Citizen" 65).

jostled with the more personal need to preserve what, in language strikingly like Warren and Brandeis's, Simmel interchangeably called one's "personality" or "spiritual private property" (454).

Simmel described human beings as the only "object of knowledge" that can decide for itself what to reveal and conceal so that while the "internal facts of a person" can be objectively known, what's known can contain both "truth and illusion" (444–5). The challenge to modern societies that rely on trust, of course, is that one can't be sure of the proportion of truthfulness and distortion comprised in this private property, which a greater quantity of information won't change. What's interesting about acquaintanceship is that by straddling strangeness and intimacy, it calls forth the self-restraint that keeps one person from even attempting to know more than what another person chooses to reveal—what, in the terms of this chapter, is the exercise of their privacy (452). Thus, Simmel calls acquaintanceship "the peculiar seat of 'discretion'" (452), which in turn he describes as the expression of an

> effective consciousness that an ideal sphere surrounds every human being, different in various directions and toward different persons; a sphere varying in extent, into which one may not venture to penetrate without disturbing the personal value of the individual. Honor locates such an area. (453)

In this formulation, honor becomes a kind of aura, an "ideal sphere" to complement the physical zone set off by private space and which, he continues, is strongest around "significant" people with higher "personal value."

That this sphere or area comes in different sizes ("varying in extent"), just like a person's house might, reinforces the links between material wealth, status, and the extent of the discretion owed to their personality. The connection is explicit:

> To penetrate this circuit by curiosity is a violation of his [the significant man's] personality. As material property is at the same time an extension of the ego . . . and as on that account every invasion of possession is resented as a violation of the personality; so there is a *spiritual private property*, to invade which signifies *violation of the ego* at its center. (453–4, emphasis mine)

The ego at the center of Simmel's significant man is the inviolate personality of Warren and Brandeis's conception: Both are harmed by—and, it should be emphasized, "resent"—the intrusion. Yet Simmel argues that an invasion of privacy reveals even more about the trespasser whose "evident lack of sensitiveness for the scale of significance among people" has led him to err: "he gives evidence of his lack of capacity for appropriate respect" (453). This lack of respect is a central feature of Warren and Brandeis's complaint that the newspaper trade in gossip is "pursued with industry as well as effrontery" and "results in a lowering of social standards and of morality" (196). Bringing the two together, we can say that the new journalism dulled its readers' effective consciousness of the ideal sphere surrounding significant figures, deadening their capacity for respect, and leading them to offend the honor of private persons.[18]

One final observation about Simmel's discussion of discretion: Much of the analysis focuses on an observer's self-restraint regarding the internal facts an acquaintance chooses not to reveal, but it comes with the caveat that no individual can "demand discretion" when "discretion would prejudice social interests" (455). What those social interests are and how those knowledge boundaries will be set are questions of "external discretion" which the law routinely regulates in terms of business but which, as Warren and Brandeis's attempt makes plain, becomes much more difficult when applied to informal or private relationships. For example, Simmel notes that over the course of an association an especially percipient acquaintance can piece together a kind of surplus information that goes beyond what the person observed voluntarily makes known—and, if possible, would have *kept* unknown—and which requires a new "internal discretion" (455). This internal "duty of discretion" requires viewers to monitor themselves and judge the extent to which their interpretation and "mental handling" of this surplus remains appropriate or becomes "morally quite as unjustifiable as listening at keyholes and prying into the letters of strangers" (455–6). The observance and the breach of both forms of discretion animate Stevenson's and Wilde's novels.

In their search for a right to privacy, Warren and Brandeis were attempting to create a legal zone around that quality that by now we can call dignity, honor, spiritual private property, ego, and inviolate personality. Out of all of them, "personality" is perhaps the trickiest term to use for denoting the inner life and special characteristics of individuals, especially insofar as it was the publication of articles about "personalities" that filled the new journalism and offended more high-minded readers. However, as James Q. Whitman explains, Warren and Brandeis borrowed it from German "personality law" and the idea of *Persönlichkeit*, or the quality of being a personage (which

---

[18] Warren and Brandeis comment on the free market approach to gossip: "In this [journalism], as in other branches of commerce, the supply creates the demand. Each crop of unseemly gossip, thus harvested, becomes the seed of more, and, in direct proportion to its circulation, results in a lowering of social standards and of morality" (196). By "crowd[ing] the space available for matters of real interest to the community" and "usurping the place of interest in brains capable of other things," gossip pages actively discourage the practice of discretion, in Simmel's terms (196).

together with French concepts of dignity and honor make up the Continental "culture of Privacy") (1183, 1205).[19] Still, it's the German idea that privacy gave individuals the freedom to explore, recognize, and develop their individual aptitudes—their personalities—that best captured Warren and Brandeis's sense of its value. For German thinkers, Whitman elaborates, freedom meant "the unfettered creation of the self," which is why artists so often figured as their "paradigmatic free actor" and why control of the publication of intellectual and artistic property made the more attractive analogy for the right to be let alone to ground the privacy protection (1181). On this thinking, the presentation of a public face, like other creative acts and performances, begins with the private development of one's inner life and is mediated by the individual's right to determine what to disclose and how much access to grant to others. This then is the paradox that one's reputation or face before the world is at bottom a matter of privacy, or the effect of one's ability to reflect on, develop, and manage access to one's inner life.

To further describe this personality as being "inviolate" establishes boundaries around the individual, of course, but more than that, it connotes a wholeness, if not precisely consistency, interior to the individual and under his control. In other words, in order for a personality to be inviolate, at least two conditions must be met: first, the individual would have to be free from *unwanted* input, influence, or control by another person such that any transgression of the boundary between people would constitute a violation. As Warren and Brandeis put it, the right to privacy is essentially "part of the more general right to the immunity of the person—the right to one's personality" (207) so that the right "to be let alone" is a not a requirement to be alone as much as the ability for one person to set those boundaries, and, drawing on Simmel, for another to observe through the exercise of discretion and guided by that "sense of justice with respect to the sphere of the intimate contents of life" (Simmel 454).

The second, more problematic condition for inviolability is really a question as to the nature of the personality as an interior essence, not what happens *between* people but *within* a person. If "inviolate" implies wholeness, must then wholeness imply uniformity, or can it denote a bundle of separable qualities united by their belonging to a specific person (not unlike the bundle of rights associated with the Roman *patria potestas*)?[20] The "reasonable man" model of legal subjectivity, along with the property qualifications entailed

---

[19] There is more to say about the French law of insult since it bears so closely on both newspaper libel and the sense of self-esteem that insult necessarily offends and was the place Warren and Brandeis instinctively looked to frame their new right. See Whitman 1183, 1205.

[20] See Sir Henry Sumner Maine on the "university" of rights in *Ancient Law* 172–3.

by possessive individualism, limit the kind of personality that can be considered inviolate. However, as I will suggest in my reading of Stevenson's and Wilde's novels, the sense of more complex personalities emerging in the new social sciences, including criminology and psychology, and the parallel development of new pleas challenge the model of inviolate personality and consequently the right to privacy based on it.[21]

Warren and Brandeis brought together a triangulated set of terms: property, personality, and privacy. In the next section, I turn to Stevenson's *Strange Case* to look at a set of related questions that begin with the novel's representation of selfhood as being conventionally based in the capacity to control property (signaled by Utterson's preoccupation with both Jekyll's house and his will). Jekyll's experiments make clear, however, that his personality is precisely *not* inviolate, which, following on the discussion above, raises questions about his right to privacy: Being a less cohesive self, is he entitled to privacy in the terms offered by Warren and Brandeis? How do Utterson's failures to observe the "duty of discretion" contribute to Jekyll's collapse? With this right an open question throughout the novel (variously posed by the suspicion of blackmail, a general reticence to speak about one's peers, and Utterson's decision to burst the cabinet doors), the way characters and information circulate in space becomes even more important. Given the emphasis in "The Right to Privacy" on domestic space and the idea of the private home, for example, the near absence of domesticity in the novel (paralleling the absence of women) makes it harder to classify spaces and hence to define the quality of the communications or disclosures made in them. The next section will consider, then, the novel's emphasis on public and private locations, including the in-between zone of the professional, as a spatial counterpart to Warren and Brandeis's emphasis on property, personality, and privacy, the main question being how the designation of professional space requires or allows different rules for the kinds of information (including intellectual property) that can be shared and its implications not only for the concept of privacy itself, but for the legal and literary characters that require privacy as a sign of inner life.

A "Story of the Door" in *The Strange Case of Dr. Jekyll and Mr. Hyde*

The story of Henry Jekyll's transformation into the savage and sadistic Edward Hyde is familiar even to those who have never read Robert Louis Stevenson's 1886 novella. The multiplicity of human character is depicted in Stevenson's "shilling shocker" as the respectable, sociable, and professional man of science

---

[21] These complex personalities align with my notion of transgressive individualism, discussed in the Introduction and Chapter 1, but as already noted some legal personalities do not enjoy immunity.

Dr. Jekyll gives way to his murderous other self, Mr. Hyde. In Jekyll's "Full Statement of the Case" (or "confession," as he calls it) in which he explains the origins of his experiment and its effects, he describes his "two characters" or "two natures" as an "original and better self" struggling to subdue a "second character" who embodies the "original evil" of fallen man (Stevenson 52, 55, 50). As a moral allegory, the tale cautions against a variety of sins: against the intellectual overreaching of scientific experiment à la Victor Frankenstein; against the moral and logical failure to control one's impulses; and also, for the lawyer Mr. Utterson, in the attempt to conceal rather than confront and expunge one's demons.

These dimensions signal the novel's gothic, literary heritage, but others point towards its deconstruction of the detective story.[22] Although the structure of the novel conforms to the model of classic mystery, Jekyll's "Full Statement" introduces rather than resolves questions. And instead of clarifying the central character's identity, or tracing the development of a unified self, as the novel tended to do, Stevenson's book documents the dissolution of a self, initiating what Ronald R. Thomas describes as "an elaborate assault on the ideals of individual personality and the cult of character that dominated the nineteenth century" ("Strange Voices" 75).

A nineteenth-century "cult of character," reflected in a range of genres including the memoir or confession, the biography, the *Bildungsroman*, or the novel itself as a "life story," nevertheless denotes more than a literary history or preoccupation (Hirsch 228–9). In *Jekyll and Hyde*'s immediate, post-Darwinian context, these investigations into character took on a distinctly evolutionary cast. From evolutionary psychology to cultural and criminal anthropology, from new studies of "mental chemistry" to medicalized concepts of "moral insanity" or "moral imbecility" and onwards to the private policing of sexuality and the graphing of class boundaries, medicine, science, and the new social sciences focused on developing physiological, psychological, and social classifications of and explanations for human behavior, all of which have been invoked by critics, nineteenth-century and contemporary, of the novel.[23]

The conjunction of medical and legal discourses in the field of criminology was especially noteworthy for the way it reflected, and contributed to, the transformation of early nineteenth-century conceptions of character into identities, largely through the evacuation of personal responsibility and

---

[22] For the gothic history of the novel, see Hirsch; Davison; and Dryden. For the detective novel, see Hirsch 223; and Cawelti.

[23] See Persak; Block; Reid; Davis; Rosner; Taylor 17; Moore; Arata, "Stevenson, Morris"; and Brantlinger and Boyle.

the naturalization of deviance. As Martin J. Wiener explains, the criminal whose behavior had once been attributed to the lack of restraint or a will run amok had become by the 1890s a depersonalized sign of "weak spots in the human (and, to a lesser degree, social) constitution" (229). One hears echoes of John Stuart Mill's ethology here with its emphasis on social reform, but the prospect of education that included *moral* reform would be out of place in a field that held moral consciousness and free will to have been bred out of the criminal mind (236).[24] Not only had these tendencies or "weak spots" been dispersed among the population, following Havelock Ellis's categorization of criminal types in *The Criminal* (1890), worse still, the ability to identify them had been transferred away from everyday citizens to medical and legal experts with the training and technology to detect them. Once anyone might harbor criminal tendencies, so might a range of hidden crimes lie behind the respectable facades of Victorian people and their homes.[25]

The criminological interest in "problem personalities" (Wiener 228) surely informs Stevenson's characterization of Henry Jekyll and Edward Hyde, but the focus on criminal character in analysis of the novel offsets a comparative lack of attention to other legal conceptions of character, such as the inviolate personality Warren and Brandeis were theorizing. After all, the principal investigator of this "strange case," the lawyer Utterson, is drawn to it not by a crime but by a "mad will," which provides a pathway from testaments to torts and law's civil side. To be sure, Utterson's professional status has not gone unnoted, nor has his attitude to Jekyll's will been ignored.[26] What I am suggesting is that a number of questions about the intimate relationship between privacy, private spaces, and the constitution of personal subjectivity have been overlooked.[27]

---

[24] See Wiener 228–42 on developments in criminology, especially Havelock Ellis's development of criminal types in *The Criminal* (1890) (237). See also R. Thomas, *Detective Fiction* 208–16 for discussion of Ellis's connection to Francis Galton and his work to individuate criminals through fingerprinting.

[25] See Wiener on the conjunction of criminality and respectability. Once street crime was felt to have been controlled, "middle-class attention [turned] inward, from the streets to the home" (244).

[26] On his status as a professional, see Davison 142; Rago 275; and Goh. On documents, reading, and writing, see Davison; R. Thomas, "Strange Voices"; Rago; Hirsch; and Garrett. On the will, see Davison 148. For the role of the media in winning social consent to laws or providing social substitutes, see Rowbotham and Stevenson xxii.

[27] One explanation for the way that law has been overlooked in considerations of Stevenson's novel is that it is always implied in criminal anthropology, forensic psychology, and medical theories that could change the kinds of (secondary) plea available to criminal defendants. A second reason that formal law is rarely discussed is precisely because Utterson's investigation is informal: accusations are made privately; trials are purposefully avoided; wills receive no

Assuming that the legal protection of privacy gives personality its substance—the creation of the *right to* calling into being the *existence of*—then one can ask what sorts of procedures for and limitations *against* accessing private space and the inner self Utterson, as a legal professional, brings to the novel. Utterson's search for evidence against Hyde amounts to the construction of a legal case against him, but his prosecution is hampered by the desire to protect Jekyll's reputation, extending even to reluctance to see Hyde formally tried for murder. How far does Utterson's professional privilege extend? When and where do his exchanges with Jekyll merge from the professional to the personal and back? And for the novel: what do *Jekyll and Hyde*'s narrative occlusions—its resistance to letting officials in at the front door—suggest about literary realism and the stylistic alternatives that were developing with the turn to modernism?

Towards the end of the novel, after Utterson has stormed Dr. Jekyll's cabinet, searched through the cellars and closets of the laboratory for Jekyll's body, and investigated the infamous alley door, he finds a packet of papers—Dr. Lanyon's letter and Jekyll's "Full Statement"—that will disclose the acts and motives of this "strange case." Although Utterson promises the butler, Poole, that, once he has read the contents, he will return and send for the police, neither happens. Were it not for the two startling documents (each a new narrative of the facts), this end of the story proper would send readers back to the beginning of the novel and its "Story of the Door."

For Dr. Jekyll's story is the story of several doors: the door that exits on the alley, the door that fronts the respectable side of the house (but which opens increasingly infrequently throughout the novel), the door of the cabinet that Utterson breaks down, even the door of Utterson's own cabinet in which he locks away Jekyll's disgraceful will.[28] It is the story of the comings and goings of Jekyll and of Hyde, as well as the passage of information about them. It is also a story of curiosity and the circulation of information between Enfield, who in Chapter 1 relates his encounter with Hyde, and Utterson, who listens, enrapt and disturbed. More particularly, Enfield's narrative is prompted by and centers on the image of the door, that point of access and egress, that bar against public intrusion, that closed door behind which the king in his castle rules.

Here we should recall that Warren and Brandeis gave pride of place to this familiar notion of the house as middle-class man's equivalent to the

---

professional sanction. A third is that the focus on criminology obscures the novel's other jurisdictions, that is, its civil engagement with testamentary law and torts.

[28] See M. Kellen Williams's discussion of Utterson's intrusion as an act of narrative revenge: "the imperative to see and to seize the deviant body in support of flagging narratives" (424).

castle. Pointing out in their conclusion to "The Right to Privacy" that even the law's "own officers engaged in the execution of its commands" often could not encroach upon the private citizen's jurisdiction in his home, they align "constituted authority" with a front-door approach, in other words, with an approach that shows appropriate respect for the sovereignty of the home by contrast to the back-door malingering of those without legal sanction (or without even the legitimate claims of servants and tradespeople to come and go from the house).[29] Like their focus on the door, Stevenson's focus on the relationship between the two doors of Jekyll's house and his laboratory draws on the physical and ideological significance of boundaries between the public and private—a spatial boundary that demarcates social relationships, but also one that extends to individuals through the division of the self into a public (sometimes professional) persona and an interior being or inner life—both of which are maintained through each person's control over how much of one's inner self to disclose and, hence, how to determine one's intimate acquaintance and shape the contours of one's private life (Bezanson 1135).

Unlike its polished and painted neighbors, the back door of Enfield's story repels rather than invites. The building itself is a "sinister block" of two "windowless storeys," a "blind forehead of discoloured wall" (Stevenson 8). Its only point of communication with the world is a door that, ironically, "was equipped with neither bell nor knocker" for the uninvited to announce their presence, seek entrance, or disturb the occupant. If the door discourages physical entrance, however, it does invite speculation. Sight of this unlikely door prompts Enfield's story (about Hyde's trampling of the little girl and, more importantly for Utterson, his ease of access both to Jekyll's house and a duly signed check), in which the absence of law—and the consequent fear as well as freedom from restraint it engenders—forms an important context. Enfield explains that his walk through the deserted street makes him "long for the sight of a policeman," yet the encounter with Hyde inspires Enfield with murderous desire that he channels into "the next best thing," a threat of scandal (9). And although Enfield freely tells Utterson that the name on Hyde's check was "very well known and often printed" (9), he demurs from actually naming Jekyll, saying the check was "drawn payable to bearer and signed with a name that I can't mention, though it's one of the points of my story." Enfield's studied incuriosity comes from an aversion to exposure, a scruple against jeopardizing and judging others, a consciousness of Jekyll's "honor," in Simmel's terms, and a sense of the justice due to Jekyll as a significant man.

---

[29] For discussion of the home and domestic privacy specifically, see Seipp, "Right to Privacy" 1894–8; and Wiener 244–7.

Put differently, he respects Jekyll's privacy and his right both to be let alone and to control his public face.

Enfield does not show the same reticence about judging Hyde or disclosing *his* name to Utterson, however; "I can't see what harm it would do," he says. The only difference between making Hyde's name "stink from one end of London to the other" (as he had threatened Hyde with doing) and linking Hyde to the incident in the first place (as Enfield does by telling Utterson this story) is the audience. There is "no harm" in Enfield's view because although the idea of a wider audience is never far away, he has confined the tale to a private circle of trusted friends. There is also "no harm" in denying Hyde the power to set limits on disclosure because the disturbing something he exudes suggests his personality is already violate and therefore not possessed of a natural right *of* privacy.

In the absence of the police, Enfield's efforts establish the unofficial justice the novel will pursue in which witness testimony is essentially a form of gossip, which designates whose privacy must be respected and who deserves none. Utterson's reaction to the story in this first scene, including his own speculation about Jekyll's relationship with Hyde, develops this justice, especially in the way Utterson attempts to quell talk by safeguarding documents, on the one hand, but to compel it within the private circles of professionals and friends on the other. Utterson's concern about Jekyll's will, for example, which Enfield's story specifically exacerbates, becomes a concern for Jekyll's character, his public reputation, and what it must suffer by the association with Hyde.

Property and privacy are thus central principles of both misgivings, in the most obvious sense that Utterson is worried about a distribution of property but also that he worries about his friend's personal secrets. Together they form the main constituents of character (of agency and reputation) in Utterson's conventional understanding; however, it is an equation that Stevenson's novel breaks down. The novel itself, as Warren and Brandeis's essay would do, experiments with new models of the subject. Unlike Warren and Brandeis, however, whose protection of privacy required the replacement of narrow definitions of property with inviolate personality, *Jekyll and Hyde* maintains the importance of property while undermining the notion of inviolability: the self may dissolve, but the physical property is left intact. By questioning the security of self-possession only, the novel poses questions about character and invites the reader to join in this speculation even as it "hydes" information and disrupts expectations readers may bring from their encounter with the omniscient narratives of realist fiction.

The novel does make one substitution, though. By converting the letter "I" to "Y," Stevenson in effect changes subjectivity from an assertion to a series of questions about character which may help to explain why it is so evasive—asking readers to pose questions but refusing to answer; using silence as a mode of protecting privacy, but also exposing documents (intellectual property) at the conclusion; dismantling notions of a unified self, but not clearly establishing an alternative basis for either a *right of* or a *right to* privacy—and why this "strange case" might equally as well be a legal case as a medical or psychiatric one.

Read through a legal lens, then, the novel's interest in the will, especially Utterson's distaste for its "startling clauses," stands out. After that evening walk with Enfield, Utterson seeks out the will where he's concealed it in an envelope, in "the most private part" of a safe, in his "business room" (12). Utterson, we learn, already knows about Hyde because Hyde has been named as sole heir to Jekyll's estate:

> it [the will] provided not only that, in case of the decease of Henry Jekyll, M.D., D.C.L., L.L.D., F.R.S., &c., all his possessions were to pass into the hands of his "friend and benefactor Edward Hyde," but that in case of Dr. Jekyll's "disappearance or unexplained absence for any period exceeding three calendar months," the said Edward Hyde should step into the said Henry Jekyll's shoes without further delay and free from any burthen or obligation . . . . (12–13)

This will "offends" Utterson, both as "a lawyer and a lover of the sane and customary sides of life" (13), so much so that, although he's taken charge of it for his client, he "had refused to lend the least assistance in the making of it" (12) with the result that the will is purely "holograph" or handwritten by the person in whose name it appears. Moreover, Utterson hides the will in a series of enclosures more and more removed from public scrutiny, not because wills have to be kept secret to be valid, but because this one makes legible a disruption in Jekyll's economic and ethical life.[30]

A vehicle for the transmission of property, the will, so called, is fundamentally an act of volition associated with character and a particular documentary form. As a lover of form—the right way to behave and the right way to make a will—Utterson has always wanted to save Jekyll's "credit," his reputation, from scandal (27). By refusing to draft the will in the first place, he denies it his professional, legal sanction: proscribing probate, withholding his approval so that neither the will nor Jekyll's relationship with Hyde can be proved. Here, the lawyer's repugnance for its form is bound up with his aversion to its content (R. Thomas, "Strange Voices" 79). To Utterson, Jekyll's will

---

[30] See R. Thomas, "Strange Voices" 75, 79; Rago 277; and Hirsch 236.

is a "mad will" (an oxymoron given that "mad" minds are not sound minds) (Stevenson 30), not solely because it would squander his estate, or because it posits Jekyll's disappearance, but also because it betrays his character. Indeed, the formation of the very characters on the page, the will being handwritten, becomes evidence of the writer's dual character insofar as the writing serves as a sign of personality or identity "in the age before fingerprints" (Hirsch 238).[31] (Indeed, by equating the "sane" with the "customary," Utterson's assumptions about crime and character belong to this earlier age as well.) Jekyll's credentials, another set of characters listed in the will, include a "D.C.L" or Doctor of Common Law degree, which suggests his own familiarity with rules and procedures that would further justify Utterson's perplexity.[32] In this context, what one owns and how one disposes of it says something about one's character, and for Utterson, Jekyll's will speaks "disgrace" (13). It suggests something shameful, perhaps an undue influence, to be suppressed (if not repressed) and kept "safe" in Utterson's "business room"—that professional parallel to Jekyll's medical cabinet—until it can be returned finally to the doctor.

If we know why the will is so compelling for Utterson and why, given his silence, the investigation must be an unofficial one, the next question is how its legal *informality* influences the literary form it can take. The validity of the will is a civil matter that raises thematic concerns about intention, property, and character, but this content is organized in a formal structure

[31] The chapter called "Incident of the Letter" goes directly to the issue of how character is made legible in material forms such as the will or, here, letters and notes, two of which reveal graphological similarities between Jekyll's and Hyde's scripts, the inverted written characters signaling the same inversion of their moral character. The anomaly of Jekyll and Hyde's identity is beyond the boundary of Utterson's comprehension, but this is less a problem with the evidentiary value of handwriting than another instance of Utterson's understandable interpretive shortcomings. See Garrett 66; Brantlinger 201; and Joel Peter Eigen on the emergence of case law on the so-called "unconscious crimes" (140).

[32] The long list of credentials Jekyll provides in his will emphasizes to the point of parody his professional status, but it's worth mentioning that he is both a Doctor of Laws (an honorary degree) and a Doctor of Civil Law in addition to being a medical doctor. If Jekyll has specific legal training, then his apparent flouting of testamentary rules further justifies Utterson's sense of the ominous fancy at work in his will. In a review in *The Athenaeum*, the journalist and editor E. T. Cook identified the will's "inopera[bility]" as a weak point in the story: "Mr. Stevenson," he wrote, "has overlooked the fact that a man's will does not come into force until he is dead, and that the fact that he has not been heard of for three months would not enable his executor to carry out his testamentary directions" (qtd. in Stevenson 96)—it hasn't been witnessed either. Notwithstanding the will's legal "impossibility," however, it still serves as the expression of Jekyll's intention or desire. It assumes the moral agency associated with character and signals the individual personality inscribed in the handwriting. Utterson understands this, which is precisely why he is so baffled by and mistrusts the desires inscribed there.

that resembles the gathering of documents preparatory to a criminal case (R. Thomas, "Strange Voices" 75).[33] Of Utterson's response to the growing evidence against Hyde, Robbie B. H. Goh notes a professional reticence, a "(juris)prudential silence" (172, 174) and Peter K. Garrett, describing Dr. Lanyon's letter, incidentally provides a way of understanding Utterson's role as narrator: "With Lanyon, we get not the lawyer's attempt at accurate testimony but a more clinical account that dwells on Hyde's effect" (65). Others have pointed out the way the novel's professional brotherhood closes ranks against Hyde, whether to protect themselves as a class, or, as Utterson's particular example illustrates, to deny responsibility for his own "buried life."[34] This sympathetic silence on Jekyll's behalf marks Utterson's attempts to protect Jekyll's character from being publicly connected to Hyde and even implicated in his crimes, but it's never entirely clear whether Utterson's decision to remain silent, to prosecute this case unofficially, is most influenced by a tacit code of gentlemanly decorum, the more personal interests of friendship, or, as these examples suggest, by a professional code of conduct or confidentiality (although his handling of the Carew murder creates doubts about how far he feels bound to professional ethics). Nevertheless, each code of silence, like the many envelopes and packets that enclose the documents, creates pockets of protected information of a kind that defines and warrants privacy. In this context, Utterson's narrative attempt to represent Jekyll, grounded as it is in attempts to get information Jekyll doesn't want to share, routinely exceeds the demands of discretion and borders on an invasion of Jekyll's privacy.[35]

The novel thus stages a problem of disclosure, one that can be overcome only by overcoming reticence, either by establishing spaces where such confidences could be given (whether these sites be professional or domestic) or by compelling disclosures through the violation of private space or private communications (as when Utterson forces the cabinet door or reads Lanyon's letter). Further, the informality of the case means that Utterson does not have to approach it in his professional capacity only, nor is he bound to strictly professional spaces. Instead, he resorts to or contemplates using all of these

---

[33] See also Manlove 88.
[34] See Rago on Hyde as a "gentleman-deviant" (281); Goh on "narrative gentility" (171–2); but also Arata on the professionals' efforts to protect Hyde ("The Sedulous Ape" 239); Davis 207 on the shift in bases of professional character from the "gentlemanly culture" of the men of science to a results-oriented reputation; Garrett 69 on Utterson's implication in Hyde's crimes; and Davison 143 on Utterson's indictability. See also Hirsch 233; R. Thomas, "Strange Voices" 80.
[35] Williams notes that most of the novel's documents "appear in the guise of 'enclosures,'" which, in spite of frequent cross-referencing, hampers the ability to connect the information they contain (419–20).

means and appeals to Jekyll in his own various guises as both man of business and friend.

This ambiguity carries over into the uses of space as well where any single site can assume a different function, so that a dinner table may become a consulting room, which complicates the relationship between the people assembled there and the quality of their communications. For example, although Hyde disappears after the murder of Sir Carew, Jekyll resurfaces ("He came out of his seclusion, renewed relations with his friends, [and] became once more their familiar guest and entertainer") and holds a dinner for a "small party" which includes Utterson and Lanyon and at which, the omniscient narrator remarks, "the face of the host had looked from one to the other as in the old days when the trio were inseparable friends" (28–9). To look backwards for a moment, this scene conjures earlier dinners among "old cronies" at which Utterson "contrived" to be the last to leave, a "thing that had befallen many scores of times" because Utterson's "unobtrusive company" and "rich silence" afford a kind of bridge or transition between sociability and solitude (19). His silence is reserved only to information about himself, however, for, recurring to the subject of the will in this earlier scene, he presents himself as an aid and confidant: "make a clean breast of this in confidence," he urges Jekyll, and the lawyer will help him out of his predicament (20). Assuring Utterson of his trust, Jekyll nevertheless explains that his interest in Hyde is "a private matter" and asks Utterson to "let it sleep." To look forward now from that friendly dinner, just a few days later Utterson finds that "the door was shut against the lawyer." The letter Jekyll sends in response to Utterson's query conveys Jekyll's intention "to lead a life of extreme seclusion" such that Utterson "must not be surprised, nor must you doubt my friendship, if my door is shut even to you" (30). Indeed, Jekyll pleads that as a friend, the one thing Utterson can do to help him will be "to respect my silence."

It is this very request which Utterson struggles against and ultimately ignores, just as he breaks his promise to help Hyde.[36] Jekyll's latest bout of

---

[36] By contrast, it's Dr. Lanyon who is concerned with Jekyll's professional secrets and whose disapproval of his colleague's experimentation makes him avoid, rather than pursue, the doctor. As his final narrative explains, however, professional curiosity gets the better of him, and he accepts Hyde's invitation to learn the secret of his formula. But it's important to note that even as Hyde taunts Lanyon with the imminent routing of his "narrow and material views," he invokes the "seal of our profession" (the "our" emphasizing Jekyll's status, not Hyde's) and binds Lanyon to keeping his secret (76). Conveyed under the mantle of professional ethics, Hyde's disclosure is both private *and* shared. The offer and the acceptance of the disclosure is a negotiation of the limits which define personality, on the one hand, and which help to maintain a kind of professional fraternity on the other. It's but another indicator of Hyde's malignity that he would offer to disclose something he knows will burden

odd behavior occurs in the chapter in which Dr. Lanyon dies. The narrative explains that after the funeral, Utterson returns to his business room, the same to which he returns at the start of the novel after hearing Enfield's story, and opens a letter from Lanyon. The letter, marked "PRIVATE: for the hand of J.G. Utterson ALONE," includes a second, this one marked with the instruction that it not be opened "till the death or disappearance of Dr. Henry Jekyll" (77). At sight of the second letter "a great curiosity came on the trustee, to disregard the prohibition and dive at once to the bottom of these mysteries; but professional honor and faith to his dead friend" lead him to place this packet "in the inmost corner of his private safe" (31). Yet, the narrator explains, "it is one thing to mortify curiosity, another to conquer it" (31). Utterson continues to call on Jekyll and, as the next chapter "Incident at the Window" reveals, assumes the privilege of friendship, enters Jekyll's courtyard with Enfield in order to gaze up at the windows, and witnesses Jekyll's moment of "terror and despair." The momentum builds, for in the next chapter Utterson, asking for "consent" but promising "brute force," rejects Jekyll's pleas for mercy and breaks down the door of the cabinet (38).

These scenes mark a progression of Jekyll's retreat and Utterson's pursuit. In the first scene, Utterson is shown to be a trusted friend and professional advisor, the most intimate of an already private group of associates. But the two roles confuse what Utterson may know as a professional and what he may ask as a friend. Disclosing nothing about himself, Utterson becomes a repository of information. He mines for secrets as he collects documents (the will, Hyde's letter, Lanyon's letter), but he conceals them not in a bedside table or bureau drawer. Rather, he hides them in his business room—a place that mingles professional and domestic space where the ambiguity of purpose in the room mirrors an ambiguity in Utterson's motivations, and certainly their results, as well.

In other novels, this private space would be framed in the familiar terms of separate spheres, but the domesticity of this male world is different: social but not public, private without necessarily being personal. Instead of what Warren and Brandeis deemed "the almost sacred realm of the domestic," Stevenson depicts an in-between zone of professional work within the home.[37]

---

the doctor, who dies from the experience of "the moral turpitude that man unveiled to [him]" (77).

[37] Brook Thomas remarks that Warren and Brandeis were most interested in protecting the "almost sacred realm of the domestic circle" and suggests himself that while that circle may be "the most sacred zone of privacy" (62, 63), the marriage contract undermines the concept of inviolate personality and hence the right of married people to claim privacy from their spouses. William M. Moddlemog notes specifically that many challengers to Warren and

I am not suggesting that a house, or its ideological counterpart the "home," is ever free from work, and of course nineteenth-century men had domestic spaces of their own (libraries, smoking rooms, the post-prandial dinner table). What interests me about this aspect of the novel is that the spaces these men consider most private double as sites for their professional work as well. Utterson doesn't go to an office (another sign of his desire to keep this work off the books, so to speak); Jekyll retreats to his cabinet where a hearthside tea service shares space with "glazed presses full of chemicals"; Lanyon examines Hyde under the "bright light" of his consulting room—within his house—and with "as fair an imitation of [his] ordinary manner to a patient" as circumstances allowed (44–5). We do see the strictly domestic space of Hyde's Soho flat, but then his *lack* of a profession is one of the traits that unsettles everyone in the novel and seems to justify this inspection (indeed, the view of this interior is the only official investigation in the novel, conducted by the inspector from Scotland Yard but also, unofficially, by Utterson who has led him there). As I've suggested, this doubling of function blurs the distinction in the kinds of conversations had or disclosures made in these spaces.

Thus, although Utterson's desire for information and his reasons for protecting Jekyll can be understood as the obligations of friendship, in more professional terms, Utterson's reasons raise questions about the relationship between the lawyer's responsibility to his client and to the broader aspirations of social justice, aspirations which return us, via the relationship of the individual to society, to questions of character, privacy, and inviolate personality.

To focus first on privacy: as Brook Thomas's distinction between a *right to* and a *right of* privacy suggests, Jekyll's multiple selves complicate the notion of inalienability required by an appeal to natural rights. The exchange of one personality for another and the distance or alienation between those personalities indicates that there is little that is intrinsic or constant in the model of individual personality, the self, that Jekyll has discovered. Therefore, this self-alienation can be read as the staging of the question of whether such split selves have anything inalienable about them that would allow them to

---

Brandeis's equation of legal personality and domestic privacy—their translation of the idea of a separate sphere within the self into the logic of separate social spheres (342)—were women anxious to "'divorce' the concept of privacy from its moorings in the home" (339). Brian Artese, in a reading of Henry James's work and its response to sentimental literature (typically associated with feminist energies), looks specifically at the quality of disclosures made in American as opposed to European novels. America "the 'land of the open door' had become a socius ruled by the discipline of confession, by a posture of transparency and full disclosure." Europe, in contrast, "comes to represent a society that has not yet anathematized the individual's prerogative to maintain a testimonial stance, whether in a public forum or before family and friends" (119).

claim a range of natural rights at the foundation of privacy. Read this way, Utterson's interventions cease to be invasions: Hyde's crimes and his aura of deformity—the notion of a personality that is in itself, essentially, a violation of legal norms of subjectivity—disqualify him in Utterson's view from these natural rights and justify his leading Inspector Newcomen to Hyde's Soho flat, even as the suspicion of a second murder will justify his breaking into Jekyll's room. The *right to* privacy, however, is a means of *preserving* the inviolate personality; as Brook Thomas says, "unless people are guaranteed the right to be left alone they will not be able to maintain an inviolate personality" (61): without the protection of privacy, everyone is susceptible to the sorts of disarticulation Jekyll undergoes. This possibility changes the question: does Jekyll collapse *because* of Utterson's pursuit?

Reading *Jekyll and Hyde* reminds us of the way that Warren and Brandeis positioned their idea that the modern individual required the protections of privacy as a reflection on the state of civilized society. Progress is not an unadulterated good, their criticism of the social world revealed. Their abhorrence of flash photography, for example, while it might seem a peculiar hobby horse, came from their sense of its being symptomatic of progress's countervailing trend of degeneration that was the *raison d'être* of the late-Victorian social sciences.[38] And yet those same social sciences suggested that the "solitude and privacy," which Warren and Brandeis deemed essential to modern man's wellbeing, had the potential to undermine both individual and social coherence.

According to evolutionary psychology and cultural anthropology, civilized man was a social man. As James Sully put it in his essay "Self-Esteem" (1876), his ability to be introspective—to "regard his or her own character '*ab extra*, just as a second person would view it'"—created also a capacity for sympathy, a "perception of analogies with one's own inner life" on which "knowledge of another's character" was founded (qtd. in Block 448).[39] Civilized man possessed a basic duality, then: through the study of imagined others he learned about himself, and through study of himself, he imagined he learned about others. According to Herbert Spencer's theories of moral

---

[38] Wiener discusses a paradox in the "consequences of success" (258). The successful control of traditional crime seemed to obviate the need for a robust penal system, but at the same time, expanded definitions of crime created a police force with longer reach, for example into commercial law and public welfare (260–1).

[39] As Ed Block Jr. puts it, the logical Utterson seeks to understand Jekyll through reference to himself, but because he cannot assimilate the "diverse characters" he sees in Jekyll and Hyde, he becomes obsessed by their mystery. Logic gives way to imagination and "monomania" (453); Utterson becomes prone to "illusions" that can only be diminished if he can relocate a stable point of orientation outside himself, in the community.

evolution and "use-inheritance"—the idea that moral "thoughts, feelings and hence motives were grounded in the nervous system" and could become heritable through repeated exercise—"sympathy" and "justice" were more likely to be promoted by "civilized life" (Persak 14).[40] In a cycle of cause and effect, communal living encouraged "'fellow-feeling,'" made it both "pleasurable and beneficial," made social approval more necessary to one's wellbeing and so promoted behaviors that would earn such approval (Persak 15–16).[41] The individualistic pursuit of self-satisfaction or excessive introspection that did *not* lead to sympathy, in contrast, suggested atavism or degeneracy that belonged to a pre-social condition, or as Havelock Ellis concluded later, at least reflected nonconformity to the social temper of the time.[42] It is no great leap from here to ideas of free will, choice, and responsibility: civilized man was a moral and logical man who could control his impulses in anticipation of the "pleasure" and "benefit" that would accrue. Anyone making a different choice was potentially morally insane or a moral imbecile.[43]

Utterson's suspicions of Hyde's character make sense in this context, as does his disturbance at the signs of the once sociable Jekyll's reclusiveness and evasiveness, both of which motivate his persistent questioning. On the one hand, he pesters Jekyll for information because he needs it, in his professional capacity, in order to build a case against Hyde.[44] At the same time, however, Utterson's attempts to make Jekyll speak, to force disclosure, amount to an unreciprocated desire for intimacy with Jekyll in a personal register. Utterson's membership in Jekyll's circle means that he will protect Jekyll from a public world of outsiders, but the trickier path to negotiate is the degree of disclosure he may expect or seek to obtain in this private world of insiders. Thus, although these theories of character are important for understanding

---

[40] Persak's analysis draws from Spencer's *First Principles* (1867) and *Principles of Psychology* (1870–2).

[41] This idea of social approval is at the foundation of Godkin's argument for the importance of reputation and for the state's interest in protecting it, "a man's regard for his reputation being one of the chief guarantees of social order and progress" ("Rights of the Citizen" 62).

[42] See Wiener's discussion of cultural relativism and Ellis's insistence that so-called savagery is only anti-social in non-savage societies (254–5).

[43] See Joel Peter Eigen as well as Mary Rosner on the concept of "moral imbecility" and the emergence of "moral insanity" as mitigating plea in legal prosecutions.

[44] Gordon Hirsch makes the remarkably simple yet illuminating observation that things would be much easier if Utterson only knew that Jekyll and Hyde were the same man. The comment is noteworthy both for justifying Utterson's efforts to defend Jekyll and revealing how flawed they are from their inception. Based on what he *can* know, Utterson has been quite right to distrust the will, to be suspicious of Hyde, to keep letters and notes safe as potential evidence. See Hirsch 234.

how much knowledge of others is aided or skewed by one's own experience or perspective, they also suggest how much easier the creation of sympathy would be if, rather than having to imagine others, those others would simply disclose themselves.[45]

Of course, sympathy may not be the only result. If we consider the adversarial model of the trial that this unofficial case is nonetheless pursuing, what we see in Utterson is a growing albeit unconscious sense of the untenable duality *forced on him* by Jekyll's identity with Hyde (again, a sign of the limits of inviolate personality). By playing "Seek" to Jekyll's "Hyde" (15), Utterson's prosecution turns back on the man he wants to defend. Thus, although he assures Poole, after they've forced their way into the cabinet and discovered Hyde's body and the doctors' documents, that "I shall be back before midnight when we shall send for the police" (41), he never returns—the letter and the confession, for all their internal ambiguities, make plain that this is not a tale Utterson can tell.

Competing personal and professional interests offer one kind of narrative problem, if not also (in light of changing evidence law) a procedural, legal problem. The more fundamental difficulty for Utterson is one that all readers share: interpretive fallibility and the related problem of simply not being able to discern true intentions, true states of mind, true statements from false, all of which is complicated, as Simmel observed, by respect for the individual's right to set the limits of disclosure (and in criminal law the right not to incriminate oneself). Sully's and Spencer's emphasis on imagination suggests an antidote to this opacity, however, which could help us gauge the social value of novel-reading as a means of creating sympathy, but which in Stevenson's hands provides a warning that imagined realities may be preferable to lived ones, that some truths are better not known. Thus, as anomalous as the Jekyll/Hyde identity is and as much as Utterson may be excused for not having divined that they were the same man (and Jekyll for declining to reveal it), the outlandishness of the thematic problem becomes in Stevenson's formal depiction a much more familiar problem of the desire to know paired with a refusal to tell, or, in terms of literary convention, a refusal to participate uncritically in the realist project of omniscience.

In traversing the surgical theater and its spectacles of anatomy (the dissection and description of bodies), Utterson and Poole make their way towards the chemical cabinet, the space of the mind, and seek to penetrate its inner workings, as Utterson says, by "consent or brute force." Even in this

---

[45] See Christine L. Krueger's point about the value of "cover stories" for infanticide defendants (*Reading for the Law* 203). Having a voice is good, but sometimes the truth also surpasseth understanding.

metaphoric movement from material to psychological realism, however, their access remains incomplete and gives only partial answers, ones that Utterson can't even interpret as both he and the narrator abandon the reader to Lanyon's letter and Jekyll's statement without integrating their contents. Dr. Lanyon dies shortly after witnessing Hyde's transformation into Jekyll, and, having read Jekyll's confession, our detective-lawyer Utterson is made speechless. At the level of character, Jekyll/Hyde stymies professional acumen, rendering their narratives incomplete.[46] Of course, bodies continue to matter—Lanyon details Hyde's stature, musculature, and pulse; Jekyll awakes to the sight of Hyde's hand and *feels* the transformation as he sits on a Regent Park bench—however, scientific description of empirical realities neither resolves questions of plot, nor provides sufficient evidence to extricate the reader from interpretive quandaries.

If science cannot explain literature, conversely, Joel Peter Eigen in his study of the history of multiple personalities rejects the usefulness of their fictional representation for understanding "medicolegal history": "For the purpose of examining law's response to multiple selves and the realities of splitting," he writes, "we would need the *trial* of Dorian Gray, or the *plea* of Dr. Jekyll, and we would need these in the form of a courtroom, not a literary, narrative" (4). Eigen's comment reminds us that even as Warren and Brandeis posited an inviolate personality as the basis for privacy, the law was also wrestling with the implications for human intention and responsibility suggested by medical and psychological theories that showed personality to be neither impenetrable nor uniform. However, his insistence that one has to look at law through explicitly legal forms (and only at trials, at that) in order to learn about its response assumes a kind of inviolable personality of law, an idea that unless its boundaries are respected it risks being undermined in the same way that Warren and Brandeis thought privacy was necessary to the maintenance of the self.

What Stevenson's novel has shown, and which Wilde's will amplify, is the way the legal conception of privacy itself relies on the idea of there being multiple aspects of personality that cohere in one person who, for a range of reasons and under a variety of conditions and circumstances, controls their disclosure. That these aspects belong to one person should not blind us to the fact that privacy is also a relational concept wherein the power to grant access to one's inner life or inner circle is also the power to shape, maintain, or even undermine a specific community. As my reading of Oscar Wilde's *The Picture*

---

[46] For analysis of Utterson's persistence in these final chapters as "notional consciousness and narrative device," see Goh 168.

of Dorian Gray will show, there is no secret without the prospect of its telling. Whether a narrative impulse, a bid for intimacy, a form of unburdening, or a source of conflict, even the voluntary sharing of personal information can expose the limits of both privacy and personality, for even private people are always members of a community, both vulnerable to and guilty of multiple forms of trespass.

"To see my soul": Voluntary Disclosure and the Problem of Influence in *The Picture of Dorian Gray*

Herbert Spencer's theory that too much introspection threatened the communal bond resonates not only in Stevenson's novel, but also in *The Picture of Dorian Gray*. If too much attention to oneself impeded sympathy for others, as Spencer held, then narcissism was surely a sign of degeneracy and Dorian the most dangerous narcissist of all. Writing in *Liberty, Equality, Fraternity* (1876) nearly a decade after Spencer's *First Principles*, James Fitzjames Stephen sounded a more cautious note about the workings of sympathy which nonetheless agreed with Spencer's assessment: "All the more intimate and delicate relations of life are of such a nature," he wrote, "that to submit them to unsympathetic observation, or to observation which is sympathetic in the wrong way, inflicts great pain, and may inflict lasting moral injury" (*Liberty* 106).[47] One hears strains of the Continental value for dignity in these lines (the potential for "unsympathetic observation"), but as a response to J. S. Mill's *On Liberty*, Stephen's treatise was also concerned with the extent and shape of the individual's power of self-determination, here to be free to limit access to one's "intimate and delicate relations."

What is curious in Stephen's turn towards privacy specifically, however, is not his concession that privacy encompasses more than physical intrusion on real property ("the intrusion of a stranger"), but that an influence may violate it:

> *Privacy may be violated not only by the intrusion of a stranger, but by compelling or persuading a person to direct too much attention to his own feelings and to attach too much importance to their analysis.* The common usage of language affords a practical test which is almost perfect upon this subject. Conduct which can be described as indecent is always in one way or another a violation of privacy. (*Liberty* 106, emphasis mine)

What Stephen seems to argue for is both a liberal idea of freedom of thought (consonant with Mill's argument about the sometimes stultifying effect of

---

[47] For discussion of morality and privacy in the American context, see J. Smith.

public opinion and groupthink) limited by Spencer's sense of the dangers of excessive introspection.[48] The real harm of violated privacy for Stephen lies in what one is *exposed to* rather than what of oneself might become visible to others. Thus, although the protection *from* sympathy seems at first to contradict the Spencerian notion that social approbation is a motivator for good (or that fellow-feeling, by contrast to solipsism, conduces to general wellbeing), Stephen's version of privacy is a seal against the kinds of intrusive influence Lord Henry, for example, exercises over Dorian Gray. That this negative influence is specified as a proclivity to self-analysis suggests that for Stephen privacy retains elements of sociality (serving "intimate and delicate *relations*") by contrast to Warren and Brandeis's emphasis on the cultivation of personality. Indeed, if one is to infer from the passage how Stephen might define "inviolate personality," here to be "inviolate" is to be free from "moral injury," from "indecen[cy]," and from the wrong kind of sympathy and pain, traits which Dorian, and Dr. Jekyll before him, cannot claim. For all that Wilde's novel is riddled with secrets, on these terms, there is no privacy in *Dorian Gray*.

I've already indicated Simmel's view of secrecy as being a social "accomplishment." Before continuing the discussion of influence, it's worth pausing here to consider how the "universal sociological form" of secrecy works and how, as a form, it could be viewed apart from "moral valuations of its content" (464). This formal approach to secrecy resonates with Wilde's novel in particular and the infamous maxim that fronts *The Picture of Dorian Gray*: "There's no such thing as a moral or immoral book. Books are well written or badly written. That is all." Attention to the mechanism of secrecy also illuminates the dynamics of secrecy and disclosure by explaining why someone might keep a secret and, equally, why they would choose to reveal it, thereby indicating not only the secret's value for its possessor, but the energies or capacities it draws out of/from those on the secret's outside.

Simmel broaches the subject of secrecy as part of a wider discussion of intimate relationships that depend on mystery for their continuation: "That which we can see through plainly to its last ground shows us therewith the limit of its attraction, and forbids our phantasy to do its utmost in adding to the reality" (461). The implication that reality cannot sustain interest unless the imagination is free "to do its utmost" explains why novels as different as *Adam Bede* and *Dorian Gray* must wind down once confessions are made. More than that, though, Simmel's key to ongoing attractiveness shares a modernist, indeed literary, ethos that "it must be presented to us in part

---

[48] Mill 61. Stephen's argument is made in the chapter "The Doctrine of Liberty in Its Application to Morals," more specifically his explanation of the limits of "useful interference," by law and public opinion, on personal morality.

in the form of vagueness or impenetrability" (461). By withholding and/or obscuring information (especially those "internal facts of the person" noted in Simmel's discussion of discretion), the aesthetics of secrecy ensure "an enormous extension of life . . . the possibility of a second world alongside of the obvious world" (462).

Simmel's view is not wholly aesthetic, however, insofar as it shares the analogy to property found in discussions of privacy generally and in Warren and Brandeis's broader conception of a property in thoughts, feelings, and personal information. Referring to secrecy as a "form of commerce" (464) circulating in the "credit-economy" of urban societies (446), Simmel outlines four features: first, secrecy makes communities by excluding others and second, it raises the stature of the person "enshrouded by it." In this sense, possessing a secret can make even the most mundane or insignificant person mysterious, just as anyone who shares in that secret can revel in the knowledge that they possess something others do not.

The two attributes of secrecy described by Simmel that apply most clearly to *Dorian Gray*, however, are those that concern the ever-present potential for loss: the paradoxical fear of and pleasure in discovery. I will reserve discussion of the pleasure of release because it best explains Dorian's revelation of the portrait. The more immediate issue is the experience of holding a secret that develops through Basil Hallward's act of painting. Through Basil's painting, Wilde introduces the subject of influence, merges it with ideas about artistic property, and explores the interplay of privacy and secrecy in the constitution of personhood and relations between people. What does the painting reveal? Whose is it, and who therefore may control access to it? How does the power of influence affect answers to these questions?

As Simmel's analysis suggests, there is no surer sign of an inner life than the possession of secrets. Privacy allows for the cultivation of personality, but secrecy gives it mystery, or so Basil Hallward explains to Lord Henry as they admire the newly finished portrait of Dorian Gray.[49] From the beginning, the picture becomes a locus of secrecy, a visual diary that records Dorian's sins, but at this point in the narrative, Basil's concern is that the painting reveals too much about himself (173, 184). "I have put too much of myself into it," he explains, "and will not put it on display" (44). In this, Basil expresses easily recognizable common law tenets of artistic property which preserve the individual's right to "fix the limits of the publicity" to be given to any material expression of his "thoughts, sentiments, and emotions" (Warren and

---

[49] Jill Lepore puts it differently: "Secrecy is what is known, but not to everyone. Privacy is what allows us to keep what we know to ourselves." See also Vincent.

Brandeis 198). As I've hinted above, the novel's title as well as the picture's genre (as portraiture) rather complicates this question of ownership, but Basil subscribes to an expressivist aesthetic theory that firmly links the painting to its creator:

> [E]very portrait that is painted with feeling is a portrait of the artist, not the sitter. The sitter is merely the accident, the occasion. It is not he who is revealed by the painter; it is rather the painter who . . . reveals himself. The reason I will not exhibit this picture is that I am afraid that I have shown in it the secret of my own soul. (Wilde 47)

Basil's theory reflects Simmel's contention that "in the case of the artist, the form of his art . . . furnishes the only possibility of presenting his entire nature" (Simmel 457), while Basil's anxiety about its exposure is precisely the malady that privacy existed to cure by providing peace of mind "or the relief afforded by the ability to prevent any publication at all" (Warren and Brandeis 200).

Of even greater interest, however, is that these fears extend to showing the painting to Dorian himself because they will reveal the secret of Basil's "artistic idolatry" (Wilde 47) and Dorian's power to influence. In the language of *Persönlichkeit*, Basil should be free to develop his capacities, not only of technical skill but also of personhood, yet he admits that Dorian's "mere personality" threatens to "absorb my whole nature, my whole soul, my very art itself"; "I did not want any external influence in my life" (48). When paired with his decision not to show the image, this assertion reflects both Warren and Brandeis's and James Fitzjames Stephen's definitions of privacy. Having been *exposed to* Dorian's personality, Basil has "given away [his] whole soul" in a Faustian exchange for aesthetic maturity. The painting is thus a matter of privacy (what Basil may choose to display or withhold), a vessel of secrecy (Basil's anxiety as an artist and what his response to the male muse might reveal about his nature), and a register of the power of influence.[50]

Well understanding Lord Henry's opium-smoking, art-collecting, and French novel-reading tendencies, Basil enjoins him not to influence the youth who gives Basil's art "whatever charm it possesses" (55), but the subject of

---

[50] Basil's anxiety of influence is not the fear T. S. Eliot would describe in "Tradition and the Individual Talent." In those terms, it's Dorian who becomes the "strong" painter-poet, even though his final act is based in a misunderstanding, or misreading, of the relationship between himself, the painting, and Basil. Where does Lord Henry fit? The irony is that although Dorian is "poisoned by a book," his own expressivism registers visually, which suggests that Basil's idealized image of Dorian has influenced Dorian more than he's aware of, and even more than Lord Henry.

Lord Henry's "bad influence" and his own theories of personality corroborate and expand on Stephen's sense that the wrong kind of fraternity can act as a violation of privacy and hence as an infringement of liberty. Henry defines the "aim of life" as "self-development" or "to realize one's nature perfectly" (58). Influence is therefore immoral, he argues,

> Because to influence a person is to give him one's own soul. He does not think his natural thoughts, or burn with his natural passions. His virtues are not real to him. His sins . . . are borrowed. He becomes an echo of some one [sic] else's music, an actor of a part that has not been written for him. (58)

Lord Henry's own influence on Dorian is fully consonant with both of these ideas. On the one hand, he imagines a richer than Arnoldian Hellenism that would emerge "if one man were to live out his life fully and completely, were to give form to every feeling, expression to every thought, reality to every dream" (59). Certainly Dorian will pursue this project, but Lord Henry claims it for himself, too, notwithstanding that he must therefore be guilty of depriving Dorian of his own soul: "There was something enthralling in the exercise of influence" (75), he muses, as he plans to be to Dorian what Dorian had been to Basil; "He would seek to dominate him—had already, indeed, half done so. He would make that wonderful spirit his own" (76). Whatever the result of his experiment might be (and he doesn't much care how it will end, his self-professed scientific interest in the process rendering him unsympathetic to his subject), he stakes his own self-development on this new sensation, "the most satisfying joy left to us in an age so limited and vulgar as our own" (76).

Lord Henry's analogy between himself and Dorian reveals Basil's and Dorian's susceptibility and recalls the distinction between a *right to* and a *right of* privacy, which in turn has implications for the novel's dynamics of disclosure. (What does *Dorian Gray* tell us that *Jekyll and Hyde* has not?) Dorian's abject(ed) self means he doesn't possess the inviolate personality that under Warren and Brandeis would entitle him to privacy, even when privacy is taken to mean only the power of controlling publication and limiting access. He has no *right of* privacy. Dorian's personality certainly also fails Stephen's test of being free from moral injury and indecency, or the wrong kind of sympathy. The novel suggests that he, like Basil, is too open to external influence and that the influence leads not just to Dorian's libertinism but also, as was true of Basil, to an excessive attachment to the analysis of his own feelings (figured most notably by Dorian's constant consultation of the portrait and fear of separation from it). By suggesting their personalities are weak in this way, the novel doesn't remove blame from Lord Henry so much as show how necessary a *right to* privacy is to the development of that inviolate personality. In other words, the right to be let alone may encompass the right to be free from undue influence because only then can one pursue freedom of thought and of expression (hence the connection to liberty). The irony, in Dorian's case at least, is that his eccentricity is not the admirable antidote to public opinion imagined by Mill. His influence on Sibyl Vane, Adrian Singleton, Alan Campbell, and others shows rather how he infringes their privacy with his own indecent conduct.

Thus far I've discussed Basil's position that on both aesthetic and legalistic grounds the picture of Dorian Gray belongs to him. Albeit a portrait of another man, the painting expresses the artist's inner life who is therefore at liberty to exhibit or conceal it. In this way the novel adheres to what James Q. Whitman characterized as the common law approach to privacy as liberty.[51] By contrast, Lord Henry articulates a more Continental approach to privacy as *Persönlichkeit*, or freedom from determinism, which Whitman explains was so often framed as an artistic, creative freedom and exemplified through the figure of the artist (with the tantalizing suggestion that Henry is more an artist than Basil). Poised between these two figures, Dorian pursues Harry's model, but his personal transformation as registered in the portrait blinds him to the painting's continued relationship to the painter. Dorian's transactional approach to the picture, his sense of its instrumentality *for him*, in other words, occludes its value as Basil's artistic property.[52] After all, it's the Picture *of* Dorian Gray, not *by* Dorian Gray. (Of course, it's tempting to think that Dorian overwrites or paints over Basil's vision, but the novel never explains by what force of agency—magic, chemistry, mildew, prayer—the transformation occurs. It's more accurate to say he exploits a power that doesn't belong to him.)

Dorian's analysis of his image is at once a visual, spiritual, and literary preoccupation. The picture "held the secret of his life, and told his story" (128), and yet Dorian asks himself "What should he do if Basil Hallward

---

[51] In the American context this liberty meant freedom from state tyranny. However, there is a question about where English law sits within these western cultures. David J. Seipp, writing on judicial recognition of the right to privacy, points out that for all that Warren and Brandeis cited numerous common law precedents, they were ahead of both the English courts and the British Parliament in recognizing a right to privacy. Rejecting calls from legal writers across the Commonwealth ("English Judicial Recognition" 327), the House of Lords turned to defamation law as the next best thing for protecting privacy, the implication being that privacy could only be protected in the breach as with libel. And as discussed in Chapter 3, the strength of the press lobby in Parliament made the prospect of a statutory protection a non-starter.

[52] See Anat Rosenberg on value assessments.

came and asked to look at his own picture?" (130–1). This question recalls Simmel's discussion of secrecy's formal properties, first, that a possessor's pleasure in and sensibility of a secret's value is highest at the moment of its revelation and, second, that the revelation which will realize the secret's value is a "danger" that can originate within the self as well as from outside it:

> Secrecy is sustained by the consciousness that it might be exploited... [T]he external danger of being discovered is interwoven with the internal danger of self-discovery, which has the fascination of the brink of a precipice. Secrecy sets barriers between men, but at the same time offers the seductive temptation to break through barriers by gossip or confession. (466)

Basil does ask to see the portrait—indeed, plans to exhibit it after all—and thus poses the "external danger" of discovery. Yet the scene, in which Dorian leads Basil to confess the reasons for his original reserve, gives way to a second, mirrored scene in which Dorian volunteers to show Basil the now degraded portrait, adding "the internal danger of self-discovery" to his list of experiences. Confronted by the painter, who doesn't recognize his friend in the terrible rumors circulated about him, Dorian catches on Basil's idea that to know someone requires accessing their inner life, or seeing the soul (184) (a point Simmel will make in respect to intimacy but which he limits by the provision of mystery). This phrase, "to see my soul," "show the soul" reverberates throughout the novel and is revealed in the painting, which in this scene Dorian calls the "diary of my life . . . [which] never leaves the room in which it's written" (185). What had included too much of Basil's soul is now a text to read, a new secret to disclose, and *Dorian*'s soul to show. Yet the fascination of the portrait, following Simmel, can be read as the "fascination of the brink of the precipice" from which vantage point Dorian experiences the temptation to confess and with it the danger that by realizing his secret's value, he will also have to lose it.[53]

It's important to emphasize two things about the dynamics of disclosure in this scene. First is that Dorian wants to make this confession, not to gain forgiveness, but to impose the burden of his knowledge, or, per Simmel, to release "the tension of reticence" (Simmel 466). In a show of nominal

---

[53] Simmel's language also eroticizes the feeling of possession: "Secrecy involves a tension which, at the moment of revelation, finds its release. This constitutes the climax in the development of the secret; in it the whole charm of secrecy concentrates and rises to its highest pitch—just as the moment of the disappearance of an object brings out the feeling of its value in the most intense degree" (465). The "danger" of discovery becomes more pointed in light of Wilde's sexuality but also more tempting as an expression of the "Art of Being Found Out" per Tóibín's discussion.

catholicity, he playfully teases Basil by calling the painting his diary, but he blames him as well and uses the disclosure to exact revenge: "the man who had painted the portrait that was the origin of all his shame was to be burdened the rest of his life . . . with what he had done" (Wilde 184). There is power here, perhaps even as Simmel imagines, in a "negative and perverted form" albeit not in actual "self-abasement and contrition" (Simmel 466). A second point is that Basil, by contrast, feels compunction about confronting Dorian; "what right had he to pry?" (Wilde 184). Where Dorian has a secret to tell, Basil invokes the privacy principle and, going further, imagines Dorian's suffering in a way that recalls Stephen's comments on the confessional and casuistry:

> That any one human creature should ever really strip his soul stark naked for the inspection of any other, and be able to hold up his head afterwards, is not, I suppose, impossible because so many people profess to do it; but to lookers-on from the outside it is inconceivable. (*Liberty* 107)

Not only is Basil's sympathy of the right kind, he also imagines, as a "looker-on from the outside," how Dorian's *self-respect* must be harmed by the truth of the rumors. This idea of being able to "hold up one's head" makes the defense of privacy a defense of dignity and the observance of privacy an act of discretion.

Basil's assumptions are not altogether well-founded, however. Dorian answers Basil's plea that they repent together by stabbing him, and the failure of Dorian's experiment with self-denial (that fails to alter the picture) moves him to stab the portrait as well. Believing he can kill the painter, the painting, the past, and his conscience all at once, he kills himself instead. An easy lesson of this famously "immoral" novel is that it's impossible to live without a conscience, or to deny one's past yet be a person in the fullest sense: "So long as a man can be said to be himself in any intelligible sense of the word," wrote Stephen, "he must more or less remember and pass judgment on his past existence" (*Liberty* 239). However, the restored perfection of the pentimento complicates this interpretation. Warren and Brandeis argued that privacy depended on and existed to protect personality, and it was personality that informed theories of artistic property. Dorian's crime, his two-fold murder of the painter and "the painter's work" (Wilde 250), is also a theft, a misappropriation of artistic property and, fundamentally, a misreading. Even when Basil himself contemplated stabbing the portrait with a palette knife, he realized "it would be murder" (67) and desisted. But Dorian's death, by restoring Basil's "ideal" to the image, allows the art object to stand; it survives its creator, as well as those who (mis)interpret it.

Dorian assumes a liberty to cultivate his personality that disregards the importance of the social body. In the most obvious sense, he becomes a criminal antagonist of the social order. In less obvious ways, his reductive version of privacy leads him to underappreciate the portrait as a shared property (his image, yes, but also an object that binds him to the painter its creator, and one that embodies Basil's "thoughts, sentiments, and ideas"), and although Dorian studies the impact of his experiences on the portrait (sensations bought at others' cost), he again underestimates the lasting impact on others of his secret self-study. Ruining the canvas cannot undo the damage it merely reflects. My point has been that *Dorian Gray* allows us to move beyond the physical or spatial dimensions of privacy towards more abstract understandings of property, but even more than *Jekyll and Hyde*, *Dorian Gray*'s emphasis on influence expresses the permeability of the boundaries around the self. There is no "multiform, complex creature" which has not had to negotiate the influences around it or which should not be mindful of its impact on others. Whether privacy depends on an inviolate personality, or on a narrower set of more interpersonal relationships that retain a role for social approbation, privacy has to wrestle with these models of personhood.

In both *The Strange Case of Dr. Jekyll and Mr. Hyde* and *The Picture of Dorian Gray*, disorders of the self (of the "soul," if not the mind) are figured in representational deformities and hidden away in private spaces where the revelation of secrets leads to murder, and misreading leads to suicide. Although the actors' intentionality is ambiguous (does Jekyll kill himself, or does Hyde murder him? Does Dorian's attempt to mortify his conscience amount to a purposeful or accidental suicide?), in the end both are wounds inflicted by one part of the self on another and, in Jekyll's case, on the shared body. In Utterson and Basil Hallward, both novels depict characters who assume the existence of a core subjectivity, a continuous and consistent self that persists in the face of superficial change, in order to depart from that notion and through Jekyll and Dorian consider the implications of new ones.[54]

These ideas about personhood place both novels in an uneasy relationship to the ideas of property and personality central to Warren and Brandeis's conception of privacy, especially in their focus on the circulation of texts—more specifically, the "thoughts, sentiments, and ideas" embedded in them—as a form of disclosure. Colm Tóibín, writing of Stevenson, Wilde, and other secret sharers at the turn of the century, attributes this impulse to give oneself

---

[54] Basil is one of those "people who go in for being consistent," while Dorian disdains "the shallow psychology of those who conceive the Ego in man as a thing, simple, permanent, reliable, and of one essence" (Wilde 147, 175). See also Lisa Rodensky on the "forensic person" (41).

away to a human need "to have something recorded and known because private life and private acts are not enough" to affirm a rounded personality ("The Art of Being Found Out"). "Without public knowledge," he continues, "even the most strong and significant [feelings] are like books imagined and sketched but not written or published. They are no use to anybody." Jekyll's will and "Full Statement" and Basil's painting of Dorian reveal secrets that comprise and confirm the inner life of their subjects, making secrets into a kind of intellectual property (the secret of the painting being a double property). And getting at the substance of these texts has been the driving compulsion of both novels. Staging scenes of disclosure and reticence, they raise questions about why some secrets are kept while others are revealed, the point often becoming less about the nature of the secret than about the choice to tell or not.

As the act of disposal is to ownership, so paradoxically is publication of one's own secret the surest sign of its possessor's inner life. A way of asserting the self, telling secrets can also serve to create relationships and establish intimacy, but it may create burdens by making others share in carrying their weight. Put differently, the sharing of secrets, whether through gossip or reading, may serve to constitute and preserve a community in the way Simmel describes and in the way the professional community in *Jekyll and Hyde* circulates information amongst its members, but the confession of secrets, to the extent that its purpose is the more insular one of constituting the individual self, puts the community in service to the self, as Dorian does when he maliciously shows Basil the picture. Instead of the sympathetic sharing that Herbert Spencer imagined would promote justice and civilized life, we see the atomistic tendencies of a pre-social world, or the coming twentieth-century world. Worse, the revelation of these secrets is coterminous with acts of destruction. Concealed throughout the narrative, these secret texts, when revealed, prove to be inassimilable or unreadable within its confines. Indeed, they remain unanalyzed *because* they exceed the boundaries of the novel, the place where reading is staged, in a dynamic that transforms both authors' concerns *in* the novel into concerns *about* the novel more broadly.

Law's own scientific turn towards making people legible transforms character into identity. For a fuller account of character, one has to turn to literature and its increasing investment in understanding and representing interiority, or the psychological realism that Henry James and the coming modernists achieved by delving directly into the mind.[55] What's surprising

---

[55] Brian Artese observes that omniscience does away with the need for characters to confess or to testify: to make spontaneous and unreserved disclosures, on the one hand, or to "craft" statements about oneself for public consumption with all the implications of a

here in pairing *Jekyll and Hyde* and *Dorian Gray* with "The Right to Privacy" is that the reduction or loss of character perpetrated by law's turn to identity is the same which Stevenson himself lamented was produced by realist techniques so that the corrective will lead to methods which depict character to a fault. The new realism must lead, ironically, to the very penetration of consciousness that, according to Warren and Brandeis, constitutes a violation of privacy, one which, if not protected by law, would lead to the disintegration of the modern legal subject. Thus, although the prospect of penetrating consciousness may give "passion" and "vitality" to the experience of reading, reading both novels through a legal lens suggests that it is literature, or the impulse to read literature, that by turning readers, in Stephen's phraseology, into "lookers-on from the outside," jeopardizes the sanctity of the home, the privacy of the legal subject, and the wellbeing of the individual.[56]

Stevenson's "strange case" is certainly not one that Warren and Brandeis consulted as a precedent for privacy, for although Stevenson shares their impulse to protect privacy, he does not ground it in a notion of inviolate personality. In fact, Stevenson doesn't seem to posit a reason to protect privacy so much as offer obfuscation and misdirection as a way to do it. A different modernist tendency, this evasiveness perpetuates the compulsion to talk, read, and share secrets—the desire for stories—that in one sense is in tension with law's articulation of the right to privacy, that is, as the creation of an inner life that needs protection from just this sort of prying. If we recall that the protection was not meant to cancel out communication, rather to allow individuals to control what could be said or known about them, then in another sense, we see that both novels have it both ways—by exposing character but making it impossible to understand thereby preserving the mystery which sustains intimate relationships, but also jeopardizes the trust on which modern society depended. This impasse begs the question as to the value of this sort of activity: what is the point or even the effect of this ambivalence?

Just as the right to be let alone did not constitute an injunction to be alone, so do different texts constellate or interpolate a particular readership

---

self-interested selection of detail, on the other (104). M. Kellen Williams, similarly, reads Stevenson's "novel of adventure" as an answer to the "novel of character" whose reliance on realist (read as scientific) techniques of observation flattens out "passion" and "vitality" which *Jekyll and Hyde* explores (414–15). Robbie B. H. Goh tackles readings of the novel's resistance to realism most directly and argues that "narrative itself" and "acts of interpretative judgment structured and sustained by the narrative" are more significant sources of meaning in this novel than "thematic concerns and simplifying social oppositions" (159).

[56] This is dangerously close to a very eighteenth-century conclusion that novel-reading is a moral hazard, and twentieth-century obscenity cases suggest the idea had currency even then.

without implying criticism of other works and their respective communities, or requiring that any single text command a mass audience. Reading *The Strange Case of Dr. Jekyll and Mr. Hyde* and *The Picture of Dorian Gray* together with "The Right to Privacy," in spite of their differing models of character, points towards an increasing insularity and atomism at the end of the nineteenth century, on the one hand. But through their specific analyses of the threats to character, they also reveal, on the other, the way communities are formed through acts of selective disclosure and silence, acts which do not eliminate social relationships between people as much as reorient and relocate them as private relationships conducted behind closed doors.

5

The English Dreyfus Case: Status as Character in an Illiberal Age

> Now we turn to the last tribunal of all, a tribunal which never errs when the facts are fairly laid before them, and we ask the public of Great Britain whether this thing [is] to go on.
> Arthur Conan Doyle, "The Case of Mr. George Edalji" (1907)

> All relationships of people to each other rest, as a matter of course, upon the precondition that they know something about each other.
> Georg Simmel, "The Sociology of Secrecy and of Secret Societies" (1906)

Hester Prynne and Hetty Sorrel didn't want to talk. Helen Graham and Samuel Rowton didn't want to be talked about. Helen Graham kept her secrets and managed their disclosure in a redacted diary, but even that gift couldn't keep Gilbert Markham from following her home, any more than Jekyll's pleas deterred Utterson from showing up uninvited at his house. Cousin Henry was also pestered by a lawyer, Phineas Finn by an editor, but the ever-encroaching press that published libels about them both encouraged two other lawyers to write a treatise about privacy. Politicians and newspapermen argued that public interest was more important than private character, and while the gossips of Wildfell and Cranford would agree with Georg Simmel that communities have a need to know the people among them, Dr. Jekyll, Basil Hallward, Dorian Gray, and many other characters encountered in this study rebutted the call for character evidence with claims to the nascent rights to silence or privacy, claims made in order to preserve their reputations, assert their liberty, or cultivate their individual personalities.

This mash-up of literary characters, historical persons, legal rules, and legislative debates highlights the close connection between, and wider applicability of, the forms of character-talk discussed in individual chapters. It reminds us that the operation of getting at character in the novel and at law depended on the dynamics of secrecy and disclosure, with its tension between an individual's capacity to limit access and law's capacity to compel, as well as on the legal allocation of responsibility, which paralleled the allocation of narrative attention in the construction of the novel. The nexus of characters and legal concepts also emphasizes the importance of each of these modes of character-building to the formation and maintenance of communal boundaries, the public life of personal reputation, and ideas about the liberty and dignity of individual persons, all of which informed an ever-shifting balance of the rights and responsibilities of the many compared with those of the one. Most importantly, these forms of character-talk are all dimensions or tools of storytelling that highlight the narrative underpinnings of legal and literary realities. If it seems self-evident that the novel is a character-system, one aim of this book has been to make it equally as obvious that law is a character-system, too.

In his 1983 essay "Nomos and Narrative," legal scholar Robert Cover sweepingly observed that narrative is foundational to all normative activity and that every aspect of the nomos or "normative world" is grounded in it. "History and literature cannot escape their location in a normative universe," he writes, "nor can prescription, even when embodied in a legal text, escape its origin and its end in experience, in the narratives that are the trajectories plotted upon material reality by our imagination" (96). Other passages have been cited more frequently, but this one—with its references to history, literature, and law—captures the power of aesthetic and cultural forms not only to shape and give meaning to experience, but also to entail "prescription" such that culture acquires a force like law. At the same time, it insists that legal texts, which might appear to reside outside "experience" so as to regulate it from afar, are inseparable from it. Rules derive from, are directed towards, and act upon experience (their "origin" and "end"), which constitutes a "material reality" upon which the "imagination" constructs or "plots" a future course of action. Sounds like fiction.

Cover contended that the work of world creating (and maintaining) is always a collective, social action. Each community locates its principles and stories, often in a central text or a dominant interpretation of that text, and commits to living out the implications of that interpretation in the present and into the future. If legal institutions, legal interpretations, or the application of law as social control seem especially directed towards making and maintaining social worlds, Cover reminds readers that the *nomos* is a world out of which law emerges and with which law is in a sense identical. Both are described as a "system of tension": *nomos* "between reality and vision," and law "linking a concept of reality to an imagined alternative" (101). And as a process or activity, both *nomos* and law are essentially aspirational, always poised between the real and ideal and always weighing the former by the latter. In this system, narrative supplies the "normative significance"; it makes the meaning that shapes understanding and inspires the commitment to live out that meaning: "To inhabit a *nomos* is to know how to *live* in it" (97). Imagine then, as Kim Lane Scheppele asked readers to do in her Foreword to the "storytelling" issue of the *Michigan Law Review*, the impact of being excluded from the creation, interpretation, or reconfiguration of the dominant narrative: "How are people to think about the law when their stories, the ones they have lived and believed, are rejected by courts, only to be replaced by other versions with different legal results?" (2080).

Cover's and Scheppele's observations make visible two sets of tensions. First is the gap between the real and the ideal that narrative seeks to mediate and which is always at work in the creation of the *nomos*. The second is variation within the "concept of reality" and even within the ideal that a community takes as its starting place and which so-called "outsider narratives"—stories that fall outside frames of legal recognition (e.g. as with excluded evidence) or which are interpolated into master narratives ("stock stories") that misrecognize or misrepresent a defendant's particular experience (Brooks, "Narrative Transactions" 1)—are poised to remediate.

In this concluding chapter, then, I want to pull together strands of what I've called a jurisprudential theory of character by turning to the once-forgotten history of George Edalji, the Staffordshire solicitor who served three years for horse-ripping before Arthur Conan Doyle took up his cause. Conan Doyle won his campaign to exculpate Edalji by using his own literary reputation and access to the press to move public opinion and the Home Office. By contrast to Trollope's skepticism about liberties of the press, Conan Doyle used its freedom to pressure the government to review the case and restore Edalji's personal and professional reputation. What becomes visible in newspaper accounts of Edalji's trial and what Conan Doyle found in the available records was a set of stock stories that predetermined not only how narrative attention would be allocated but also the kind of character evidence that was admitted or ignored.

To appreciate and extend the impact that the interplay of competing legal, literary, fictional, and non-fictional stories has on both individual character and national culture, this chapter also takes up Julian Barnes's 2005 novel *Arthur & George* which, like Hawthorne's and Eliot's historical novels with which this study began, offers both a fictional story of the past and an implied story of the real present. The final section turns to recent work on the "resurgence of character" in narratives of national and cultural identity that illustrate the legal force of cultural narratives, the cultural force of legal narratives, and the necessity of counter-narrative in an age of renewed essentialism.

"A kind of squalid Dreyfus case": George Edalji, Arthur Conan Doyle, and the Court of Public Appeal

In 1906, when George Edalji was convicted of mutilating a colliery pony and terrorizing his family and neighborhood, Great Britain had no court of criminal appeal. Questions of law arising from civil cases could be "reserved" and from 1848 referred to the Court for Crown Cases Reserved, but these questions did not pertain to facts established in the original trial and were not mooted by the defendant. Only in 1907, and partly through the influence of Edalji's case, did defendants gain a right of appeal to a new Court of Criminal Appeals (Baker 139). But appeals were certainly made. In this section I survey the story as it was emplotted at law, and the alternative story as it was debated in government and in the press before moving finally to Julian Barnes's fictional recreation. What were the stock stories that informed the investigation into Edalji and his trial? What was George Edalji's "self-believed story" (to borrow Erving Goffman's term), and what structural and historical conditions prevented it from being heard and endorsed at law? (qtd. in Scheppele 2079). In other words, how did his outsider story counter them, and how, in the absence of formal mechanisms of appeal, did his partial success nevertheless depend on the advocacy of strong insiders in a way that leaves his own story still unheard?

George Edalji was sentenced to seven years' hard labor for slashing a horse and for participating in, if not masterminding, a years-long campaign of harassment and threatening letters directed towards members of his Staffordshire community, his family, and even himself: a strange pastime for the bookish solicitor and author of *Railway Law for the "Man in the Train"* whose father was also the vicar of Great Wyrley. But such anomalies were cited by prosecution and defense alike, and especially by Edalji's most famous advocate Sir Arthur Conan Doyle, as evidence in their favor.

Accounts of the pre-history of the trial and of subsequent measures to overturn the conviction point first to Edalji's ethnicity. George's father, Bombay-born Shapurji Edalji, had converted to Christianity and trained in England as an Anglican clergyman (Risinger 3–4). Following his marriage to Charlotte Stoneham, Charlotte's uncle gave him the living of St. Mark's. No official, public account pointed to the Rev. Edalji's ethnicity as having impaired his reputation in the community (his politics and management of local affairs were sufficiently controversial), and none cited George's Anglo-Indian heritage as being directly at issue (34–5). However, the letters that began to plague the Edaljis, first in the period 1888–9 and again in 1892–5, routinely employed variations on their "blackness" (36).[1] Certainly, racial prejudice dominates Conan Doyle's explanation of the reasons George Edalji was targeted. In a community of farmers and miners such as Great Wyrley, George's education and gentlemanly status were also poised to rankle British attitudes about class. Add ethnic difference and prominent social position to the effect of extreme myopia on his facial expression and, in Conan Doyle's view, George must have "seem[ed] a very queer man to the eyes of an English village, and therefore to be associated with any queer event" ("The Strange Case of George Edalji").

Further queering George, the prosecutor Mr. Disturnal referred in his summation to the "extraordinary arrangement" by which George and his father had slept in the same bedroom for more than seventeen years ("The Great Wyrley Outrages," Oct. 30). Speculation about the reason for this arrangement ran the gamut from Mrs. Edalji's left-over habit of nursing George's sister to the Rev. and Mrs. Edalji's passionless relationship to the possibility of child sexual abuse. Clearly incommensurate with one another, the reasons' irregularity marked yet another form of George's difference and predisposed belief in his guilt. During the three-day trial, more than one witness was reported to have said he "was not a right sort" ("The Great Wyrley Outrages," Oct. 23), and in the summing up Chairman of the Sessions Reginald Hardy ventured that "the offense had been committed by some person possessed of a peculiar twist in the brain" and found it "impossible to arrive at any motive why the prisoner should have committed such a horrible act" ("Outrages," Oct. 30).

The verdict did locate a motive, or at least a disposition, however, in Edalji's character as an Oriental and in this way reinserted the "very queer man" into a stock story that could explain his behavior. The jury returned a guilty verdict but recommended mercy because of Edalji's "personal position"; however, Hardy weighed the "disgrace inflicted on the neighbourhood" more heavily and passed a sentence of seven years' penal servitude ("Outrages," Oct. 30). Litchfield's *The Mercury* devotes a full section to Edalji's demeanor in which the verdict transforms him from a composed and candid professional into an Oriental type. A "slight pallor" enters his face when he first hears the sentence, but then he "seemed to become darker, almost black, as he leaned over the edge of the dock"; his light suit "emphasized the black face

---

[1] See also Risinger 40n164. Risinger relies heavily on two works that compile personal, public, and formerly confidential Home Office records: Gordon Weaver's *Conan Doyle and the Parson's Son* (2006) and Stephen Hines and Steven Womack's *The True Crime Files of Sir Arthur Conan Doyle* (2001). I sample newspaper accounts and parliamentary records directly from the original source.

and the staring, wide-opened gleaming eyes"; he "pass[es] into a hypnotic trance" and at last, moved by the warder, "sighed ... and visibly relaxed into resignation. It was the Oriental's acceptance of fate" ("Outrages," Oct. 30). Here George's physical transformation is keyed to his new (or rediscovered) character, not merely as a criminal, but as an Oriental whose criminality is un-English.[2]

Because "character" in the nineteenth century was not so inconsistent as to be altered by a single event, the press's narrative suggests rather that it is Edalji's English mask that drains away with the verdict. Shifting to the *Daily Mail*'s coverage, *The Mercury* report of October 30, 1903 finally reveals the operative stock story. The ending of the trial ("now that Edalji is convicted") validates the prosecution's story, but *The Mercury*'s coverage goes even further by adding information which had not been introduced at trial, namely, that Edalji's name had been connected, purportedly from the start twelve years before, with the "gross" and "coarse" series of anonymous letters. The paper asks readers to interpret this new information in an old way, however. Playing up its own objectivity (the revelation about the letters becomes "permissible" only once the conviction is reached), it also positions readers to draw on what the discourses of a racialized criminology suggested was known all along. George's appearance is claimed to be patently criminal: "Those who closely studied this extraordinary criminal in the dock would have no doubt that he is a degenerate of the worst type. His jaw and mouth are those of a man of very debased life" and, further, he is said to have "gained for himself the reputation of being a lover of mystery—*another* Oriental trait, and one that goes far to explain the anonymous letters" (emphasis mine). Ronald R. Thomas's analysis of Havelock Ellis confirms that representations of the criminal increasingly assumed the "physical characteristics of colonial subjects" and offered to public imagination a "fragment of the prehistoric past that [had] mysteriously found its way from foreign places into the modern, civilized world" (*Detective Fiction* 210). Thus, while George Edalji relaxed into resignation, *The Mercury*'s use of stock stories about "the subtle Eastern mind" made it possible for readers to relax as well by attributing all the anomalies of the Wyrley outrages—starting with the mixed marriage of a Parsee convert to Christianity and his prestigious position as vicar—to a recognizable type.

---

[2] Daniel D. Blinka observes that even in modern evidence law "Character estimations loom large in our daily 'factfinding' outside the courthouse, and predictably, juries crave such information in the courtroom as well. The expectation of such proof cannot be turned off like a light switch. Absent formal character proof, the factfinder will fill in the gaps with whatever is more readily available, especially demeanor" (104).

Efforts for Edalji's release began almost immediately following the conviction, but it was not until May 1907, following the report of a Committee of Inquiry, that Home Secretary Herbert Gladstone recommended a free pardon, albeit without compensation. The process of petition and review as well as the peculiarities of the committee's findings are interesting by themselves, but two aspects are especially noteworthy. One is that the committee, led by Arthur Wilson, lamented the curious absence of a trial report that would have clarified the jury's position, particularly regarding the letters but without which leads to inference if not guesswork. Drawing on press coverage instead, their report routinely refers to what they "take to be" the jury's conclusion, what the jury "must be taken to have held," or "the finding at which we think the jury arrived" about Edalji's authorship of the so-called "Greatorex letters of 1903" (Wilson et al. 5).[3] In an appendix to the Committee's report, Sir Kenelm Digby explains that recourse to "the best newspaper reports" (7–9) was part of the usual practice of review, which both heightens the legal significance of cultural narratives and shows how in this instance they actually effected Edalji's pardon (even as the committee used their vagaries to blame him for having contributed to his own misery).[4] A second observation concerns the procedure of returning the committee's assessment to the Chairman of the sessions, the judge, and even to the investigating police for commentary (Digby 7). This practice in particular drew criticism from Conan Doyle. Indeed, it's no wonder that he took his version of Edalji's case directly to the papers since they had standing within existing practices of review and yet remained outside the potential corruptions of officialdom.

This is not to suggest, of course, that government intervention was inherently flawed or that public opinion was foolproof, however much Conan Doyle pandered to his readers' self-complacency. In his peroration, Conan Doyle praises an unerring, rational-minded public in an effort to create conscientious readers freed from the self-interest of government insiders (in effect, he creates a new group to claim solidarity with the outsider Edalji).

---

[3] Denying that George's authorship of the letters makes him guilty of the maimings, Wilson observes: "We think it quite as likely that they are the letter of an innocent man, but a wrong-headed and malicious man, indulging in a piece of impish mischief, pretending to know what he may know nothing of, in order to puzzle the police, and increasing their difficulties in a very difficult investigation": Edalji "to some extent brought his troubles on himself" (5).

[4] See Sir Kenelm Digby, "Note to the Home Office in Dealing with Criminal Petitions," a memorandum on the procedure of the Home Office and the Home Secretary written in regard to the Adolf Beck case (one of four, including Edalji's, usually cited as having led to the creation of a Court of Criminal Appeal).

At the same time, he regrets pitting a public tribunal against the Home Office because the implied criticism might "weaken the power of the forces that make for law and order by shaking the confidence of the public" ("Strange Case," Feb. 3). Yet as a representative body, the House *was* the public and, particularly in the matter of appeals, the only conduit between it, the Home Secretary, and the Crown. Before Conan Doyle concerned himself in the case, the exposé journal *Truth*, edited by Henry Labouchère, Liberal MP for Northampton, had been active in its support of Edalji. In July 1907, F. E. Smith (MP for Liverpool, Walton) diverted a discussion of vivisection towards one about Edalji (a grim irony, given the mutilation of the pit ponies), during which he called attention to the 10,000 signatories who petitioned the Home Secretary to review the case and called for a new public inquiry to remove the last smirch on Edalji's character left by the attribution of the Greatorex letters ("Civil Services and Revenue Departments Estimates," c. 1004).[5] We've seen one way that the newspapers framed Edalji's story; how then did Edalji's story look to Conan Doyle?

In a perhaps unfortunate echo of Stevenson's novella, Conan Doyle's "The Strange Case of George Edalji" appeared first in the *Daily Telegraph* on January 11 and 12, 1907 with the *New York Times* running a similar spread on February 2 and 3. The opening paragraph of the first installment in *The Times* proclaims that one look at George sufficed to show both why he was suspected and why he must have been innocent of the crimes. As noted above, Conan Doyle makes much of George's physical appearance: the "vacant bulge-eyed staring appearance" that came of his extreme myopia and his dark skin signal the otherness on which Conan Doyle grounds his defense ("Strange Case," Feb. 2). While he ends by buttering up his readers, he starts by offering himself as the most objective investigator, abjuring "preconceived theory"—a charge leveled against the Staffordshire constabulary first by the Wilson committee and again by Conan Doyle—in favor of an impartial study of the evidence on both sides. If the investigation itself had been neutral, it nevertheless led to his current partisanship. Begging to "tell the strange story from the beginning," he "hope[s] that the effect of my narrative will be to

---

[5] The debate was ostensibly about the Home Secretary's salary but was really a vehicle to call attention to the recent report of a Royal Commission on Vivisection and its findings that the law was not being properly administered. See "Civil Services and Revenue Departments Estimates." See also "The Edalji Case," in which Viscount Castlereagh refers to Digby's memo and asks Gladstone whether he will call the public inquiry, to which the Home Secretary replies, basically, he would if he could.

raise such a wave of feeling in this country as will make some public reconsideration of the case inevitable."

And let it be said that Conan Doyle's account is curious in its own right, too. The narrative maintains that differences of race and class marked George Edalji and influenced the case from the beginning:

> It is this studious youth, who touches neither alcohol nor tobacco, and is so blind that he gropes his way in the dusk, who is the dangerous barbarian who scours the country at night, ripping up horses. Is it not perfectly clear, looking at his strange swarthy face and bulging eyes, that it is not the village ruffian, but rather the unfortunate village scapegoat, who stands before you?

Yet Conan Doyle's criticism of Home Office protocols in the second installment deploys the same discriminatory tropes used in *The Mercury* reportage. Calling for an inquiry into the fate of the R. D. Yelverton petition, Conan Doyle marvels at the practice of referring an investigation of police procedure to the police; "I cannot imagine anything more absurd and unjust in an Oriental despotism than this" ("Strange Case," Feb. 3). No rhetorical lapse here, Conan Doyle reverses the relationship between outward appearance and true Englishness: George is visibly othered but thoroughly English, while the face of "British justice" hides Oriental despotism. If George was Hyde on the outside, Conan Doyle's own detective work would reveal the Jekyll at his core.

To illustrate this pattern of behavior more clearly, Conan Doyle cites the recent Adolf Beck case and turns to yet "a more classic example, for in all its details this seems to me to form a kind of squalid Dreyfus case." The outsider targeted, the professional reputation maligned, a campaign for redress (led by another literary light, no less), and questions of forgery all support the analogy, but Conan Doyle turns regretfully to the worst point of comparison:

> that in the one case you have a clique of French officials going from excess to excess in order to cover an initial mistake, and that in the other you have the Staffordshire police acting in the way I have described.

Conan Doyle's narrative marshals the outrage of a liberal, English lover of justice and defender of the weak, but even here it is possible to see a stock story of honor and chivalry fighting corruption at work. The tale was effective and by May of that year Edalji had his pardon (although as noted already the campaign for full redress continued). But why? Paul Gewirtz asks what, in a "culture of argument," wins a legal decision-maker's acceptance, especially when that story comes from an avowed outsider who by definition may encounter barriers of unfamiliarity, skepticism, or discomfort in his listeners (6)? How did Edalji's outsider's story manage to gain public support and to reach decision-makers within government?[6]

First, the comparison to Dreyfus resonated with Edalji's other supporters. The *New York Times* proclaimed "Conan Doyle Solves a New Dreyfus Case." F. E. Smith, in his July 18 address to the House, "recalled a time when we involved ourselves in our own virtue and talked of the secret dossier in France . . . they [in Britain] had also the *chose jugée*, and for the 'honour of the Army' had only to substitute the 'honour of the police'" ("Civil Services and Revenue Departments Estimates," c. 1015).[7] Indeed, it was historian Douglas Johnson's reference to Edalji in his own account of the Dreyfus affair that piqued Julian Barnes's interest. So, one reason the story worked is because it was already familiar. Conan Doyle took a story that should have reflected the superiority of British institutions, especially the common law, and used it to indict, if not the whole system, then the corrupt officials who were harming it. Second, his tone is both chivalric and regretful. He doesn't want to impugn the government, but his belief in law and order requires him to demand a public inquiry (with the full conviction that it could and would be conducted fairly). The third reason combines the story's familiarity with Conan Doyle's ethos: this is a story of Britain's historical relationship with France, of Britain's Imperial identity, and a true detective story written by the creator of Britain's most famous consulting detective. "The Strange Case of George Edalji" appealed because, as the *New York Times* reported, it "reads like a new adventure of Sherlock Holmes . . . which, were it fiction, would be as breathlessly interesting as any of the author's stories and which, being an accurate statement of an actual case loudly calling for rectification, is doubly thrilling" ("Conan Doyle Solves a New Dreyfus Case" 1).[8] Nevertheless, one

---

[6] In *Law's Stories: Narrative and Rhetoric in the Law*, Peter Brooks and Paul Gewirtz move beyond the then dominant way of thinking about law as literature into the "form, structure, and rhetoric" of legal argument and caution that "storytelling in law is narrative within a culture of argument" that directs the affective and descriptive elements of storytelling towards drawing the "coercive force of the state" to one's side (Gewirtz 4–5).

[7] Conan Doyle also refers to the "wickedness of the concealed dossier" ("Strange Case," Feb. 3) because he and Yelverton before him were denied access to the Home Office files. He surmised that a pardon was slow in coming because the file included other evidence or reports, which Edalji's defenders were not allowed to examine or refute. For discussion of Conan Doyle's intervention in the Oscar Slater case, also compared with Dreyfus, see Farmer, "Arthur and Oscar (and Sherlock)" 12–13, 16.

[8] Even Peter Brooks cannot resist the Holmes comparison. In a comment on narrative, meaning, and retrospection, he notes: "it is only in hindsight . . . that one can establish a 'chain of events,' in the manner of Sherlock Holmes concluding one of his cases . . . In this sense, there are no principles to guide you; there is only the causal and sequential linkage of events, the concrete particulars which narrative alone can convey" (this by comparison with the

also has to wonder whether this version came appreciably nearer the story Edalji himself would have told. Sometimes quoted in other reports, Edalji wrote few accounts, the most notable of which appeared in the sporting magazine *Umpire*—a marginal paper for a marginal figure when compared with the high-profile advocacy of Conan Doyle and an international press.[9]

Thus far I have presented select documents that illustrate Edalji's story as it appeared in the press, in official public debate, and in the literary nonfiction of Conan Doyle's true crime narrative. I turn now to its further retelling in Julian Barnes's novel *Arthur & George* (2005). As an alternative form of legal storytelling, the novel's exploration of Englishness, its structural emphasis on beginnings and endings, and its alternating narrative point of view imaginatively voice George Edalji's story, reinserting his case—and others like it—into public consciousness.

"Three quarters of justice": Plot, Character, and the Self-Believed Story in *Arthur & George*

Julian Barnes described the development of *Arthur & George* in a 2006 interview with Xesús Fraga. Originally planned as a short piece, he opted for a novel instead and even considered placing "a contemporary story of racial prejudice" alongside the historical fiction (Barnes, Interview 135). The idea was abandoned, however, on the thinking that only a poor reader would miss the connections. Barnes positions good readers, then, to see the parallels by emphasizing two elements of Conan Doyle's narrative of the case—the importance of race in that account as well as its comparison to Dreyfus—and by playing with the causal chain of its narrative structure and the perspective through which it is told.

Part three of the novel, "Ending with a Beginning," reimagines Arthur's first meeting with George and emphasizes Conan Doyle's suppositions about race in the 1907 articles. Whether teased by his office mates or ridiculed by "a loutish element" on the train, George's racial difference draws commentary throughout the novel (*AG* 94). At the same time, his thoughts reveal a persistent conviction of his own Englishness alongside resistance to Shapurji Edalji's observation that "others may not always entirely agree" with that belief (52). In the exchange between Arthur and George that opens part three, George is surprised to hear that Arthur concurs with his father. George denies that "race prejudice has anything to do with my case" (264);

---

strategy of many judges to "recas[t] the story events" into "a narrative recognizable in terms of legal principle") ("Narrative Transactions," 14).

[9] Bernard O'Donnell took notice of the *Umpire* piece in *Cavalcade of Justice* (Macmillan, 1952), which is reprinted in Glashan.

"I was brought up as an Englishman," he explains. Through the omniscient point of view, Arthur is shown to understand this rational approach but also to dismiss the conclusion George draws from it: "It is not his fault if he is unable to see what others can" (267). Instead, Arthur suggests that both he and George are "unofficial Englishmen" (268). Glimmerings of George's self-believed story and the question of his insider or outsider status emerge from this exchange. George enlists Arthur's help precisely because he "appeared to be part of official England" (268) whereas he, by contrast, was *made* an outsider—convicted and struck from the Roll of Solicitors—by official acts and could only be reinstated by them.

Nevertheless, this external recategorization has no bearing, as yet, on his self-understanding. If George misses the irony in Arthur's comment—indeed, he thinks it "impolite to question a man's categorization *of himself*" (268)—it nevertheless causes him to reconsider his own position:

> How is he less than a full Englishman? He is one by birth, by citizenship, by education, by religion, by profession. Does Sir Arthur mean that when they took away his freedom and struck him off the Rolls, they also struck him off the Roll of Englishmen? If so, he has no other land. He cannot go back two generations. (268)

Here George confronts the incompatibility of his self-believed story with the official story suggested by the verdict and even with the more sympathetic view of his latest advocate which, the narrative voice reveals, harbors still different views, which he means to exploit.

Arthur's strategy for effecting an official revision is to embarrass the government—"the official English do not like noise" (269)—and he resolves to "make the Edalji Case into as big a stir as they did with Dreyfus over there in France" (299). Following publication of the *Daily Telegraph* articles (which analogized the case equally with Sherlock Holmes as with Dreyfus), George and Arthur meet again and the scene is repeated, this time from George's revisionary perspective. The articles, George thinks, "made him feel like several overlapping people at the same time: a victim seeking redress; a solicitor facing the highest tribunal in the country; and a character in a novel" (366). And of course Barnes's "George," Conan Doyle's "George as Dreyfus," and the historical George Edalji have been all those things. In this sense, Barnes's metafictional layering of stories offers yet another variation on what was already a multiform construction of Edalji's character. The Dreyfus analogy remains particularly telling, however. Barnes comments on the lack of historical attention to Edalji's case, but also on an English response that even at the time was comparatively less noisy than French reaction to Dreyfus. Considering the prominence of the comparison, however, Barnes suggests that Edalji's defenders might have learned, first, that the "the establishment doesn't give up" and, second, that their own efforts were equally as likely as the original trial to end in uncertainty and partial justice (Interview 146).

The novel amplifies this point in George's assessment of Arthur's case against Royden Sharp. Barnes delineates Arthur's increasing frustration with George's skepticism about, and apparent lack of gratitude for, the case he's built against Sharp as the actual culprit. George, like Dreyfus, disappoints by not being "up to the mystique of his own affair" (*AG* 372). George is similarly dissatisfied with the interview because, try as he may to soften the comparison, Sir Arthur's case (with its reliance on circumstantial evidence, contamination of material evidence, and identification of the letter-writer with the horse-ripper) is too much like the Staffordshire constabulary's case against him (374). Barnes's depiction of Arthur's thoughts and George's comparison constructs a Conan Doyle caught up in and capitalizing on his own literary reputation, beguiled by the mystique of his more famous literary creation, Sherlock Holmes, into thinking he can catch the real culprits. George's comparison also reminds readers that what Alexander Welsh called "strong representations" of evidence are rhetorically designed to prosecute or defend; no story is uninterested. Was justice achieved the first time that Edalji went to court? In the press or the Home Office? In Barnes's novel? Barnes sums it up: "In life you don't necessarily find out who did it, you don't necessarily get justice—you get three quarters of justice, half justice. And you don't really know who the bad guy was in the end" (Interview 146).

Perhaps for that reason, the novel is preoccupied with beginnings and endings. "How can you make sense of the beginning if you don't know what the ending is?" Arthur asks (*AG* 239). Animating everything from questions of spiritualism to his methods of fictional narrative and the construction of legal argument, this question dominates Barnes's development of Arthur's worldview (and is memorably challenged by Capt. Anson who points out that Arthur's case for George proceeded from his own theory that George had been targeted). It informs the novel's four-part structure as well, the titles of which—"Beginnings," "Beginning with an Ending," "Ending with a Beginning," "Endings"—are all variants on the theme.[10] Applied to narratives of justice, the predicament (of law, of literature, of life) becomes clear: we need an ending to make sense of the beginning, but we don't really know what the ending is. What we have are prospective and provisional endings that put a premium on the way those conclusions are reached. This premium is especially high when story elements are adapted to stock stories or, per Brooks,

---

[10] It's worth noting that Barnes won the 2011 Man Booker Prize with *The Sense of an Ending*.

"standard narrative sequences" whose meaning is predetermined ("Narrative Transactions" 26). By juxtaposing several stock stories yet undercutting their narrative sequence, their beginnings and ends, *Arthur & George* destabilizes the power of any one of them to show "what really happened" (*AG* 336).

Barnes has been criticized for playing fast and loose (from a legal point of view) with the historical record and thus breaking a tacit compact with the reader, his dereliction in this instance held to illustrate just one of the "dangers of relying on fiction in the teaching of evidence" (Risinger 4, 31). But the value of even realist fiction does not lie in its identification with or adherence to legal rules of evidence, whose exclusionary nature contributes to the silencing of stories that scholars of narrative jurisprudence critique. Recalling that the creation of a *nomos* is a collective, aspirational activity in which the present is evaluated in reference to an alternative vision of what may or ought to be, one may conclude that fiction does its best work *because* it has greater latitude. Robert A. Ferguson is instructive on this point. Describing a "continuum of publication" through which a trial comes to inhabit public consciousness, he suggests that fiction is the final and perhaps most effective way of working through its meaning ("Untold Stories" 84).[11]

What then does fiction's latitude teach about history, evidence, and legal storytelling? As Lisa Rodensky argued for the nineteenth-century novel, narrative omniscience makes states of mind, especially criminal intention, available to the reader in distinction to the limited access of legal counsel and expert witnesses. Thus, Barnes's recourse to a third-person narrator in *Arthur & George* gives readers an innocent, victimized "George." D. Michael Risinger suggests that this foreknowledge voids the narrative of its "evidentiary interest" (32). On the contrary, this strategy gives readers access to what Scheppele refers to as the "self-believed story" (2079). Read with the aims of narrative jurisprudence in mind, Barnes's depiction of George's hapless innocence puts into relief the ways elements of his story can be—and were—emplotted, how evidentiary elements from handwriting and horse hairs to character and culture could be organized into different narratives. The result is not a relativistic allowance for all perspectives, however: trials end in decisions, and appeals "judge the frameworks in which the verdict was reached" (Brooks, "Narrative Transactions" 21). Rather, the stakes are high because only some self-believed stories are "officially approved, accepted, transformed into *fact*," while others are "officially distrusted, rejected, found to be untrue, or perhaps not heard at all" (Scheppele 2080).

---

[11] He continues, "A story wrongly refused by law will return in a republic of laws as cultural narrative and, often enough, as renewed legal event. The law does not get beyond what it has not worked through" ("Untold Stories" 97).

I have focused discussion of the relationship between narrative and law on their world-creating potential and on the stories that contribute to the maintenance of the normative world. In concluding, I want to gesture towards the implications of this pairing by thinking of the call for outsiders' stories in the context of both the continuous and the aspirational goals of the *nomos*. That is, by comparing individuated, real experiences with a collective ideal, outsider narratives promise to reframe or in some cases to authenticate that vision by making it more inclusive. At the same time, the aspirational nature of the *nomos* suggests that narrators must consent to seeing that visionary ideal in a sense remain unrealized or only partially realized so that it can always offer an alternative to real life. What then should various legal actors do with the stories they tell and hear? Julian Barnes doesn't say, but his attention in the many cases of George Edalji to the various narrators' motives and assumptions—as well as the historical and contextual pressures framing the way their arguments could be heard, understood, and acted upon—offers a compelling experiment in the ineluctable "imposition of narrative form on life" (Brooks, "Narrative Transactions" 26). Perhaps he would agree with Peter Brooks that "the best we can hope for is a more critical awareness of the storied nature of our thinking, as well as the material presented to our thought" (26).

Victorian Character Again

Robin West's work in *Narrative, Authority, and Law* (1993) discusses the distinctions between "economic man" and "literary woman" and the different kinds of (inter)subjectivity each presupposes: their capacity for self-understanding, the value each places on rationality or empathy respectively, and the kind of community each is likely to constitute, promote, or sustain (chapter 5). The "moral promise" of each of these types connects also to the "moral value" of modes of dispute resolution, namely, rights talk and storytelling (257). Arguing that both are necessary, West observes that stories are told in order to attribute or deflect responsibility, while rights talk prevails when the goal is to make responsibility appear irrelevant (426). The legal stories told for and against George Edalji coincided with questions of responsibility, and although much of my discussion has focused on the emplotment of narrative elements, the idea of character—the central figure the telling of whose story motivates that plotting—has never been far behind. As George tells Arthur, "I want my name back again," a name he surrendered to "the court's right to decide a prisoner's name" (*AG* 261). As his solicitor explains, "What you call mispronouncing, I would call . . . making you more English" (148).

Nicola Lacey's work on responsibility attribution, although not connected with legal storytelling per se, is especially important in this regard because on the one hand, it emphasizes the allocation, not the discovery, of criminal responsibility, while on the other, it explicitly links that assignment to the resurgence of "character essentialism" or character as "status" when deciding or even trying to prevent crime ("Resurgence of Character" 151–78, 156, 160). Comparing a contemporary "crisis of security" with the late nineteenth century, Lacey observes a similar response in the "construction of criminal classifications" today:

> Just as the late nineteenth-century classifications reflected prevailing anxieties and contemporary scientific theories and technologies, so today's categories—the anti-social youth, the sex offender, the migrant, and, above all, the terrorist—are appropriate symbols of otherness relative to contemporary anxieties and technologies. (173)[12]

In Chief Constable Capt. Anson's assessment of the case, George ticks all these boxes.[13] In his interview with Xesús Fraga, Barnes comments on the novel's putative connection to the 9/11 attacks:

> I've had *Arthur & George* put to me as being in part post-9/11 because it deals with how people with the wrong skin colour are always suspected. And I said, "Well, I'm sorry, but I never thought of it. I didn't think it for a moment." (144)

What he did appear to think of, however, was a set of themes that are transhistorical, even as their particular expression is historically contingent. In the early twentieth century, Arthur Conan Doyle saw racial prejudice at the root of a white constabulary's investigation of an Anglo-Indian British citizen. In the early twenty-first century, Julian Barnes considered, then abandoned, setting a contemporary mirror against Edalji's story. If only poor readers could miss the theme's relevance, as he suggested, then good readers can surely see its parallels in modern racism, Islamophobia, and distrust of asylum seekers and of immigrants full stop.

This essentialism extends beyond criminal classification into the rules of character evidence and across common law jurisdictions. Although it goes by many names—propensity evidence (Sevier 441), similar fact evidence

---

[12] Lacey's notes provide several examples of contemporary cases relating to detention of suspected terrorists (164n37) and past "reprehensible but non-criminal conduct" (166n41), for example.

[13] Anson makes miscegenation and atavism the source of all George's troubles but quickly moves to physical unattractiveness combined with a sexual repression that found no outlet in "the great manly English games" (Barnes, *AG* 341), as further explanations of his behavior.

(Keyes 195), other-acts evidence (Cicchini and White)—character evidence is more often discussed in terms of the prejudicial impact of bad character than the mitigating potential of good, due in large part to empirical and social science findings of its increased role in the denial of asylum applications, conviction rates, sentencing, and parole hearings, and in the treatment of victims of color in cases of police shootings and other violence.[14] Where the probative value of such evidence has outweighed the risk of prejudice, instruction from the bench (in jury trial) is offered as a curative to misapplication or overemphasis (Cicchini and White 368), but critics of this approach argue that such instructions can be difficult for the layperson to understand, and, moreover, run counter both to the informal ways character enters the court and to the layperson's *desire for* precisely this kind of information.[15]

It has not been my purpose, nor in my purview, to take a position about whether character should be "abolish[ed] . . . as a consideration" (Wolf and Bagaric 567), about the right kind of reform of rules of evidence to implement (Rhode), or indeed whether character evidence is a necessary component of the perceived legitimacy of specific verdicts or of legal process generally (Sevier). What does stand out, though, is the persistent narrative attraction of character in spite of formal rules to control or exclude it, for example when evidence to character that would otherwise be disallowed is permitted when it serves a "narrative" purpose of contextualizing other evidence (Elias 574). Describing such background evidence as "character-'lite'" (114), Daniel D. Blinka observes that the modern legal system's effort to move away from character founders on a failure to recognize it as a fundamentally social, cultural construct whose form varies but whose hermeneutic value for a lay audience persists:

> Curiously, the law of evidence is uncomfortable with popular thought and culture. We invite lay people into the courtroom as witnesses and jurors

---

[14] On Australia's adherence to international non-refoulement rules, particularly the "doubling up of character provisions" in the domestic Migration Act, see Lillian Robb 282. See Ryan Elias on wrongful conviction in Canada and Michael Cicchini and Lawrence T. White on other-acts evidence, "'character evidence in disguise'" (354), in U.S. convictions. On the use of character evidence in sentencing and disciplinary hearings in Australia, see Gabrielle Wolf and Mirko Bagaric. On parole and other criminal justice proceedings in the U.S., see Deborah Rhode. For the use of racial character evidence in pre-verdict evidence law, see Jasmine B. Gonzalez Rose 374. See also Finn Keyes's discussion of the UK's Criminal Justice Act 2003 and the sharp uptick in the use of similar fact evidence (219).

[15] See Rose on the way character evidence enters the courtroom "passively," for example "the way implicit racial bias takes on evidentiary value" without having been formally submitted into evidence (404).

yet ... demand that they abandon familiar ways of thinking, especially with regard to character. (148)

From debates about the competency of the accused in the 1850s to worry over the close relationship between gossip and hearsay when allowing evidence of general reputation, from attempts to promote public benefit while protecting individuals from libel to locating a right to develop one's personality in private: As this study has argued, the Victorian novel's jurisprudence of character has been an essential way of making our thinking about character familiar in the first place.

Works Cited

"Alleged Libels in Newspapers." *Leader and Saturday Analyst*, Jun. 23, 1869, pp. 589–90.
Allen, Christopher J. W. *The Law of Evidence in Victorian England*. Cambridge UP, 1997.
Alsop, Elizabeth. "Refusal to Tell: Withholding Heroines in Hawthorne, Wharton, and Coetzee." *College Literature*, vol. 39, no. 3, Summer 2012, pp. 84–105.
Altick, Richard. *The English Common Reader*. U of Chicago P, 1957.
Ambrosini, Richard and Richard Dury, eds. *Robert Louis Stevenson: Writer of Boundaries*. U of Wisconsin P, 2006.
Appleton, John. *The Rules of Evidence: Stated and Discussed*. Johnson & Co., 1860.
—. "Rules of Evidence-No.6." *American Jurist and Law Magazine*, vol. 13, 1835, pp. 46ff.
Arata, Stephen. "The Sedulous Ape: Atavism, Professionalism, and Stevenson's Jekyll and Hyde." *Criticism*, vol. 37, no. 2, 1995, pp. 233–59.
—. "Stevenson, Morris, and the Value of Idleness." *Robert Louis Stevenson: Writer of Boundaries*, edited by Richard Ambrosini and Richard Dury. U of Wisconsin P, 2006, pp. 3–12.
Armstrong, Nancy. *How Novels Think: The Limits of Individualism, 1719–1900*. Columbia UP, 2005.
Artese, Brian. "Overhearing Testimony: James in the Shadow of Sentimentalism." *The Henry James Review*, vol. 27, 2006, pp. 103–25.
Baker, J. H. *An Introduction to English Legal History*. 4th ed., Butterworths, 2002.
Bannet, Eve Tavor, and Susan Manning, eds. *Transatlantic Literary Studies, 1660–1830*. Cambridge UP, 2012.
Barnes, Julian. *Arthur & George*. Vintage, 2005.
—. Interview by Xesús Fraga, Jul. 10, 2006. *Conversations with Julian Barnes*, edited by Vanessa Guignery and Ryan Roberts. U of Mississippi P, 2009, pp. 134–47.
—. *The Sense of an Ending*. Vintage, 2011.
Baym, Nina. "Revisiting Hawthorne's Feminism." *Hawthorne*, edited by Person, pp. 541–58.
Beer, Gillian. *Darwin's Plots: Evolutionary Narrative in Darwin, George Eliot, and Nineteenth-Century Fiction*. 2nd ed., Cambridge UP, 2000.
Berger, Courtney. "When Bad Things Happen to Bad People: Liability and Individual Consciousness in *Adam Bede* and *Silas Marner*." *Novel*, vol. 33, no. 3, 2000, pp. 307–27.
Berry, Laura C. *The Child, the State, and the Victorian Novel*. U of Virginia P, 1999.

Bezanson, Randall P. "*The Right to Privacy* Revisited: Privacy, News, and Social Change, 1890–1990." *California Law Review*, vol. 80, Oct. 1992, pp. 1133–75.

Blinka, Daniel D. "Character, Liberalism, and the Protean Culture of Evidence Law." *Seattle University Law Review*, vol. 37, no. 1, Fall 2013, pp. 87–154. HeinOnline.

Block, Ed Jr. "James Sully, Evolutionary Psychology, and Late Victorian Gothic Fiction." *Victorian Studies*, vol. 25, 1982, pp. 443–67.

Boase, George Clement. "James Anthony Lawson." *Dictionary of National Biography, 1885–1900*, vol. 32. Smith, Elder & Co., p. 292. <https://en.wikisource.org/wiki/Dictionary_of_National_Biography,_18851900/Lawson,_James_Anthony> (accessed Mar. 23, 2021).

Bowlby, Rachel. "'Hetty Had Never Read a Novel': *Adam Bede* and Realism." *George Eliot Review*, vol. 41, 2010, pp. 16–29.

Brantlinger, Patrick. "An Unconscious Allegory about the Masses and Mass Literacy." Stevenson, pp. 197–204.

Brantlinger, Patrick and Richard Boyle. "The Education of Edward Hyde." Veeder and Hirsch, pp. 265–82.

Brewer, David A. *The Afterlife of Character, 1726–1825*. U of Pennsylvania P, 2005.

Brontë, Anne. *The Tenant of Wildfell Hall*. Edited by Herbert Rosengarten and Josephine McDonagh. Oxford UP, 2008.

Brooks, Peter. "Narrative Transactions: Does the Law Need a Narratology?" *Yale Journal of Law and Humanities*, vol. 18, no. 1, 2006, pp. 1–28.

—. *Troubling Confessions: Speaking Guilt in Literature and Law*. U of Chicago P, 2000.

Brooks, Peter and Paul Gewirtz, eds. *Law's Stories: Narrative and Rhetoric in the Law*. Yale UP, 1996.

Campbell v Spottiswood. English Reports, vol. 122, 1863, pp. 288–93. <http://www.uniset.ca/other/cs3/122ER288.html> (accessed May 23, 2021).

Campbell, Sarah. "Loyalty and Disloyalty: The Fenian Treason Trials, 1865–67 and the Evolution of British Counter-Insurgency Policies in Nineteenth-Century Ireland." Houses of the Oireachtas Services, Nov. 17, 2014. <http://opac.oireachtas.ie/AWData/Library3/sarahCampbellLoyalty_and_Disloyalty_Report_112435.pdf> (accessed Mar. 23, 2021).

Carlisle, Janice. *John Stuart Mill and the Writing of Character*. U of Georgia P, 1991.

—. "On the Second Reform Act, 1867." *BRANCH: Britain, Representation and Nineteenth-Century History*, edited by Dino Franco Felluga. <http://www.branchcollective.org/?ps_articles=janice-carlisle-on-the-second-reform-act-1867> (accessed Mar. 12, 2018).

"The Case of the Clergyman Convicted of an Indecent Assault." *The Times* [London], Oct. 4, 1864, "Middlesex Sessions," p. 9.

Casson, Allan. "*The Scarlet Letter* and *Adam Bede*." *Victorian Newsletter*, vol. 20, 1961, pp. 18–19.

Cawelti, John. *Adventure, Mystery, and Romance: Formula Stories as Art and Popular Culture*. U of Chicago P, 1976.

Cicchini, Michael D. and Lawrence T. White. "Convictions Based on Character: An Empirical Test of Other-Acts Evidence." *Florida Law Review*, vol. 70, no. 2, Mar. 2018, pp. 347–78. HeinOnline.

"Civil Services and Revenue Departments Estimates." HC Deb, Jul. 18, 1907, vol. 178, cc. 994–1017.

Cockle, Ernest. *Leading Cases on the Law of Evidence.* Sweet and Maxwell, 1907.
Cocks, H. G. "Trials of Character: The Use of Character Evidence in Victorian Sodomy Trials." *Domestic and International Trials, 1700–2000: The Trial in History*, vol. 2, edited by R. A. Melikan. Manchester UP, 2003, pp. 36–53.
Collini, Stefan. *Public Moralists: Political Thought and Intellectual Life in Britain, 1850–1930.* Clarendon P, 1991.
Colón, Christine. "Beginning Where Charlotte Left Off: Visions of Community in Anne Brontë's *The Tenant of Wildfell Hall.*" *Brontë Studies*, vol. 33, Mar. 2008, pp. 20–9.
Conan Doyle, Arthur. "The Strange Case of George Edalji." *New York Times*, Feb. 2–3, 1907, p. SM6.
"Conan Doyle Solves a New Dreyfus Case." *New York Times*, 2 Feb. 1907, p. 1.
Cook, E. T. "Not Merely Strange but Impossible." Stevenson, pp. 95–6.
Cover, Robert. "Nomos and Narrative." *Narrative, Violence and the Law: The Essays of Robert Cover*, edited by Martha Minow, Michael Ryan, and Austin Sarat. U of Michigan P, 1993, pp. 95–173.
Davis, Michael. "Incongruous Compounds: Re-reading *Jekyll and Hyde* and Late-Victorian Psychology." *Journal of Victorian Culture*, vol. 11, 2006, pp. 207–25.
Davison, Carol Margaret. "A Battle of Wills: Solving *The Strange Case of Dr. Jekyll and Mr. Hyde.*" *Troubled Legacies: Narrative and Inheritance*, edited by Allan Hepburn. U of Toronto P, 2007, pp. 137–62.
Defamation of Private Character Bill. Bill 99. HC Deb, Jun. 5, 1872, vol. 211, cc. 1254–8.
"Defamation of Private Character Bill." *Law Times*, vol. 53, 1872, p. 95.
Digby, Sir Kenelm. "Note to the Home Office in Dealing with Criminal Petitions." Appendix, Wilson et al., pp. 7–9.
Dixon v Holden (1869). *Law Times Reports*, vol. 20, N.S., pp. 357–8.
Dolin, Kieran, ed. *Law and Literature.* Cambridge UP, 2018.
Dryden, Linda "'City of Dreadful Night': Stevenson's Gothic London." Ambrosini and Dury, pp. 253–64.
Eagleton, Terry. *The English Novel.* Blackwell, 2005.
Eardley-Wilmot, John E. *Lord Brougham's Acts and Bills: From 1811 to the Present Time.* Longman, 1857.
"The Edalji Case." HC Deb, Jun. 10, 1907, vol. 175, cc. 1079–80.
Eigen, Joel Peter. *Unconscious Crimes: Mental Absence and Criminal Responsibility in Victorian London.* Johns Hopkins UP, 2003.
Elias, Ryan. "Unlikable and before the Jury: Does Non-probative Character Evidence Increase the Risk of Wrongful Conviction?" *Criminal Law Quarterly*, vol. 63, no. 4, Oct. 2016, pp. 567–86. HeinOnline.
Eliot, George. *Adam Bede.* 1859. Edited by Mary Waldron. Broadview P, 2005.
—. Letter to John Blackwood. Dec. 1858. Haight, vol. 2, p. 505.
—. "Silly Novels by Lady Novelists." *Westminster Review*, vol. 10, Oct. 1856, pp. 442–61.
"Evidence as to Character." *Central Law Journal*, vol. 12, Jan.–Jun. 1881, pp. 414–16.
"Evidence as to Character." *The Examiner*, Feb. 4, 1865, p. 67.
"Evidence as to Character-I." Criminal Law and Procedure, *The Law Times*, vol. 70, Nov. 1880–Apr. 1881, p. 59.
Ellmann, Richard. *Oscar Wilde.* Knopf, 1988.

Farina, Jonathan. "Character." *Victorian Literature and Culture*, vol. 46, no. 2/3, Fall/Winter 2018, pp. 609–12.

—. *Everyday Words and the Character of Prose in Nineteenth-Century Britain.* Cambridge UP, 2017.

Farmer, Lindsay. "Arthur and Oscar (and Sherlock): The Reconstructive Trial and the Hermeneutics of Suspicion." *International Commentary on Evidence*, vol. 5, no. 1, 2007, pp. [i]–17.

—. "Trials." *Law and the Humanities: An Introduction*, edited by Austin Sarat, Matthew Anderson, and Cathrine O. Frank. Cambridge UP, 2010, pp. 455–77.

Felski, Rita. "Introduction." Special issue on Character. *New Literary History*, vol. 42, no. 2, Spring 2011, pp. v–ix.

Ferguson, Rex. *Criminal Law and the Modernist Novel: Experience on Trial.* Cambridge UP, 2013.

Ferguson, Robert A. *Law and Letters in American Culture.* Harvard UP, 1984.

—. "Untold Stories in the Law." Brooks and Gewirtz, pp. 84–98.

Finn, Margot, *The Character of Credit: Personal Debt in English Culture, 1740–1910.*

Fludernik, Monika. "A Narratology of the Law? Narratives in Legal Discourse." *Critical Analysis of Law and the New Interdisciplinarity*, vol. 1, no. 1, 2014 <https://cal.library.utoronto.ca/index.php/cal/article/view/21024>.

Forster, E. M. *Aspects of the Novel.* 1927. Harcourt, 1985.

Fowler, Elizabeth, *Literary Character: The Human Figure in Early English Writing.* Cornell UP, 2003.

Frank, Cathrine O. *Law, Literature, and the Transmission of Culture in England, 1837–1925.* Routledge, 2016.

Frow, John. *Character and Person.* Oxford UP, 2014.

Gallagher, Catherine. "The Rise of Fictionality." *The Novel*, vol. 1, edited by Franco Moretti. Princeton UP, 2006, pp. 336–62.

Gallanis, Thomas P. "The Rise of Modern Evidence Law." *Iowa Law Review*, vol. 84, Mar. 1999, pp. 499–560.

Galvan, Jill. "Character." *Victorian Literature and Culture*, vol. 46, no. 2/3, Fall/Winter 2018, pp. 612–16.

Garrett, Peter K. "Cries and Voices: Reading *Jekyll and Hyde*." Veeder and Hirsch, pp. 59–71.

Gaskell, Elizabeth. *Cranford.* Edited by Elizabeth Porges Watson. Oxford UP, 1980.

Gewirtz, Paul. "Narrative and Rhetoric in the Law." Brooks and Gewirtz, pp. 4–5.

Glashan, Roy. *The Case of Mr. George Edalji.* Project Gutenberg of Australia eBook, eBook No. 1201671h.html, Jul. 2012. <http://gutenberg.net.au/ebooks12/1202671h.html#pt3> (accessed May 23, 2021).

Godkin, E. L. "The Right to Privacy." *The Nation*, Dec. 25, 1890, pp. 496–7.

—. "The Rights of the Citizen IV: To His Own Reputation." *Scribner's Magazine*, vol. 8, Jul.–Dec. 1890, pp. 58–67.

Goh, Robbie B. H. "Textual Hyde and Seek: 'Gentility,' Narrative Play and Proscription in Stevenson's *Dr. Jekyll and Mr. Hyde*." *Journal of Narrative Theory*, vol. 29, 1999, pp. 158–83.

Gold, David. *The Shaping of Nineteenth-Century Law: John Appleton and Responsible Individualism.* Greenwood P, 1990.

Gollin, Rita K. "Hester, Hetty, and the Two Arthurs." *The Nathaniel Hawthorne Journal*, 1977, pp. 319–22.

Goodlad, Lauren. *Victorian Literature and the Victorian State: Character and Governance in a Liberal Society.* Johns Hopkins UP, 2003.
Gordon, Jan B. "Gossip, Letter, Text: Anne Brontë's Narrative Tenant and the Problematic of the Gothic Sequel." *English Literary History*, vol. 4, Winter 1984, pp. 719–45.
Great Britain. An Act to Amend the Law Respecting Defamatory Words and Libel (1843) 6 & 7 Vict. c. 96.
—. Criminal Evidence Act (1898) 61 & 62 Vict. c. 36.
—. Law of Libel Amendment Act (1888) 51 & 52 Vict. c. 64.
—. Newspaper Libel and Registration Act (1881) 44 & 45 Vict. c. 60.
"The Great Wyrley Outrages." *Mercury* [Litchfield], Oct. 23, 1903.
—. *Mercury* [Litchfield], Oct. 30, 1903.
Greenwood, Elisha. "The Admissibility of Evidence of Character in Civil Actions." *Central Law Journal*, vol. 16, Jan.–Jun. 1883, pp. 202–7.
Grossman, Jonathan. *The Art of Alibi: English Law Courts and the Novel.* Johns Hopkins UP, 2002.
Haight, Gordon S., ed. *The George Eliot Letters.* 7 vols. Yale UP, 1954–5.
Hall, Donald, ed. *Muscular Christianity: Embodying the Victorian Age.* Cambridge UP, 1994.
Hawthorne, Nathaniel. *The Scarlet Letter.* Edited by Leland S. Person. W.W. Norton, 2005.
Healy, Meghan. "Weak-Willed Lover and Deformed Masculinities in *The Scarlet Letter* and *Ruth*." *The Gaskell Journal*, vol. 28, Jan. 2014, pp. 17–34.
Heinzelman, Susan Sage. "Imagining the Law: The Novel." *Law and the Humanities: An Introduction*, edited by Austin Sarat, Matthew Anderson, and Cathrine O. Frank. Cambridge UP, 2010, pp. 213–40.
Henderson, Andrea K. *Romantic Identities: Varieties of Subjectivity, 1774–1830.* Cambridge UP, 1996.
Henry, Nancy. *The Life of George Eliot.* Blackwell, 2015.
Hewitt, Martin. "The Press and the Law." *Journalism and the Periodical Press*, edited by Joanne Shattock. Cambridge UP, 2017, pp. 147–64.
Hines, Stephen and Steven Womack. *The True Crime Files of Sir Arthur Conan Doyle.* Berkeley Prime Crime, 2001.
Hirsch, Gordon. "*Frankenstein*, Detective Fiction, and *Jekyll and Hyde*." Veeder and Hirsch, pp. 223–8.
Holland, Merlin. *The Real Trial of Oscar Wilde.* HarperCollins, 2004.
Hughes, Linda K. and Sarah R. Robbins, eds. *Teaching Transatlanticism: Resources for Nineteenth-Century Anglo-American Print Culture.* Edinburgh UP, 2015.
Hull, Raymona. *Nathaniel Hawthorne: The English Experience, 1853–64.* U of Pittsburgh P, 1980
Hunt, Aeron. "Calculations and Concealments: Infanticide in Mid-Nineteenth Century Britain." *Victorian Literature and Culture*, vol. 34, no. 1, 2006, pp. 71–94.
Hunter, J. Paul. *Before Novels: The Cultural Contexts of Eighteenth-Century Fiction.* W.W. Norton, 1990.
Hyde, H. Montgomery. *The Trials of Oscar Wilde.* Dover, 1973.
"Imaginative Literature: The Author of *Adam Bede* and Nathaniel Hawthorne." *North British Review*, vol. 33, 1860, pp. 160–85.

"Ireland—Fenian Prisoners at Waterford—Observations." HC Deb, Mar. 16, 1866, vol. 182, cc. 440–7.

Jones, Miriam. "'The Usual Sad Catastrophe': From the Street to the Parlor in *Adam Bede*." *Victorian Literature and Culture*, vol. 32, no. 2, Sept. 2004, pp. 305–26.

Joshi, Priti. "Masculinity and Gossip in Anne Brontë's *Tenant*." *Studies in English Literature*, vol. 49, no. 4, 2009, pp. 907–24.

Judge, Elizabeth. *Character Witnesses: Credibility and Testimony in the Eighteenth Century Novel*. Dissertation. 2004.

Kalinevitch, Karen. "Hawthorne and George Eliot." *The Nathanial Hawthorne Review*, vol. 3, 1997, pp. 6–7.

Kalsem, Kristin. *In Contempt: Nineteenth Century Women, Law & Literature*. Ohio State UP, 2012.

Kemp, Melody J. "Helen's Diary and the Method(ism) of Character Formation in *The Tenant of Wildfell Hall*." *New Approaches to the Literary Art of Anne Brontë*, edited by Julie Nash and Barbara Ann Seuss. Ashgate, 2011, pp. 195–211.

Keyes, Finn. "Unloosing the Gordian Knot: The Scope of the Exclusionary Rule for Bad Character Evidence in Irish Law." *King's Inns Law Review*, vol. 8, 2019, pp. 195–226. HeinOnline.

Knezevic, Boris. "An Ethnography of the Provincial: The Social Geography of Gentility in Elizabeth Gaskell's *Cranford*." *Victorian Studies*, vol. 41, no. 3, 1998, pp. 405–27.

Korobkin, Laura Hanft. "The Scarlet Letter of the Law: Hawthorne and Criminal Justice." Hawthorne, edited by Person, pp. 426–51.

Krueger, Christine L. "Literary Defenses and Medical Prosecutions: Representing Infanticide in Nineteenth-Century Britain." *Victorian Studies*, vol. 40, no. 2, Winter 1997, pp. 271–94.

—. *Reading for the Law: British Literary History and Gender Advocacy*. U of Virginia P, 2010.

—. "Witnessing Women: Trial Testimony in Novels by Tonna, Gaskell, and Eliot." *Representing Women: Law, Literature, Feminism*, edited by Susan Sage Heinzelman and Zipporah Batshaw Wiseman. Duke UP, 1994, pp. 337–55.

Lacey, Nicola. "In Search of the Responsible Subject: History, Philosophy and Social Sciences in Criminal Law Theory." *The Modern Law Review*, vol. 64, May 2001, pp. 350–71.

—. "Responsibility and Modernity in Criminal Law." *The Journal of Political Philosophy*, vol. 9, no. 3, 2001, pp. 249–76.

—. "The Resurgence of Character: Responsibility in the Context of Criminalization." *Philosophical Foundations of Criminal Law*, edited by R. A. Duff and Stuart Green. Oxford UP, 2011, pp. 157–78.

—. *Women, Crime, and Character: From* Moll Flanders *to* Tess of the D'Urbervilles. Oxford UP, 2008.

Lake, Jessica. "Privacy, Property or Propriety: The Case of 'Pretty Portraits' in Late Nineteenth-Century America." *Law, Culture and the Humanities*, vol. 10, no. 1, 2014, pp. 111–29.

Langbein, John. "The Historical Origins of the Privilege Against Self-Incrimination at Common Law." *Michigan Law Review*, vol. 92, 1994, pp. 1047–85.

—. *The Origins of Adversary Criminal Trial*. Oxford UP, 2003. Rpt. 2010.

Lapides, Robert. Comment on "How to Divide the Victorian Era." *Victoria Listserv*, Aug. 25, 2009. <https://list.indiana.edu/sympa/arc/victoria/2009-08/msg00141.html> (accessed May 23, 2021).
Latham, Sean. *The Art of Scandal: Modernism, Libel Law and the Roman à Clef.* Oxford UP, 2009.
"Law." *The Times* [London], Jan. 30, 1865, p. 11.
Law, Graham. "Trollope and the Newspapers." *Media History*, vol. 9, no. 1, 2010, pp. 47–62.
Law of Evidence and Procedure Bill. Second Reading. HL Deb, Mar. 10, 1853, vol. 124, cc. 1363–82.
"Law of Libel." *Law Times*, vol. 1, no. 9, Jun. 3, 1843, pp. 236–8.
"The Law of Libel." *Law Times*, vol. 1, no. 10, Jun. 10, 1843, p. 265.
"The Law of Libel." *The Saturday Review of Politics, Literature, Science and Art*, vol. 23, Apr. 27, 1867, p. 600. British Periodicals, p. 527.
Leavis, F. R. "Foreword." George Eliot, *Adam Bede*. Signet Classics, 1961.
"Legal Epidemics." *The Saturday Review of Politics, Literature, Science and Art*, Aug. 17. 1872, vol. 34, p. 877. British Periodicals, p. 213.
LePore, Jill. "The Prism: Privacy in an Age of Publicity." *The New Yorker*, Jun. 24, 2013. <https://www.newyorker.com/magazine/2013/06/24/the-prism> (accessed May 23, 2021).
Libel Bill. HL Deb, Feb. 4, 1858, vol. 148, cc. 685–6.
—. Second Reading. Negatived. HL Deb, Apr. 13, 1858, vol. 149, cc. 947–82.
Libel Bill. Bill 3. Committee. HC Deb, May 20, 1868, vol. 192, cc. 592–618.
—. Second Reading. HC Deb, Nov. 27, 1867, vol. 190, cc. 306–13.
—. Second Reading. HC Deb, Apr. 1, 1868, vol. 191, cc. 664–72.
Libel Bill. Bill 11. Second Reading. HC Deb, Mar. 13, 1867, vol. 185, cc. 1716–41.
Libel Bill. Bill 17. Second Reading. HC Deb, Mar. 17, 1869, vol. 194, cc. 1599–617.
Libel Bill. Bill 33. First Reading. HC Deb, Feb. 21, 1865, vol. 177, cc. 561–3.
—. Second Reading. HC Deb, May 23, 1865, vol. 179, cc. 785–7.
Libel Bill (re-committed). Bill 112. HC Deb, Jun. 25, 1867, vol. 188, cc. 539–49.
Libel Bill. Bill 215. Third Reading. HC Deb, Aug. 7, 1867, vol. 189, cc. 1050–69.
"The Libel Bill Which Passed through Committee." *The Times* [London], Jun. 27, 1867, p. 8.
"The Libel Bill, of Which the Second Reading." *The Times* [London], Nov. 29, 1867, p. 8.
"Libeling the Beauties." *New York Times*, Oct. 26, 1879, pp. 9ff.
"Libels on Personal Dignity." *The Spectator*, Oct. 18, 1879, pp. 10ff.
"Liberty of Criticism, and the Law of Libel." *Fraser's Magazine for Town and Country*, vol. 68, Jul. 1863, pp. 35–45.
Liddle, Dallas. *The Dynamics of Genre: Journalism and the Practice of Literature in Mid-Victorian Britain*. U of Virginia P, 2009.
Loveland, Ian. *Political Libels: A Comparative Study*. Hart, 2000.
Lynch, Deidre Shauna. *The Economy of Character: Novels, Market Culture, and the Business of Inner Meaning*. U of Chicago P, 1998.
McDonagh, Josephine. "Child-Murder Narratives in George Eliot's *Adam Bede*: Embedded Histories and Fictional Representation." *Nineteenth-Century Literature*, vol. 56, no. 2, Sept. 2001, pp. 228–59.

McGill, Meredith. Roundtable. *Journal of American Studies*, vol. 49, no. 1, 2015, pp. 161–5.
Maine, Henry Sumner. *Ancient Law: Its Connection to the Early History of Society and Its Relation to Modern Ideas*. Edited by Frederick Pollock. Henry Holt, 1906, pp. 172–3.
Manlove, Colin. "'Closer Than an Eye': The Interconnection of Stevenson's *Dr. Jekyll and Mr. Hyde*." *Studies in Scottish Literature*, vol. 23, 1988, pp. 87–103.
Manning, Henry Edward. *The Internal Mission of the Holy Ghost*. Burns and Oates, 1875.
Manning, Susan. *Poetics of Character: Transatlantic Encounters 1700–1900*. Cambridge UP, 2013.
Manning, Susan and Andrew Taylor, eds. *Transatlantic Literary Studies*. Edinburgh UP, 2007.
"Middlesex Sessions." *The Times* [London], Oct. 1, 1864, p. 11.
"Middlesex Sessions." *The Times* [London], Dec. 8, 1864, p. 11.
Milder, Robert. "In the Belly of the Beast: Hawthorne in England." *The New England Quarterly*, vol. 84, no. 1, Mar. 2011, pp. 60–103.
Mill, John Stuart. *On Liberty and Other Writings*. Edited by Stefan Collini. Cambridge, 1989.
Miller, D. A., *Narrative and Its Discontents: Problems of Closure in the Traditional Novel*. Princeton UP, 1981.
Mitchell, Paul. *The Making of the Modern Law of Defamation*. Hart, 2005.
—. "Nineteenth Century Defamation: Was It a Law of the Press?" *Amicus Curiae*, vol. 75, Autumn 2008, pp. 27–32.
Moddlemog, William M. "'Disowning Personality': Privacy and Subjectivity in *The House of Mirth*." *American Literature*, vol. 70, Jun. 1998, pp. 337–63.
Moglen, Eben. "The Privilege in British North America: The Colonial Period to the Fifth Amendment." *The Privilege Against Self-Incrimination: Its Origins and Development*, edited by R. H. Helmholz et al. U of Chicago P, 1997, pp. 109–44.
Moore, Grace. "Something to Hyde: The 'Strange Preference' of Henry Jekyll." *Victorian Crime, Madness and Sensation*, edited by Andrew Maunder and Grace Moore. Ashgate, 2004, pp. 147–61.
"Newspaper Reporting and the Law of Libel." *The London Review of Politics, Society, Literature, Art, and Science*, vol. 14, Mar. 23, 1867, p. 351. British Periodicals, p. 340.
Newspapers (Law of Libel) Bill. Bill 5. HC Deb, Aug. 20, 1881, vol. 265, c. 604.
Norton, Caroline. "Art. IX.—1. Adam Bede. By George Eliot. 3 vols. 1859. 2. Scenes of Clerical Life. By George Eliot. 2 vols. 1858." *The Edinburgh Review*, vol. 110, Jul. 1859, pp. 223–46. British Periodicals Online. British Library. Sept. 14, 2010.
"Nothing Can be Simpler than the Law of Libel." *The Times* [London], Apr. 21, 1863, p. 9.
Odgers, William Blake. *A Digest of the Law of Libel and Slander*. 3rd ed., Stevens & Son, 1886.
Pace, Joel. "Wordsworth, the Lyrical Ballads, and Literary and Social Reform in Nineteenth-Century America." *The "Honourable Characteristic of Poetry": Two Hundred Years of Lyrical Ballads*, edited by Marcy L. Tanter. Nov. 1999,

paras. 1–33. *Romantic Circles*, Jun. 26, 2014. <https://romantic-circles.org/praxis/lyrical/pace/wordsworth.html> (accessed May 23, 2021).

"Papers Moved for." HL Deb, Mar. 18, 1858, vol. 149, cc. 313–19.

Persak, Christine. "Spencer's Doctrines and Mr. Hyde: Moral Evolution in Stevenson's 'Strange Case.'" *The Victorian Newsletter*, vol. 86, 1994, pp. 13–18.

Person, Leland. "Hester's Revenge: The Power of Silence in *The Scarlet Letter*." *Nineteenth-Century Literature*, vol. 43, no. 4, 1989, pp. 465–83.

Petition of Rigby Wason, Esquire. HL Deb, Feb. 12, 1867, vol. 185, cc. 257–73.

Phelan, James. "Narrative Theory, 1966–2006: A Narrative." Robert Scholes, James Phelan, and Robert Kellogg, *The Nature of Narrative*. 40th anniversary ed. Oxford UP, 2006, pp. 283–336.

Pionke, Albert D. and Denise Tischler Millstein, eds. *Victorian Secrecy: Economies of Knowledge and Concealment*. Routledge, 2016.

"Police-Rowton, James for Indecent Assault." "Police." *The Times* [London], Sept. 10, 1864, p. 11e.

Poovey, Mary. "Trollope's Barsetshire Series." *The Cambridge Companion to Anthony Trollope*, edited by Carolyn Dever and Lisa Niles. Cambridge UP, 2011, pp. 31–43.

—. "Writing about Finance in Victorian England: Disclosure and Secrecy in the Culture of Investment." *Victorian Investments: New Perspectives on Finance and Culture*, edited by Nancy Henry and Cannon Schmitt. Indiana UP, 2009, pp. 39–57.

Powers, Edwin. *Crime and Punishment in Early Massachusetts, 1620–1692: A Documentary History*. Beacon Press, 1966.

Pringle, Matthew. "The Scarlet Lever: Hester's Civil Disobedience." *ESQ: A Journal of the American Renaissance*, vol. 53, no. 1, 2007, pp. 31–55.

Quick, Jonathan R. "*Silas Marner* as Romance: The Example of Hawthorne." *Nineteenth Century Fiction*, vol. 29, no. 3, Dec. 1974, pp. 287–98.

Rae, William Fraser. "John Arthur Roebuck." *DNB*, vol. 49, 1897, pp. 95–6.

Rafferty, Oliver. "Fenianism in North America in the 1860s: The Problems for Church and State." *History*, vol. 84, no. 274, 1999, pp. 257–77.

Rago, Jane V. "Dr. Jekyll and Mr. Hyde: A 'Men's Narrative' of Hysteria and Containment." Ambrosini and Dury, pp. 275–85.

Railton, Stephen. "The Address of *The Scarlet Letter*." Hawthorne, *The Scarlet Letter*, edited by Person, pp. 481–500.

Regina v Rowton. English Reports, vol. 169, 1865, pp. 1497ff.

Reid, Julia. "Robert Louis Stevenson and the 'Romance of Anthropology.'" *Journal of Victorian Culture*, vol. 10, 2005, pp. 46–71.

Report from the Select Committee of the House of Lords Appointed to Consider the Law of Defamation and Libel, Jun. 1, 1843.

Report from the Select Committee on the Law of Libel, Aug. 6, 1879. Reports from Committees. 7 vols. Vol. 4, Session 5, Dec. 1878–Aug. 15, 1879.

Reynolds, Larry J. "*The Scarlet Letter* and Revolutions Abroad." *American Literature*, vol. 57, no. 1, 1985, pp. 44–67.

Rezek, Joseph. *London and the Making of Provincial Literature: Aesthetics and the Transatlantic Book Trade, 1800–1850*. U of Pennsylvania P, 2015.

Rhode, Deborah L. "Character in Criminal Justice Proceedings: Rethinking its Role in Rules Governing Evidence, Punishment, Prosecutors, and Parole."

American Journal of Criminal Law, vol. 45, no. 2, Spring 2019, pp. 353–406. HeinOnline.

Risinger, D. Michael. "Boxes in Boxes: Julian Barnes, Conan Doyle, Sherlock Holmes and the Edalji Case." *International Commentary on Evidence*, vol. 4, no. 2, 2006, pp. 1–90.

Robb, Lillian. "From Cancellation to Removal: The Protection of Migrants of Bad Character in Australia." *American University International Law Review*, vol. 35, no. 2, 2020, pp. 259–96. HeinOnline.

Rodensky, Lisa. *The Crime in Mind: Criminal Responsibility and the Victorian Novel*. Oxford UP, 2003.

Rorty, Amelie Okensberg. "Characters, Persons, Selves, Individuals." *Theory of the Novel*, edited by Michael McKeon. Johns Hopkins UP, 2000, pp. 537–53.

Rose, Jasmine B. Gonzalez. "Racial Character Evidence in Police Killing Cases." *Wisconsin Law Review*, vol. 2018, no. 3, 2018, pp. 369–440. HeinOnline.

Rosenberg, Anat. "The Realism of the Balance Sheet: Value Assessments between the Debtors Act and *The Picture of Dorian Gray*." *Critical Analysis of Law*, vol. 2, 2015, pp. 363. <https://ssrn.com/abstract=2691329> (accessed May 23, 2021).

Rosner, Mary. "'A Total Subversion of Character': Dr. Jekyll's Moral Insanity." *The Victorian Newsletter*, vol. 93, 1998, pp. 27–31.

Rowbotham, Judith and Kim Stevenson, eds. *Criminal Conversations: Victorian Crimes, Social Panic, and Moral Outrage*. The Ohio State UP, 2005.

"Rowton (Samuel James) Not the Rowton in the Police Court." "Police." *The Times* [London], Sept. 13, 1864, p. 12e.

Rubery, Matthew. *The Novelty of Newspapers: Victorian Fiction After the Invention of the News*. Oxford UP, 2009.

Scheppele, Kim Lane. "Foreword: Telling Stories." *Michigan Law Review*, vol. 87, no. 8, 1989, pp. 2073–98.

Schramm, Jan-Melissa. *Testimony and Advocacy in Victorian Law, Literature and Theology*. Cambridge UP, 2000.

Schulkind, Jeanne, ed. *Moments of Being*. Sussex University Press, 1976.

Seipp, David J. "English Judicial Recognition of a Right to Privacy." *Oxford Journal of Legal Studies*, vol. 3, no. 3, Winter 1983, pp. 325–70. HeinOnline.

—. "The Right to Privacy in Nineteenth-Century America." *Harvard Law Review*, vol. 94, no. 8, Jun. 1981, pp. 1892–910. HeinOnline.

Sennett, Richard. *The Fall of Public Man*. W.W. Norton, 1992.

Sevier, Justin. "Legitimizing Character Evidence." *Emory Law Journal*, vol. 68, no. 3, 2019, pp. 441–508. HeinOnline.

Sheasby, Ronald E. "The Black Veil Lifted: A Note on Eliot and Hawthorne." *CLA Journal*, vol. 44, no. 3, 2001, pp. 383–90.

Simmel, Georg. "The Sociology of Secrecy and of Secret Societies." *The American Journal of Sociology*, vol. 11, no. 4, 1906, pp. 441–98.

Siskin, Clifford. *The Historicity of Romantic Discourse*. Oxford UP, 1988.

Smith, Henry E. "The Modern Privilege: Its Nineteenth-Century Origins." *The Privilege Against Self-Incrimination: Its Origins and Development*, edited by R. H. Helmholz et al. U of Chicago P, 1997, pp. 145–80.

Smith, Jeffrey A. "Moral Guardians and the Origins of the Right to Privacy." *Journalism and Communication Monographs*, vol. 10, 2008, pp. 65–110.

Spacks, Patricia Meyer. *Gossip*. Knopf, 1985.

"State Prosecutions Against the Press." *The Times* [London], Mar. 21, 1860, p. 9.

Stephen, James Fitzjames. "The Law of Libel." *The Cornhill Magazine*, vol. 15, Jan. 1867. British Periodicals, p. 36.

—. *Liberty, Equality, Fraternity*. 1873. Edited by Stuart D. Warner. Liberty Fund, 1993.

Stephen, Leslie. "Anonymous Journalism." *Saint Pauls Magazine*, vol. 2, May 1868, pp. 217–30.

Stevenson, Robert Louis. *The Strange Case of Dr. Jekyll and Mr. Hyde*. Edited by Katherine Linehan. W.W. Norton, 2003.

Stokes, Edward. *Hawthorne's Influence on Dickens and George Eliot*. U of Queensland P, 1985.

Straub, Julia, ed. *Handbook of Transatlantic North American Studies*. Walter de Gruyter, 2016.

Sutherland, John. *Victorian Fiction: Writers, Publishers, Readers*. St. Martin's P, 1995.

Taylor, David. "Beyond the Bounds of Respectable Society: The 'Dangerous Classes' in Victorian and Edwardian England." Rowbotham and Stevenson, pp. 3–22.

Thomas, Brook. *American Literary Realism and the Failed Promise of Contract*. U of California P, 1997.

Thomas, Ronald R. *Detective Fiction and the Rise of Forensic Science*. Cambridge UP, 1999.

—. "The Strange Voices in the Strange Case: Dr. Jekyll, Mr. Hyde, and the Voices of Modern Fiction." Veeder and Hirsch, pp. 73–93.

Tóibín, Colm. "The Art of Being Found Out." *London Review of Books*, vol. 30, no. 6, Mar. 20, 2008. <https://www.lrb.co.uk/the-paper/v30/n06/colm-toibin/the-art-of-being-found-out> (accessed May 23, 2021).

"The Town Talk Libels." *The Saturday Review of Politics, Literature, Science and Art*, Nov. 1, 1879, vol. 48, p. 1253. British Periodicals, p. 527.

Tracy, Robert. "Trollope Redux: the Later Novels." *The Cambridge Companion to Anthony Trollope*, edited by Carolyn Dever and Lisa Niles. Cambridge UP, 2011, pp. 58–70.

Trial of Adolphus Rosenberg. Oct. 1879. Ref. t18791020-932. *Old Bailey Proceedings Online*. <https://www.oldbaileyonline.org>, version 6.0, Apr. 17, 2011 (accessed May 23, 2021).

Trollope, Anthony. *An Autobiography*. Edited by David Skilton. Penguin, 1996.

—. *Cousin Henry*. Edited by Julian Thompson. Oxford UP, 1987.

—. *Dr. Wortle's School*, edited by Mick Imlah. Penguin, 1999.

—. "Introduction." *Saint Pauls Magazine*, vol. 1, Oct. 1867, pp. 1–7.

—. "On Anonymous Literature." *Fortnightly Review*, vol. 1, May–Aug. 1865, pp. 491–8.

—. *Phineas Finn*. Edited by Jacques Berthoud. Oxford UP, 1982.

—. *Phineas Redux*. Edited by John C. Whale. Oxford UP, 1983.

—. "The Press." *The New Zealander*. Edited by N. John Hall. The Trollope Society, 1995, pp. 31–52.

—. *The Prime Minister*. Edited by David Skilton. Penguin, 1994.

—. *The Warden*, edited by Robin Gilmour. Penguin, 1984.

—. *The Way We Live Now*. Edited by Frank Kermode. Penguin, 1994.

Turner, Mark. *Trollope and the Magazines: Gendered Issues in Mid-Victorian Britain*, St. Martin's P, 2000.

Veeder, William and Gordon Hirsch, eds. *Dr. Jekyll and Mr. Hyde After One Hundred Years*. U of Chicago P, 1988.
Vincent, David. *"I Hope I Don't Intrude": Privacy and Its Dilemmas in Nineteenth-Century Britain*. Oxford UP, 2015.
Waddams, S. M. *Sexual Slander in Nineteenth-Century England: Defamation in Ecclesiastical Courts, 1815–1855*. U of Toronto P, 2000.
Wahrman, Dror. *The Making of the Modern Self: Identity and Culture in Eighteenth-Century England*. Yale UP, 2004.
Wall, Stephen. *Trollope: Living with Character*. Henry Holt, 1988.
Warhol, Robyn R. "Toward a Theory of the Engaging Narrator: Earnest Interventions in Gaskell, Stowe, and Eliot." *PMLA*, vol. 101, no. 5, 1986, pp. 811–18.
Warren, Samuel D. and Louis D. Brandeis. "The Right to Privacy." *Harvard Law Review*, vol. 4, no. 5, Dec. 15, 1890, pp. 193–220.
Wason v Walter. *Law Times Reports*, vol. 17, N.S., Jan. 4, 1868, pp. 386–91.
Watt, Ian. *The Rise of the Novel*. Berkeley: U of California Press, 1959.
Weaver, Gordon. *Conan Doyle and the Parson's Son*. Vanguard Press, 2006.
Weisbruch, Robert. "Cultural Time in England and America." Manning and Taylor, pp. 97–104.
Welsh, Alexander. *George Eliot and Blackmail*. Harvard UP, 1985.
—. *Strong Representations: Narrative and Circumstantial Evidence in England*. Johns Hopkins UP, 1992.
West, Robin. *Caring for Justice*. New York UP, 1997.
—. *Narrative, Authority, and Law*. U of Michigan P, 1993.
Wharton, Robin and Derek Miller. "New Directions in Law and Narrative." *Law, Culture, and the Humanities*, DOI: 10.1177/1743872116652865, Jun. 5, 2016, pp. 1–10.
Whitman, James Q. "The Two Western Cultures of Privacy: Dignity Versus Liberty." Paper 649, *Faculty Scholarship Series*, Yale Law School Legal Scholarship Repository, 2004, pp. 1151–221. <https://digitalcommons.law.yale.edu/cgi/viewcontent.cgi?article=1647&context=fss_papers>, Apr. 23, 2018 (accessed May 23, 2021).
Wiener, Martin J. *Reconstructing the Criminal Character: Culture, Law, and Policy in England 1830–1914*. Cambridge UP, 1990.
Wigmore, John H. "The History of the Hearsay Rule." *Harvard Law Review*, vol. 17, no. 7, May 1904, pp. 437–58.
Wilde, Oscar. *The Picture of Dorian Gray*. Edited by Norman Page. Broadview P, 1998.
Williams, M. Kellen. "'Down with the Door, Poole': Designating Deviance in Stevenson's *Strange Case of Dr. Jekyll and Mr. Hyde*." *ELT*, vol. 39, no. 4, 1996, pp. 412–29.
Wills, William. *The Theory and Practice of the Law of Evidence*. Stevens & Sons, 1894.
Willson, Andrew. "Mediation, Authority, and Critical Reading in *The Warden*." *Studies in the Novel*, vol. 48, no. 2, Summer 2016, pp. 168–85.
Wilson, Arthur, John Lloyd Wharton, and Albert de Rutzen. "Papers Relating to the Case of George Edalji." Eyre and Spottiswoode, 1907. Great Britain, Parliament, House of Commons Papers, Cd 3503, vol. 67, 1907, p. 403. <https://books.google.com/books?id=XOgLAQAAIAAJ&q=edalji+case#v=snippet&q=edalji%20case&f=false> (accessed May 23, 2021).

"Witnesses to Character." *The Saturday Review of Politics, Literature, Science, and Art*, vol. 19, Feb. 4, 1865, p. 133.

Wolf, Gabrielle and Mirko Bagaric. "Nice Or Nasty: Reasons to Abolish Character as a Consideration in Australian Sentencing Hearings and Professionals' Disciplinary Proceedings." *Monash University Law Review*, vol. 44, no. 3, 2018, pp. 567–601. HeinOnline.

Woloch, Alex. *The One vs. the Many: Minor Characters and the Space of the Protagonist in the Novel.* Princeton UP, 2003.

Index

Page numbers followed by n are notes

accused speaks model, 91, 111
Adam Bede, 6–7, 22, 31–82, 110–11, 112;
  see also Sorrel, Hetty (character)
Allen, Christopher J. W., 40, 42n, 44, 68
Alsop, Elizabeth, 35n, 47–8, 66n
American Jurist and Law Magazine, 42
Appleton, John, 34, 42n, 43, 71
  "Admission of Parties in Criminal
    Procedure", 42
  The Rules of Evidence: Stated and Discussed,
    40–2, 43n
Armstrong, Nancy, 7–8, 22, 23n, 74
"art of being found out", 170, 203–4
Artese, Brian, 190n, 204–5n
The Athenaeum, 186n
Ayrton, Acton, 128–9, 130–2, 151

Bagaric, Mirko, 101n
Bain, Alexander, *On the Study of Character*,
  6n
Baines, Edward, 125, 133n, 135
Barnes, Julian, *Arthur & George*, 209, 216,
  217–21, 222
Baym, Nina, 50n
Beck, Adolf, 215
Bentham, Jeremy, 75
  Rationale of Judicial Evidence, 40
Berry, Laura C., 51n
Blackburn, Justice, 124
Blackburn, Samuel, 120–1
Blackstone, William, *Commentaries*, 24
Blackwood, 57, 78–9
Blinka, Daniel D., 18n, 212n, 223–4
Block, Ed, Jr, 191n
Borthwick, Sir Algernon, 164
Brandeis, Louis D.
  domestic spaces, 189
  free market approach to gossip, 177n
  house as castle, 182–3
  inviolate personality, 21, 194
  press, 162–3
  privacy, 170, 198–9, 200n
  privacy and personality, 202–3
  property and personhood, 20–1n, 117n,
    171–9
  "right to be let alone", 108–9n
  "The Right to Privacy", 165–8, 175n, 205
  society papers, 164
  solitude and privacy, 191
Bray, Caroline, 32n
Brewer, David A., *The Afterlife of Character,
  1726-1825*, 17n
The British Ensign, 123–4
Brooks, Peter, 11, 77n, 216–17n, 219–20,
  221
  *Law's Stories: Narrative and Rhetoric in the
    Law*, 216n
Brougham, Lord, 42–3
Brougham's Act *see* Evidence Amendment
  Act (Lord Brougham's Act) 1851
Brougham's Law of Evidence and Procedure
  Bill 1853 *see* Law of Evidence and
  Procedure Bill (Lord Brougham) 1853
The Broughton Gazette (fictional newspaper),
  142

Campbell, Lord, 119, 121, 122, 123–4,
  134n
  bill 1858, 125
Campbell, Sarah, 137–8n
Campbell v Spottiswood, 123–4, 129
Campbell's Act *see* Libel Act (Lord
  Campbell's Act) 1843
Carlisle, Janice, 3, 57
Carmarthen Herald (fictional newspaper),
  141, 142–3, 155–9

INDEX

Central Criminal court, London, 139n
The Central Law Journal, 103
Chambers, Thomas, 126, 130–1, 135–6
character, 9–30, 221–4
   and conduct, 73–82
   criminal, 54n, 55, 57–8, 100, 181
   development, 7–8
   evidence, 98–101, 104n, 110–11, 114–15, 223n
   exception, 83–115
   forming through law, 101–8
   idea of, 1–30
   incriminating, 31–82
   mobilizing, 13–14
   mode for distributing, 10–11
   moral, 186n
   natural, 108, 110, 112n
   pragmatics of, 16
   private, 119–38
   as property, 121–2
   Rorty, Amelie Oksenberg, 2–3n
   roundedness, 15–16, 19n
   rule, 99n
   status as, 207–24
   strange, 165–206
   transformation into personality, 93–4
   transgressive, 22–3
character essentialism, 108n, 222–3
character-spaces, 10, 14
   private, 172–9, 179–95
character-systems, 10–11, 12–30
   law as, 208
character-talk, 3–4, 10–11, 13, 84–5, 207–8
Chaucer, Geoffrey
   The Canterbury Tales, 15, 19
Chelmsford, Lord, 134
Cockburn, Chief Justice
   character evidence, 81, 103–4n, 105–6, 106n
   public interest, 135, 138, 152n
   public man, 123n, 124, 159
   reputation and character, 85
   utilitarianism, 135n
Collini, Stefan, 3, 84–5
Colón, Christine, 88
Committee of Inquiry, 213
community, 109–10
   gossip, 86–95
compellability, 43–4n, 76–7
complex personalities, 179
compulsive intimacy, 109–10
consequences of success, 191n
consequentialism, 53, 57–8

Conway, Moncure D., 32n
Cook, E. T., 186n
copyright laws, 144–5n, 166, 168n, 174n
The Cornhill Magazine, 123n, 136
Cornwallis-West, Patsy, 160–1, 165–6
counsel
   as character, 12
   character evidence, 104n
   cross-examination, 67–8, 97n
   deprivation of, 48n
   exception, 97–103
   infanticide, 65
   Sorrel, Hetty (character), 51–3
   witness testimony, 39–40, 48
Court for Crown Cases Reserved, 210
Court of Appeal, 210–17
Court of Criminal Appeals, 210
Cover, Robert, "Nomos and Narrative," 208–9
cover stories, 67, 76, 193n
Cranford, 22, 85–6, 92–5, 108, 108–15
Cranworth, Lord, 43, 43n
criminal character, 54n, 55, 57–8, 100, 181
Criminal Evidence Act 1898, 43
criminal intention, 18n, 36, 54n, 220
criminology, 180–2
cross-examination, 42n, 97–98
cult of character, 180
culture of privacy, Continental, 177–8
Custody of Infants Act 1839, 86

Daily Mail, 212
Daily Telegraph, 163, 214, 218
Dallas, E. S., 65
Darwin, Charles, 6, 57, 58, 110–11, 180
defamation of character, 116–64, 171–2, 174, 200n
Denham's Act *see* Evidence Act (Lord Denham's Act) 1843
Dickens, Charles
   Bleak House, 113
   Oliver Twist, 53n
   A Tale of Two Cities, 6
"difference" and guilt, 210–12, 214–15
Digby, Sir Kenelm, 213
dignity, 165–206
disclosure, 20n, 165–206
   in American context, 190n
   and secrecy, dynamics of, 20–1
   voluntary, 195–206
discretion, 175–7
Divorce and Matrimonial Causes Act 1857, 86

Dixon v Holden, 121n
domestic spaces, 179–95
Doyle, Arthur Conan, 163, 209–24
   "The Strange Case of George Edalji", 207, 214–224
Duke, Sir John, 1st Baron Coleridge, 132
dynamics of secrecy and disclosure, 10–11, 20–1

Edalji, George, 163, 209–24
Edinburgh Review, 31, 79–80, 80
Eigen, Joel Peter, 194
Eliot, George, 31–82
   Adam Bede, 6–7, 22, 31–82, 110–11, 112
   Hawthorne's influence on, 31–2n
   rumour, 80–2
   Scenes of Clerical Life, 31
   secret identity, 78–82
   "Silly Novels by Lady Novellists", 72–3, 110
   Sorrel, Hetty (character), 10, 22, 31–82
   transgression, 78–82
Ellenborough, Lord, 105
Ellis, Havelock, 192, 212
   The Criminal, 181
English Dreyfus case, 207–24
Erle, Justice, 106–7
Erskine, Lord, 52, 104–5
ethics of representation, 115, 145–7, 162
Everybody's Business (fictional newspaper), 142
evidence
   character, 98–101, 104n, 110–11, 114–15, 223n
   circumstantial or indirect, 111
   hearsay, 95–101
   legal rules of, 95–101
   novel, 112
   withholding, 40
Evidence Act 1843 (Lord Denman's Act), 40
Evidence Act (Lord Denham's Act) 1843, 42
Evidence Amendment Act (Lord Brougham's Act) 1851, 40, 42, 43–4, 113
evolutionary psychology, 54, 180, 191–2
The Examiner, 103
exception, 83–115
exchange of stories, 86–95

Farina, Jonathan, 3–4
Fenian, 137
Ferguson, Robert A., 24, 95, 220
fictionality, 17–20

Fifth Amendment, 77n
Finn, Phineas (character), 10–11
first-person narration, 19n, 87–8
Flux, William, 160, 160n
Forster, E. M., 17–18n, 25n
   Aspects of the Novel, 9–10, 14
Fowler, Elizabeth, 15, 19
Fraga, Xesús, 217, 222
Fraser's Magazine, 124
freedom from determinism, 172, 200
freedom of the press, 116–164
Frow, John, *Character and Person*, 3n

Gallagher, Catherine, 15–17, 18–20
Gallanis, Thomas P., 96–100, 114
Galvan, Jill, 15n
Garrett, Peter K., 187
Gaselee, Stephen, 131n
Gaskell, Elizabeth, 21
Gewirtz, Paul, 215–16
   Law's Stories: Narrative and Rhetoric in the Law, 216n
Gifford, Sir Hardinge, 163n
Gilbert, Geoffrey, 95n
Gladstone, Herbert, 213
The Glasgow Weekly, 155
The Globe, 120–1
Godkin, E. L., 172–4, 192n
Goh, Robbie B. H., 187, 205n
Gold, David, 42n, 44
Google N-gram Viewer, 3
Gordon, Jan B., 87, 88, 90
gossip, 22, 83–115
   character evidence, 104n
   communities, 86–95
   as entertainment, 89–90
   free market approach to, 177n
   outsiders, 89n
   serious, 87, 93n
   witness testimony, 184
Graham, Helen (character), 83–115
The Graphic, 139, 143
Gray, Dorian (character), 11, 22–3, 165–206
Great Reform Act, 129
"Greatorex letters of 1903", 213–14
Greenleaf, Simon, 41
Greenwood, Elisha, 104n
Grossman, Jonathan, 111, 113

Hansard's Debates, 133–4, 138
Hardy, Reginald, 211

Hardy, Thomas, 52, 104–5
Harvard Law Review, 163
Hawthorne, Nathaniel, 31–82
   "The Custom House", 38, 69, 72
   feminist readings of, 50n
   influence on Eliot, 31–2n
   Prynne, Hester (character), 10, 22, 31–82
   The Scarlet Letter, 22, 31–82
   writer's block, 70
hearsay, 83–115
Heinzelman, Susan, 73n
Henderson, Andrea K., 7
Henley, Joseph, 134
Hewitt, Martin, 119
Hirsch, Gordon, 192n
Holmes, Sherlock (character), 216–19
Home Office, 209, 214, 215, 216n
house as castle, 158–9, 165, 182–95
House Committee, 130–3
House of Commons, 134–5, 164
House of Lords, 120, 122, 125, 133–4, 134–5, 164
Hull, Raymona, 32n
Hunt, Aeron, 65
Hunter, J. Paul, 9–10
Hunter v Sharpe, 123n
Huntingdon, Helen (character), 10
Hutchinson, John, 159
Hyde, Edward (character), 4, 165–206

immunity, 168–9, 179n
individualism, 7–8, 22–3, 76
   liberal, 75, 168
   responsible, 44
infanticide, 50–69, 76
influence, 195–206
injury caused by libel, 117n, 121–2, 166–7, 172n, 174
intellectual property, 144–5n, 174–5
inviolate personality, 21, 108–9n, 168–9, 174–5, 178–9, 184, 189–90n, 191, 196, 199–200, 205
The Irish People, 137
Irish politics, 131n, 136–7
Irish Republican Brotherhood (IRB), 137

James, Henry, 23n, 190n
Jekyll, Dr (character), 11, 165–206
   will, 179, 181–7
Jesuitism, 131n, 137
Johnson, Douglas, 216
Jones, Miriam, 51n, 65, 76n

Joshi, Priti, 87, 91–2
journalism, 116–64, 177n
   financial, 20n
   political, 152n
Judge, Elizabeth, 16
The Jupiter (fictional newspaper), 142

Kalsem, Kristin, 36n, 65
Kelly, Sir Fitzroy, 133–4, 138
Kemp, Melody J., 92
Kingsley, Charles, 2
knowledge industry, 19n
Korobkin, Laura Hanft, 45, 66n
Krueger, Christine L.
   cover stories, 67, 76, 193n
   "extralegal" moments, 66n
   feminist narrative jurisprudence, 36–7n
   infanticide, 51n, 65
   narrative jurisprudence, 11, 25

Labouchère, Henry, 214
Lacey, Nicola
   character, 3n
   culpable ignorance, 38
   Hetty as "doubly deviant", 53–4
   responsibility attribution, 73n, 75n, 221–2
   social attitudes, 74
   transgression, 75
   women's criminality, 34
Ladd, Mason, 104n
Langbein, John
   "accused speaks" model, 111
   character evidence, 100
   character rule, 99n
   confessions, 77n
   defense counsel, 97
   hearsay, 97n
   law of evidence, 98n
   self-incrimination, 39n, 68
   Wigmore, John H., 95n
Langtry, Edward, 160, 165–6
Lapides, Robert, 5n
Law, Graham, 139
Law of Evidence and Procedure Bill (Lord Brougham) 1853, 43n
law of insult, French, 178n
Law of Libel Amendment Act 1888, 119, 159–64
The Law Times, 103–4n, 122
The Law Times Reports, 133–4
Lawson, James, 137

Leader and Saturday Analyst, 122–3
Leavis, F. R., 32, 50–1
libel
    American laws, 162
    and dignity, 165–6, 175
    French laws, 162
    injury caused by, 117n, 121–2, 166–7, 172n, 174
    number of cases, 139n
    and privacy, 159–64, 171–2
    private character and public interest, 119–38
    and slander, 117n
    Trollope and, 116–64
Libel Act (Lord Campbell's Act) 1843, 120–1, 125, 128, 131, 143, 153, 159, 162, 164
liberal individualism, 23n, 75, 168
Liddle, Dallas, 116, 138, 140, 145
literary professionals, 78–82
literary reviews, 78–82
Locke, John, "forensic person", 60n
The London Review, 126–7
Loveland, Ian, 129, 135, 152n
Low, George, 83–115
Lynch, Deidre Shauna, 16, 17–18n, 94
Lyndhurst, Lord, 134

Maine, 34, 40–1, 42n, 43, 76n, 113n
The Manchester Courier, 164
The Manchester Weekly Times, 155
manifest criminality, 57–8, 61n, 75
Manning, Cardinal, 4, 21
Markham, Gilbert (character), 10
McDonagh, Josephine, 51n
The Mercury, 211–12, 215
Michigan Law Review, 209
Mill, John Stuart, 1–2, 6, 57, 181
    On Liberty, 6, 195–6
Mitchell, Paul, 119, 135, 164
Moddlemog, William M., 173, 189–90n
moral and legal guilt, 61–3, 68n
moral character, 186n
Morning Chronicle, 126n

narration
    first-person, 19n, 87–8
    third-person, 35–6, 56–7, 65–6, 71–2, 220
narrative jurisprudence, 1–30
    feminist, 36n
narrative realism, 75n
narrative theory, 1–30

The Nation, 172
National Association of Journalists, 164
natural character, 108, 110, 112n
"nature", 57–9
Neate, Charles, 127, 130n, 136
negations, 59n
New Dreyfus Case, 207–24
"new journalism", 164, 177
The New York Times, 160, 214, 216–17
Newdegate, Charles, 126, 128–9, 131n
Newspaper Libel and Registration Act 1881, 143, 163
Newspaper Press Fund, 164
newspapers, 116–64, 170n, 209–24
    American, and Irish politics, 137
    gossip, 176–7
nomos, 208–9, 220, 221
North British Review, 31–2
Norton, Caroline, 31, 79–80
nostalgia, 94

Odgers, William Blake, *A Digest of the Law of Libel and Slander*, 116, 163–4
Old Bailey cases, 139
O'Loghlen, Sir Colman, 122, 124–5, 129n, 131–4, 136–8, 151
    bill, 128–30, 139
Orley Farm, 118
outsider jurisprudence, 12n, 25n
outsiders, 88–90, 170n

Pankhurst v Sowler, 164
The People's Banner (fictional newspaper), 140–1, 142, 143–55
"person", 2–3n
Person, Leland, 47
personality, 93–4, 108, 108–15, 171–9
personhood, and property, 20–1n, 203
Persönlichkeit, 177–8, 198, 200
Phineas Finn, 139n, 140, 143
Phineas novels, 140–1, 143–55
Phineas Redux, 21–2, 116, 139, 140, 143
The Picture of Dorian Gray, 22–3, 165–206
Pollock, Baron, 163
Poovey, Mary, 20n, 118, 118n
Pope, Alexander, "Epistle to a Lady", 65
Powers, Edwin, *The Body of Liberties*, 48
press
    freedom of the, 116–64
    liberties of the, 140–1
    and social improvement, 128
presumption of guilt, 48, 68, 75
presumption of innocence, 41, 55

Prisoner's Counsel Act 1836, 39–40, 76
privacy, 159–64, 165–206
  compulsive intimacy, 108
  Continental culture of, 177–8
  development of characters, 18–19
  and disclosure, 20–1
  first-person narration, 19n
  intellectual property, 144–5n
  knowledge industry, 19n
  and personality, 23
  and property, 117n
  right to silence, 12–14
  Seipp, David J., 170n
  The Tenant of Wildfell Hall, 91–2
  tort, 167n
  Whitman, James Q., 173n
privacy laws, American, 170–3, 175n
private character, 119–38
private properties, 171–9, 179–95
private spaces, 172–9, 179–95
privilege, 124, 135
"problem personalities", 181
property
  and capitalism, 20–1n
  character as, 121–2
  intellectual, 144–5n, 174–5
  and personhood, 20–1n, 203
  private, 171–9, 179–95
  reputation as, 117n, 121–2n
  and selfhood, 179
Provincial Newspaper Press Association, 129–30, 159–60
Prynne, Hester (character), 10, 22, 31–82
psychological realism, 204
public face, 165–206
public interest, 119–38
Pue, Surveyor, 49, 70
Purcell v Sowler, 163

Quolquhon, Patrick, 1

R v Garbett, 39n, 43–4
R v Jane Warwickshall, 77n
R v Rowton, 52, 80–1, 83–115
racial prejudice, 210–12, 214–15, 217–21, 222
Raikes, Henry, 138n
reader as jury member, 71, 85–6
realism
  Adam Bede, 66–7
  dynamics of secrecy and disclosure, 20n
  Eliot, George, 110
  high, 109n

narrative, 75n
psychological, 204
The Scarlet Letter, 70–1
Stevenson, Robert Louis, 204–5
The Tenant of Wildfell Hall, 88, 95–6
Reform Bill, 125, 129, 135n
reputation
  and community, 58, 68
  narrative, 16–18
  and privacy, 21
  as property, 117n
  R v Rowton, 80, 101–8
  right to, 172–3
  social approval, 192n
  Sorrel, Hetty (character), 52–3
  on trial, 83–115
"reserved" civil cases, 210
responsibility attribution, 10–11, 73n, 221–2
responsible individualism, 44
Rezek, Joseph, 93
"right to be let alone", 108–9n, 175, 191
Risinger, D. Michael, 220
Rodensky, Lisa
  character evidence, 104n, 106n, 111, 114
  The Crime in Mind, 35–6
  criminal intention, 18n, 54n, 220
  deeds and intentions, 55n, 56–8, 59
  "forensic person", 60n
  negations, 59n
  novel evidence, 112
  Oliver Twist, 53n
  Sorrel, Hetty (character), 53–4
Rodwell, B. B. Hunter, 160
Roebuck, John A., 126
Rollit, Albert Kaye, 159–60
Romanticism, 17–18n, 94
Romantics, 17–18
Rorty, Amelie Oksenberg, 2–3n
Rosenberg, Adolphus, 160–2
Rowton, James, 83–115
Rowton, Samuel James, 83–115
Rubery, Matthew, 147, 153n, 155, 162
rumour, 80–2, 90–1, 106–8, 202

Saint Pauls Magazine, 118–19, 138, 139–40
Salem Custom House, 49, 70
The Saturday Review, 103, 124, 127, 143, 160
The Scarlet Letter, 22, 31–82; *see also* Prynne, Hester (character)

Scheppele, Kim Lane, 209, 220
Schramm, Jan-Melissa, 75n, 111, 112–13
Scott, Walter, 31, 78–9, 80
Second Reform Bill, 136, 138
secrecy, 10–11, 20n, 108, 196–8, 201
Seipp, David J., 166, 167n, 170, 171, 172n, 200n
Select Committees, 134n, 163
   House of Lords, 120, 125
   1843, 159
   1879, 130n
   on the Law of Libel, 159–60, 159n
self-believed story, 210, 217–21
selfhood, 8, 179
self-incrimination, 39–40, 42–3, 68
self-possession, 64
Seneca Falls Convention 1848, 45n
Sennett, Richard, 93–4, 112n, 115
   The Fall of Public Man, 80, 108, 110
serious gossip, 87, 93n
Sevier, Justin, 104n
silence, 12, 31–82
silence promoting measures, 44
silence threatening measures, 43–4
Simmel, Georg, 193, 196–8, 201–2
   "The Sociology of Secrecy and of Secret Societies", 1, 175–8, 207
Siskin, Clifford, 7–9, 16–17, 32–3
slander, 124–42
   character, 98
   injury caused by, 121, 167n
   Jesuitism, 131n
   and libel, 117n, 128–29n
   and privacy, 171
   The Tenant of Wildfell Hall, 90
   Wason, Rigby, 134n
   Welsh, Alexander, 142n
Slide, Quintus (character), 22, 140–2, 143–55
Smiles, Samuel, 58
   Self-Help, 6, 110–11
Smith, F. E., 214, 216
Smith, Henry E., 39, 43–4, 76
Soames, Francis Larkin, 130n
society papers, 160–4
solitude and privacy, 173, 188, 191
Sorrel, Hetty (character), 10, 22, 31–82
Spacks, Patricia Meyer, 87, 89n, 90, 93n, 108
The Spectator, 160–2, 164, 165–6, 175
Spencer, Herbert, 191–2, 195, 204
spiritual autobiography, 91–2

Starkie, Thomas, 98, 100n
   Practical Treatise of the Law of Evidence, 96, 100
   Treatise on the Law of Libel and Slander, and Incidentally of Malicious Prosecutions, 121
Stephen, James Fitzjames, 2, 104n, 136, 149, 198–9, 202
   Liberty, Equality, Fraternity, 165, 195–6
Stephen, Leslie, 145
   "Anonymous Journalism", 140
Stevenson, Robert Louis, 165–206
stories of experience, 109n, 112
story of the door, 179–95
The Strange Case of Dr. Jekyll and Mr. Hyde, 4, 22–3, 165–206
Sully, James, 193
   "The Aesthetics of Human Character", 6n
   "Self-Esteem", 191
sympathy, 8, 59–60, 67–8, 72n, 76n, 191–3, 195–6

telling one's story, 36–8
The Tenant of Wildfell Hall, 22, 83–115; see also Graham, Helen (character)
Thesiger, Lord Chief Justice, 125
third-person narrator, 35–6, 56–7, 65–6, 71–2, 220
Thomas, Brook, 35, 37, 174–5, 189–90n, 190–1
Thomas, Ronald R., 112n, 180, 212
thresholds, 45, 179–95
The Times
   Edalji, George, 214
   freedom of the press, 122–4
   libel, 127–8, 130, 133–4
   power of the press, 138, 139
   R v Rowton, 83–4, 102–3, 115
   Trollope, Anthony, 151
Tóibín, Colm, 170, 203–4
Town Talk libels, 159–64, 165–6
Trollope, Anthony
   "On Anonymous Literture", 151
   Autobiography, 156
   confusion between author and characters, 138–59
   Cousin Henry, 141, 143, 155–9, 162
   development of characters, 153–4n
   Dr. Wortle's School, 118, 142
   "Editors' Tales", 140
   ethics of representation, 115
   and libel laws, 21–2, 116–64

liberties of the press, 138–59
"newspaper novelist", 139
newspapers, 139n
Orley Farm, 155
The People's Banner (fictional newspaper), 140–1, 142, 143–55
Phineas Finn, 139n, 140, 143
Phineas novels, 140–1, 143–55
Phineas Redux, 21–2, 116, 139, 140, 143
"The Press", 138
The Prime Minister, 22, 142, 153–4, 156
recurring characters, 118n
Saint Pauls Magazine, 140n
Slide, Quintus (character), 22, 140–2, 143–55
The Warden, 139n, 141–2, 146n
The Way We Live Now, 163
Truth, 214
Turner, Mark, 154n

Umpire, 217
unreal knowability, 18–19

Virtue, James, 140
Voce, Mary, 52, 64n, 68–9
voluntariness, 76
voluntary disclosure, 195–206

Waddams, S. M., 144n
Wahrman, Dror, 7–9, 15n
Waldron, Mary, 57
Wall, Stephen, 116
Warhol, Robyn R., 72n
Warren, Robert, 137
Warren, Samuel D.
    domestic spaces, 189
    free market approach to gossip, 177n
    house as castle, 182–3
    inviolate personality, 21, 194
    press, 162–3
    privacy, 170, 198–9, 200n
    property and personality, 202–3
    property and personhood, 20–1n, 117n, 171–9
    "right to be let alone", 108–9n
    "The Right to Privacy", 165–8, 175n, 205
    society papers, 164
    solitude and privacy, 191
Wason, Rigby, 133–5

Wason v Walter, 133–5, 138, 139, 152n, 159
Watt, Ian, 71, 73
    The Rise of the Novel, 86
Weisbruch, Robert, 32n
Welsh, Alexander, 32, 71, 87–8, 111, 112–13, 219
    George Eliot and Blackmail, 19n, 142n
    Strong Representations, 111
Wensleydale, Lord, 134
West, Robin, *Narrative, Authority, and Law*, 221
Whalley, George, 131n, 137
Whitman, James Q., 166, 167n, 173n, 175n, 177–8, 200
Wiener, Martin J., 1, 2n, 5–6, 57–8, 181, 191n
Wigmore, John H., 95n
Wilde, Oscar, 165–206, 167n
Willes, Justice, 106–7, 114–15
Williams, M. Kellen, 205n
Wills, William, 95n, 102n
Willson, Andrew, 139n, 141, 145, 146n, 147
Wilson, Arthur, 213
witness testimony, 96–101
    Cockburn, Chief Justice, 106n
    competence versus credibility, 39–44
    competency, 36–8
    The Scarlet Letter, 70–3
    Schramm, Jan-Melissa, 113
    Smith, Henry E., 39n
    The Strange Case of Dr. Jekyll and Mr. Hyde, 184
    Wills, William, 95n
Wolf, Gabrielle, 101n
Woloch, Alex, 8, 14–15, 21, 22–3, 25n, 86
    The One vs. the Many: Minor Characters and the Space of the Protagonist in the Novel, 10–11
women
    activism, 77
    as characterless, 65
    criminal, 33–4
    talk, 35n
Wordsworth, William, 50–1
    Preface to *Lyrical Ballads*, 72–3
written evidence, 91–2, 95n, 108

Yelverton, R. D., 215, 216n